THE UNITY *of the* BIBLE

DANIEL P. FULLER

THE UNITY of the BIBLE

Unfolding God's Plan for Humanity

ZondervanPublishingHouse
Grand Rapids, Michigan

A Division of HarperCollins*Publishers*

The Unity of the Bible
Copyright © 1992 by Daniel P. Fuller

Requests for information should be addressed to:
Zondervan Publishing House
Academic and Professional Books
Grand Rapids, Michigan 49530

Library of Congress Cataloging-in-Publication Data

Fuller, Daniel P.
The unity of the Bible / Daniel P. Fuller.
p.   cm.
Includes bibliographical references and index.
ISBN 0-310-23404-2
1. Bible–Criticism, interpretation, etc. 2. Bible. N.T.-
-Relation to the Old Testament. I. Title.
BS511.F85 1992
220.6–dc20   91-42393
CIP

Edited by Craig Noll and Leonard G. Goss

Cover designed by Church Art Works

Printed in the United States of America

97 98 99 00 01 /DC / 12 11 10 9 8 7 6 5 4 3

This edition is printed on acid-free paper and meets the American National
Standards Institute Z39.48 standard.

*. . .the ethics or dogmatics of redemptive history
ought to be written someday.*
Oscar Cullmann, *Salvation in History*

Contents

Acknowledgments

A number of people have rendered indispensable help in preparing this material for publication, and to all of them I owe a great debt of gratitude. At the top of the list is Janet Gathright, who spent the entire summer of 1984 keying the written text of my "Unity of the Bible" syllabus onto a computer disk so that I could rework it on my word processor. I tremble to think of how hard it would have been to write and revise all this on a typewriter! Then there were the numerous editings that my wife, Ruth, has made of the manuscript at various stages, which have added greatly to its readability. And very special thanks are due to John Piper, senior pastor at Bethlehem Baptist Church of Minneapolis, who in the midst of his many pastoral responsibilities took three full days to scrutinize an early draft of the first twelve chapters. He gave another six days of a sabbatical in the summer of 1990 to taping numerous queries concerning the basic outline of the manuscript. He also gave several days of his 1991 vacation to making queries of the final draft of the manuscript. These efforts helped me correct and clarify a number of important matters. His writing of the Foreword reflects his deep investment in this work.

Also important are several people who helped to clarify my understanding of the religions of Hinduism, Buddhism, and Islam. I am particularly indebted to Eric J. Sharpe, professor of religious studies at the University of Sydney, Australia, for his lengthy letters criticizing my early drafts on Hinduism and Buddhism. James Stephens, who is connected with the United States Center for World Mission in Pasadena, California, also aided me greatly in understanding Buddhism. Both of these men were recommended by Ralph D. Winter, director of the USCWM and my close friend since high-school days. I also wish to thank Dudley Woodberry, professor of Islamic studies at the Fuller Seminary School of World Missions, for helping me gain a better grasp of Islam.

Many former students have also played a crucial role in the preparation of this book. As over the years they have taken my "Unity of the Bible" course, they have continually prodded me to turn the photocopied syllabus into a book. Several have used this earlier form in actual church situations and given me valuable feedback on how the material is received by laypeople who give promise of leadership ability. Special mention is due Larry Allen, a beloved pastor. In teaching this material to his laypeople over the years, he has developed his own series of questions for each and has constantly encouraged me to go ahead with this project, focusing the book on people like those with whom he has been working. To all these who have contributed so substantially to the appearance of *Unity of the Bible* in its present form, I therefore express my great thanks, and my gratitude to God for providing them.

Foreword

No book besides the Bible has had a greater influence on my life than Daniel Fuller's *The Unity of the Bible*. When I first read it as a classroom syllabus over twenty years ago, everything began to change.

The hallowing of God's name (Matthew 6:9) flamed up as the center of my prayers. God's passion for his glory (Isaiah 48:9–11) stopped seeming selfish and became the very fountain of grace that flings all wonders of love into being. God's law stopped being at odds with the gospel. It stopped being a job description for earning wages under a so-called covenant of works (which I never could find in the Bible) and became a precious doctor's prescription that flows from faith in the divine Physician (Romans 9:32).

God's commitment to work with omnipotent power for those who wait for him (Isaiah 64:4) became my main weapon against worry. The discovery that "God is not served by human hands as though he needed anything" (Acts 17:25) stunned me with the thought that the apex of God's glory is not in being served but in serving (1 Peter 4:11). It has never ceased to be breathtaking that the God who made the galaxies is pursuing me with goodness and mercy all the days of my life (Psalm 23:6)—that he rejoices in doing me good with all his heart and with all his soul (Jeremiah 32:41).

Again and again it has seemed almost too good to be true that God is most glorified in us when we are most satisfied in him. He takes pleasure in those who hope in him (Psalm 147:11). What could turn life upside down more radically than the discovery that the chief duty of man is to be full of hope in God—that the first and great commandment translates best not as drudge and duty under divine demands, but as "delight yourself in the Lord" (Psalm 37:4)?

It seems so obvious now, but what a revolution it was

then: that saving faith is not merely the historical confidence that Christ died for me and rose again, but is also, and more powerfully, the assurance of things hoped for (Hebrews 11:1).

The whole question of how saving faith relates to obedience was transformed. Obedience is not just tacked on to faith as a disconnected evidence. It is a "work of faith" (1 Thessalonians 1:3). Faith in God's commitment to work for me in the future (Romans 8:28) is the power to break the enslaving allurements of sin. Sin promises happiness. But I came to see that the very meaning of saving faith is nothing less than being satisfied with all that God promises to be for us in Christ. So faith breaks the power of sin. Fleeting pleasures of sin are stripped of their luring power when we trust in the everlasting joys promised by God (Hebrews 11:25–26). So all preaching and teaching that aims to make people holy aims to increase the "joy of faith" (Philippians 1:25).

The life-changing effects of Fuller's *The Unity of the Bible* are not a fluke. They flow from Jesus' promise that the truth of God's word makes us holy (John 17:17); the truth makes us free (John 8:32). This book is passionately concerned with the truth of Scripture. Its power lies in the relentless pursuit of reality. There is no academic gamesmanship. The issue is not what the latest scholars think, but rather, what is God really doing in history? When the question of hell rises there is not just textual analysis but trembling. When the question of faith and obedience rises I have to come to terms with *my* anxiety and *my* greed and *my* lust. The book is about ultimate reality and how I (and you!) fit in.

It changed my life because it is so honest. No hard questions are dodged. No troubling texts are swept under the rug. There is a passion for seeing all of Scripture as a whole. It is easy (and often cheap) to toy with the parts of Scripture with no reference to how one part fits with another. Too much academic labor passes for mature scholarship while dealing only piecemeal with the reality of God's work in redemptive history. Daniel Fuller has given his life to seeing the connections, and pursuing the coherence of "the whole counsel of God."

The book will be of immense value to the church. It will be useful in seminaries, colleges, and Bible schools where teachers and students struggle to see the Bible as a whole and discover what gives unity to these sixty-six inspired books and these thousands of years of world history. But not only there, the book will also serve the local church directly in classes and small study groups that will profit not only from its grand vision of God's unifying work in history, but also from its stream of life-changing insights into the problems we all face in the daily fight of faith.

Over 100 people at our church have worked their way through *The Unity of the Bible* in pastor-led small group settings. The vision of God and his purposes in this book is the theological backbone of our life together. And, perhaps most important of all, the great global plan of God unfolded in this book has become the flame that drives the missionary engine of our church.

The one thing that God is doing throughout all redemptive history is to show forth his mercy in such a way that the greatest number of people from all the nations might come to delight in him with all their heart and mind throughout eternity and thus reflect the infinite worth of his glory. When the new heavens and the new earth are filled with such people from every tongue and tribe and people and nation, then the objective that God wanted to achieve in showing forth his mercy will have been achieved.

And it *will* be achieved! For thus says the Lord,

> I am God, and there is no other;
>   I am God, and there is none like me...
> saying, My counsel shall stand,
>   and I will accomplish all my purpose.
>   Isaiah 46:9–10

John Piper, Th.D.
Pastor
Bethlehem Baptist Church
Minneapolis, Minnesota
August 1991

Preface

It was in the spring of 1946 that I first felt the need for a book like this. As an ensign in the navy, I was the assisting officer of the deck on the bridge of a troop transport. Hostilities had ended about eight months earlier, and now we were bringing five thousand service personnel back from the Pacific islands. On this particular evening we were steaming along and were together on the midnight to 4:00 A.M. watch. Since there was little to do, the senior deck officer and I helped pass the time by talking.

As a Navigator in high school, I had been challenged to learn hundreds of Scripture verses and in addition had received valuable instruction in the importance of prayer and obedience to God's Word. Dawson Trotman, the founder of the Navigators, also laid great emphasis on the need to be aggressive in talking to others about Jesus and in urging them to make a definite decision that assured them that their sins were forgiven. So I had familiarized myself with his "seven steps" for winning people to Christ.

And now on a quiet bridge in the early morning hours, I began talking to this senior officer about his need for Christ and the assurance that his sins had been forgiven. He seemed interested, and after I had gone through the seven steps with him and answered several questions, he did accept Christ as his Savior.

Desiring to give him a good start in his Christian life, I then invited him to begin meeting with me in my cabin on off-duty hours. And the very next day he did show up, flopped down in a chair, and said, "Teach me the whole Bible." I was taken completely aback. Although I knew a few key biblical concepts, I certainly did not have a grasp of the Bible as a unified whole. Therefore it was not long until I had told him everything I did know. And at that point, realizing that my well had run dry, he lost interest in meeting with me.

How I wished then, and thereafter, for some book that would have set forth the logic behind God's unfolding revelation, starting with Genesis and ending with Revelation, so I could have been more help to him. Several years later while a student at Fuller Theological Seminary, I did get a much better knowledge of Bible content from a course taught by Wilbur M. Smith. But still I lacked a grasp of the inner logic that must have existed in the body of teaching Paul called "the whole [purpose] of God" (Acts 20:27), from which he had "not hesitated to preach anything that would be helpful" (v. 20), and because of which he could continue teaching night and day for three years without running dry (v. 31).

I had made an earlier attempt to understand God's plan of the ages as it was set forth sporadically in the endnotes and introductory paragraphs of the *Scofield Reference Bible* but found this approach unsatisfactory. Therefore in my doctoral thesis in the Old Testament, written at Northern Baptist Seminary in 1957, I tried to spell out an alternative. Through this study, along with the help of George E. Ladd at Fuller Seminary, I came to see the close relationship between the "church" and the "kingdom of God" and realized that there was no difference between the "gospel of the kingdom" (Matt. 24:14) preached by Jesus during his earthly ministry and the "gospel of God's grace" (Acts 20:24) preached by Paul after Jesus' ascension and the establishment of the church.

During this time I also saw that the keynote of the Bible was expressed in verses like Psalm 46:10: "Be still, and know that I am God; I will be exalted among the nations, I will be exalted in the earth." Then God's workings in history from Genesis to Revelation and the various teachings of the Bible began to fall into place as I saw that he did everything in the creation of the world and its history in order to uphold fully the glory of his name. This insight became the foundation for my course entitled "Unity of the Bible," which I have been teaching since 1965. At the end of one class a student remarked that my course could be boiled down to Isaiah 48:9-11: "For the sake of my praise I hold [my wrath] back from you. . . . For my own sake, for my own sake, I do this. How can I let [my glory] be defamed? I will not yield my glory to another."

Further insights came in the 1960s during my studies for a New Testament doctorate at the University of Basel in Switzerland. There in lecture after lecture, as well as in his prolific writings, Oscar Cullmann emphasized the need to summarize the whole Bible along the timeline of redemptive history, instead of reverting to the timeless categories of God, humankind, Christ, church, and last things that has characterized the organization of systematic theology down through the ages.

But perhaps the most crucial illumination in seeing the Bible as a unity, with no reversal or new start in moving from the Old Testament to the New, was the insight given me in the spring of 1972 by a student in a Greek exegesis course on Romans 9–11. He pointed to the statement in 9:32, "Why [has Israel] not [attained the law of righteousness they pursued so zealously]? Because they pursued it not by faith but *as if* it were by works." Then he asked, "How can systematic theology talk of the Old Testament (moral) law as a hypothetical way people could earn their salvation if they complied with it perfectly? This verse makes it clear that the law does not call for works performed in service for God. Rather, it tells us how we ought to obey God as people who trust his promise to pursue after us to do us good every day of our lives." Such a question had never occurred to me, and I was at a loss to give a satisfactory answer.

Providentially, however, a fifteen-month leave of absence began a few weeks later, and this was the time I needed to rethink my theology and work my way carefully through crucial passages on the gospel and law in the canonical Scriptures, as well as through such primary interpreters of Scripture as Calvin and Luther. In the process I discovered that only Luther, especially in his "Freedom of a Christian" and "Preface to Romans," had any inkling that the law was a law of faith (Rom. 9:32), calling for an "obedience that comes from faith" (1:5) and yielding a "work produced by faith" (1 Thess. 1:3). During this time I began to revise my 1957 dissertation, which in 1980 yielded the book *Gospel and Law: Contrast or Continuum? The Hermeneutics of Dispensationalism and Covenant Theology.*

Since then I have labored to find a way to produce a book on the unity of the Bible. During a nine-month sabbatical in 1985 I tried to do the scholarly reading pertaining to the many things about which such a book should speak. But soon I realized that the enormous amount of relevant material constantly being published made it humanly impossible to cover the whole field adequately.

Then while composing the charge to be given at the ordination of one of my students, the thought struck me that a book on the unity of the Bible would better help this young pastor and many like him to train promising laypersons if it was halfway between the scholarly style of technical theology and the popular style of the many Christian books written for the laity. With the help of such a book, he would be able to teach his lay leaders the "whole Bible," just as that newly converted officer in my cabin had asked me to do.

These leaders in turn could be most effective in training others in the church. The ordained clergy are simply too few ever to fulfill Jesus' last command in the Great Commission to teach others "to obey everything I have commanded you" (Matt. 28:20). That fact may be why Paul gave the following exhortation to Timothy and all pastors after him: "The things you have heard me say in the presence of many witnesses entrust to reliable [people] who will also be qualified to teach others" (2 Tim. 2:2).

The Unity of the Bible is therefore designed to be a text that will facilitate this task. A number of former students who are now pastors have used the photocopied syllabus of earlier versions in teaching their most promising laypersons, and they report that it has been of great help in enabling them "to prepare God's people for works of service . . . until we all reach unity in the faith" (Eph. 4:12–13).

Perhaps the best way to profit from this book is to take a chapter at a time and, in conjunction with several others, meet once a week with a "coach" who has already worked his or her way through the material. It should be made clear to such people that they are being coached so that they can

in turn be guides to yet another small group of people who
need to grasp the whole purpose of God.

In commencing this study, it will be helpful to understand
that my approach follows the inductive method of reasoning.
This method is particularly followed in chapters 1–4, where
I establish the authority of the sixty-six books of the Bible.
Following this method means that rather than simply stating
at the outset that the Bible is indeed the verbally inspired,
inerrant Word of God, I arrive at this conclusion by beginning with facts and axioms and then work upward from these
to establish the Bible's verbal inspiration.

My basic reason for proceeding by this inductive method
is the conviction that it is the way the early church went
about its missionary task. Peter, for example, began his first
sermon at Pentecost (Acts 2:14–36) by pointing out an
evidence—a fact—that both he and his hearers shared in
common: Jewish Christians were miraculously preaching the
gospel of Jesus in the mother tongues of people who had
come to Jerusalem from all over the Mediterranean world to
celebrate Pentecost, the Feast of Weeks (Ex. 34:22), fifty
days after Passover (Acts 2:5–15). This fact, he declared,
could be explained as the partial fulfillment of Joel's
prophecy that a time was coming when God would pour out
his Spirit on all people, enabling them to prophesy and edify
others (vv. 16–21).

Peter then reminded his hearers of the miracles Jesus had
recently performed in Jerusalem, "as you yourselves know,"
and argued that these acts proved Jesus was "accredited by
God" (Acts 2:22). Recalling how Jesus had been crucified
and then raised from the dead (vv. 23–24), Peter then quoted
David's statement in Psalm 16 that God would not let his
"Holy One see decay" (v. 27). Since the location of David's
tomb was common knowledge, this statement clearly referred not to David himself but to one of his descendants
who would sit on his throne (vv. 29–31). Thus Peter argued
that the prophecy in Psalm 16 could refer only to Jesus. Now
seated at God's right hand, Jesus was the cause for this
manifest outpouring of the Holy Spirit, so that people of

many nationalities were hearing the gospel in their own languages.

Then came his climax: *"Therefore* let all Israel be assured of this: God has made this Jesus, whom you crucified, both Lord and Christ" (Acts 2:36). When the people heard this affirmation, many were "cut to the heart" and asked Peter and the other disciples who had seen the resurrected Jesus (v. 32), "Brothers, what shall we do?" Peter replied, "Repent and be baptized, every one of you, in the name of Jesus Christ for the forgiveness of your sins. And you will receive the gift of the Holy Spirit" (vv. 37–38). At that point three thousand people responded and joined the apostles' fellowship.

Therefore, since God blessed the inductive approach in Peter's evangelistic strategy for founding the church, I have felt that to follow this method was most appropriate in establishing the Bible's inerrancy and unity. Not only does it honor Scripture's own approach, but it provides an even greater ability to give to others "the reason for the hope that [we] have" (1 Peter 3:15).

Review Questions

1. What is the purpose for which *Unity of the Bible* was written?

2. How is the evangelistic purpose of this book aided by arguing for the Bible's truth inductively?

PART 1

THE VALUE
OF THE INQUIRY

1

Evidence for the Bible's Unity

The goal of this book is to discover and express the basic theme that gives coherence to the Bible's teachings. It seeks to put the Bible together so that people can make better sense out of it as a whole. This understanding is vital, for when Paul urged the Corinthian church to proclaim the biblical message in a way best suited to make people stronger Christians, he argued, "If the trumpet does not sound a clear call, who will get ready for battle? . . . Unless you speak intelligible words with your tongue, how will anyone know what you are saying?" (1 Cor. 14:8–9).

It is obvious from this appeal for a clear presentation of biblical truth that the more coherent an understanding people receive, the more mature they will become as Christians. But just as soldiers in battle would become confused if, after sounding "Advance," the trumpet immediately sounded "Retreat," so Christians will be weakened if their successive exposures to the biblical message leave them contradictory notions about God and his purpose for humankind.

Indeed, searching for the Bible's coherent teaching appears as a formidable task when one considers its content: writings in different literary styles from thirty or more people living in diverse life-situations over a period of more than a thousand years in places extending from Rome to the Euphrates River. A cursory examination, however, soon provides one with several encouragements to carry out this search. First, the Bible proceeds according to a plan. Beginning with the creation of the world, it then relates and interprets a series of historical events that lead to the grand climax and goal of the world's history. One writer has compared the phenomenon of the Bible with the scriptures of other religions as follows:

> The Koran, for instance, is a miscellany of disjointed pieces, out of which it is impossible to extract any order, progress, or arrangement. The 114 Suras or chapters of which it is composed are arranged chiefly according to length—the longer in general preceding the shorter. It is not otherwise with the Zoroastrian and Buddhist Scriptures. These are equally destitute of beginning, middle or end. They are, for the most part, collections of heterogeneous materials, loosely placed together. How different everyone must acknowledge it to be with the Bible! From Genesis to Revelation we feel that this book is in a real sense a unity. It is not a collection of fragments, but has, as we say, an organic character. It has one connected story to tell from beginning to end; we see something growing before our eyes; there is plan, purpose, progress; the end folds back on the beginning, and, when the whole is finished, we feel that here again, as in the primal creation, God has finished all his works, and behold, they are very good.[1]

Even stronger encouragement to look for an organic unity in the Bible comes from statements made by its last spokespersons. These authors indicate their conviction that they were speaking in concert with every other biblical spokesperson. Two such statements are Luke's quotation of Paul in Acts and Paul's own testimony.

Acts 20:27

In Paul's farewell message to the elders of the Ephesian church (Acts 20:17–35) he said, "I have not hesitated to proclaim to you the whole [purpose] of God (v. 27)." The phrase "the whole purpose of God" represented the vast amount of teaching Paul had given at Ephesus during the three years he preached there day and night. Something of the magnitude and nature of this teaching is indicated by other statements: "I have not hesitated to preach anything that would be helpful to you but have taught you publicly and from house to house" (v. 20); "if only I may . . . complete the task the Lord Jesus has given me—the task of testifying to the gospel of God's grace" (v. 24); "I declare to you today that I am innocent of the blood of all men [in preaching the kingdom of God]" (v. 26); "remember that for three years I never stopped warning each of you night and day with tears" (v. 31).

In such extended preaching Paul must have taught his *entire message*—summed up by the phrase "the whole purpose of God." Elements of it would naturally reappear in his farewell address: (1) the need to "turn to God in repentance" and to "have faith in our Lord Jesus" (Acts 20:21); (2) the responsibility for church elders to guard themselves from evil so they can keep a proper watch and protect God's people from the ravages of sin (vv. 28–31); (3) God's having purchased believers with his own blood (v. 28); (4) his holding in store an inheritance for all those who continue to build themselves up spiritually by heeding the word of God's grace (v. 32); (5) Paul's modeling Christian love in earning money to help the weak (v. 35); and (6) Jesus' teaching that "it is more blessed to give than to receive" (v. 35).

Additional elements of this whole purpose of God must also appear in Paul's other speeches recorded in Acts. The message in his sermon at Antioch of Pisidia (Acts 13:16–47) of how Jesus Christ had fulfilled God's Old Testament promises to Abraham and David,[2] so that salvation was now available to Israelites as well as Gentiles who would believe in Jesus, was doubtless part of what was taught at Ephesus. Also the two basic points in Paul's message at Athens (17:22–31)—that God is not served by human hands, and that everyone must repent, since God had guaranteed a future judgment by raising Jesus from the dead—must have been part of the whole purpose of God. And the same would be true for his remaining speeches in Acts 24:10–24 and 25:24–26:29.

Since Paul summarized his message as the whole purpose of God, it is clear that he regarded it as a unity. The Greek word for "purpose" (*boulē*, "will" in the NIV) in this phrase implies the deliberate choice to pursue a certain goal step-by-step, in a methodical way. A statement in Acts 2:23 uses the same Greek word to indicate a deliberate plan of action: "This man [Jesus] was handed over to you [Jews] by God's set purpose and foreknowledge." Since Jesus' crucifixion was not the goal of God's plan but an indispensable step for realizing it, we understand that God's *boulē* implies taking successive steps toward realizing his goal. This same point is also made in Acts 13:36, where Paul spoke about how "David had served God's purpose [*boulē*] in his own generation." There were steps in God's purpose for the world that had to be taken during David's lifetime, and David served God in the way he helped carry out those steps. So the phrase "the whole purpose of God" implies the steps God takes in creation and afterward in bringing world history to his intended goal.

This plan includes not only the many elements of Paul's teaching but also all that was taught in the Old Testament. In making his defense before King Agrippa, Paul declared, "I am saying nothing beyond what the prophets and Moses said would happen" (Acts 26:22). In Paul's thinking, then, all that the Old Testament taught was included in the phrase "the whole purpose of God." This conviction is found also in his epistles. In 2 Timothy 3:16–17 Paul said, "All Scripture is God-breathed and is useful for teaching, rebuking, correcting, and training in righteousness, so that the man of God may be thoroughly equipped for every good work." In the next I argue that the Old Testament canon with its thirty-nine books was closed about 150 years before the Christian era. So in making this statement Paul was saying that the whole Old Testament was verbally inspired by God. In chapters 3 and 4, then, I conclude that the twenty-seven books composing the New Testament canon are also inerrantly and verbally inspired by God.

Galatians 1:8–9

Paul's statement in Galatians 1:8 also necessarily implies that the whole Bible, both Old Testament and New Testa-

ment, sets forth a coherent message: "Even if we or an angel
from heaven should preach a gospel other than the one we
preached to you, let him be eternally condemned." The
words "if we or an angel from heaven" imply that the people
included in the "we" must have been the primary spokespersons of the Christian message at that time, since they
could be classed with the angels. (Ordinary teachers, that is,
people who had been taught the gospel by the primary
spokespersons or their pupils, are the ones included in the
"anybody" of v. 9.) So Galatians 1:8 implies that Paul and
the other contemporary revelatory New Testament spokespersons regarded themselves as speaking in concert, since
each regarded the message they preached as being God's
message. All were conscious that if any of them veered from
this message and persisted in some alien teaching, they
would suffer eternal condemnation. Each of these primary
spokespersons—Paul, Peter, John, James, and so on—also
frequently supported their message by quoting from the Old
Testament. Our first task, however, is to learn from certain
statements in Galatians and other Pauline Epistles just how
these primary revelatory spokespersons related to each
other.

That Paul meant to include Peter and James in the "we" of
Galatians 1:8 is implied by verse 18: "[When I went back to
Jerusalem] I saw none of the other apostles—only James, the
Lord's brother." Then in recounting a later visit to Jerusalem
(2:1–10), Paul speaks of John as also being a pillar in the
Jerusalem church (v. 9). By saying "Whatever they [once]
were makes no difference to me" (v. 6), Paul implies that
John and Peter had been with Jesus during his earthly
ministry. Paul spoke of them in this way to affirm that he was
no less an apostle (or revelatory spokesperson) than they,
even though, unlike them, he had not been taught by Jesus
for three years. So from Galatians 1:18 and 2:6, 9, we infer
that Paul also meant to include John and "the other apostles"
among the "we" of 1:8.

As for James the Lord's brother, he was an unbeliever
during Jesus' ministry (John 7:5). But according to 1 Corinthians 15:7, Jesus, after his resurrection, appeared to this
James, and as a result he was regarded as an apostle and

became a leader in the Jerusalem church. Paul then was the last person to be appointed as an apostle: "Last of all [Jesus] appeared to me also, as to one abnormally born" (1 Cor. 15:8).[3]

In the thinking of the early church, the term "apostle" was applied to those who had been personally commissioned by the risen Jesus to stand in his stead and preach his message to the world. Except for Paul and James, those who received this title had followed Jesus during his three-year public ministry. Matthew 10:2–4 lists the names of the twelve apostles; according to verses 5–8, "These twelve Jesus sent out with the following instructions: 'As you go, preach this message: "The kingdom of heaven is near." Heal the sick, raise the dead, cleanse those who have leprosy, drive out demons.'"

Toward the end of his public ministry, Jesus told his disciples he would rise again after being put to death. But when he was arrested, they all forsook him; not one had the courage to be near when Jesus was crucified and buried (Matt. 27:55–61). Then they went into hiding because of fear of the Jews (John 20:19). After Jesus rose from the dead, however, he appeared to these same apostles and commanded them to be his spokespersons to the whole world (Matt. 28:18–20; Luke 24:44–49; Acts 1:6–8). "The Gospels and Acts make it quite clear that it was exclusively the act of the risen Lord that this scattered group became a community full of hope and ready for action. The act of the risen Lord, however, was the renewal of the commission of the disciples in their definitive institution as *apostoloi* [apostles]."[4]

As was noted, classing the "we" of Galatians 1:8 with an angel implies that they were the primary Christian spokespersons: Peter, the chief apostle (1:18); James, the brother of Jesus, (1:19); the apostle John (2:9); and of course Paul. He certainly regarded himself as a revelatory spokesperson, for he declared, "I did not receive [the gospel] from any man, nor was I taught it; rather, I received it by revelation from Jesus Christ" (1:12). With the exception of Judas Iscariot, the apostles listed in Matthew 10:2–4 should also be included in this "we."

Galatians 2:9 then speaks of how these primary leaders—

Peter, James, and John—by extending the right hand of fellowship to Paul and his coworker Barnabas, openly demonstrated their complete agreement with them on the teaching comprising the gospel. This agreement was emphatic because it was given in connection with their decision that the baptized but uncircumcised Gentile Titus, brought by Paul to Jerusalem as a concrete example of the extremely successful Gentile mission, was as legitimate a church member as any circumcised Jew who had been baptized in the name of Jesus (Gal. 2:3). Though this was a very sensitive issue for the Jewish mother church at Jerusalem, Galatians 2:9 shows that even here its primary leaders were in total agreement.[5]

And this fact implies that the teaching of the Bible is a unity. These who signified agreement regarding the gospel at the Jerusalem conference composed part of the last group of revelatory spokespersons that God had ordained to report and interpret his plan in culminating redemptive history. The time during which God transmitted revelatory information to his people was therefore almost at an end. Soon his people would have a fixed body of revelatory data from which to learn all that was necessary for building them up in their faith. This point was made explicit by Jude, who spoke in his small epistle written at the close of the apostolic age (c. A.D. 90) of "the faith that was once for all entrusted to the saints" (v. 3). The very fact that Jude regarded all that was authoritative for the saints as "faith" in the sense of doctrine and practice necessarily implies that he too was convinced that God had been giving his people a coherent and unified body of teaching from the beginning of the Old Testament down to the close of the first century when the last apostle (John?) died.

This agreement among these last revelatory spokespersons also means that everything said through earlier spokespersons coheres to form a unity, for these final writers always held the teaching of the Old Testament as authoritative. Consequently in the Old Testament and New Testament of the biblical canon, the people of God have that all-important "clear [trumpet] call" (1 Cor. 14:8) upon which to build and strengthen their Christian lives to play the role that God has for each in carrying out his great plan for the world.

Thus in these statements of the Bible's final spokespersons there is good evidence of its unity, consisting in the steps God takes in carrying out his plan for the world. The case for its unity will be further strengthened as we consider in following chapters the circumstances that led to the formation of the canons of both the Old Testament and the New Testament.

Review Questions

1. If the message that Christian ministers preach is called the whole purpose of God, what are some of the fundamental teachings of this unified message?

2. Drawing upon the other Pauline speeches in Acts, explain what other thinking besides that of Paul himself must have been included in the phrase the "whole purpose of God"?

3. What is said in 2 Timothy 3:16–17 that strengthens your conviction about the indispensability of the Old Testament?

4. How do we know that the "we" in Galatians 1:8 must have been the most prominent Christian spokespersons?

5. Why is the unity of the whole Bible a necessary implication from Galatians 1:8?

6. What misleading understanding about the Old Testament was introduced by Melito of Sardis in A.D. 180?

7. How does the context of the public display of agreement in Galatians 2:9 strengthen our conviction about the Bible's unity?

8. How do 1 Corinthians 15:9 and Jude 3 argue that the canon was closed with the death of the last apostle?

9. Why would it be much more difficult to build the church if apostles appeared continually to add canonical teaching to our Bibles?

NOTES

[1] James Orr, *The Problem of the Old Testament* (New York: Charles Scribner's Sons, 1907), 31–32.

[2] In 4 below, mention is made of a certain Melito, bishop of Sardis (a city in the western part of what is today Turkey), who sometime before A.D. 180 went east, where there were more Jewish synagogues, to determine the exact books in the Jewish Bible. For some unknown reason he called these books the Old Testament, in contrast to the books of the so-called New Testament then regarded as canonical. His choice of the term "Old Testament" was unfortunate, for it implies that some sort of new start was made in the New Testament and thus discourages people from regarding the whole Bible as a unity. At this point we certainly cannot rename the Bible's first thirty-nine books. When I refer in this book to the Old and New Testaments, however, readers should understand that I intend to imply no gulf between these two parts of the Bible; similarly, in using "New Testament," I do not imply that God is making some new beginning in carrying out his plan of redemption.

[3] Paul's commissioning as an apostle took place some six years after that of the other apostles, who were commissioned during the forty days Jesus spent on earth after his resurrection. Paul thus regarded his appointment as an apostle like the birth of a baby at an abnormal time.

[4] K. H. Rengstorf, "Apostolos," in *Theological Dictionary of the New Testament*, 10 vols., ed. Gerhard Kittel and Gerhard Friedrich, trans. Geoffrey W. Bromiley (Grand Rapids: Eerdmans, 1964–76), 1:430.

[5] Nor could Paul have been lying about this agreement. He knew that when his Galatian epistle was read in the churches there, his enemies the Judaizers from Jerusalem would be in the audience and would be only too glad to contradict anything he said that was not true.

2

The Old Testament Canon and the Bible's Unity

The next three chapters deal with the legitimacy of the books composing the Old Testament and New Testament canons. Since we are concerned with the coherency of the message these books set forth, we must consider the circumstances that made them canonical. What caused the Jews to settle on the books composing the Old Testament canon, and the Christian churches to settle on the books of the New Testament canon? The answers to these questions are important for knowing whether or not we should expect the Bible's message to be a unity. We thus consider here the situation in Israel that gave rise to its Old Testament canon, a situation that provides a fundamental argument for the coherency of the Old Testament.

Israel's Sense of Historical Destiny

Israel is unique among the nations of earth in understanding its history as the result of a supernatural intervention of God that began when he founded the nation by singling out Abraham. In the eighth century B.C. the prophet Amos expressed this confidence when he quoted God as saying, "You only [Israel] have I chosen of all the families of the earth" (Amos 3:2). God's first move in implementing this decision is recorded in Genesis 12:1–3, where he said to Abraham, "Leave your country, your people and your father's household and go to the land I will show you. I will

make you into a great nation and I will bless you; I will make
your name great, and you will be a blessing. I will bless
those who bless you, and whoever curses you I will curse;
and all peoples on earth will be blessed through you." Most
of Genesis then tells how Abraham, his son Isaac, and his
grandson Jacob lived as foreigners in the land of Canaan.
The book ends with the account of how Jacob's twelve sons
settled in the land of Egypt, where the regular supply of food
made it possible for this rapidly expanding clan to survive.

During the four hundred years they stayed in Egypt, the
Israelites fell into disfavor with the Egyptians, who made
them slaves. But as the books of Exodus through Deuteronomy relate, God raised up Moses and through miraculous
works delivered his people from Egypt, bringing them back
to Canaan, the land of the patriarchs Abraham, Isaac, and
Jacob. There God enabled them to conquer the Canaanites
so the land could become their own, a marvel that finds
expression in Moses' words to the people: "The Lord did not
set his affection on you and choose you because you were
more numerous than other peoples, for you were the fewest
of all peoples. But it was because the Lord loved you and
kept the oath he swore to your forefathers that he brought
you out with a mighty hand and redeemed you from the land
of slavery" (Deut. 7:7–8).

Another example of Israel's conviction that its entire
history was being governed by God was the preaching of the
prophet Jeremiah (639–575 B.C.). When the people were
about to be led off into captivity in Babylon for their sins,
Jeremiah declared that the punishment was only temporary
and that God would continue to carry out his purposes for
Israel. Quoting God, he said, "If I have not established my
covenant with day and night and the fixed laws of heaven
and earth, then I will reject the descendants of Jacob and
David my servant and will not choose one of his sons to rule
over the descendants of Abraham, Isaac, and Jacob. For I
will restore their fortunes and have compassion on them"
(Jer. 33:25–26).

In addition, at least three of the 150 psalms, which so often
echo Israel's deep convictions, relate how God has worked
throughout its history. Psalm 78 tells of his working for his

people, despite their repeated sinning, from Abraham down through the Exodus from Egypt and on to the establishment of David as king. Psalm 105 recounts God's actions from Abraham to the Exodus, and Psalm 106 his dealings with Israel from the Exodus to the Exile, sometime after 587 B.C.

The Formation of the Old Testament Canon

The people's sense of historical destiny thus was clear, and their scribes and scholars recorded that history, producing a literature more complete and better preserved than that of any other ancient nation. The likeliest reason that Israel preserved its literature so well was the people's strong conviction that God had founded it as a nation through Abraham and had often intervened in its history to save it from destruction, because he was going to fulfill his promise to Abraham that in Israel all the nations of the world would eventually be blessed. Such happenings were far too significant to be forgotten and so impressive that the people developed a literature recounting God's dealings with them.

But this conviction of God's supernatural intervention as the root explanation for Israel's history was not shared by the surrounding nations. Thus Old Testament theologian Walther Eichrodt has remarked on the uniqueness of Israel's conviction that it was to play a crucial role in bringing the history of the world to a grand climax. He noted how Israel's consciousness of having a purpose to fulfill in world history, regularly reinforced by God's supernatural interventions and declarations, excluded "the fear that constantly haunts the pagan world, the fear of arbitrariness and caprice in the Godhead." Israel viewed itself as God's people, "that is to say, [as] a people possessing unity in their situation as *clients* of a common God."[1]

Three statements in the Old Testament are of particular help in making clear this unique relationship. One is Isaiah 64:4: "Since ancient times no one has heard, no ear has perceived, no eye has seen any God besides you, who acts on behalf of those who wait for him." None of the religions of the world knows anything of a God who is transcendent or personal and who works for the benefit of those who have committed themselves to him in that they willingly wait for him to act. In all other religions—and also in a Christianity that has not read its Bible carefully enough—there is talk only of working for God and of acting on behalf of his interests.[2]

Isaiah's theme is expanded upon by Jeremiah 32:40–41, where God promises, "I will make an everlasting covenant with [Israel]: I will never stop doing good to them. . . . I will rejoice in doing them good and will assuredly plant them in this land with all my heart and soul." This unique relationship between Israel and God is voiced also by the psalmist, here in a most startling way: "As the eyes of slaves look to the hand of their master, as the eyes of a maid look to the hand of her mistress, so our eyes look to the Lord our God, till he shows us his mercy" (Ps. 123:2). What we would naturally expect to find following the two "as" clauses is, "So our eyes look to you, O God, to catch every signal for what you want each of us to do." But instead the main clause radically breaks with this normal expectation to affirm that Israel was to look to God to work mercifully *for them,* instead of their working for him.

Why is the Bible the only place where one hears of such a God? Every historian is faced with the problem of explaining Israel's unique conviction about its relationship to God, for it is axiomatic that every effect must have a commensurate cause. I argue that Israel's holding to such a conviction, and carefully preserving the literature telling of the sequence and meaning of these divine interventions in its history, cannot be explained by any natural circumstance in its past. But since every effect must have a cause, the conclusion can only be that God did indeed intervene supernaturally in Israel's history and that the Old Testament canon is a result of a phenomenon that can be explained only by this miraculous intervention.

The Closing of the Old Testament Canon

The supernatural, divine interventions that gave rise to the compilation of Israel's canonical books continued in its history until about a century after being led off to captivity and exile in Babylon. Either Malachi, the last of the so-called minor prophets, or Ezra or Nehemiah, eminent leaders in postexilic Israel, received the last prophetic word from God. But as Israel passed from the control of the Persians (539–331 B.C.) to that of the Greeks (331–164), it gradually dawned on them that for many years they had received no prophetic revelation from God. So when in 164 B.C. Judas Maccabaeus cleansed and rededicated the temple desecrated by the Greeks, he had the stones for the altar piled to one side "until a prophet should come and decide [as to what should be done] concerning them" (1 Macc. 4:46; cf. 9:27 and 14:41).

Further testimony for this cessation of revelation comes from the Jewish historian Josephus (*Against Apion* 1.8), writing around A.D. 95. He also spoke of there being no "exact succession of the prophets" since the reign of the Persian Artaxerxes in the fifth century B.C., which was about the time when Malachi, Ezra, and Nehemiah were active.

Explicit Evidences of a Pre-Christian Closing of the Jewish Canon

A number of early Jewish writings, however, such as 1 Maccabees just cited, do not appear in our Bible. How and when was a decision made as to which books should be considered authoritative, or *canonical?* The first evidence of a closed canon[3] comes from a writing of Jesus ben Sira—an Old Testament apocryphal book often called Ecclesiasticus.[4] What we have today is the translation from Hebrew into Greek that ben Sira's grandson made when he moved from Jerusalem to Egypt and wanted the Greek-speaking Jews there to profit from his grandfather's wisdom.

In the prologue the grandson alludes to the Egyptian king reigning at the time, which enables scholars to date the translation as not later than 130 B.C. Three times the grandson alludes to the Jews' foundational books as falling into three categories: (1) "the Law and the Prophets and the others who have followed in their steps"; (2) "the Law and the Prophets and the other Books of the fathers"; and (3) "the

Law itself and the Prophecies and the rest of the Books."
The prologue begins as follows:

> Whereas many and great things have been delivered unto us
> by the Law and the Prophets and the others that have
> followed in their steps . . . my grandfather Jesus, having much
> given himself to the reading of the Law and the Prophets and
> the other Books of the fathers and having gained much
> familiarity after acquiring considerable proficiency in them,
> was himself led to write something [of these things] pertain-
> ing to instruction and wisdom; in order that, by becoming
> conversant with this [exposition] also, those who love learning
> should make even greater progress in living according to the
> Law.[5]

It should be noted that what the grandfather wrote was
"something of *these things.*" In that he was writing only
something of the Law, the Prophets, and the Books, the
grandson was making it clear that the grandfather did not
regard his book as taking its place alongside the books of the
third division. Instead he regarded it as an exposition of the
Jews' foundational books that would help people gain a
clearer understanding of them. In thus speaking, the grandson indicated that to add to these authoritative, canonical
books had never entered his grandfather's mind.

Ben Sira wrote his book perhaps as late as 160 B.C., or about
the time that Judas Maccabaeus said Israel had been without
a prophet for some time (see above). So the prologue to
Ecclesiasticus, as well as 1 Maccabees, contains statements
necessarily implying both that the Old Testament canon was
closed about 150 years before the Christian era and that it
was regarded as falling into three divisions.

This threefold division is further supported by Jesus'
statement in Luke 24:44–45 that "everything must be
fulfilled that is written about me in the Law of Moses, the
Prophets and the Psalms." Evidence is also found in his
statement in Matthew 23:34–35: "Therefore I am sending
you prophets and wise men and teachers. Some of them you
will kill and crucify; others you will flog in your synagogues
and pursue from town to town. And so upon you will come
all the righteous blood that has been shed on earth, from the

blood of righteous Abel [Gen. 4] to the blood of Zechariah son of Berekiah [2 Chron. 24], whom you murdered between the temple and the altar" (cf. Luke 11:51). Now as far as canonical *chronology* is concerned, the last martyr in the Old Testament was Uriah the son of Shemaiah, killed by King Jehoiakim (Jer. 26:20–23), who reigned in Judah 609–598 B.C. But according to a *baraita* (or very ancient tradition) in the Babylonian Talmud (Baba Bathra 14b),[6] the last book of the third division of the Jewish canon was 2 Chronicles, and the last martyr in that book was in fact this Zechariah. Jesus' reference to Zechariah implies that he was perfectly familiar with the structure of the long-since-closed Old Testament canon.[7] And in order to show how rebellious against God Israel had been all along, Jesus cited the first and last persons martyred according to the *official Jewish canonical sequence*. In this sense Zechariah was the last, as Abel was the first.

The Significance of a Closed Jewish Canon

Israel's conviction that God's prophetic interventions in its life had ceased is as remarkable a phenomenon as the conviction that its history and destiny had been shaped by these interventions. It is most comforting to feel that God is intervening on one's behalf, and human nature would, if it could, find a way to assure itself that this relationship was continuing. Thus if the conviction that God was supernaturally intervening in its history had been simply a part of Israel's cultural pattern, the nation might well have contrived a way to assure itself that this intervention had not stopped. But Israel could not maintain such a conviction because this phenomenon was not the product of human imagination but was initiated by God. So its inability to go on thinking that God was supernaturally intervening in its history confirms the conclusion that the record of these interventions and their interpretation could be explained only as a supernatural act of God. And if God's activity alone is capable of explaining the origin and closing of the Old Testament canon, then there is every reason to suppose that there is a unity and singleness of purpose in these books.

Thus an effort to understand the unity underlying these books will not be in vain.

The Problem of Jewish Wisdom Literature

It may be objected, however, that the inclusion of the wisdom literature—Proverbs and Ecclesiastes in particular—is out of place in a canon regarded as having arisen in a sequence of divine, supernatural interventions in history, which only the Psalms refer to explicitly. Old Testament theologian Gerhard Hasel alludes to the problem as follows:

> The wisdom materials of the Old Testament must be allowed to stand side by side with other [historical] theologies. [The wisdom materials] make their own special contributions to Old Testament theology on [an] equal basis with those more recognized ones [e.g., the Deuteronomist history]. . . . It would appear that where conceptual unity seems impossible the creative tension thereby produced will turn out to be a most fruitful one for Old Testament theology.[8]

Gerhard von Rad, another Old Testament theologian, has observed that Proverbs and Ecclesiastes do help to fill out a theology based on God's acts in history. He notes that the laws given in conjunction with the deliverance from Egypt could deal only with the most fundamental issues in life. Consequently "a wide sphere still remained unconditioned and unregulated by the [laws] . . . and yet in this sphere so many decisions had daily to be made."[9] The Egyptians and other nations around Israel had large collections of wisdom-literature maxims for acting wisely in given situations. And Israel likewise had its collection in the book of Proverbs. Here one finds an array of wise sayings to show how life should be lived with regard to matters either too commonplace or not well-suited to be addressed by the commands found in the Mosaic legislation. For example, Proverbs 15:1 declares, "A gentle answer turns away wrath, but a harsh word stirs up anger." A proverb is better suited than one of the Mosaic laws for teaching this essential element of wise living. And so it is with hundreds of other maxims found in the book of Proverbs.

Perhaps the reason that so much of Israel's wisdom literature was written without reference to the redemptive acts by which God carries out his plan for world history is that the truth of this literature can be gained and validated simply by observing life and does not depend upon a supernatural intervention. One does not need special revelation to know the pacifying effect of a soft answer. But such is not the case with the tenth commandment of the Decalogue: "You shall not covet your neighbor's house . . . or anything that belongs to your neighbor"(Ex. 20:17). The validity of this rule could certainly be questioned in a world where lack of life's necessities is widespread, and misery and death commonplace. To have credibility, therefore, such a command needs the revelatory knowledge implied a few verses earlier in Exodus, "I am the Lord your God, who brought you out of Egypt" (v. 2) and made explicit in similar statements in Leviticus (11:45; 22:33; 25:38; 26:45), which add that God's purpose in bringing Israel out of Egypt was to continue to be its God in the future. So for him to be Israel's God means he will intervene in future crises to deliver them. Therefore they do not need to covet, for when such a promise, known only by revelation, is true for a people, then it certainly follows that they should be content with what they now have. God as *their* God will surely supply what they need in the time of trouble.

Consequently, that a number of books in the Writings of the Old Testament canon do not allude specifically to God's supernatural interventions in Israel's history does not weaken the argument that this entire canon was formed because of Israel's acute awareness that God had frequently acted supernaturally on its behalf to make it a blessing to all nations of the earth. A considerable part of the canon does recount these prophetic interventions and provides revelation showing why, for example, people should not covet. But it was also essential that Israel have books detailing wise conduct that experience proves valid in a great variety of life situations. Not to have had an extensive collection of proverbs like the nations around it would have deprived Israel of the help such maxims provide to cope with life in a praiseworthy and fulfilling manner.

Moreover it is significant that some passages in Proverbs expressly affirm that much knowledge about how to live wisely comes only from God's special providential guidance. So, for example, Proverbs 16:2 says, "All a man's ways seem innocent to him, but motives are weighed by the Lord." And 21:30–31 makes it clear that living wisely is possible only with the help of God: "There is no wisdom, no insight, no plan that can succeed against the Lord. The horse is made ready for the day of battle, but victory rests with the Lord." This truth is also affirmed in 20:24: "A man's steps are directed by the Lord. How then can anyone understand his own way?" These are precisely the sorts of statements one would expect in the verbally inspired books of a nation whose existence and destiny is being determined by God's supernatural intervention.

Von Rad remarks how, in the Old Testament wisdom books, "all the teaching and lessons of experience which wise men impart to their pupils are designed to the end of 'strengthening trust in Jahweh' (Prov. 22:19)." As such, Israel's wisdom and proverbs avoid the sense of tragedy that is found in those of Egypt, and especially of Babylon, where suicide is recommended as the wisest course of action, given the meaninglessness of life.[10] Not even Ecclesiastes, the most pessimistic of Israel's wisdom literature, is without its hopeful side. True, the emphasis is that trying to make sense out of all that is "under the sun" (1:3 and throughout) will lead to the conclusion that "everything is meaningless" (1:2; 12:8). The sense of life's meaning, however, cannot come from what is seen, but only from what God makes known. And throughout Ecclesiastes it is emphasized that people should keep God in their thinking and not consider just what is "under the sun." Divine retribution from God comes to those who break vows (5:4–6), and so people are to "stand in awe of [him]" (v. 7). Furthermore, a person who acts wisely is sheltered (7:12), and "it will go better with God-fearing men, who are reverent before God" (8:12). The key to the apparent pessimism of Ecclesiastes may well be the statement that "God tests [people] so that they may see that they are like the animals" (3:18). The purpose of Ecclesiastes would thus be to teach people the ultimate wisdom of having no confidence in themselves but only in what God will providentially do for them as he intervenes supernaturally on their behalf.

In that Proverbs and, most explicitly, Ecclesiastes acknowledge that people on their own cannot come even close to deriving all the wisdom necessary for attaining a fulfilled future, they fit in well with the rest of the Old Testament canon, whose books are based on God's supernatural activities in Israel's history. In so doing, they (along with Job, the Song of Solomon, and Lamentations) are gold mines of maxims for wise living. In Job, for example, we find the statement, "Where can wisdom be found? . . . It cannot be found in the land of the living. . . . God understands the way to [wisdom]. . . . And he said to man, 'The fear of the Lord—that is wisdom, and to shun evil is understanding'" (28:12, 23, 28).

Review Questions

1. What common-ground evidence is there that the Old Testament gives a unified message regarding what God has said and done?

2. How does Israel's conviction that God's prophetic intervention ceased around 400 B.C. argue for the Old Testament's being a unity comprising a word from God?

3. How does the introduction to Ecclesiasticus argue for a closed Old Testament canon by the year 150 B.C.?

4. How does Jesus' statement about the martyrs from Abel to Zechariah provide evidence that the Old Testament canon was closed at that time?

5. Why do laws based on God's intervention in Israel's history need to be supplemented by proverbs and maxims in books making no reference to God's acts in redemptive history?

6. How does the pessimism of Ecclesiastes actually argue that it belongs in a canon controlled by the sequence of God's redemptive and hope-giving acts?

NOTES

[1]Walther Eichrodt, *Theology of the Old Testament*, trans. J. A. Baker, 2 vols. (Philadelphia: Westminster, 1961), 1:38, 40, italics added.

[2]Chapters 5 and 6 below, which briefly survey Hinduism, Buddhism, and Islam (after Christianity, the three largest religions of the world), demonstrate this point.

[3]By a "closed" canon I mean that at a certain point in time, "such general agreement has been reached [regarding which books are canonical], both among the leaders of the community and in the body of the faithful, that any contrary voices raised, however eminent, have no significant effect upon religious belief or practice" (Roger Beckwith, *The Old Testament Canon of the New Testament Church* [Grand Rapids: Eerdmans, 1985], 275). Beckwith's is the most extensively researched book on the Old Testament canon to appear so far in this century.

[4]The so-called apocryphal (or "hidden") books are the fourteen or fifteen books written in the two centuries before Christ and into the first century A.D. They were called hidden either because they were to be kept separated from the canonical books or because their value warranted their being kept in a safe place where only those who could truly profit from them would have access to them. Some of the better-known apocryphal books are 1–2 Maccabees, Tobit, Judith, Ecclesiasticus, and Baruch.

[5]Beckwith's translation (*Old Testament Canon*, 110–11), with additions in brackets based on the original in the LXX.

[6]The Talmud was the codification of the massive amount of Jewish civil and religious teaching derived from the Torah. This task was finally completed between the fourth and sixth centuries A.D.

[7]The Jewish Bible today (the Christian Old Testament) still follows this threefold division, in which the last book is 2 Chronicles. Jews call their Bible the "Tenach," an acronym for its three parts: "T" is for *Torah*, or the law composed by the first five books (Genesis through Deuteronomy); "N" stands for *Nebaim*, or "prophets" (Joshua through Malachi); and "CH" is for *Chethabim*, or "writings," the name for the rest of the Old Testament, including such books as Psalms, Job, Proverbs, Ecclesiastes, Daniel, Ruth, and 1–2 Chronicles.

[8]Gerhard F. Hasel, *Old Testament Theology: Basic Issues in the Current Debate* (Grand Rapids: Eerdmans, 1972), 94. Though I cite this quotation as evidence of the problem of seeing the

Writings as part of redemptive history, I am not happy with Hasel's implication that there are several theologies in the Old Testament.

[9]Gerhard von Rad, *Old Testament Theology*, trans. D. M. G. Stalker, 2 vols. (New York, Harper & Row, 1962–65), 1:433.

[10]Ibid., 440, 457 n. 8.

3

The Climax of Prophetic Interventions

In describing the circumstances that led to the formation of the Old Testament canon, we noted that beginning around 400 B.C., Israel was forced to conclude that God had ceased visiting it with supernatural interventions. But commencing with the preaching of John the Baptist four hundred years later, there was unmistakable evidence that God had resumed these interventions. Something of the indisputableness of this evidence comes from Matthew 21:23–27, where the Pharisees, sorely vexed by the great popularity Jesus was enjoying with the multitudes, asked him, "By what authority are you doing these things?" Jesus agreed to tell them if they would publicly answer one question: "John's [the Baptist] baptism—where did it come from?" They refused to answer the question, however, for they reasoned, "If we say, 'From heaven,' [Jesus] will ask, 'Then why didn't you believe him?' But if we say, 'From men'—we are afraid of the people, for they all hold that John was a prophet."

The Ultimacy of Jesus' Authority

Thus the manifest spiritual power of John the Baptist was surely a proof that someone at least as great as any Old Testament prophet was again on the scene. Other passages in the Gospels, too, cite evidence that this man was the climactic prophet. For example, in the announcement of

John's birth to his father, the priest Zechariah, the angel said, "[John the Baptist] will go on before the Lord, in the spirit and power of Elijah [the prophet]" (Luke 1:17). Then when John was born, Zechariah prophesied that "you, my child, will be called a prophet of the Most High; for you will go on before the Lord to prepare the way for him [Jesus]" (v. 76). He also foresaw that God had raised up John "to show mercy to our fathers and to remember his holy covenant, the oath he swore to our father Abraham" (vv. 69–73). Therefore John the Baptist had a crucial role to play in carrying out Israel's mission for world history, a mission that God had first indicated to the patriarch Abraham back in Genesis 12.

This significance was affirmed when Jesus arrived on the scene, for he declared that John the Baptist was the climax of the Old Testament supernatural interventions that had ended with the prophet Malachi. "[John is] more than a prophet. This is the one about whom it is written [Mal. 3:1]: 'I will send my messenger ahead of you, who will prepare your way before you'" (Matt. 11:9–10). The One for whom John prepared the way was none other than the Son of God, the second person of the Trinity, who came into the world as a man and ministered with great power for three years before his crucifixion, resurrection, and ascension back to heaven. And the writer of Hebrews testified to the supreme and ultimate authority of Jesus in affirming how he climaxed all previous revelation: "In the past God spoke to our fore-fathers through the prophets at many times and in various ways, but in these last days he has spoken to us by his Son" (Heb. 1:1).

John was more than a prophet because he declared that a person who was God himself was shortly to appear on the scene. Jesus himself could not be regarded merely as a prophet because he did not speak *for* God but *as being* God himself. Of all the biblical spokespersons, only Jesus attached "Amen" to his own statements, thereby declaring that he himself as God had the authority to affirm his teachings as reliable and true.[1] Matthew 18:3 is but one example of many in the Gospels: "I tell you the truth [*amēn*], unless you change and become like little children, you will never enter the kingdom of heaven."

Jesus justified this note of supreme authority by declaring himself to be the fulfillment of what the earlier revelatory spokespersons had been talking about. Thus as he preached in the synagogue of Nazareth early in his ministry, he cited Isaiah 61:1–2, "The Spirit of the Lord is on me, . . ." and then declared, "Today this scripture is fulfilled in your hearing" (Luke 4:16–21). This note of authority characterized all of Jesus' ministry. "He even gives orders to evil spirits and they obey him" (Mark 1:27), exclaimed the people after Jesus cast out demons. And at the conclusion of the Sermon on the Mount, they marveled that he "taught as one who had authority, and not as their teachers of the law" (Matt. 7:29).

It is noteworthy, however, that we have no written words directly from Jesus. Our knowledge of his words and deeds has come to us through the apostles he commissioned and through their close associates like Luke, Paul's coworker, and Mark, who was Peter's companion. These apostles faithfully sounded Jesus' note of authority in the traditions about him that they passed on, which today exist in the four gospels.

The Full Authority of New Testament Apostles

The apostles could speak thus on Jesus' behalf because in making them his spokespersons, he had channeled his full authority through them. In citing some specifics of this authority, we should note especially the example of Paul, whose many epistles in the New Testament and pivotal role in the book of Acts provide the most information about what it meant to be an apostle. His experience with Jesus on the Damascus road sets forth the two requirements for one to be an apostle: one must have seen the risen Jesus and must have been commissioned by him as his spokesperson. Thus Jesus said to Paul, "I have *appeared* to you to *appoint* you as a servant and as a witness of what you have seen of me and what I will show you" (Acts 26:16).[2] So it is not surprising to hear Paul declare that "Christ is speaking through me" (2 Cor. 13:3). He was so aware of being Jesus' spokesperson that on the very few occasions when he was less than fully sure of just what Christ would say, he warned his readers of that fact. In 1 Corinthians, where Paul is handling some difficult matters relating to marriage, he twice warned his readers that he was relying in part on his own wisdom, not the explicit teaching of Christ (1 Cor. 7:10–16, 40). But then after completing these instructions in verse 40, Paul added confidently, "And I think that I too have the Spirit of God [in saying what I have just said]."

Therefore in understanding himself to be an apostle, a spokesperson for Jesus Christ, it was only natural that Paul would regard his teaching and that of the other apostles as being the verbally inspired Word of God. Hence we read in 1 Corinthians 2:13, "[What God has freely given us] we [revelatory spokespersons] speak, not in words taught us by human wisdom but in words taught by the Spirit."[3] Paul was so convinced that the Lord Jesus, rather than himself, was the originator of his teaching that he said to the Thessalonians, "If anyone does not obey our instruction in this letter, take special note of him. Do not associate with him, in order that he may feel ashamed. Yet do not regard him as an enemy, but warn him as a brother" (2 Thess. 3:14–15). The same note of authority is sounded in 1 Thessalonians 5:27: "I charge you before the Lord to have this letter read to all the brothers." Paul could also assert his apostolic authority positively, without any implicit threats: "We have confidence in the Lord that you are doing and will continue to do the things we command" (2 Thess. 3:4).

The Collegiality of Apostolic Authority

In the passages just cited Paul used the pronoun "we" in affirming his authority, thereby affirming that there were other apostles and teachers with similar authority. We also encounter the phenomenon of individual apostles as having a specialty in certain aspects of God's whole counsel. One instance emerges from reflecting upon Galatians 1:18, which relates how Paul, three years after his conversion on the Damascus road, finally returned to Jerusalem and "visited" *(historēsai)* Peter for two weeks. Translators from the early church onward have taken this word to mean nothing more than a time for getting acquainted. It was felt necessary to give this almost-impossible meaning to *historēsai* because back in Galatians 1:11–12 Paul had said, "I want you to know, brothers, that the gospel I preached is not something that man made up. I did not receive it from any man, nor was I taught it; rather, I received it by revelation from Jesus Christ." Translators felt that if Paul had spent these two weeks with Peter conversing about Jesus Christ and the gospel, he would naturally have learned much from *him* and thus could not say that he received the gospel directly from Jesus Christ.

But the Greek word *historēsai,* from which our word "history" comes, means "visit a person for the purpose of inquiry."[4] So, for example, in referring to "natural history" we are talking about knowledge that results from *careful, painstaking* inquiry into the many facets of nature. This verb in Galatians 1:18 therefore indicates that during the two weeks Paul was with Peter, he must have cross-examined and grilled him hour after hour to learn all he possibly could about what Jesus taught and did from his baptism onward. It would be impossible to suppose that Paul could spend two whole weeks with Peter and not talk about Jesus, who had so radically changed the purpose of each of their lives!

How, then, could Paul say that the gospel he preached came directly from Jesus Christ, if he had had an intensive two-week course about Jesus from Peter, the chief apostle? The answer comes from understanding the particular ministry Paul had. In Galatians 1:16 he declared that God's primary purpose in revealing Christ to him and commissioning him as an apostle was "so that I might preach [Jesus] among the Gentiles." Therefore Paul's unique contribution as an apostle was to show how the gospel was to be taken by Jews, despite their peculiar culture pattern, to all the various culture patterns of the peoples of earth, so that churches could be formed in them as well. This task required a clear understanding of how baptism alone, rather than circumcision, was now to be the sign of those embracing God's gracious covenant as the gospel spread through the Mediterranean world. It also required understanding the truth that newly evangelized peoples were not required to forgo anything harmless in their dietary practices so as to conform to the Jewish kosher diet commanded in Leviticus 11.

It is also important to understand that the sticking point between Paul and the Judaizers at Galatia, who were trying to convince those churches that their founder, Paul, was a false teacher, was his refusal to allow Gentile Christians to be circumcised. Thus he declared, "I, Paul, tell you that if you let yourselves be circumcised, Christ will be of no value to you at all" (Gal. 5:2). Though the Judaizers regarded this insistence of Paul's as a proof that he was not a genuine apostle, in fact his refusal to permit circumcision was a most vital aspect of the gospel that he had received directly from Jesus.[5] He alone had received complete instruction from Jesus on this all-important matter of not enforcing Jewish culture patterns on Gentiles.

With these facts in mind, we can now understand how Paul could give the usual meaning to the word *historēsai* in Galatians 1:18, even after saying in verses 11–12 that he had received the gospel only from Jesus Christ and not from another apostle. It was his special understanding concerning the mission to the Gentiles, certainly a most crucial part of the gospel, that was the message Paul had received directly from Jesus Christ. So Paul's answer to the Judaizers, who cited this teaching as an argument against his being an apostle, was that he was simply passing on what Christ had uniquely given him as one of his spokespersons. But receiving this unique message did not rule out his learning many other things about the gospel from Peter.

So Paul forthrightly declared to the churches at Corinth,

> What I received [by way of tradition] I passed on to you as of first importance: that Christ died for our sins according to the Scriptures, that he was buried, that he was raised on the third day according to the Scriptures, and that he appeared to Peter, and then to the twelve. After that he appeared to more than five hundred of the brothers at the same time, most of whom are still living. . . . Then he appeared to James, then to all the apostles, and last of all he appeared to me also, as to one abnormally born. (1 Cor. 15:3–8)

In 1 Corinthians 11:23–25 we find this same theme:

> I received from the Lord [by way of tradition] what I also passed on to you: The Lord Jesus, on the night he was betrayed, took bread, and when he had given thanks, he broke it and said, "This is my body, which is for you; do this in remembrance of me." In the same way, after supper he took the cup, saying, "This cup is the new covenant in my blood; do this, whenever you drink it, in remembrance of me." For whenever you eat this bread and drink this cup, you proclaim the Lord's death until he comes.

Indeed, this report of the Last Supper could have been given directly by Jesus to Paul, but it seems more likely that it was told him by Peter.

Here, then, are two instances where Paul was teaching a part of the gospel that he had learned from at least one other apostle. Two matters are particularly noteworthy. First, in both instances he speaks of having "received" these traditions and "passed them on" to the Corinthians. The Greek word for "received" is *parelabon*, the very word that he used in Galatians 1:12 when he said that he had not been taught the gospel by any other apostles. But we have now seen that the gospel Paul had *not* received from other apostles concerned Jewish behavior in founding churches with Gentile believers. Therefore there is no contradiction between Galatians 1:12 and all that Paul must have learned during his two weeks with Peter (v. 18).

The second noteworthy matter is that Paul regarded what he had received from Peter as "from the Lord" (1 Cor. 11:23). That he thus passed on to the church at Corinth the tradition regarding the Lord's Supper indicates that Paul regarded Peter's teachings to be as much from the Lord as the particular teaching he had received immediately from Christ. And that the apostles Peter, James, and John gave Paul the right hand of fellowship (Gal. 2:9) implies that they regarded his understanding of how to carry out the Gentile mission to be as completely "from the Lord" as what each of them had learned immediately from Christ. So these other apostles did not make the mistake of the Judaizers at Galatia, faulting Paul because he had something unique to contribute in the matter of getting the gospel out to the Gentiles.

Therefore both the phenomenon of a resumption of

supernatural intervention that even its detractors could not publicly deny and the melding together of the particular teachings of the different apostles provide a powerful incentive for investigating the coherency of biblical teaching. In ordinary human experience people who regard themselves as authorities on certain subjects often clash, rather than cooperate, with others who are also authorities on these subjects. But while Peter, James, John, and Paul all claimed the authority of being Jesus' spokespersons, yet each deferred to the particular teachings of the other. This behavior can be explained only by their conviction that Jesus was responsible (1) for the apostolic authority each of them possessed and (2) also for the special teachings an apostle like Paul had received for carrying out his specific task of heading up the Gentile mission. So their record of cooperating with and supporting one other is a compelling evidence that they believed themselves to be teaching God's work in concert.

The Apostles and the Old Testament

Another compelling evidence for the unity of the Bible is the way the New Testament apostles regarded their teachings to fit in with and enrich the teachings of the Old Testament. Perhaps Paul, having been the most promising student of the great rabbinic scholar Gamaliel (Acts 22:3; cf. Gal. 1:14), had the hardest task harmonizing the Old Testament with what he had learned about the gospel from Jesus and the other apostles. It should be noted that Paul talks of his learning as training in Jewish tradition; according to Jesus, such tradition had replaced the commands of God in the Old Testament itself (Mark 7:8).

With such a background Paul obviously needed sufficient time to unlearn the rabbinic traditions and to learn what the Old Testament really taught. This process most likely took place during the three-year period that he spent alone in Arabia (Gal. 1:17–18). Among other things, he came to understand that the Messiah must first suffer before entering into his glory (cf. Luke 24:26; 1 Peter 1:11). He also had to realize that none of the commandments of God is ever to be understood as a "law of works," a job description, but as a "law of faith" (cf. Rom. 3:27; 9:32), a doctor's prescription. In declaring that God shows "love ['mercy' in the original] to a thousand generations of those who love [him] and keep [his] commandments," Exodus 20:6 clearly proves that all of God's commands are a law of faith, calling for an obedience of faith (Rom. 1:5) and subsequent works of faith (1 Thess. 1:3; 2 Thess. 1:11). Mercy, or grace, is therefore conditional, though never meritorious.[6]

We find, then, that one of the most striking encouragements to regard the New Testament as a unity with the Old Testament is the conversion of the young Pharisee, Paul, whose epistles compose a substantial part of the New Testament. For him to unlearn all his Pharisaic understanding of the Old Testament, "[their] own traditions," and relearn the Old Testament as "the commands of God" (Mark 7:8–9) constitutes one of the essential elements of the Bible's unity.

Paul's conversion also upholds the truth of what he and the Old Testament taught. We have firm evidence both for Paul's earlier life as a young rabbinic scholar and his later heading up of the Gentile mission. We cannot doubt his earlier involvement in Judaism (Gal. 1:13–14); otherwise the Judaizers at Galatia would have had an incontrovertible argument for refuting Paul. There is also historical evidence for Paul's spearheading of the Gentile mission. Early church history has many independent affirmations for this role, and no historian denies that Paul was the chief mover in establishing the churches in the Gentile world.

But the historian must also explain how a person so involved in Judaism could then act in completely non-Jewish ways, rejecting circumcision as the sign of the covenant for believing Jews and Gentiles (Gal. 2:3–5) and willingly eating nonkosher food as he maintained table fellowship with the Gentiles (vv. 11–14). Nothing in his background as one totally immersed in the traditions of Judaism can explain such a profound reversal of conduct. The only alternative for explaining how Paul came to eat pork is to accept his own explanation: this profound change resulted from his being confronted by the risen Jesus as he journeyed to Damascus to destroy the Christian church there.[7]

This complete reversal in Paul's goal in life is part of God's supernatural intervention, resumed with the birth of Jesus Christ some four hundred years after the cessation of the divine visitations resulting in the compilation of the Old Testament canon. I have argued that both the beginning and the termination of the Old Testament prophetic interventions can be explained only as acts of God rather than as the product of human imagination, and this argument supports the truth and therefore the unity of the Old Testament. Likewise the mighty resumption of supernatural intervention in the life and ministry of Jesus Christ, of which the conversion of Paul to head up the Gentile mission was one of its most lasting effects, argues for the truth and therefore the unity of the New Testament, which reports and interprets this final intervention.

Review Questions

1. What evidence is there that a supernatural intervention greater than those recorded in the Old Testament resumed during the first century of the Christian era?

2. What is the significance of Jesus attaching "amen" to his own statements?

3. How could Paul and James be apostles when both, unlike the other apostles such as Peter and John, were unbelievers during Jesus' ministry upon earth? (Hint: What two qualifications were necessary for one to claim to be an apostle?)

4. How does verbal inspiration differ from a dictation theory of inspiration?

5. Be able to show that Galatians 1:11–12 is not contradicted by verse 18, even though the Greek word *historēsai* in that verse means that Paul questioned Peter thoroughly when he was with him.

6. How can Paul say he received information about the Lord's Supper "from the Lord" when it really came to him via other apostles such as Peter?

7. How does the answer to number 6 encourage you to regard the Bible as a unity?

8. How does Exodus 20:6 prove that grace is conditional but not merited (a basic thesis of this book)?

9. Why is Paul's great adherence to Judaism in his preconversion days common-ground knowledge that all should accept?

10. Why is the termination of a supernatural intervention at the end of the apostolic age an argument for the truth of the Bible?

NOTES

[1] In the Old Testament "amen" was used only to affirm complete agreement with and confirmation of what *another* had said. For example, after each of the twelve crimes cited in Deut. 27:14–26 as punishable by death or deportation, the injunction is added, "Then all the people shall say, 'Amen.'" Likewise, Ps. 106:48 concludes, "Praise be to the Lord, the God of Israel, from everlasting to everlasting. Let all the people say 'Amen!'" This usage continued in the early church. For example, 1 Cor. 14:16 addresses the need for public worship to be carried on in an intelligible language so that new converts could understand and say "Amen" to what they heard.

[2] See also 1 Cor. 9:1, where Paul said, "Am I not an apostle? Have I not seen Jesus our Lord? Are you [converts at Corinth] not the result of my work in the Lord?"

[3] It should be emphasized that verbal inspiration was not divine dictation, such as the Koran, the Muslim scriptures, claims for itself. The verbal inspiration Paul claimed for himself and the other revelatory spokespersons in 1 Cor. 2:13 was one in which the Holy Spirit used the particular vocabulary and speech pattern of each biblical writer in a way best suited to convey, inerrantly, God's teachings in the Bible.

[4] Henry George Liddell and Robert Scott, *A Greek-English Lexicon*, rev. H. S. Jones and R. McKenzie, 9th ed. (Oxford: Clarendon Press, 1940), 842.

[5] See Eph. 3:1-13 and Rom. 15:15-18 for Paul's elaboration on the particular ministry Jesus had given him.

[6] The commands of God throughout the Bible are the conditions for receiving God's *mercy*. Hence the law and all other commands

can never be regarded as elements of a job description, where one receives a wage equivalent to the worth of the service rendered an employer (Rom. 4:4–5). Mercy is never something one earns or works for. Furthermore, people cannot work for God and do things for him, for God "is not served by human hands, as if he needed anything, because he himself gives all men life and breath and everything else" (Acts 17:25). But we certainly can follow the commands he gives as being the health regimen he prescribes so that we might overcome our spiritual sickness. See Daniel P. Fuller, *Gospel and Law: Contrast or Continuum?* (Grand Rapids: Eerdmans, 1980), 65–120, 199–204, and also the Appendix below for the exegetical arguments that God's commands are not for works but are always laws of faith.

[7]See Daniel P. Fuller, *Easter Faith and History* (Grand Rapids: Eerdmans, 1965), 208–29, for the complete argument that only the risen Jesus could have so changed Paul's life direction.

4

The Emergence of
the New Testament Canon

As chapter 2 has shown, God's supernatural interventions in Israel's history were the root cause for the formation of the Old Testament canon. The writing of the books that completed the biblical canon then began as this divine activity was resumed with John the Baptist, "more than a prophet" in that he introduced Jesus, who spoke as God's only Son (chap. 3). After Jesus' ascension these interventions continued in the work and teaching of his apostles, whom he appointed to be his spokespersons and to spread the gospel to the nations of earth. And when these interventions ceased, the churches found in this fact a most important guideline in deciding upon the canonical books of the New Testament. The remarkable awareness that the early church had that with the death of the last apostle, there would be no more prophetic interventions to impart revelation to them represents the final piece of evidence needed to motivate a person to search out the unity of the Bible.

Attestations of the Close of the Apostolic Age

With the death of the last apostle at the close of the first century, there was consensus in the Christian community that no further revelation would be given the church, which meant that the canon was now closed. The churches had been forewarned of this development by Paul, who declared that he was the *last* person to have been appointed as an apostle (see chap. 1 above). Jesus also implied this closing in John 17:20, where he made a sharp distinction between his apostles and those who would hear their preaching and believe: "My prayer is not for [my apostles] alone. I pray also for those who will believe in me through their message." And Jude, writing toward the end of the first century, spoke of "the faith [body of teaching] that was *once for all* entrusted to the saints" (v. 3).

The churches knew that people became apostles only because Jesus had appointed them. They in turn could and did appoint elders and bishops, but had no authority to appoint new apostles. So when the last apostle died, the churches knew that revelation had ceased and that now they must bring together the teachings and writings of the apostles and their close associates. Only through these teachings as the capstone to the Old Testament could they continue to be instructed by the whole counsel of God. Another reason for assembling the apostolic teachings was that so many writings falsely claiming to be apostolic were appearing. The *Epistle of Barnabas,* the *Teaching of the Twelve,* and the *Shepherd of Hermas,* for example, all claimed apostolic authority, and so the church had to draw a line between truly apostolic teachings and those that were spurious.

That the church recognized this need is evident from the writings of two of its leaders at the end of the first century. They clearly separated themselves from the apostles, thus implying that revelation had come to an end. First consider Clement, probably the bishop for the household churches in and near Rome, as he wrote to the Corinthian church around A.D. 95. Here he explicitly distinguished himself from the apostles: "The apostles received the gospel for us from the Lord Jesus Christ" (*1 Clem.* 42:1). Then in 42:2 he declared how only Christ, and not a bishop like himself, could appoint people to be apostles. In verse 5 he then stated that the apostles, after founding churches, did not appoint other apostles, but rather "bishops" and "deacons" to rule these churches and carry on evangelism to those yet to hear the gospel.

Further evidence that Clement saw himself as standing

outside the apostolic age is seen in his saying, "With true inspiration [Paul] charged you concerning himself and Cephas [Peter] and Apollos, because even then you had made yourself partisans. But that partisanship entailed less guilt on you; for you were partisans of apostles of high reputation [Paul and Cephas] and of a man approved by them [Apollos]. [But now you have taken sides with mere nonapostles, and so your guilt is much greater]" (*1 Clem.* 47:3–5).

How the church at the end of the first century regarded the teachings of Paul and Jesus in comparison with the Old Testament likewise has important implications for the formation of the New Testament canon and the unity of the Bible as a whole. Clement, for example, introduced his quotation of Jeremiah 9:23–24 ("Let not the wise man boast himself in his wisdom . . .") with the words "for the Holy Spirit says" (*1 Clem.* 13:1). Then he attributed the same level of inspiration to Paul when he declared that in 1 Corinthians Paul spoke in "true *spirituality*" [lit. trans. of 47:3], which I interpret to mean that Paul spoke with an inspiration that only a revelatory spokesperson had. In 13:1 Clement likewise affirms that the inspiration of Jeremiah and Paul extends to the words of Jesus as reported by the gospel writers, for after exhorting his readers to obey Jeremiah's command, Clement said, ". . . especially remembering the words of the Lord Jesus which he spoke when he was teaching gentleness and longsuffering." In the next verse Clement then cites several of Jesus' statements found in Matthew and Luke, such as, "Be merciful that ye may obtain mercy" (Matt. 5:7), and "With what measure ye mete, it shall be measured to you" (Luke 6:38). Further evidence is found in 16:2, where in introducing Isaiah 53:1–12 ("Lord, who has believed our report, and to whom was the arm of the Lord revealed?"), he said, "The scepter of the greatness of God, the Lord Jesus Christ, came not with the pomp of pride or of arrogance, for all his power, but was humbleminded, as the Holy Spirit spake concerning [Jesus in Isa. 53]."

The second early church leader we should notice is Ignatius, bishop at Antioch in Syria, who likewise distinguished himself from the apostles. Writing during his journey from Syria to Rome as a prisoner condemned to fight wild beasts in the Colosseum (c. A.D. 105), he said, "I do not order you as did Peter and Paul; they were apostles, I am a convict" (*To the Romans* 4:3). He also regarded "the gospel" as an ultimate authority. "Give heed to the prophets and especially to the gospel, in which the Passion has been revealed to us and the Resurrection has been accomplished" (*To the Smyrnaeans* 7:2). This statement implies that tradition regarding the death and resurrection of Christ, existing for the church today in the four gospels, was already being proclaimed either from memory or from written records and would be as authoritative as the writings of Peter and Paul. So we see how these two bishops differentiate their own authority and teaching from an entity that had finally been given "once for all" to the saints during the apostolic age and that put the Old Testament, Jesus, and Paul on the same level of ultimate authority.

The Formation of the New Testament

It is against this backdrop of a relatively brief period of prophetic intervention during the first century A.D. that we obtain an understanding of the emergence of the New Testament canon.

The Need for a Canonical New Testament

With the termination of the apostolic age, the churches of the early second century naturally felt deprived in that they could no longer hear the "living voice" of one of Jesus' apostles. This sense of change is evident in the writings of Papias, whose works themselves are lost but are known from their quotation by the fourth-century historian Eusebius in his *Ecclesiastical History*. The following quotation from Papias helps us understand how Christians of that time felt:

> I shall not regret to subjoin to my interpretations [of Jesus' teachings], also for your benefit, whatsoever I have at any time accurately ascertained and treasured up in my memory, as I have received it from the elders, and have recorded it in order to give additional confirmation to the truth, by my testimony.

For I have never, like *many*, delighted to hear those that tell many things, but those that teach the truth, neither those that record foreign precepts, but those that are given from the Lord, to our faith, and that came from the truth itself. But if I met with any one who had been a follower of the elders anywhere, I made it a point to inquire what were the declarations of the elders. What was said by Andrew, Peter or Philip. What by Thomas, James, John, Matthew, or any other of the disciples of the Lord. What was said by Ariston, and the presbyter John, disciples of our Lord; for I do not think I derived so much benefit from books as from the *living voice* of those that are still surviving. (3.39, italics added)

The latest probable date for this statement is A.D. 130. Though Papias revealed his preference for the "living voice" of those who had known the apostles, he knew that that voice had died out. So henceforth the church must live by the written voice of the Old Testament and of Jesus' apostles and close associates.

Therefore one driving force in the formation of the New Testament canon was the need to conserve the apostolic tradition in writing. Oscar Cullmann has stated that A.D. 150 was "already too far away [from the apostolic age] for the living tradition still to offer in itself the least guarantee of authenticity."[1] Written *apostolic* tradition alone could instruct the church from this time on.

The second driving force is indicated by Papias's statement about the proliferation of books "that record foreign precepts." Gnosticism, with its claim of a secret, unwritten apostolic tradition, was creating much confusion among the churches and had to be rejected because of its inability to validate its claim.

Apocryphal gospels had also been appearing in writing during the early decades of the second century, relating such bizarre tales as that the infant Jesus created sparrows and that he had miraculously killed his companions who were annoying him. According to Eusebius, even Papias's *Oracles*, which was about Jesus' ministry, was untrustworthy, since he had included "certain strange parables of our Lord . . . and some other matters rather too fabulous [to be credited]" (3.39). There were also numerous apocryphal books of Acts in circulation. Consequently the churches had to draw a line between valid and specious writings.

Thus the middle of the second century was a decisive moment in the church's history. The "living voice" of the apostles had now died out. But as Cullmann has observed,

> About the year 150 [Christians] were still near enough to the apostolic age to be able, with the help of the Holy Spirit, to make a selection among the oral and written traditions; on the other hand, the bewildering multiplication of Gnostic and legendary traditions had made the church ripe for this act of humility in submitting *all* later inspiration [purported transmission and exposition of apostolic teaching] to a norm. At no other time in the history of the Church could the fixing of the canon have been undertaken. It was at that very time that God granted to the Church the grace of recognizing the difference between the period of incarnation [of God's Word in Christ mediated by his apostles] and the period of the Church.[2]

Such decisions singling out those documents that "teach the truth" were not made in some church council attended by representatives from church districts scattered far and wide, as is sometimes claimed. Instead they were made informally at the grass-roots level, by small groups of Christians networked with each other in household churches located mostly around the eastern half of the Mediterranean.[3] No doubt the decisions of one network would be transmitted by a traveler to networks elsewhere. Thus there must have been many lists of the New Testament canon made up, but only two from that period are extant.

Indications of the Content of the Second-Century New Testament Canon

The first indication comes from Papias as quoted by Eusebius: "John the Presbyter [at Ephesus] also said this, Mark being the interpreter of Peter, whatsoever he [Mark] recorded he recorded with great accuracy. . . . Wherefore Mark has not erred in anything. . . . Matthew composed his history in the Hebrew dialect, and every one translated it as he was able." Eusebius then noted that Papias also made use of testimonies from "the first epistle of John and from [the first epistle] of Peter" (3.39).

This quotation from Papias mentions only two of the four gospels, but Irenaeus in his *Against Heresies* (c. A.D. 185) described the distinct features of each of the four gospels. And Eusebius (4.29) remarked that a certain Tatian (c. 170) had put these four gospels together into what was called a Diatessaron (lit. "through four"), an interweaving of the three Synoptic Gospels (Matthew, Mark, and Luke) into the sequence of the gospel of John.

The second and more complete list of the content of the second-century New Testament canon is the Muratorian Fragment, discovered in 1720 in a library in Milan by Cardinal Muratori. The opinion of scholars is that it was a list made up around A.D. 170 to indicate what books a group of churches in a certain geographic area held as canonical. The opening lines, where Matthew and Mark would be listed, are missing. But the first words of the extant list are ". . . at some he [Mark?] was present [with Peter], and so he set them down. The third book of the Gospel, that according to Luke. . . ." This wording implies that originally the gospels of Matthew and Mark had commenced the list. The fragment then justifies Luke's canonicity by saying that Paul had taken Luke "like a legal expert [*quasi ut iuris studiosum*]," who wrote "in his own name on Paul's authority [*nomine suo ex opinione*]." New Testament scholar F. F. Bruce remarked that it required a former professor of Roman law, Arnold Ehrhardt, to understand the significance of these words. Writing in 1953, Ehrhardt recognized them as the ones used to designate the legal expert *(iuris studiosus)* who accompanied a Roman provincial governor. This expert would issue documents in his own name that accorded with the opinion *(nomine suo ex opinione)* of the governor. So the Muratorian Fragment was explaining that Luke, who was not an apostle himself, nevertheless had a relationship with Paul like that of a legal expert with a Roman governor.[4] Therefore even though he put his own name to his gospel, it was apostolic in that it reflected the opinion of Paul and therefore had as much authority as the gospels of Matthew and John.

The Muratorian Fragment went on to speak of how the

disciple John wrote his gospel. This John was also regarded as the author of the epistle of First John. The epistles of Paul are then listed, including Philemon and the Pastoral Epistles (1–2 Timothy and Titus). The fragment justifies the canonicity of these letters by saying, "These were written in personal affliction, but they have been hallowed by being held in honour by the catholic church, for the regulation of church discipline."[5]

Then came mention of some of the so-called Catholic Epistles, specifically two by John. These may be 2 and 3 John, since 1 John had been mentioned earlier. Jude too is included. The fragment also noted that the churches had received "the Apocalypse also of John and of [2?] Peter which some of our friends will not have read in the Church." There is an outright rejection of the *Shepherd of Hermas* as having no apostolic backing, so that it should not be read publicly in the churches. Its listing of the Old Testament apocryphal book the Wisdom of Solomon as canonical is singular.

Some Characteristics of Second-Century Canonical Books

Thus the Papias quotation and the Muratorian Fragment validate many New Testament writings, but not all. What about Hebrews and James? Hebrews must have been written before the close of the apostolic age, because Clement, writing in A.D. 95, quotes from it, and its unnamed author claims to have been taught by the apostles of Jesus (Heb. 2:3). Possibly the uncertainty regarding its author was responsible for its being omitted from the two lists. It is significant that Papias regarded James as an apostle and mentioned his desire to learn everything he could about James. James's epistle, however, was written specifically for Jewish Christians and thus did not get a firm foothold in the West until the fourth century—probably the reason it was not included in the two extant lists. Beyond these disputed books there was also some opposition to the Revelation of John and to 2 Peter.

But such a situation was inevitable during those early

years. There was no way the persecuted churches in that century could all send representatives to a conference where careful deliberation could decide upon the canonicity of these disputed books. Therefore the incompleteness and ambiguity concerning certain books alluded to by Papias and the Muratorian Fragment is something that would be expected.

Then too, since the second-century canon came together in the informal, grass-roots manner alluded to above, we do not know how many other lists there may have been. In any event it is highly unlikely that all the networks of churches throughout the Roman empire would have reached immediate agreement regarding the disputed books, and the Muratorian Fragment's inclusion of the Old Testament apocryphal Wisdom of Solomon would surely have created a lively discussion resulting in its exclusion from the canon. But the crucial point about the formation of the canon in the second century is that it acknowledged that apostolic revelation had ceased and that for the church to survive, every effort must be made to gather together the writings of the apostles and their close associates. In subsequent years decisions leading to a settlement about the disputed books could be made, and in the meantime the churches could live with an as-yet-incomplete New Testament canon.

Another characteristic of the second-century New Testament canon was that it continued the apostolic practice of regarding the canonical books of the Old Testament as the Word of God. The Old Testament had been the church's basic Scriptures from the beginning. Paul, for example, reminded his younger helper, Timothy, "how from infancy you have known the holy Scriptures, which are able to make you wise for salvation through faith in Christ Jesus" (2 Tim. 3:15). The reference here could only be to the Old Testament canon, which the churches, too, continued to regard as their Scriptures. Since by around A.D. 60 a rift had developed between the synagogues and the churches, it is not surprising that Eusebius (4.26) relates how a certain Melito, bishop of Sardis during the reign of Marcus Aurelius (161–180), was asked by his brother, Onesimus, to provide him with "an exact statement of the Old Testament [books]." All ancient copies of the Septuagint, the Greek translation of the Old Testament, include apocryphal books alongside the canonical ones, because these books had always been held in esteem, and a scribe making a new copy of the Septuagint would want to fill any remaining space with edifying material. So it was natural for Onesimus to wonder about the precise listing of the Old Testament canon. In response Melito said,

> I have endeavoured to perform this, for I know your zeal . . . to acquire knowledge. When therefore I went to the East and came as far as where these things are proclaimed and done [a Jewish community in Syria?], I accurately ascertained the books of the Old Testament and send them to thee here below. Of Moses, five books, Genesis, Exodus, Leviticus, Numbers, Deuteronomy. Jesus Nave [Joshua, the son of Nun], Judges, Ruth. Four of Kings [1–2 Samuel and 1–2 Kings]. Two of Paralipomena [Chronicles], Psalms of David, Proverbs of Solomon . . . Ecclesiastes, Song of Songs, Job. Of prophets, Isaiah, Jeremiah. Of the twelve prophets, [all] one book. [Also] Daniel, Ezekiel, Esdras.[6]

A third characteristic of the second-century New Testament canon was that it readily admitted writings composed by nonapostles who worked in close association with an apostle. Thus Luke, who wrote his gospel and Acts, has more in writing in the New Testament than any other author. We have also seen how Mark was regarded as apostolic because of his close connection with Peter. As for Hebrews, the author's statement in 2:3 that he had been taught by the apostles, plus its use by Clement at the early date of A.D. 95, argues strongly for an author who, like Mark and Luke, was in close association with the apostles.

The Significance of the Appearance of the New Testament Canon

It is noteworthy that the New Testament canon emerged in much the same way as that of the Old Testament. Like the cessation of supernatural intervention after the time of Malachi, Ezra, and Nehemiah, its cessation with the death of the last apostle points up that this second series of divine visitations too was something that happened only to Israel, not to humankind in general. Neither its beginning nor its ending can be explained by forces already at work in the Palestine of that day. We can postulate only be the initiative of God himself. And since the writings of the New Testament canon embody the message God gave in that intervention, we have a compelling reason to believe that the New Testament forms a unity with the message of the Old Testament canon, whose origin, as argued in chapter 2, could only be God himself.

This concludes the inductive reasoning mentioned in the Preface for arriving at the conclusion that the Bible is the Word of God and true. But just because something is true does not mean that everyone should take the time and energy necessary to grasp its truth. Only if the nature of the message is so important that one's future fulfillment and happiness depend on knowing it and responding to it properly should such an effort be made. That the biblical message is indeed that important will now be shown by contrasting the blessings promised by the God of the Bible with the prospects for happiness that one would have as an adherent of each of three other great world religions: Hinduism, Buddhism, and Islam.

Review Questions

1. Cite two elements from 1 Clement to prove that the church at the close of the first century regarded revelation to have ceased and therefore the canonical record of it (when assembled) to be closed.

2. What does Clement say that argues for the unity of the Old Testament and the New Testament?

3. In what sense was the New Testament canon closed in A.D. 150? In what sense was it not closed then?

4. Why was there incompleteness and diversity in the listing of the New Testament canonical books coming out of the second century?

5. What was there about Greek copies of the Old Testament (i.e., the Septuagint, or LXX) that c. A.D. 175 caused

Onesimus, the bishop of Melito's brother, to question the exact extent of the Old Testament canon?

6. How does the final prophetic intervention, which ceased with the death of the last apostle, argue for the divine origin and truth of the New Testament?

NOTES

[1] Oscar Cullmann, "The Tradition," in *The Early Church*, ed. A. J. B. Higgins, trans. A. J. B. Higgins and S. Godman (Philadelphia: Westminster, 1956), 89.

[2] Ibid., 91–92.

[3] Two and a half centuries later, when Christians were no longer persecuted and Christianity had become the state religion of the Roman empire, the Third Council of Carthage was convened (A.D. 397). This ecumenical council declared officially that the twenty-seven books we now have in the New Testament represented the New Testament canon.

[4] F. F. Bruce, "Some Thoughts on the Beginning of the New Testament Canon," *Bulletin of the John Rylands Library* 65, 2 (Spring 1983): 56. See also his *Canon of Scripture* (Downers Grove, Ill.: InterVarsity Press, 1988), 161.

[5] At that time in history, "catholic church" meant the majority of churches in which there was consensus regarding fundamental matters, not, as is often the case today, the Roman Catholic church.

[6] Esdras included our present Ezra-Nehemiah. The only book omitted from this list was Esther. Some have thought that the Jews with whom Melito consulted had kept that book out of sight because the recent third war with Rome, the revolt under Bar Cocheba (A.D. 132–35), made it inexpedient to have a book that mentioned an earlier Jewish uprising.

5

One's Future in
Hinduism and Buddhism

Two remarkable aspects of God's purpose for his creation are found in Isaiah 64:4: "Since ancient times no one has heard, no ear has perceived, no eye has seen any God besides you, who acts on behalf of those who wait for him." The first aspect is his promise that for those who trust him, he will work to do them good. The encouragement this gives is made even greater by a further promise in Jeremiah 32:41: "I will rejoice in doing them good . . . with all my heart and soul." The Almighty God, the Creator of the universe, thus wants nothing so much as to work for people's benefit; doing so brings him complete and unsurpassed joy. And the more we consider this truth, the more we become assured of enjoying an eternity of happy tomorrows.

The second remarkable teaching in Isaiah 64:4 is that God works for the benefit of those who *wait* for him. It must be emphasized that enjoying the blessing of having God work for our benefit is conditioned upon ceasing to trust in our own wisdom and efforts to attain a happy future, waiting instead for him to bring it to pass.

The uniqueness of God's promise to work beneficially for those who wait for him can be verified in large measure by comparing Christianity with the three other great religions in the world: Hinduism, Buddhism, and Islam. This comparison will show that only in one of Buddhism's two branches is there anything faintly resembling the idea of Isaiah 64:4, though closer examination will show that it, too, falls short of providing lasting happiness. First, however, we look at Hinduism, probably the oldest of these three religions.

Hinduism

Some 630 million people (13.1 percent of the world's population), most of them in India, espouse this ancient religion. Since its religious leaders are pictured as content and serene, one might infer that Hinduism provides the sort of peace and joy that people would have whose God is acting benevolently on their behalf. But a consideration of its tenets makes clear that, to the contrary, this serenity comes from learning to *suppress* the desire for happiness by disciplines designed to enable one both to become detached from this present world and to be indifferent to one's welfare in the future.

This detachment is illustrated in the "Song of God," a famous passage in the Bhagavad Gita that has been called the Gospel of Hinduism.[1] The song begins by telling how Arjuna, a member of the noble warrior caste (Kshatriya), was poised with his four brothers to do battle with an army made up of close relatives. Previously Arjuna had been robbed of his land and exiled for thirteen years by his cousin Duryodhana. Upon his return he sought to reclaim his land, but not even his uncle could prevail upon Duryodhana to restore it. So Arjuna prepared to do battle with his relatives, and the story opens as the two armies confront each other.

But Arjuna was troubled as he faced these men whom he would soon be trying to kill. Therefore he asked Krishna, his charioteer, who was actually the ninth incarnation of the god Vishnu, to delay the battle by halting between the two forces. As Arjuna looked at these "fathers, grandfathers, uncles, cousins, sons, grandsons, teachers, friends, fathers-in-law and benefactors" arrayed against him, he confessed to Vishnu, "My limbs fail me, ... my body trembles and my hair stands on end. [My bow] slips from my hand, and my skin burns. I cannot keep quiet, for my mind is in tumult. . . . What good can come from the slaughter of my people on this battlefield?" (8). "If, on the contrary, [my cousins] . . . should slay me, unarmed and unresisting, surely that would be better for my welfare!" (10).

To these questions Krishna replied,

The wise grieve neither for the dead nor for the living. There was never a time when I was not, nor thou, nor these princes [in the opposing army] were not; there will never be a time when we shall cease to be. . . . Those external relations which bring cold and heat, pain and happiness, they come and go; they are not permanent. Endure them bravely, O Prince! The hero whose soul is unmoved by circumstance, who accepts pleasure and pain with equanimity, only he is fit for immortality. . . . The Spirit [the ultimate reality, Brahman], which pervades all that we see, is imperishable. Nothing can destroy the Spirit. The material bodies which this Eternal, Indestructible, Immeasurable Spirit inhabits are all finite. Therefore fight, O Valiant Man! (16).

He who thinks that the Spirit kills, and he who thinks of It as killed, are both ignorant. The spirit kills not, nor is It killed. . . . Even if thou thinkest of It as constantly being born, constantly dying, even then, O Mighty Man, thou still hast not cause to grieve. For death is as sure for that which is born, as birth is for that which is dead. Therefore grieve not for what is inevitable. (17)

[Brahman] the end and beginning of beings [is] unknown. We see only the intervening formations. . . . Though many are told about [Brahman], scarcely is there one who knows It. . . . [Therefore] thou must look at thy duty. Nothing can be more welcome to a soldier than a righteous war. . . . Refuse to fight in this righteous cause, and thou wilt be a traitor . . . incurring only sin. . . . To the noble, dishonour is worse than death. . . . If killed, thou shalt attain Heaven; if victorious, enjoy the kingdom of earth. . . . Look upon pleasure and pain, victory and defeat, with an equal eye. Make ready for combat, and thou shalt commit no sin. (18)

Several facets of Hindu thinking are apparent in this exchange between Arjuna and Krishna. First, there is Brahman, an impersonal reality at the heart of everything in the universe. Here all the apparent opposites of the visible world—for example, "cold and heat, pain and happiness, victory and defeat"—meld together as one. Second, between phenomenal individuals and the noumenal, impersonal

Brahman are "intervening formations." These are caused by what Hinduism calls *maya*, something of an illusion, so that people find it easy to regard as real the opposites in the phenomenal world around them.

The Hindu concept of righteousness also becomes evident. It is one's relationship to *dharma* (the "law," "custom," or "order") that spells out the duties the members of each caste are obliged to perform. Thus in the Bhagavad Gita we see Krishna's argument to Arjuna that sin is not killing revered relatives and friends but failing to behave as one who is a member of the warrior caste.

Another facet of Hindu thinking is *yoga*, the discipline necessary for going beyond the illusory phenomenal world and becoming conscious of the noumenal world of Brahman. "But thou hast only the right to work, but none to the fruit thereof. Let not then the fruit of thy action be thy motive; nor yet be thou enamoured of inaction. Perform all thy actions with mind concentrated on the Divine [Brahman], renouncing attachment and looking upon success and failure with an equal eye. Spirituality [yoga] implies equanimity" (21).

Arjuna, however, regarded this teaching as hard to follow and thus objected to Krishna. "I do not see how I can attain this state of equanimity which Thou hast revealed, owing to the restlessness of my mind. My Lord! Verily, the mind is fickle and turbulent, obstinate and strong, yea extremely difficult as the wind to control." Krishna agreed that the mind is "exceedingly difficult to restrain, but . . . with practice and renunciation it can be done" (65).

> Verily this Divine Illusion of Phenomenon manifesting itself in the Qualities is difficult to surmount. Only they who devote themselves to Me and to Me alone can accomplish it. . . . Who meditates on Me without ceasing, devoting himself only to Me, he is the best. . . . After many lives, at last the wise man realises Me as I am. A man so enlightened that he sees God [Brahman] everywhere is very difficult to find. . . . I am not visible to all, for I am enveloped by the illusion of Phenomenon. This deluded world does not know Me as the Unborn and the Imperishable [i.e. Brahman]. (72)
>
> [But] to him who thinks constantly of Me, and of nothing else, to such an ever-faithful devotee, O Arjuna, am I ever

accessible. Coming thus to Me, these great souls go no more
to the misery and death of earthly life, for they have gained
perfection. The worlds, with the whole realm of creation,
come and go; but, O Arjuna, whoso comes to Me, for him there
is no rebirth. (80)

In truth, therefore, there is the Eternal Unmanifest, which is
beyond and above the Unmanifest Spirit of Creation. . . . The
wise say that the Unmanifest and Indestructible [Brahman] is
the highest goal of all; when once That is reached, there is no
return. That is My Blessed Home. (82)

Karma and "rebirth" are also important facets of Hindu
thinking. Karma is the degree of merit in achieving detachment from the phenomenal world that one has achieved in
previous lifetimes and to date in the present life. Krishna
spoke of it to Arjuna as follows:

No evil fate awaits him who treads the path of righteousness.
Having reached the world where the righteous dwell, and
having remained there for many years, he who has slipped
away from the path of spirituality will be born again in the
family of the pure, benevolent and prosperous. . . . Then the
experience acquired in his former life will revive, and with its
help he will strive for perfection more eagerly than before.
Unconsciously he will return to the practices of his old life; so
that he who tries to realise spiritual consciousness is certainly
superior to one who only talks of it. Then, after many lives, the
student of spirituality, who earnestly strives, and whose sins
are absolved, attains perfection and reaches the Supreme. (66)

The task of reaching the "Supreme" or the "Blessed
Home" of Brahman thus is formidable. Only a "very few"
devote all efforts to becoming spiritual. These must meditate
without ceasing on the noumenal aspect of Krishna or on one
of the other aspects of Brahman such as the gods Shiva or
Brahmin. They must also renounce all thought of the
rewards they will gain from their labor to sustain life. No
doubt the "restless mind" can be stilled for a few hours by
rigorous exercises in meditating on the illusory nature of the
phenomenal world pressing in on all sides. But such
awesome forces as one's complete immersion in this phenomenal world and the mind's instinctive inclination to
choose activities that will bring gain from one's work will

soon again concentrate one's thoughts upon the illusory phenomenal world. Thus one's karma rating will decline. And the painful knowledge that one tends to live life exactly as it was lived in previous incarnations would tend to extinguish any hope of success in constantly meditating on the noumenal Brahman.

In contrast, all that is required of those who desire blessings from the omnipotent and omniscient God of the Bible is to wait for him in the sense of banking all their confidence for a happy future on the many promises he has made. So the future happiness one may have as set forth in the Bible is vastly more attainable than that offered to the Hindu. And since all humanity craves happiness, all—Hindus included—are therefore well advised to expend the time and effort necessary to learn God's whole purpose in history as set forth in the Bible.

Buddhism

Buddhism emerged from a Hindu context in the person of Siddharta Gautama, born around 560 B.C. in a town in Nepal, near the northern border of India. Currently 556 million people (11.5 percent of the world's population) adhere generally to one of two basic forms of Buddhism. The original teachings of Gautama are most recognizable in southern Asia (Sri Lanka, Burma, Thailand, Kampuchea, and Laos), although even here it has undergone variations. In Sri Lanka, for example, it is combined with astrology and many elements of primitive animism—ideas that Buddha himself would have spurned.

> Fear of unknown forces is a very powerful controlling factor in the lives of many Buddhists and Hindus in Sri Lanka. They go regularly to astrologers, shrines, medicine men, exorcists, or such people, who claim to have power to control or direct supernatural forces. When the people are faced with sickness or some such trouble, they ask, "Is this because of a charm or an evil spirit?" If so, they want to counteract the evil forces, using whatever means available to them.[2]

A different sort of Buddhism is found in Tibet, parts of the Soviet Union, Mongolia, China, Taiwan, Vietnam, Korea, and Japan. In distinction to that of much of southern Asia, this northern form calls itself Mahayana ("Upper Vehicle") Buddhism. Since this title implies that the Buddhism in parts of southern Asia is inferior, its followers in the South prefer to call their religion Theravada Buddhism, or "The Buddhism of the Elders." A consideration of this earlier form is necessary in order to understand Mahayana Buddhism.

The Buddhism of the Elders

Siddharta Gautama, or Buddha ("the enlightened one"), a name Gautama received from his followers, was born into a wealthy family living in a palace as isolated as possible from the misery, poverty, and death in the world outside.[3] But one day at age twenty-nine, married and the father of a small child, Siddharta disobeyed his father's order never to leave the palace grounds and went out to see how the rest of the world lived. So profoundly shocked was he at the spectacle of death, poverty, and human suffering outside his palace that a few nights later he left his sleeping wife and child and departed, never to return.

Donning the saffron robes of a wandering beggar, shaving his head, and generally following Hindu teaching, he tried to block out the phenomenal world of suffering and reach Brahman through meditating and subjecting himself to ascetic extremes. But though he persisted in this regimen for six years, he found no relief from the problem of suffering.

Therefore he abandoned such efforts, and while sitting under a tree, later called the Bodhi ("knowledge") Tree, he decided upon a new approach. The previous six years, he was convinced, had brought no enlightenment because he had sought it with the very same selfish desire that causes so much suffering in the world. Therefore he abandoned his efforts to get through to Brahman by rigorous efforts to concentrate on one of its manifestations such as Krishna, choosing instead to follow a more relaxed "middle way" of living. And seven weeks later full enlightenment finally came. Going then to a public place in the nearby city of

Benares, India, he began to teach this new way to attain peace in a world of suffering. As he taught, he radiated such calm and self-possession that ascetics who had known him during the first six years became convinced that he truly had received a remarkable enlightenment. And so for the remaining forty-five years of his life, he tirelessly traveled throughout northern India preaching his message and radiating his serenity. An increasingly large number of men from different castes began to follow his precepts, and in time women too were allowed to become initiated into an order.

Siddharta summarized his enlightenment in "Four Noble Truths": (1) suffering is universal; (2) the cause of suffering is attachment to things or a craving for them; (3) the cure for suffering is the elimination of craving and attachment by (4) following the "middle way." This middle way obviously meant avoiding one extreme of giving in to carnal lusts. But it also meant avoiding the opposite extreme of craving knowledge of Brahman in the Hindu way of asceticism. To elucidate this middle way Siddharta advocated the Eightfold Path.

The first step is *right belief.* Part of this right belief is to waste no time and energy trying to answer metaphysical questions as to whether the world is created and temporal or eternal, finite or infinite, or whether the life principle of a person is identical with the body or distinct from it. Suffering still exists no matter what answers are given to such theoretical questions. Effort should therefore be devoted instead to fostering worthy attitudes and practical ethical behavior. One must avoid modes of behavior that cause suffering such as killing, stealing, immorality, lying, talebearing, harsh language, covetousness, and ill will. The second step, *right mindedness,* requires carrying on one's activities from a proper motive. While this step naturally includes rejecting the motives that lead to forbidden behavior, it also emphasizes the need to carry on one's activities with a wisdom that will alleviate suffering in oneself and others.

The third and fourth steps, *right speech* and *right action,* repeat much of step 1. The fifth step of *right living* concerns choosing a life vocation that brings benefit rather than hurt to society. *Right effort,* the sixth step, spells out the four virtues one needs to foster: avoidance of evil, overcoming of lust and bad habits, development of helpful words and actions, and maintenance of the sort of behavior that will help eradicate suffering. The seventh step of *right attentiveness* also singles out four objects—the body, the emotions, the mind, and worldly phenomena—from which so much suffering can come until one learns, for example, not to love the beautiful or strong parts of the body, because they will wither and die as readily as the body's uglier and weaker parts. *Right concentration* then brings the Eightfold Path to a climax. Those making progress into this eighth step should begin to experience the joy of trances that are a foretaste of nirvana, where one never again has to be reborn into the world of suffering.

True to his distaste for metaphysical speculation, Buddha was vague in describing nirvana, which means literally the "blowing out" of existence. This concept would seem to imply annihilation, a conclusion that Buddha never affirmed. All that mattered to him concerning this subject was that it marked the end of painful becoming and the beginning of the peace of an eternal, changeless state of being. Those destined for nirvana after their last lifetime would await death with calm detachment and contentment.

In distinction to the Hinduism from which it sprang, Buddhism could be characterized as a humanistic, even atheistic, religion. It did, however, carry over into its teaching two somewhat revised features of Hinduism: karma and rebirth. Buddha reiterated the concept of karma, whereby one's merit from a preceding life would determine the status attained in a future one. But his understanding of karma allowed people to be much more optimistic about their future than they could be in Hinduism. "In [Buddha's] view a man of any caste or class could experience so complete a change of heart or disposition as to escape the full consequences of sins committed in previous existences. . . . [The Law of Karma] could not lay hold upon a man . . . who had achieved arahatship, 'the state of him that is worthy,'"[4] the last step of the Eightfold Path. This arahatship, or spirituality, canceled out the past karma that heretofore had determined the quality of one's next life. So in Buddha's teaching a spiritual person, or arahat, would live eternally in nirvana and never become a part of the painful world of flux again.

Buddhism also distinguished itself from Hinduism in that Buddha and his followers were to foster a benevolent attitude toward others. So, for example, the sixth step of the Eightfold Path decreed that one should choose a vocation that contributed to the well-being of society. Buddhists were also to maintain a loving rather than an unconcerned or vengeful attitude toward others, which was essential to have peace of soul. This emphasis on love figured largely in the rise of "Upper Vehicle" Buddhism, which became prominent around A.D. 100 after going through several modifications.

Mahayana ("Upper Vehicle") Buddhism

The first modification came from the strong influence of King Asoka, who became ruler of all India in the third century B.C. To secure such power required his dealing cruelly with the people who lived alongside the Bay of Bengal, though the Buddhist teaching he had already received condemned him for such violence. Asoka decided to make Buddhism the official religion of India but expounded it as a system of piety whereby people could be good Buddhists simply by carrying on normal lives, without having to become monks or nuns.

Another step toward Mahayana Buddhism was the virtual deification of Buddha. Although Buddha himself had asserted that there were many gods in the universe, he discouraged prayer or devotion to any of them, since they, like human beings, were finite and subject to the pain that comes from the flux of life. Buddha himself never encouraged people to direct prayers to him after he died and entered nirvana. But in order to spread his teachings, his followers had come to build sanctuaries called *wats*, where ordinary people could assemble to be instructed by monks. Most of these wats had an image of Buddha seated above the altar. And though the well-trained monks regarded prayers as nothing more than repetitions that earned merit, the common people began to direct their prayers toward Buddha himself. They saw him as one who would help them in their need because he had fostered a benevolent attitude toward others and now enjoyed the transcendence of being in the changeless nirvana. It was then but a short step to think of Buddha as having preexisted before coming down to earth to tell people how to gain alleviation from suffering. To this notion was added the idea that he was a divine, omniscient being who had repeatedly volunteered to be incarnated on earth to bless people with his teachings. It was then another short step to the belief that Buddha had lived sinlessly during these incarnations and therefore had earned enough merit to dwell in Tusita, the most desirable heaven.

The third step in Buddhism's modification came with the belief that many such buddhas had come to earth before Siddharta Gautama and that others would come after him. Thus the idea took shape that the universe was full of compassionate beings who wanted to aid suffering humanity. Now people sought salvation not just by the Four Noble Truths and the Eightfold Path but by looking to these buddhas as divine beings with vast stores of merit that they were eager to share with the faithful so they too could enjoy the blessings of heaven. This exceedingly hopeful message carried by Mahayana Buddhism caused it to spread much more rapidly than the original form. By the second century A.D. it was found throughout the lands generally north of the Himalayas—Tibet, China (including Vietnam), Mongolia, Korea, and Japan.

Mahayana Buddhism taught that ordinary people who were well on their way toward the final step on the Eightfold Path were *bodhisattvas* ("Buddhas in the making"). But when they died, instead of entering nirvana, they would choose another rebirth, so that they might help thousands more learn the way to nirvana. The greatest of these bodhisattvas had chosen rebirth rather than nirvana thousands of times, and as a result had acquired so such merit that they dispensed it from a heavenly place to those who worshiped them and directed prayers to them. Noss observes that "this merit is so great that they could readily achieve the full status of Buddhas and pass into nirvana; but they are compassionate beings; out of love and pity for suffering humanity they postpone their entrance into nirvana and transfer their merit, as need arises, to those who call upon them in prayer and give devotional thought to them."[5]

The following statement from a Prajnaparamita Sutra ("teachings concerning transcendental wisdom"), written soon after the first century A.D., explains the motivation of such a being.

> Doers of what is hard are the Bodhisattvas, the great beings who have set out to win supreme enlightenment. They do not wish to attain their own private nirvana. On the contrary, they have surveyed the highly painful world of being, and yet, desirous to win supreme enlightenment, they do not tremble at birth-and-death [of future lives on earth]. They have set out for the benefit of the world, for the ease of the world, out of pity for the world. They have resolved: "We will become a shelter for the world, a refuge for the world, the world's place of rest, the final relief of the world, islands of the world, lights of the world, leaders of the world, the world's means of salvation."[6]

One such bodhisattva is Amitabha, a great god revered in China, Korea, and Japan. According to Noss,

> The hopeful devotee . . . turns to Amitabha, and has merit transferred to him from the great being's store. . . . A Mahayana treatise widely read in China and Japan, *A Description of the Land of Bliss* . . . says distinctly that faith in Amitabha, quite apart from meritorious works and deeds, is alone sufficient unto salvation. It declares:

> Beings are not born in that Buddha country as a reward and result of good works performed in this present life. No, all men or women who hear and bear in mind for one, two, three, four, five, six, or seven nights the name of Amitayus [an emanation from Amitabha], when they come to die, Amitayus will stand before them in the hour of death, [and] they will depart this life with quiet minds, and after death they will be born in Paradise.[7]

Is Mahayana Buddhism, then, like Christianity, a religion of hope for the future?

An Evaluation of Buddhism

Unquestionably the original Buddhism, the Teaching of the Elders, is more encouraging than Hinduism in that it affirms that one can break out of the destiny one's karma, gained through countless previous rebirths, would otherwise decree for one. Through a far-reaching repentance, one could be born instead into a much better form of existence in the next life. It is also more encouraging in that it clearly teaches that with the attainment of nirvana, one will never again be reborn into this world of flux and suffering. But the very changes that took place in the years following Buddha's death indicate that this earlier form too left much to be desired.

Ordinary people simply could not be satisfied with its indifference to transcendental matters. Their needs impel them to reach out for an omniscient, omnipotent, and loving God to answer their prayers and deliver them from the difficulties of this life. People also want definite teachings about the afterlife, and so later Buddhism came to talk about specific heavens whose inhabitants have not lost their identity as individuals. Also necessary is a religion in which men and women can participate fully without becoming monks or nuns but can carry on the ordinary vocations essential for society's well-being.

The subsequent changes both in the original Teaching of the Elders and in the development of Mahayana Buddhism demonstrate how Buddhism added those features for which people yearn. As a result the teaching regarding the foremost bodhisattvas of Mahayana Buddhism comes close to competing with the Bible's teaching that God will rejoice with his whole heart and soul to work for the welfare of the people who wait for him. That the great Bodhisattva, Amitabha, will bring to paradise a person who does nothing more than meditate on his name for one day before death surely sounds as if divine blessing could be received by grace. It is open to abuse, however, by those who wish to live sinfully during this life but nevertheless spend eternity in paradise—provided they could accurately predict when they would die. I certainly do not suggest that all who revere Amitabha are like that, for the teachers of Mahayana Buddhism urge people to be full of good works and to aspire to become bodhisattvas themselves.

Nevertheless the problem arising from the possible abuse of Amitabha's grace does exist, though it could never arise with the God of the Bible, who works for those who simply wait for him. Waiting for God means banking one's hope for an eternity of happy tomorrows exclusively upon what God has promised to do; it means having him as one's hope for the future. According to Psalm 33:20, "We wait in hope for the Lord; he is our help and our shield." A pronounced change of conduct then occurs in those having such confidence in what the loving and supreme Creator-God of the universe will do for them, for such a hope is the root cause of all virtuous living. People who confidently wait for God to bring them the desired fulfillment for their lives will not abuse others and use them as means whereby they might gain some happiness for the future. Instead they seek to serve others, because they know that God will provide for every need. All would feel at ease living alongside a person with such a hope in God.

So the Bible teaches that the condition people must fulfill in order to have the loving God work for them is not to wait for him just for one day but to make waiting on him their purpose from the time they first trust him until death. To be sure, the Christian believes in the validity of deathbed conversions, for Jesus told the thief on the cross who believed in him that he would dwell with him that very day in paradise (Luke 23:43). But the Bible gives no encouragement whatsoever to think that one could live sinfully for most of life and then be assured of paradise by thinking about God for a day or so before death.

However, an important advantage Christianity has over Mahayana Buddhism is that people need never feel ashamed to go to heaven. In Mahayana Buddhism a person could never refuse rebirth without feeling guilty that in so doing he or she was being selfish by denying others help so they too could find paradise. But there is no reincarnation taught in the Bible: "[A person] is destined to die once" (Heb.

9:27). Therefore Christians need never choose between enjoying heaven and acting lovingly toward others.

We also noted the tendency in Buddhism toward a personal transcendence. Thus Buddha himself became personalized, even though much of his individuality may have been lost in the indefinite nirvana. Herein lies Christianity's biggest advantage over Mahayana Buddhism: it explicitly teaches people to worship a living Lord now and to look forward to the enjoyment of a close family relationship with him for eternity.

During his life on earth Jesus was subjected to much suffering, personally experiencing all the hurts life can bring. So we Christians "do not have a high priest who is unable to sympathize with our weaknesses, but we have one who has been tempted in every way, just as we are—yet without sin" (Heb. 4:15). Indeed, in Mahayana Buddhism there are highly personal beings who have experienced the full range of suffering during their innumerable reincarnations. Amitabha, for example, dwells in a land one step removed from nirvana. He remains there because he still wants to use his vast store of merit, constantly increased by his unselfishness in postponing nirvana for himself, to bring millions and millions of people to his place next door to nirvana—the ultimate hope in Buddhism.

So the impersonal and individual-suppressing nirvana is still held to be the final goal of salvation, even though the history of Buddhism gives ample evidence that its adherents yearn not for cessation of individuality but rather for contact with a highly personal, transcendent being. Hence this tension, lying at the very heart of Buddhism, remains unresolved.

In Christianity, however, this tension is resolved. According to Revelation 21:1–5, the Christian will finally be in the closest fellowship with God, who "will wipe every tear from their eyes. There will be no more death or mourning or crying or pain, for the old order of things has passed away."

Review Questions

1. Contrast the bases for the experience of peace as set forth in Christianity and Hinduism. Which would you prefer, and why?

2. Though Hinduism sees good and bad as merged together in Brahman, the impersonal, ultimate reality underlying all things, nonetheless it does teach that there is "sin." In what does this sin consist?

3. Why would Krishna's exhortation quoted above, to behave as a true warrior and not to worry about killing relatives and friends, be a counsel of despair?

4. What tends to be discouraging about the Hindu teaching of karma?

5. Why would it be wrong for a Hindu to aspire to the highest (Brahmin) caste?

6. How might a Hindu argue against Buddha's teaching that the desire to become one with Brahman was fostering a desire for attachment rather than detachment?

7. What is more hopeful about "the Buddhism of the Elders" than Hinduism?

8. Contrast the Buddhist nirvana with the biblical heaven? What would cause you to choose one rather than the other?

9. What is the strongest objection to Buddhism, which led to the development of "Upper Vehicle Buddhism"?

10. How does Christianity avoid the objection that one is selfish to want to go to heaven?

11. Under what circumstances can a Christian's desire to go to heaven be an extreme form of selfishness?

12. What great problem confronts both forms of Buddhism and causes Upper Vehicle Buddhism to teach something that at first glance seems to be a gospel of grace?

13. Why must it take as long as 1.25 billion years for one to become a bodhisattva, an "enlightenment being"? Why cannot one who renounces nirvana for the good of

others start preaching Buddhism in the near future as soon as reaching maturity in his or her next reincarnation?

14. The teaching of Mahayana Buddhism about the god Amitabha sounds like salvation by grace, which would seem to prove Isaiah 64:4 false. But why does Isaiah 64:4 remain true?

15. Why do the bodhisattvas, despite all the merit for others they have accumulated, finally become valueless in Upper Vehicle Buddhism?

NOTES

[1] *The Bhagavad Gita*, trans. Shri Purohit Swami (London: Faber & Faber, 1978). This song is part of the Mahabharata, a 100,000-verse epic composed 400 B.C.–A.D. 400. According to John B. Noss, scholars estimate that the Bhagavad Gita was composed around A.D. 100 (*Man's Religions*, 3d ed. [New York: Macmillan, 1963], 266).

[2] Ajith Fernando, *The Christian's Attitude Toward World Religions* (Wheaton, Ill.: Tyndale House, 1987), 43. The author is a native of Sri Lanka.

[3] The information regarding Buddhism for this summary comes from Noss, *Man's Religions*, 167–252, and from *A Buddhist Bible*, ed. Dwight Goddard (New York: E. F. Dutton, 1952).

[4] Noss, *Man's Religions*, 180.

[5] Ibid., 217.

[6] Edward Conze, *Buddhism: Its Essence and Development* (New York: Harper & Row, 1959), 128.

[7] Noss, *Man's Religions*, 221, citing Sir Charles Eliot, *Hinduism and Buddhism*, 3 vols. (London: Edward Arnold, 1921), 2:30. The quotation is from the Lesser Sukhavati-vyuha.

6

The World of Islam

Islam, or "submission to the will of God," is the most recent of the world's great religions and claims 970 million followers, or 18.4 percent of the world's population. This monotheistic religion directs all worship to Allah as the creator and almighty God and regards Muhammad, whose teachings are set forth in the Koran, as the final prophet, superseding all previous prophets such as Abraham, Moses, and Jesus.

The Origin of Islam

Muhammad was born around A.D. 570 in the region of Mecca in Arabia. With no acting father and a mother who died when he was six, he was cared for by his grandfather for a short time and then by his uncle. Becoming a shepherd boy, he lived in poverty as a nomad near Mecca. Some verses in the Koran may echo this time: "Did [Allah] not find thee an orphan and shelter thee? Did he not find thee erring, and guide thee? Did he not find thee needy, and suffice thee?" (93:6–8).[1]

Later Muhammad accompanied caravans organized by his uncle; these took him as far north as Syria and as far south as Yemen. In this work he gained a reputation for being dependable and honest, and around 595 these qualities caught the attention of the wealthy widow Khadija, who entrusted her business affairs to him and later married him, though fifteen years his senior. With her wealth supporting him, he now had more leisure time.

By the seventh century both Judaism and Christianity had extended their influences into Arabia, and the frequent references to the Old Testament and to Jesus in the Koran indicate that Muhammad had been exposed to them both as a dweller in Mecca and during his travels as a caravaner. Their teaching of the one God who was not to be represented by any image or picture may have aroused within him a loathing for the idolatry of the pagan Bedouins. In any event, around 610 Muhammad formed the habit of withdrawing at night to a cave at the foot of a mountain north of Mecca, where he meditated and prayed. About a year later on the night of 26–27 Ramadan, he received his first revelation when the angel Gabriel appeared to him and said, "Recite: In the Name of thy Lord who created, created Man of a blood-clot. Recite: And thy Lord is the Most Generous, who taught by the Pen, taught Man that he knew not" (96:2–5).

Mecca had long been the destination of the pagan, polytheistic Bedouins because of the sacred black meteorite resting in the corner of the Kaabah, a cube-shaped sanctuary for their gods. Since the economy of the town depended heavily on the money brought by these pilgrims, at first Muhammad was reluctant to repeat the messages he had been receiving from this monotheistic God. Such teaching would clash with the polytheism of the Bedouin pilgrims and would probably deter them from visiting Mecca and enriching its economy. But as Muhammad continued to receive revelations, his assurance that they were genuine increased. The resulting conviction that he had therefore become a prophet of the one and only God may be indicated by the following: "I swear . . . by the night swarming, by the dawn sighing, [that] truly this is the word of a noble Messenger having power, with the Lord of the Throne secure, obeyed, moreover trusty" (81:15–21).[2]

With his calling assured, around the year 613 Muhammad began to declare that there was one supreme God and that he was that God's final prophet. He seems also to have denounced the Bedouin practice of burying alive baby girls thought to be superfluous (81:9). As expected, his preaching infuriated the people of Mecca. But his wife, Khadija, encouraged him to keep on preaching Allah as the only supreme God, a God of mercy and justice who would judge all people for their behavior. Earlier this God had been proclaimed by Abraham, Moses, and Jesus, but now he, Muhammad, had superseded them. "It is He [Allah] who has sent His Messenger [Muhammad] with the guidance and the religion of truth, that he may uplift it above every religion. God suffices as a witness" (48:25).

Opposition at Mecca to Muhammad and his followers (now called Muslims, or "those who have submitted to Allah") became so pronounced that in 619 he and many of his converts fled two hundred miles north to the city now called Medina. After his arrival he was invited to umpire disputes between tribes, and his success paved the way for more refugee Muslims to join him. Their number was then swelled by additional converts at Medina.

A number of battles then ensued between the Muslims of Medina and the pagans of Mecca, but finally Muhammad reached an agreement with the Meccans that allowed him and his followers to return as Muslim pilgrims. Thus Mecca became the Muslim sanctuary, and Muhammad now undertook to subjugate all of Arabia to Islam. For him there was no division between church and state. Jews and Christians could practice their faith as second-class citizens as long as they remained loyal to the state, but pagans were to be conquered. As "idolaters," they were to be given a few months to turn to Islam. If they failed to do so, however, the word was clear: "Slay the idolaters wherever you find them. . . . But if they repent, and perform the [Muslim] prayer, and pay the alms, then let them go their way; God is All-forgiving, All-compassionate" (9:5). Another directive reads, "O believers, fight the unbelievers who are near to you, and let them find in you a harshness" (9:125). With such statements it is no wonder that Islam was soon called the religion of the sword.

The Teaching of Islam

This use of the sword was one reason why, after only a century, Islam reigned from Spain to India. It almost engulfed France as well, being turned back only after its forces suffered a decisive defeat in 732 at the hands of Charles Martel. Another reason for its amazingly rapid advance was the simplicity of its teaching, so that today it is the world's largest religion next to Christianity. Only five things are required to be a Muslim: (1) confess the unity of God and the apostleship of Muhammad; (2) pray five times a day facing toward Mecca; (3) give the prescribed alms; (4) observe a fast during the month of Ramadan, when no food is eaten from dawn until evening;[3] and (5) if at all possible, make one pilgrimage to Mecca before death.

There are also high ethical commands in the Koran. For example, in 2:272 one hears an echo of the Christian teaching to conceal one's good deeds: "If you publish your freewill offerings, it is excellent; but if you conceal them, and give them to the poor, that is better for you, and will acquit you of your evil deeds." This passage is significant not only as a likely instance of Christian influence on Islam but also as evidence that in Islam, salvation is attained as one performs more good deeds than bad ones: evil deeds are canceled out, or acquitted, by the performance of good deeds. But there is no hope of salvation for those denying the tenets of Islam.

The metaphor of the pan-balances of a scale appears several times in the Koran to emphasize that entrance into paradise depends on a preponderance of good works over evil ones.

> For when the Trumpet is blown . . . then he whose scales are heavy—they are the prosperors, and he whose scales are light—they have lost their souls in Gehenna [hell] dwelling forever, the Fire smiting their faces. (23:104–5)
>
> We shall set up the just balances for the Resurrection Day, so that not one soul shall be wronged anything; even if it be the weight of one grain of mustard-seed [to determine whether the good outweighs the bad or vice versa]. We shall produce it, and sufficient are We for reckoners. (21:48)

If the pan-balance shows that one's good works outweigh the bad, then at the Judgment Day that one will be admitted to paradise with blessings far exceeding the tit-for-tat good works performed on earth: "Whosoever does an evil deed shall be recompensed only with the like of it, but whosoever does a righteous deed, be it male or female believing—those shall enter Paradise, therein provided without reckoning [in a tit-for-tat way]" (40:44).[4] For those who earn this paradise pleasures abound:

> O which of your Lord's bounties will you and you deny? [I.e., it will be hard to choose which of the abundance of Paradise's bounties are to be enjoyed.] Therein [are] two fountains of running water, . . . therein of every fruit two kinds. . . . [Therein you shall be] reclining upon couches lined with brocade, the fruit of the gardens nigh to gather [whenever one wishes them], . . . therein [are] maidens restraining their glances, untouched before them by any man. . . . [They are] lovely as rubies, beautiful as coral. . . . Shall the *recompense* of goodness be other than [such] goodness? (55:49–60, italics added)

> [The Godfearing] shall have whatsoever they will with their Lord; that is the *recompense* of the good-doers, that God may acquit them of the worst of what they did, and recompense them with the *wages* of the fairest of what they were doing. (39:35–36, italics added)

The Value of Islam

There is no denying that the blessings of the Islamic paradise are enticing. But attention should be directed toward two drawbacks in these blessings as Koranic teaching presents them.

The Inability to Satisfy the Heart Fully

In perusing the paradise passages in the Koran, one notes that the ultimate blessings for the Muslim do not go beyond a superabundance of the most pleasurable things to be enjoyed in this life. There is no indication whatsoever that heaven's joys culminate in fellowship with God.

In comparing Islam with Christianity, we may find it helpful to reflect on one of the Pensées (or "thoughts") of Blaise Pascal (1623–62), the famous French mathematician and philosopher.[5]

All men seek happiness, without exception; they all aim at this goal, however different the means they use to attain it. . . . The will never makes the smallest move but with this as its goal. [The quest for happiness] is the motive of the actions of all men, even of those who contemplate suicide.

And yet, for centuries past, never has anyone, lacking faith, reached the mark at which all continually aim. All men murmur: princes, subjects, nobles, commoners; old and young; learned, ignorant; sound and sick; of every clime, of every time, of every age, of every state. . . .

What is it then that this eager desire, and this incapacity, cry aloud to us but that man once possessed true happiness, of which nothing now remains save the mark and empty outline [*la trace toute vuide*], which he vainly tries to fill in with his circumstances, seeking from things [ahead in the future] the help which he fails to find in things present, [but] all of them incapable of giving [contentment and joy], because the infinite abyss [*goufre infini*] can only be filled by one infinite and steadfast object, i.e., by God Himself? (Thought 250)

Pascal argued that a philosophy contrived by human reflection could never succeed in filling this "infinite abyss" because philosophy can talk only about things either in this world or imaginatively by analogy to these things. But since human experience proves that nothing in this world succeeds in silencing humankind's universal complaint, it follows that to fill the abyss, attention must be directed to the great religions, with their claims to know of transcendent things that human imagination cannot concoct. As Pascal said in Thought 249, "Let us examine all the religions of the world, and see whether there is any other than Christianity which satisfies our need."[6]

On the subject of the ultimate blessings the Christian is to enjoy, the Bible's teaching contrasts sharply with the Koran's message for Muslim faithful. During this life, fellowship with God is the only thing that satisfies: "Whom have I in heaven but you? And earth has nothing I desire besides you. My flesh and my heart may fail, but God is the strength of my heart and my portion forever" (Ps. 73:25–26). The same great hope is held out for the hereafter: "And I—in righteousness I will see your face; when I awake, I will be satisfied with seeing your likeness" (Ps. 17:15). As does the Koran, the Bible refers to heaven as a place free from the miseries of this world; only the heaven of the Bible, however, includes enjoyment of intimate fellowship with God: "No longer will there be any curse. The throne of God and of the Lamb [Christ] will be in the city, and his servants will serve him. They will see his face, and his name will be on their foreheads" (Rev. 22:3–4).

Pascal's reasoning seems sound that the inner desire of humankind can never be met by earthly pleasures but only by such fellowship with God. How, then, could one living in a Muslim heaven find contentment for eternity doing nothing more than lounging in gardens through which cool streams flow, being served refreshing drinks by beautiful and diffident maidens? But to have fellowship with a God who is like Jesus Christ would constitute a joy that could never become commonplace.[7]

Why does the Koran lay no emphasis on the ultimate blessing of having fellowship with God? One plausible explanation is that the blessings of a Muslim heaven are regarded as wages paid by God. They honor the individual as a workperson who has had the skills, strength, and character necessary to meet some need of God the employer. So it would be incongruous in this system to consider fellowship with such a deficient God as a reward for one's praiseworthiness in meeting his needs.

Precisely at this point the uniqueness of the God of the Bible becomes most evident, for he "is not served by human hands as if he needed anything" (Acts 17:25). To the contrary, this God works on behalf of, or for the benefit of, those who trust and hope in him. And he is so complete in himself that in thus working he finds his greatest joy. As Old Testament theologian Walther Eichrodt observed (see chap. 2 above), Israel's religion was the direct opposite of those practiced by the surrounding peoples. In their religions God was the client for whom the people must work in order to get from him certain blessings regarded as wages, something earned. But for Israel it was just the reverse: Israel was to regard itself as the client for whom God was

working, as long as the people trustingly obeyed his direc-
tives for their welfare.

So when the situation in Islam is exactly reversed in
Christianity and God is the praiseworthy worker who meets
the needs of believing people, then having fellowship with
such a good God becomes most desirable. We thus can
conclude that Islam, in comparison with Christianity, promises a heaven that falls far short of being what the human
heart craves for most.

The Impossibility of Having Assurance in Islam

This second drawback is made clear by the Koran, which
teaches that it is only the pan-balances at the future
judgment that will determine those Muslims who will be
saved. In the meantime one can only hope that his or her
good works will outweigh the evil. But no one can be sure,
and this fear of failure tends to keep one somewhat nervous
about the future and to that extent unconcerned about the
needs of others. Thus the very lack of assurance reduces a
person's potential for being loving, and the less benevolent
one is to others, the fewer good works will be in the pan-
balance to counteract the evil ones. This situation in Islam
and even in some branches of Christianity (i.e., Roman
Catholicism) can easily create a vicious circle, where the
lack of assurance of being God's child keeps uncertainty
reigning in the heart, which in turn lessens one's chances for
doing good works. And the more people realize that this fear
is keeping them from looking for opportunities to be benevolent, the more they lack assurance that God will be pleased
with them.

Here, then, is another striking contrast between Islam and
the religion of the Bible. Hebrews 6:11–12 says, "We want
each of you to prove the same diligence as before in
maintaining full assurance of hope unto the end of your lives,
in order that . . . you may be imitators of those who through
faith and patience inherit the promises" (author's own
translation). The Bible makes full confidence that God is for
us and not against us the foundation on which to build a life
of good works, whereas Islam teaches that one must try to

amass as many good works as possible without any such assurance, since only at the final judgment can it be known whether one is to spend eternity in paradise or in hell.

These two drawbacks in Islam underscore the superior value of the religion taught in the Bible, as do the difficulties inherent in Hinduism and Buddhism. We conclude, therefore, that the Bible, for whose truth we earlier provided sufficient evidence, sets forth a message well worth our expending the time and energy to understand. Only by appropriating its message will the God-shaped vacuum of the heart be satisfied, completely and forever.

Thus the way is now clear for us to commence a study of the Bible in order to learn its unity, that is, God's will, the purpose he is carrying out step by step in creation and history.

Review Questions

1. In what sense is Allah merciful, even though paradise is reserved only for those whose good deeds outweigh the bad? (Hint: See the section "The Teaching of Islam.")

2. What is the most significant omission in the Muslim description of paradise (heaven) in contrast to the Christian description?

3. Who is the client in Islam—God or the Muslim? Who is the client in the biblical religion—God or the believer?

4. When should one gain full assurance of sins forgiven in Christianity? When is it gained in Islam?

5. Explain why the Christian doctrine of assurance helps one to be more benevolent than does the Muslim doctrine.

NOTES

[1]The 114 suras, or chapters, in the Koran ("Reading") are arranged not chronologically but generally by length (e.g., the second is 15 percent of the whole Koran; the last one consists of only seven lines). Quotations from the Koran are taken from *The*

Koran Interpreted, trans. Arthur J. Arberry (New York: Macmillan, 1955), a translation regarded as of the highest quality.

[2] Muhammad never regarded himself as an inspired revelatory spokesperson, but only as one who repeated what the angel Gabriel, the "noble Messenger," told him.

[3] Because Muslims have a lunar calendar, over the course of several years Ramadan occurs at every season of the year.

[4] The "believing" here is limited to the affirmation of Muslim beliefs and the denial of others; for example, "They are unbelievers who say, 'God is the Messiah, Mary's Son'" (5:19). Unlike the Bible, the Koran says nothing about the power of faith, understood as hope and confidence in God's promises, to produce works pleasing to God and helpful to others.

[5] Blaise Pascal was a genius who, in his twenties, developed analytical geometry and the principles of probability. At the age of thirty-two, he pursued more actively his longtime interest in religion and entered the reform-inclined, monastic Jansenist community of Port Royal, France. At the risk of his life, he wrote a score of pseudonymous letters exposing the devious practices the Jesuits were successfully using to silence all dissent against the papacy. Overtaken by cancer in his late thirties, he began his lifelong ambition of writing a book on the evidence for the truth of the Christian religion. His deteriorating health, however, allowed him only to jot down about one thousand "thoughts," which were to be basic themes and arguments for this book. Though death intervened at age thirty-nine, his "thoughts" have been regarded ever since as theological thinking at its best. The source for quotations here, both English and French, is *Pascal's Pensées,* trans. H. F. Stewart (New York: Pantheon Books, 1950).

[6] In this chapter and the preceding one I have attempted to carry out, on a small scale, such an examination of the world's four major religions—Hinduism, Buddhism, Islam, and Christianity. Chapters 2–4 conclude that Christianity is true. Now we have seen that, unlike the other three great religions, Christianity satisfies the craving of the heart and enhances the welfare of society, thus making its truth of the greatest relevance.

[7] In chapter 10, see the section "Why Only God Can Meet Our Need-Love." Only a century after Islam's founding, a mystical movement arose in a group called the Sufis, who sought to gain a sense of fellowship with Allah. Such a development indicates the insatiable desire of the human heart to have close communion with what is ultimately transcendent in one's religion.

PART 2

THE FOUNDATIONS OF REDEMPTIVE HISTORY

7

An Inductive Study
of Genesis 1:1–2:3

In approaching the study of the Bible, we are naturally concerned to grasp what the writers themselves were trying to communicate in the books they wrote or formed from materials already at hand. But a big obstacle in accomplishing this goal is the presuppositions each of us readers has, for everyone already has something of a belief system in place. Yet if we study the Bible simply to have it reinforce convictions we already have, we gain little from our efforts. Therefore we should do our utmost to set aside previous ideas relevant to a text so that new understandings have a chance to illumine our minds.

To be sure, none of us can distance ourselves completely from our presuppositions. But we must make the strongest possible effort to hold them at bay. As the French theologian Oscar Cullmann has said,

> The fact that complete absence of presuppositions is impossible must not excuse us from striving for objectivity altogether. . . . On the contrary, a *special effort* is needed if I am not simply to ascribe [for example] my own love experiences of a particular kind to the writer of a love song, who could have had very different experiences. . . . [The perennial principle of all sound exegesis] is, not to interpret myself into the text. . . . Obviously as a Christian I shall interpret [see the significance of?] the Koran differently from a Moslem. Yet in my interpreting, I shall try continually not to impose my Christian questions and notions of faith upon it.

Furthermore, Cullmann declared that it was quite possible to "interpret a text of a pagan religion correctly without belonging to this religion. Otherwise, all scholarship on the history of religions would be impossible."[1]

Cullmann also affirmed that to hear what the Bible has to say, "I may not consider it certain that my Church's faith in Christ is in its essence really that of the New Testament. . . . We cannot exclude the possibility that some sources of error have been accepted into the church of the present."[2]

Interpretational Policies to Be Followed

Since the possibility exists for interpretive error, no "rule of faith" we bring to the Bible can guarantee that we will interpret it correctly. There are, however, three interpretational policies that, when followed, offer the best chance for grasping what the Bible means, rather than making it echo convictions already held.

Honoring the Time Sequence of Biblical Events

In the preceding chapters we have seen several instances of the Bible's regarding its message as the reportage and interpretation of the events God initiated in carrying out his plan for the world he created. We have emphasized how Paul characterized his entire message as the "will" or "purpose" of God in history. Such an emphasis necessarily implies that to understand biblical theology we must start at the beginning, with what God did first. Then we should move on through the Bible, following its own time sequence and interpretation of God's supernatural interventions.

Unfortunately the church has seldom followed this approach in the almost two thousand years of its history. At the outset it had to deal with the thinking of the ancient Greek world, where succession in a time sequence was regarded as part of the flux of this world and therefore irrelevant to eternal, unchanging truth. Therefore to make the gospel meaningful to that culture, scriptural truths were set forth in timeless categories. This approach has continued to influence theologians such as Calvin, who in his *Institutes* outlined his systematic theology in categories (e.g., God, Christ, the Holy Spirit, the church) with no reference to time.

At least two theologians in the Western church, however, have rebelled against the timelessness in which the Bible's teaching has traditionally been summarized. In 1739 Jonathan Edwards (1703–58), a revivalist and America's greatest theologian to date, set forth the outline of a different kind of theology in a series of sermons entitled "A History of the Work of Redemption." As he began the series, he said,

> In order to see how any design is carried on, we must first know what it is. To know for instance, how a workman proceeds, and to understand the various steps he takes in order to accomplish a piece of work, we need to be informed what he *intends* to accomplish; otherwise we may stand by, seeing him do one thing after another, and be quite puzzled and in the dark, because we see nothing of his scheme. Suppose an architect, with a great number of hands, were building some great palace; and one that was a stranger to such things should stand by, and see some men digging in the earth, others bringing timber, others hewing stones, and the like, he might see that there was a great deal done; but if he knew not the *design*, it would all appear to him confusion. And therefore, that the great works and dispensations of God which belong to this great affair of redemption may not appear like confusion to you, I would set before you briefly the main things designed to be accomplished [in this great work, to accomplish which God began to work presently after the fall of man, and will continue working to the end of the world, when the whole work will appear completely finished].[3]

Edwards hoped to be able to rework these sermons into a system of theology, but his untimely death prevented this. His son, however, put them together so as to have some continuity, and in his introduction to them stated that his father "had planned a body of divinity, in a *new* method, and in the form of a *history*."[4]

I intend to follow Edwards's plan for writing theology: to set forth a coherency of biblical teaching by understanding the steps God took to attain his purpose in redemption. Thus this chapter commences an exposition of the history of redemption with an inductive study (as explained below) of Genesis 1:1–2:3 that raises the question, "Why did God create the world?" From that point we move to the Fall (Gen. 2:4–4:26), the Flood (5:1–11:26), the call of Abraham (11:27–25:18), and on through the other crucial steps leading to the goal of redemption reached in Revelation 21 and 22.

In more recent times Cullmann has also broken ranks with the way theology has been written in the Western church, urging that the sequence necessarily involved in time be taken as the basis for understanding the Bible. In such books as *Christ and Time* (trans. 1950) and *Salvation in History* (trans. 1967), he has performed invaluable service in showing just how such a summarization of the Bible might be carried out. Toward the end of the latter book, he concluded that "a dogmatics or ethics of salvation history . . . ought to be written some day." It should be noted that for Cullmann, the dogmatics of redemptive history necessarily involves ethics. And so he emphasizes that God's plan of redemption requires a radical response from people: "If the decision of faith intended in the *New Testament* [and the Old Testament] asks us to align ourselves with that *sequence of events,* then the sequence may not be demythologized, de-historicized, and de-objectified [but taken as it is given]." Cullmann often quotes the maxim of J. A. Bengel (1687–1782), the father of textual criticism and a revivalist: "Give yourself wholly to the text, and apply all you learn to yourself."[5]

Ignoring the Units of Reference

In commencing this study of Genesis, readers should understand that since the versification was added long after the book was composed, the author may not have approved of such later editing. This observation leads to the second policy of interpretation to be followed, as stated by the Baptist scholar A. T. Robertson: "The first step in interpretation is to ignore the [relatively] modern chapters and verses."[6] The present chapter divisions for both the Old Testament and the New Testament were not decided upon until 1205. At that time Stephen Langton, a professor in Paris engaged in editing a Latin version of the Bible, introduced them to make it easier for people to locate a passage. In 1330 his system was then adopted by the Jews for a new hand-copied manuscript of the Hebrew Old Testament, and in 1516 these same chapter divisions were used in the first Hebrew Bible printed. The verse divisions in the Old Testament had been inserted much earlier (c. A.D. 200), to make it easier for a scholar reading the Hebrew text in a synagogue to know where to stop so that the sentence just read could then be translated into Aramaic, the spoken language of the Jews since their return from exile in Babylon six centuries earlier.

The New Testament's verse divisions were the work of Robert Stephanus, a Parisian printer, in 1551. Using Langton's chapter divisions, he then divided the New Testament into verses as he rode on horseback in the rain from Paris to Lyons to meet a printer's deadline. Given the inexactness that would necessarily result from performing this task under such circumstances, we should never allow the Bible's units of *reference* to determine its various units of *composition* (propositions, paragraphs, and larger units). At times, in fact, Stephanus's verse divisions sunder a single proposition. Versions that indent each verse thus are defective in that they imply to untrained readers that one must work with these verse divisions as the basic literary units for under-standing a passage.

Chapter divisions must also be regarded as mere units of reference, for they often begin or end at a point not corresponding to the beginning or ending of a chapter-sized literary unit. For example, the inductive study of the first four chapters of Genesis that follows will show that in Genesis, neither 2:1 nor 3:1 accurately delimits literary units.

We should also ignore the punctuation and paragraphing in our Bibles, whether in our mother tongue or in the original Hebrew and Greek. These too are the work of recent scholars, and there are differences of opinion regarding these matters among those responsible for the various editions. So the first step in the inductive method is to delimit the various sizes of compositional units composing a passage, a task that requires ignoring editorial additions.

Searching for the Author's Intended Meaning

The most important reason for ignoring these later units of reference in interpretation is that our goal is to find the meanings that *authors* wanted to impart to readers as they composed their manuscripts. We can best accomplish this task by concentrating on their train of thought, looking for the intended meaning first in the predication of each clause, and then in each of the larger literary units. There is consensus, for example, that Paul was developing a single theme in writing Galatians; in interpreting that book, we will want to see how his clauses and paragraphs helped him transmit his intended meaning. But it would be a mistake to attempt to understand 1 Corinthians in the same way, for there we discover that Paul was dealing sequentially with several different problems. Therefore in studying that book the interpreter will need to grasp each of these points in order, to determine the boundary of the separate units.

The final shape of some parts of our Bibles, however, is the work of authors who sometimes worked with the materials of others to get their own messages across.[7] So we interpreters look for intended meanings not only in books composed immediately by one person, like Galatians, but also in books whose final shape is more than the work of an editor, such as the Pentateuch or one of the Gospels. So to simplify matters we will henceforth use the term "author" for every person finally responsible for a biblical writing; the primary task of a interpreter is to grasp that person's intended meaning in each unit of composition.

In affirming that the early chapters of Genesis as they appear in our Bibles are the work of an editor using sources provided by others, we are aligning ourselves with an important emphasis of present-day biblical scholarship, namely, that the Bible student is completely dependent on the work of the final editor of a book or group of books. Thus for example an eminent Old Testament scholar has said in the introduction to his commentary on Genesis, "Basically we are dependent *only* on [the editor], on his great work of compilation and his theology, and we receive the Hexateuch at all *only* from his hands."[8]

In conducting our inductive study of Genesis 1:1–2:3, we will follow a sequence of four steps.[9] In posing the questions under these four steps, the teacher assumes the role of a Socrates (470–399 B.C.), the ancient Greek philosopher whose aim was to get people to think for themselves by asking them questions. One following this Socratic method of teaching must constantly insist that people's conclusions about the author's intended meaning be supported by *reasons* derived from the text and, if possible, also by pertinent historical information regarding the life-situation of the author and original readers. People will become like the noble Bereans (Acts 17:11) only as they learn to base their conclusions on solid evidence.[10] As the original Bereans "examined the [Old Testament] Scriptures every day to see if what Paul said was true," they had to evaluate arguments, pro and con, to make their interpretational decisions. In today's churches time and energy must be given to train promising people to do likewise. Christians must be taught to accept no conclusions about what the Bible teaches without evaluating the arguments used to support them. Teaching people to be Bereans should surely be one of the essential tasks in preparing "God's people for works of [the ministry]" (Eph. 4:12).

NOTE. Unfortunately it is virtually impossible to find any further instances of Berean Bible study through the history of the church right up to the present day. One exception was the unique curriculum of the Biblical Seminary in New York City. Founded in 1902 by Wilbert W. White, this seminary devoted at least half of its curriculum to the inductive study of biblical books in the English language. White recalled how W. R. Harper, a Hebrew scholar at Yale, had sent out a questionnaire to some 1,000 pastors, asking them to identify the greatest deficiency in their seminary training. Fully 888 responded that their greatest lack was in knowledge of the Bible and of a method of studying it. White himself had first been a pastor for four years, then a teacher in seminary, where he felt that far too little time was given to the study of the Bible.

To remedy this deficiency, White began to follow

Harper's method of teaching entire books, so that students
could see the details in the broad perspective of the whole.
White's teaching was soon in great demand, taking him
even to India. There he sent out a questionnaire to three
hundred missionaries in that land, asking what their
greatest need was. They replied that it was a better
knowledge of biblical books. These missionaries wanted
him to start a school in India, but White felt that with such
a demand for a biblical curriculum, such a school should
start in America. Biblical Seminary thus opened its doors
in New York City in 1902 and in subsequent years made
its influence felt at Wheaton and Westmont colleges and at
Eastern, Princeton, and Fuller seminaries. My own life-
work of teaching inductive book studies in seminary
resulted from a class taught in 1946–47 at Princeton by
Howard T. Kuist, formerly a professor at Biblical Seminary. A number of other professors at Fuller have pro-
moted this method as well. Sadly, however, through lack
of sufficient funds, Biblical Seminary felt it had to change
its curriculum to address the social problems of the inner
city and in 1965 became the New York Theological
Seminary.

The Inductive Method in Four Steps (Gen. 1:1–2:3)

*Ask Questions to Determine a Passage's
Compositional Units*

Q: Why do you think Langton ended the first chapter of
Genesis after verse 31?

A: Because it would seem, at first sight, that the high point
of creation comes with the creation of the first man and
woman. God's words "and it was very good" (1:31), when
heretofore it was simply said, "God saw that it was
good," imply that some sort of climax has been reached.

Q: But why would Langton have been better advised to end
chapter 1 at 2:3?

A: It is clear that the author of chapter 1 was working on a
sequence of days, and so what happened on the seventh

day (2:1–3) should have been regarded as the climax, and chapter 2 should have commenced at 2:4.

Q: What, then, are the basic compositional units in 1:1–2:3?

A: Draw arcs showing the boundaries of what happened on each of the seven days. Show verses 1–2 as a separate arc. A larger arc embracing all seven days should then be drawn from 1:3 to 2:3. (See fig. 1.)

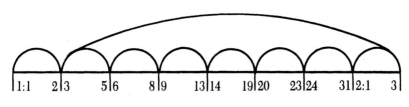

Figure 1

Q: What is the relationship between 1:1–2 and 1:3–2:3?

A: Verses 1–2 tell how chaotic and useless the earth was originally; 1:3–2:3 then set forth the steps God took to make the earth so pleasing that he could be completely at rest on the seventh day.

Q: What happens on each of the successive days?

A: Draw arcs for each day, with units of references (as in fig. 1), and insert a word or phrase to identify the happenings of each day.

Determine the Author's Basic Point

(Note that repetition reaching a climax often signifies an author's purpose.)

Q: What statement is repeated in the course of God's actions on most of the days?

A: "It was good" appears once on day 1 (v. 4); twice on day 3 (vv. 10, 12); once on day 4 (v. 18); once on day 5 (v. 21); twice on day 6 (v. 25 and, at the climax in v. 31, "[All that God had made] was very good").

Q: But what are the works of these days really good for? That is, why is God carrying on these works of creation, which end so conclusively with the "very good" at the end of the sixth day that he can rest with complete contentment on the seventh day?

A: The events of days 1–5 prepare the earth for the creation of human beings, each day contributing vitally to the "very good" of verse 31. (See the next section below, which spells out these contributions.) Verses 26–31 then cite the reasons for the climactic "very good" of verse 31. First, God creates a man and a woman in his image (v. 26).[11]

Second, in expressing the command to create people in God's image, the author shifts from the "let there be" mode of expression used in 1:3–25 to what the Hebrew grammarians call the plural of majesty: "Let us make ..." (v. 26). (Other instances of this mode of expression are Gen. 11:7, "Let us go down and confuse their language," and Isa. 6:8, "Whom shall I send, and who will go for us?") According to the Hebrew grammarians Gesenius and Kautzsch, this plural "is best explained as a plural of *self-deliberation*."[12] The usage of this grammatical form thus expresses God's entering into an act with the fullness of his being, which would suit the creation of people "in his image." Also, the word for "God" in the Hebrew language is often *elohim*, the last two letters being a plural suffix. This plural, which implies a complexity in the one and only God, fits in with the New Testament revelation that God is a Trinity.

Third, God commands people made in his image to subdue the earth and have dominion over the creatures in the sea, on the land, and in the air (v. 26). Since people in his image subdue the earth and rule over the living creatures, the natural inference is that the earth and its creatures will be controlled in a praiseworthy manner that will help the whole earth to reflect God's image fully.

Fourth, God commands these people, made in his image, to multiply so that they, and thus God's image, will fill the earth (v. 28). From this command we conclude that the meaning the author intended to transmit in 1:1–2:3 is that the superlative goodness achieved, especially in connection with the creation of a man and a woman made in God's image, is that the created earth is now established to display outwardly, far and wide, the goodness of God, which is his glory or praiseworthiness.

Ask Questions to Show How the Larger Units Support the Basic Point

Q: How are the needs of the earth as described in 1:2 met in the works of the successive days?

A: The problem of darkness is solved on day 1; that of water and formlessness on days 2 and 3.

Q: Why was the work of days 1 and 2 necessary for the support of what was accomplished on day 3?

A: Plants need the light of day 1 and the atmospheric water of day 2.

Q: The dry land and vegetation of day 3 is said to be good— but good for what?

A: It provides food for humans and animals (1:30). Everything is working toward the climax of verse 31, "God saw all that he had made, and it was very good."

Q: What phrase is repeated on day 4 that shows the ultimate purpose for the luminaries created on that day?

A: "To give light on the earth" (vv. 15, 17)—so the people who are to fill the earth (v. 28) will be benefited by the time measurements provided by the sun, moon, and stars.

Q: What is the main thing that the birds, fishes, and land animals are to do?

A: The waters are to swarm with the great variety of creatures living there (vv. 20, 22); the birds are to occupy the space above the earth, that is, "the expanse of the sky" (v. 20), and also to multiply on the earth (v. 22); and the command for the land creatures to reproduce also implies filling up the earth (vv. 24–25). Thus as these creatures fill the earth on land, sea, and air and are ruled by people in God's image who are everywhere, God's image is also going to be in evidence everywhere. (Note:

We have already construed the significance of 1:26–31 in the section above.)

Q: What is climatic about God's resting on the seventh day?

A: This resting on the seventh day fully emphasizes that the earth now had been established in such a way that its final outcome will fully honor God, without the fear that any fault in it would at all detract from God's perfection. Consequently God was perfectly content with what he had brought to a climax on day 6 and so could rest completely on day 7.

State the Basic Thrust of the Unit and
Its Practical Application

Chapters 8–11 below are devoted to inquiring more fully into why God created the world, and what should be our appropriate response to this purpose.

NOTE. The foregoing questions and answers indicate my concern to let the Bible speak for itself. Nevertheless I acknowledge that the interpretations given here are my own constructions of what I believe were the intended meanings of the biblical writer; often these were hammered out with a few seminary students in Berean situations. Such situations are normal; all interpretations of the Bible and, indeed, of all other verbal communications are only the result of what a human mind has construed to be their intended meanings. There is no "public meaning" of the Bible; all statements regarding its meanings are humanly construed. For this reason readers of this book should be Bereans, carefully scrutinizing the interpretations given in it before they agree or disagree with any of them. During my more-than-thirty years of teaching the Bible inductively in small seminars, my Berean seminary students have on a number of occasions caused me to see that I was overlooking some datum vital to the understanding of a text; when I have thus been convinced that their arguments are compelling, I have changed my interpretation. This Berean, then, has been taught by many other

Bereans and hopes that he and the Bereans who read this book will always be open to the possibility of changing their way of construing the Bible to bring their theology ever closer to the Bible's fixed original meaning.

NOTE. From what has just been said, the question of the Holy Spirit's role in biblical interpretation is bound to rise. I believe that the Holy Spirit is indispensable for an interpreter's reaching a correct interpretation of a text. The Spirit must work in the interpreter's heart so that he or she *welcomes* the biblical message that one's egotistic, sinful heart otherwise hates with a vengeance. According to 1 Corinthians 2:14, "The man without the Spirit does not [welcome] the things that come from the Spirit of God, for they are foolishness to him, and he cannot understand them because they are spiritually discerned." When *dechetai*, the Greek word translated "accept" (NIV), is given its more accurate meaning "welcome,"we understand that an unregenerate person can gain cognition of what any part of the Bible intends to say. But since no part of the Bible, whose God works for those who wait for him, allows the ego to boast in having pleased him, unbelievers will therefore regard the clearly understandable biblical teaching as foolishness. They refuse to agree with the perfectly rational idea that God "lives in the high and holy place, but also with him who is contrite and lowly in spirit" (Isa. 57:15). Consequently such people lack the discernment necessary to value the Bible's spiritual teachings. And if demands such as those of a vocation require them to teach the Bible, they will inevitably twist its meanings to cater to their and their hearers' egos, and the Bible's intended message will not be heard. Only those who have no confidence in themselves and have banked all their hope for a happy future on what the loving God of the Bible will do for them will expound its message faithfully.

A further requirement for accurate exposition is that all interpretations of Scripture must find their support only in pertinent historical and textual data. If the statement "the Holy Spirit gave me this interpretation" could be used as an argument for its validity, then everyone's interpretation of a text would have an equal claim to be right. The result would be total confusion, and all efforts toward edifying Christ's sheep would fail. So the attempt is made in this book to base all conclusions on data in the text or its original historical surroundings. Then one's fellow Bereans can argue from the philological and historical data alone for the validity of an interpretation.

Review Questions

1. What is the chief obstacle that stands in the way of our grasping what a biblical author wanted to say in a literary unit such as Genesis 1:1–2:3?
2. How can Cullmann say (1) that he will interpret the Koran differently from a Muslim, and yet also say, (2) "I can interpret the text of a pagan religion correctly"? (Hint: There are two meanings for the term "interpret.") Be able to state Cullmann's meaning in your own words so there is no ambiguity.
3. What is the only use for the Bible's units of reference such as Genesis 12:1?
4. Why must these units of reference be ignored in interpreting the Bible?
5. List and explain the four steps of inductive Bible study.
6. Cite three reasons from Genesis 1:1–2:3 and especially 1:26–31 for saying that God's goal in creating the world was to extend his glory as far and as widely as possible.

NOTES

[1] Oscar Cullmann, *Salvation in History*, trans. Sidney G. Sowers (New York: Harper & Row, 1967), 67, 71.

[2] Ibid., 68.

[3] Jonathan Edwards, "A History of the Work of Redemption," in *The Works of Jonathan Edwards*, rev. and corrected by Edward Hickman, 2 vols. (Carlisle, Pa.: Banner of Truth Trust, 1974), 1:535. The material in brackets was omitted from this more recent edition but is found in *The Works of President Edwards*, 4 vols. (New York: Leavitt & Allen, 1858), 1:302. Unless noted otherwise, references to Edwards's *Works* are to the 1974 edition.

4 Edwards, *Works*, 1:532, italics added.

5 Cullmann, *Salvation in History*, 292, 70, 69.

6 A. T. Robertson, *An Introduction to the Textual Criticism of the New Testament* (Nashville: Broadman Press, 1925), 101.

7 This observation, however, by no means invalidates the Bible's verbal inspiration and truthfulness. In the prologue to his gospel, Luke writes of having used materials that were gathered through painstaking research (1:1–4), which covered the virgin birth, life, ministry, death, and resurrection of Jesus Christ. A comparison between his gospel and certain accounts found in Matthew and Mark provides evidence that each of these authors functioned also as an editor, modifying somewhat both the tradition he had received and its chronological arrangement in order to get his particular message across more effectively. As for the early parts of Genesis, the position I take in seeking to understand the author's intended meaning is that the biblical editor was verbally inspired by the Holy Spirit (2 Tim. 3:16–17) to do this arranging and editing in order to transmit a determinate meaning in each literary unit. The difference between this verbal inspiration and a dictation theory of inspiration was explained above in chapter 3, note 3.

8 Gerhard von Rad, *Genesis*, trans. J. H. Marks, rev. ed. (Philadelphia: Westminster, 1972), 42, italics added. Von Rad speaks of the "Hexateuch" (Genesis through Joshua) rather than the Pentateuch (Genesis through Deuteronomy) because he was convinced that the redactor responsible for Genesis through Deuteronomy completed his work with Joshua, since that book records the fulfillment of the promises made to Abraham regarding Israel's possession of the land of Canaan.

9 Philosophers know that it is impossible to be purely inductive, reaching conclusions simply by drawing inferences from brute facts. In coming to the Bible, however, I still want to work from the textual and historical data upward to our conclusions. I have no interest in coming to the Bible with a system of theology already in place, so that one's interpretations never differ from that system. The method to be followed is thus what E. D. Hirsch, Jr., calls the hypothetico-deductive process: "Our self-confirming pre-understanding needs to be tested against all the relevant data we can find, for our idea of genre is ultimately a hypothesis like any other, and the best hypothesis is the one that best explains the relevant data. This idea of genre, pre-understanding, and hypothesis suggests that the much-advertised cleavage between thinking in the sciences and the humanities does not exist. The hypothetico-deductive process is fundamental in both of them, as it is in all

thinking that aspires to knowledge" (*Validity in Interpretation* [New Haven: Yale University Press, 1967], 263–64). Accordingly, in attempting to determine the author's intended meaning in a text, we try out various hypotheses to see if they square with all the pertinent data. Most hypotheses do not, but the interpreter continues to try new ones until finding one that does justice to all the historical and linguistic data. Ideally, this process should occur in what I will call a Berean situation, where other minds can argue the merits and demerits of various hypotheses.

[10]The example of the Bereans given in Acts 17:11 bears out Hirsch's insistence that the interpretation of a text gains more claim to credibility when a given hypothesis is challenged by four or five other interpreters who have also worked hard at construing the text. Hirsch says, for example, "The hermeneutic hypothesis is not completely self-confirming since it has to compete with rival hypotheses about the same text and is continuously measured against those components of the text which are least dependent on the hypothesis" (ibid., 261). See the following note in the main text for how little the Bible has been subjected to the scrutiny of *contemporary* hypotheses that differ. Those rival views that do exist are in the main separated by lengthy intervals, so that meaningful interaction and correction have been difficult. Thus the situation of the "noble Bereans" has seen few revivals in church history. Biblical interpretation would be vastly advanced, however, if interpreters of generally equal skill could carry on an oral discussion about the meaning of a text over a period of several days. And seminary education would be greatly improved if students and the "teacher" of a biblical text could argue out, for example, the meaning of the prologue in 1 John (1:1–4) or the significance of the "therefore" or "so" introducing the Golden Rule (Matt. 7:12).

[11]See chapter 10 below on a promising way to explain how people are made in God's image.

[12]*Gesenius' Hebrew Grammar*, ed. E. Kautzsch and A. E. Cowley, 2d ed. (Oxford: Clarendon Press, 1910), 398 n. 2.

8

God's Necessary Work of
Being a Trinity

The inductive study of Genesis 1:1–2:3 in chapter 7 led to the conclusion that God had a purpose or goal in creating and establishing the world and that he had laid the foundation for this purpose so well that he found complete delight in his contemplation of it. Now in this chapter and the next we will look elsewhere in the Bible for help in answering the question of why God created the world, so that we might have as clear an understanding as possible of God's whole plan.

Some may object that interrupting our journey along the Bible's timeline to reflect on material from other parts of the Bible is a reversion to the timelessness that has characterized theology from the beginning of church history. In Edwards's analogy (cited above in chapter 7) to describe his "body of divinity, in a *new* method and in the form of a *history*," he wrote of a passerby's seeing workers busily engaged in erecting some sort of building. But "in order to see how a design is carried on, we must first know what the design [of that building] is." In Genesis 1:1–2:3 we have seen all that God did in the beginning to create an earth reflecting his image on land, in the sea, and in the air. But to fill in more details of the Architect's plan for the whole and the motive that led him to carry out this plan, we should now look elsewhere. The better we understand why God regarded his creation as very good at the beginning of history, the better able we will be to worship him in freedom now.

115

Scripture explicitly states that "surely . . . the glory of the Lord [will fill] the whole earth" (Num. 14:21). And Habakkuk 2:14 declares that "the earth will be filled with the knowledge of the glory of the Lord, as the waters cover the sea." But just what is this glory of God? Exodus 33:18–19 helps answer the question in a way that also provides a tie-in with Genesis 1:1–2:3: "Moses said [to God], 'Now show me your glory.' And the Lord said, 'I will cause all my *goodness* to pass in front of you, and I will proclaim my name, the Lord, in your presence.'" Here we note that God's "goodness" is used as a synonym for his glory, and we remember that the predicate "good" was the main emphasis of Genesis 1:1–2:3.

Goodness is the quality that makes a person or an object useful and beneficial for meeting a need. A good pen is one that writes smoothly and whose flow of ink begins as soon as its owner starts to write. A good person is one who makes life easier for others by having such desirable qualities as dependability, cheerfulness, intelligence, and diligence. As we shall see, in filling the earth with his glory, God will do the ultimately good thing for people made in his image by sharing with them the very joy that he has in himself.

In this chapter, then, I will try to explain what God's greatest joy is; in the next, we will consider what will bring the greatest joy to people, whom God has created in his image. In order to understand the source of God's joy, we must first distinguish his *necessary* work of being the Trinity that he is, from his *free* work of then going outside the Trinity to create the world and share his joy with people he made in his image.

The best place to begin in understanding God as a Trinity is with the scriptural assertion that God's wisdom is foundational for his whole being. In Proverbs 8 wisdom is personified and talks about herself as follows: "The Lord brought me forth as the first of his works, before his deeds of old; I was appointed from eternity, from the beginning, before the world began" (vv. 22–23). Then in verse 30 wisdom speaks of her joy in enabling God to plan the world: "Then I was the craftsman at his side. I was filled with delight day after day, rejoicing always in his presence." Such a personification of wisdom means that God found complete delight in the decisions his perfect wisdom led him to make in creating the world and ordaining its history. But according to verses 22–23, wisdom was the foundation of God from all eternity, and so just as God later delighted in the way wisdom enabled him to plan the world, so God's wisdom has always caused him to delight fully in using his infinite power to be just the sort of God who would be most pleasing to himself.

But for God to be wholly pleasing to himself in seeing himself as the embodiment of perfect wisdom, he also had to have a completely clear and undistorted knowledge of himself. The self he beheld had to be totally separate from himself as the knowing subject. According to Jonathan Edwards, "If God beholds himself so as thence to have delight and joy in himself he must become his own Object."[1] God accomplished this absolutely necessary work for his being God by begetting Jesus Christ, his only Son. Thus we now need to examine closely the biblical basis for understanding Jesus Christ as begotten of the Father.

The Only Begotten Son

It is chiefly from John's four uses of the Greek word *monogenēs* that we find support for understanding Jesus as the only begotten from the Father in a manner that has some analogy to people's begetting children. The key passages are the following: "We have seen [Jesus'] glory, the glory of the One and Only [*monogenous*] . . . from the Father" (John 1:14); "No one has ever seen God, but God the One and Only [*monogenēs*], who is at the Father's side, has made [God] known" (John 1:18); "God so loved the world that he gave his one and only [*monogenē*] Son" (John 3:16); "This is how God showed his love among us: He sent his one and only [*monogenē*] Son into the world that we might live through him" (1 John 4:9).

In these four usages of *monogenēs* the first part of the word, *mono-*, means "only." The second part, *-genēs*, does not come from the Greek *gennaō*, "to beget," but from *genos*, "descendant," or "offspring." So the translation "beget" is not actually supported etymologically from *monogenēs*. The word nevertheless implies "beget" because *monogenēs* obviously includes the idea of the only descendant or reduplication of the source, who is God the Father. This conclusion is further supported by John 5:18: "For this reason the Jews tried all the harder to kill [Jesus]; not only was he breaking the Sabbath, but he was even calling God his own [*idion*] Father, making himself equal with God." In Romans 8:3 Paul uses very similar language: "For what the law was powerless to do in that it was weakened by the sinful nature, God did by sending his own [*heautou*] Son." Thus the early Nicene Creed of 325 reads, "We believe . . . in the Lord Jesus Christ, the Son of God, the only one [*monogenē*] begotten [*gennēthenta*] of the Father . . . very God of very God, begotten [*gennēthenta*], not made [*poiēthenta*]."

John's statements make it clear that Jesus was himself fully God and that he was a completely separate person, or center of consciousness, from the Father. When John 1:18 says that "God the One and Only, who is at the Father's side, has made [God] known," there is no other way to construe this proposition than to understand that Jesus, from all eternity, was both God and also a separate person from God the Father. John 1:1 mentions the "Word" (whom the context [see v. 14] regards as Jesus) as having existed always, alongside of God: "In the beginning was the Word, and the Word was with [*pros*, 'over against'] God, and the Word was God."

C. S. Lewis, perhaps the most popular Christian writer of the twentieth century, casts much light on the Nicene Creed's statement "begotten, not made."

When you beget, you beget something of the same kind as yourself. A man begets human babies, a beaver begets little beavers, and a bird begets eggs which turn into little birds. But when you make, you make something of a different kind from yourself. A bird makes a nest, a beaver builds a dam, a man makes a wireless set—or he may make something more like himself than a wireless set: say, a statue. If he's a clever enough carver he may make a statue which is very like a man indeed. But, of course, it's not a real man; it only looks like one. It can't breathe or think. It's not alive.[2]

There is, however, a great problem in using the figure of speech "begotten" in making clear Jesus' unique relation to God: as far as human experience is concerned, the begetter always exists for a period of time before the one who is begotten. Yet the Scriptures are clear that Jesus the Son has always existed as the only begotten of the Father. Again Lewis is helpful in pointing out how this can be so:

> I asked you just now to imagine . . . two books. . . . You made an act of imagination and as a result you had a mental picture. Quite obviously your act of imagining was the cause and the mental picture the result. But that doesn't mean that you first did the imagining and *then* got the picture. The moment you did it, the picture was there. . . . That act of will and the picture began at exactly the same moment and ended at the same moment. If there were a Being who had always existed and had always been imagining one thing, his act would always have been producing a mental picture; but the picture would be just as eternal as the act.[3]

Thus we can see how John's gospel is not speaking nonsense in declaring Jesus to be the only begotten of the Father who was himself God, and then to say that he is the Word who, like God the Father, has always existed alongside of and over against the Father.

Indeed, Jesus differs from the Father in that he is the begotten while the Father is the begetter, yet every attribute of deity that is ascribed to the Father is likewise ascribed to Jesus. In John 5:26, for example, Jesus said, "As the Father has life in himself, so he has granted the Son to have life in himself." In emphasizing Jesus' complete reduplication of the Father, the reformation theologian John Calvin declared, "When we speak simply of the Son, without reference to the Father, we well and properly declare him to be of himself, and for this reason we call him the sole beginning. But when we mark the relation that he has with the Father, we rightly make the Father the beginning of the Son."[4] Therefore, though the Son does proceed from the Father, yet the life that he receives from the Father is life that the Son has "of himself" to such an extent that he possesses it in and of himself just as the Father possesses it in and of himself.

Were the Son's life constantly to exist by derivation from the Father, then he would not be the exact representation of the Father, and consequently the Father could not delight fully in the perfection of his own being by beholding the Son. Furthermore God, who surely has the ability to bring into existence an exact reduplication of himself, would be unrighteous not to do what was necessary for fully delighting in himself.

Upon hearing this line of thought, people sometimes object that God would be egotistic and therefore sinful in wanting to delight fully in himself. Indeed, no human being should ever delight in his or her own self, for there is nothing in any of us creatures that deserves to be worshiped. Everything we creatures have, we have only as a gift, and so we should never glory in anything about ourselves as though we had produced it on our own (1 Cor. 4:7). Rather, we should give thanks to God for the innumerable good things we enjoy as his creation: sight, hearing, remembering, having particular skills and gifts, companionship with others, and much more. But the situation is entirely different with God, for his wisdom is not something he received as a gift. To the contrary, he is himself the source and cause of the wisdom that is displayed in his character and conduct. And since he represents perfect wisdom, he would be sinful indeed if he did not delight in himself, formed by his perfect wisdom, with the full energy of his omnipotence. So whereas for human beings self-worship is the worst sin, for God it is the epitome of his righteousness.

Hence he would be unrighteous if he had the power to reduplicate himself but remained a single center of consciousness as he is thought to be in Judaism and Islam. It is doubtful that the teachers of these other religions would deny that God had the power to "beget" his own counterpart. But if they affirm that he has such power yet deny that he used it to attain full knowledge of himself as the embodiment of perfect wisdom, then they do so at the expense of implying his sinfulness in failing to render to himself the full worship he deserves.

Another problem Judaism and Islam face by denying that God is more than one center of consciousness is that he could then not be love without creating the world. Thus Lewis has argued, "The words 'God is love' have no real meaning unless God contains at least two Persons. Love is something that one *person* has for another *person*. If God was a single person then before the world was made, he was *not* love."[5]

But these problems are avoided by taking seriously John's affirmation that Jesus is the only begotten Son of the Father who has always existed alongside him. Likewise Hebrews 1:3 declares, "The Son is the radiance of God's glory and the exact representation of his being." From this affirmation Edwards reasoned that since the Son "is the brightness of His glory, the very image of the Father, the express and perfect image of His Person . . . therefore the Father's infinite happiness is in Him [the Son], and the way that the Father enjoys the glory of the deity is in enjoying Him."[6] Since God found "infinite happiness in [Jesus, the Son]," then it becomes clear that from all eternity God has enjoyed his Son's love and companionship. Therefore the creation of the world was not a necessary act that God undertook to overcome loneliness. To the contrary, creation is God's free act, a concept that will be explained in the next chapter. But first we must show that God is truly God only by being a Trinity, and so we now turn to a consideration of the Holy Spirit's generation.

The Holy Spirit

The New Testament speaks of the Holy Spirit as proceeding both from the Father and the Son. According to Galatians 4:6, "God sent the Spirit of his Son into our hearts"; John 15:26 makes the same basic affirmation: "When the Counselor comes, whom I [Jesus] will send to you from the Father, the Spirit of truth who goes out from the Father, he will testify about me." Hence the Westminster Confession (1647) makes the following distinction between the three persons of the Trinity: "The Father is of none, neither begotten nor proceeding; the Son is eternally begotten of the Father; the Holy Spirit [is] eternally proceeding from the Father and the Son" (2.3).

A comprehension of God's necessary work in having the Spirit proceed from both the Father and the Son begins with understanding the love the Father and the Son have for each other. John 3:35 affirms that "the Father loves the Son," as do Matthew 3:17 and 17:5, where the Father says, "This is my Son, whom I love; with him I am well pleased." And Jesus acknowledged this love when he said, in praying to the Father, "Father, I want those you have given me to be with me where I am, and to see my glory, the glory you have given me because you loved me before the creation of the world" (John 17:24). The Scriptures also make it clear that the Son loves the Father: "The world must learn that I love the Father and that I do exactly what my Father has commanded me" (14:31). This love is also evident when Jesus said, "The one who sent me is with me; he has not left me alone, for I always do what pleases him" (8:29). From this love of the Father and the Son for each other, we understand in what sense God is, and always has been, love. "God's love is primarily to Himself," said Jonathan Edwards, "and His infinite delight is in Himself, in the Father and the Son loving and delighting in each other. . . . The happiness of the Deity, as all other true happiness, consists in love and society."[7]

From our experience as humans we know that the stronger the ties that bind a society, the stronger is the spirit characterizing that society. Service organizations, churches, clubs, military units, and all other kinds of groups each have their distinctive atmosphere or spirit that arises from the way its members feel about the ideals and purposes that bring them together. The strength of a group's esprit de corps depends on the degree of dedication its purpose calls forth from its members.

But the esprit de corps of every human group always leaves much to be desired. No society on earth even comes close to the vitality of spirit that arises from the love the Father and the Son have for each other. When we consider that the Son, like the Father, is the perfection of beauty, that both have the omniscience to appreciate fully the perfection of the other's glory, and that both are able to summon the energy of omnipotence to render proper adoration to each other with appropriate zeal, we can glimpse why the Scriptures speak of such a society as having a most vital spirit. In fact the "spirit" of this community is so strong that a separate center of consciousness called the Holy *Spirit* proceeds both from the Father and the Son in such a way that a third person exists, who himself is a center of consciousness and has all the divine attributes of the Father and the Son.

And why should not the Spirit, with whom the Father and the Son delight so in each other, be himself a person, especially since both the Father and the Son enter into this delight with all the energy of their beings? Thus Edwards argued:

> The Godhead being thus begotten by God's loving an Idea of himself and showing forth in a distinct subsistence or Person in that Idea, there proceeds a most pure act, and an infinitely holy and sacred energy arises between the Father and Son in mutually loving and delighting in each other. . . . This is the eternal and most Perfect and essential act of the divine nature, wherein the Godhead acts to an infinite degree and in the most perfect manner possible. The deity becomes all act, the divine essence itself flows out and is as it were breathed forth in love and joy. So that the Godhead therein stands forth in yet another manner of subsistence, and there proceeds the third Person in the Trinity, the Holy Spirit.[8]

Lewis follows the same line of argument:

> Perhaps the most important difference between Christianity and all other religions [is] that in Christianity God is not a static *thing*—not even a person—but a dynamic, pulsating activity, a life, almost a kind of drama. Almost, if you won't think me irreverent, a kind of dance. The union between the Father and the Son is such a live concrete thing that this union itself is also a Person. I know that's almost inconceivable, but look at it this way. You know that among human beings, when they get together in a family, or a club, or a trades union, people talk about the "spirit" of that family, or club, or trades union. They talk about its "spirit" because the individual members, when they're together, do really develop particular ways of talking and behaving which they wouldn't have if they were apart. It is as if a sort of communal personality came

into existence. Of course it isn't a real person: it is only rather like a person. But that's just one of the differences between God and us. What grows out of the joint life of the Father and Son is a *real* Person, is in fact the Third of the three Persons who are God.[9]

Therefore in order for God to be God, the Holy Spirit must proceed as a person who is himself God. He must proceed from the Father and the Son and himself be God because of the omnipotently fervent love the Father and the Son each has for the other. Had this mutual love not produced the third person of the Trinity, the Holy Spirit, the inference would be that neither the Father nor the Son enjoyed each other sufficiently to generate a Spirit of companionship strong enough to be a person. But in that this mutual fellowship did produce a Spirit so intense that he was himself a person who reduplicated the Father and the Son in every way, we know that in begetting the Son, God was able to satisfy fully his "need-love," finding complete delight in himself.[10] Hence for God to be God, it was absolutely necessary for him to be a Trinity.

Consequently, since the Holy Spirit proceeds from the Father and the Son because of the love each has for the other, it is not surprising that he is spoken of in Scripture as the embodiment of the love of God: "God has poured out his love into our hearts by the Holy Spirit, whom he has given us" (Rom. 5:5). This love of God is the love between the Father and the Son, for significantly, while we have seen passages in which the Father loves the Son and vice versa, nowhere does one read of the Father or the Son loving the Holy Spirit, or vice versa. Thus when the Holy Spirit comes to dwell in the heart of the believer, the very delight that the Father and the Son have for each other, the supreme delight of God himself (which delight, empowered by divine omnipotence, is so perfect that it must be embodied in one who is himself a person), becomes ours to enjoy as well.

It is no wonder, then, that in Scripture the Holy Spirit is spoken of as the great promise or gift that God gives people (Luke 11:13; Acts 1:4–5; 2:33; Gal. 3:14). By giving believers the Holy Spirit, God has done nothing less than give them the very delight that he has in himself. Just as the gift of the Holy Spirit in John 7:38 is likened to "streams of living water," so the psalmist, speaking to God, says, "You give [people] drink from your river of delights" (Ps. 36:8). This meaning of the Holy Spirit is also well expressed by Charles Wesley (1707–88) in one of his hymns:

> Love Divine, all loves excelling,
>   Joy of heaven to earth come down
> Fix in us thy humble dwelling,
>   All thy faithful mercies crown.

It is now possible, therefore, to understand why God enjoyed complete rest on the seventh day. After concluding toward sundown the day before that he had so established the earth that people made in his image would fill it and then subdue both it and the ocean, land, and sky creatures dwelling in it, he knew he had set in motion a process that would eventually extend the superlative worth of his glory throughout the earth. As we have seen in Exodus 33:18–19, God's glory consists in his goodness, that is, in that he alone is both able and disposed to bring people, made in his image, into the ultimate happiness of sharing with him his delight in his glory.

In seeing that an earth now existed that eventually would be filled with people representing his glory, God had done what would forever keep him in a state of complete joy and contentment. In other words, he had acted in freedom— engaged in a task as an end, where the activity itself brings a final joy that needs no supplement. In carrying out the sequence of the events of earth's history, reaching their climax in the new heaven and earth (Rev. 21:1–4), God was doing a work that was free in that he found total satisfaction simply in the doing of it.

In chapter 9 we consider more fully just how the establishment of the earth was God's *free* work, in contrast to the work of begetting the Son and generating the Holy Spirit, which were *necessary* works performed so that God would then be able to carry out his free work.

Review Questions

1. Explain what the glory of God is by using Exodus 33:18–19 and the repetition of "it is good" in Genesis 1:1–2:3.

2. Explain what is meant in this book by saying that God's being a Trinity is a necessary work, while his creating the world and ordaining its history is a free work. Be sure you can explain in everyday language what a "free" work is (as used in this sense) and be able to give an illustration of a free work from your own experience.

3. Why was it necessary for God to be at least a diunity in order to be God?

4. What is the difference between "making" and "begetting"?

5. Why is it important to emphasize that Jesus was begotten and not made?

6. What difficulty does the analogical predicate "begotten" raise concerning Jesus, and how does C. S. Lewis suggest that the problem be solved?

7. In worshiping himself, why is God righteous and not sinfully egotistic?

8. Understanding that we use the word "necessary" in at least two different senses in different contexts in this book, explain in your own words the following: God's creation of the world was a free work, yet he created the world out of necessity. Be able to link these two senses up with "need-love" (see n. 10) and benevolent love.

9. Why are the Jewish and Muslim monotheisms in danger of making creation a necessary work of God, rather than a free one?

10. Explain why the Holy Spirit is the greatest blessing God can give a believer.

11. In teaching junior highers about the Holy Spirit, what would be something in their experience that would help them understand in what sense the third person of the Trinity is a spirit?

12. How does the existence of the Holy Spirit prove that God's need-love was satisfied?

NOTES

[1] Jonathan Edwards, *An Unpublished Essay of Edwards on the Trinity*, ed. George P. Fisher (New York: Scribner's, 1903), 80.

[2] C. S. Lewis, *Beyond Personality* (New York: Macmillan, 1948), 5. Permission to quote C. S. Lewis in this chapter kindly granted by the Macmillan Company.

[3] Ibid., 20.

[4] John Calvin, *Institutes of the Christian Religion*, ed. John T. McNeill, trans. Ford Lewis Battles, The Library of Christian Classics, vols. 20 and 21 (Philadelphia: Westminster, 1960), 20:144 (1.13.19). References throughout to Calvin's *Institutes* will be both to volume and page number of this edition and to book, chapter, and paragraph numbers of the work itself.

[5] Lewis, *Beyond Personality*, 21.

[6] Jonathan Edwards, *Observations Concerning the Scripture Economy of the Trinity and Covenant of Redemption* (New York: Scribner's, 1880), 22.

[7] Jonathan Edwards, "Treatise on Grace," in *Puritan Sage: Collected Writings of Jonathan Edwards*, ed. Vergilius Ferm (New York: Library Publishers, 1953), 561, 564.

[8] Edwards, *Unpublished Essay*, 93–94.

[9] Lewis, *Beyond Personality*, 21–22.

[10] To distinguish the love between the Father and the Son from the benevolence God has for his creatures, I have coined the word "need-love" for the former, signifying love in the sense of finding great delight in another.

9

God's Free Work of Creation

We have seen how essential it was from all eternity for God to beget the Son and, by reduplicating himself as another person standing alongside, thus be able to enjoy himself as the full embodiment of perfect wisdom. In the same way it was necessary for the omnipotently fervent spirit of community and love between the Father and the Son to become a divine person, the Holy Spirit. But this understanding of the Trinity raises three questions as we seek to understand why the triune God willed to create an earth in the terms set forth in Genesis 1:1–2:3.

How Could the Triune God Have Any Desire to Create a World?

If God's delight in himself as a Trinity was so complete, why was he not perfectly content to remain simply as that fully happy Trinity? How could there be any remaining unfulfilled desire to move him to display his glory in a world he would then create? God certainly did not create the world in order to become more glorious, for Jesus prayed shortly before his return to heaven, "And now, Father, glorify me in your presence with the glory I had with you before the world began" (John 17:5). So not even Jesus' ministry on earth increased the glory he enjoyed with the Father before creation. Nevertheless Genesis 1:1–2:3 speaks of God's having embarked on achieving a goal so desirable that he

129

could not rest until all had been set in place to diffuse his glory throughout the created world. To resolve this apparent contradiction between God's being both a Trinity and also the Creator, it is foundational that we grasp his whole purpose in creation and redemptive history.

A good place to begin this task is to consider briefly how the Swiss theologian Karl Barth (1886-1968), under whom I studied for three years, and the early American theologian Jonathan Edwards understood God's motive in creating the world. Their quite opposite answers to this question pinpoint the pitfalls to be avoided.

Karl Barth's response to this question fails, in my opinion, to cast any direct light on the subject. Nevertheless a consideration of the inadequacy of his answer helps to acquire a better understanding and appreciation of what I believe to be the solution, for which Edwards laid the foundation. In attempting to answer the question, Barth said, "[God] has no need of a creation. He might well have been satisfied with the inner glory of His threefold being. . . . The fact that He is not satisfied, but that His inner glory overflows and becomes outward, the fact that He wills creation . . . is grace, sovereign grace, a condescension inconceivably tender." The difficulty here is that Barth seems to say that God had no motive or desirable goal to attain in creating the world. The following statement further supports this conclusion:

> [God maintains creation] in the freedom of his love. He does not do it, therefore, because in His essence He is under the necessity of having the world as well, outside Himself, perhaps as His fellow-worker or even as His playmate. He does not do it because He is not great or rich enough in Himself, or because His omnipotence—the omnipotence of the divine knowledge and will—needs an object distinct from itself, or space for its activity outside itself. Nor does He do it because of a superabundance which has to find an outlet, as it were, and if it did not overflow in the creation of a world would be an imperfection, discord or suffering. He does not in any sense do it because He stands in need of an improvement or enlargement of Himself and must provide it for Him-

self. . . . He does it in love. But His love is free. It does not have to do what it does.[1]

According to Barth, every attribute in God functions inside the Trinity without there having to be a creation. His omnipotence is expressed in the generation of the Son; his omnipresence, in the fact that though the Son is distinct from the Father, yet God is equally in both. God is also love because of the delight the Father has in the Son. And Barth claims that he can account for all of God's attributes without going outside the Trinity. Yet obviously God's mercy or grace, which is the desire to render aid to those with a great need that they cannot supply for themselves, could never be exercised within the Trinity, where the Father and the Son find only a full delight, the meeting of their need-love, in beholding the completion and perfection of one another.[2] How, then, could it be at all possible for the Father and the Son ever to show mercy, or benevolence, to each other when both are fully God? Thus in every passage that I have come across in Barth's more than nine thousand pages of dogmatics where he speaks of God's mercy or grace, he must go outside the Trinity and speak of creation. For example, he defines mercy as "a determination of the love and grace of God manifested *in time* as God's effectual participation in the misery of another."[3]

In that Barth speaks of God's mercy or grace only in connection with what God does for the dependent creation,[4] never in terms of the love between the Father and Son, he necessarily implies that mercy is God's love exercised toward creation. But we have just seen that for Barth, this action is done for no reason (i.e., with no desirable goal in view), for he defined God's grace as a freedom of acting without a motive. But then God's acts done in grace and mercy are nothing more than whims.

However, from the way the author of Genesis 1:1–2:3 described the work of creation, one would never think of God as acting capriciously, for he expressed great enthusiasm and delight in what he had accomplished by the end of the sixth day. And this fact is comforting, for it would be most distressing for us creatures to conclude that, at root, we exist on this earth only from some act of whimsy on God's part. In such a case we might be tempted to wish God had remained blissfully happy inside his Trinity instead of creating, for no reason, a world that he in his omniscience knew would have so much hurting in it for so long. Therefore I argue that defining mercy or grace as acting without a motive, or out of caprice, is the first pitfall to be avoided in understanding God's purpose in creation.

Though Edwards too wanted to avoid understanding creation as a necessary act, like God's begetting the Son, he avoided this first pitfall by distinguishing between the need-love involved in that begetting and the benevolent love involved in God's diffusing his glory and goodness in creation. Of the begetting of the Son Edwards had said, "The Father's infinite happiness is in him,"[5] which is certainly an expression of need-love. But concerning the work of creation, he declared that "God's rejoicing in creation is rather a rejoicing in his own acts, and his own glory expressed in those acts, than a joy derived from the creature. God's joy [in creation] is dependent on nothing besides his own act which he exerts with an absolute and independent power."[6]

I interpret this statement to mean that creation itself is not the source of God's happiness, as is the only begotten Son, but that God does find great joy in the activity of extending his glory throughout creation. In other words, what motivates him is not the need for something he does not have or has incompletely but his delight in displaying what he already possesses. This is benevolent love, a love that is distinct from need-love; it is the desire to take the blessing that one enjoys and extend it beyond oneself so that others will also benefit from it.

To be sure, Edwards did say, "Without [the creation of man and the redemption of the elect, God] is as alone, as Adam was before Eve was created." The words of this statement, if taken by themselves, could lead us to think that in creating Adam, God satisfied a need-love in himself such as he satisfied in Adam by creating Eve as his wife. But this statement was made in a context of God's having a strong desire to exercise benevolent love by diffusing and extending his glory outward toward his creation. And so Edwards avoided the pitfall of regarding the created world as a necessary work like that of begetting the Son. And to show clearly that the love motivating God to create was a benevolent love, Edwards said,

> After the creatures are *intended* to be created, God may be conceived of as being moved by benevolence to [these as yet uncreated creatures]. . . . His exercising his goodness, and gratifying his benevolence to them in particular, may [then] be the spring of all God's proceedings through the universe; as being now the determined way of gratifying his general inclination to diffuse himself. Here God acting for *himself*, or making himself his last end, and his acting for their sake, are not to be set in opposition; they are rather to be considered as coinciding one with the other, and implied one in the other.[7]

Thus Edwards regarded as the mainspring behind all of God's acts in creation and redemption his benevolent love— his merciful and gracious desire to diffuse his glory and goodness throughout all the earth. Moreover in speaking of God's loving the people in the created world before creation took place, Edwards is able to talk about God's desire to be merciful from all eternity, thus showing how mercy exists in the Trinity even before the actual creation of the world. That God had always planned to create a world is clear, for 1 Peter 1:20 says that Jesus was destined before the foundation of the world to be the redeemer. But this reference to God's *eternal* purpose to create raises another question.

Why Did God Wait So Long to Create the World?

We have seen how John 1:1 views Jesus, the Word, as always having existed alongside God. Verses 3–5 then relate the role the Word played in creation, and the unmistakable implication is that creation took place after God's necessary works in being a Trinity. The declaration in Psalm 90:2 that "before the mountains were born or you [God] brought forth the earth and the world, from everlasting to everlasting you are God" also indicates that vast aeons of time elapsed before God acted to establish the earth so it would reflect his glory.

But Irenaeus, Augustine, and Calvin—some of the

church's greatest leaders—have sternly warned people not to ask what God was doing before he created, or to wonder why he waited to create. As Calvin saw it, "It is neither lawful nor expedient for us to inquire why God delayed so long, because if the human mind strives to penetrate thus far, it will fail a hundred times on the way. . . . When a certain shameless fellow mockingly asked a pious old man what God had done before the creation of the world, the latter aptly countered that he had been building hell for the curious."[8]

I believe, however, that it is both lawful and expedient to ask why the triune God waited a long time to create the world. From the very fact that he waited, we know that he did not create us out of the necessity involved in need-love, but only in the freedom involved in benevolent love. It would be threatening to our future happiness to know that God had created us to meet some need in himself, which might mean our having to fulfill a purpose contrary to our own welfare. But the moment we understand that all of God's need-love was met in being a Trinity, then we see that he is free to act toward us, his creation, solely in terms of the freedom of a benevolent love.

A striking way to represent the difference is to say that if God were to have created us out of need-love, it would be like his inviting us to a banquet, only to inform us that we were to be one of the courses for the meal. But when God invites us to a banquet out of benevolent love, he wants us to join with him as guests at his table, to enjoy the feast along with him—as the psalmist put it, to drink from the river of his delights (Ps. 36:8).

So God's having delayed creation for a long while makes it unmistakably clear that he created us not out of need but in the freedom of his benevolent love, out of mercy and grace. Therefore contrary to Irenaeus, Augustine, and Calvin, it is most edifying to know why a long period elapsed before God created the world. This reason provides one of the most encouraging emphases that emerges from studying theology in terms of a sequence on a timeline: God, in his benevolent love toward creation, wants to serve the very best interests of as many people as possible. This desire to be a means to people's own ends is strongly affirmed when God says, "I will rejoice in doing them good ... with all my heart and soul" (Jer. 32:41).

Such considerations, however, lead to a third question.

Did God Then Become Subordinate to Creation?

An illustration drawn from everyday life may help to show that God's desire to benefit his creation does not, on that account, make creation superior to God. In producing a play, people with many different skills—the scriptwriter, costume designers, carpenters, painters, actors, the director, and many others—commence work months before the opening night. As that date draws near, the tension increases because they want everything to be in readiness. If the dress rehearsal is flawless, then all the participants can say of the play, "It is very good" and can rest well before the all-important opening night.

It should be noted that before opening night all effort in producing this play has been directed toward the completely necessary task of having a dress rehearsal that takes place without a hitch. But all this months-long effort was not for the joy of the dress rehearsal itself, even though all the glory and praiseworthiness of the play was already evident there. Rather, it was to lay the necessary groundwork so the cast could then have the freedom of greatly increased joy as they extended the goodness of this play to the audiences for what all hoped would be a long run of performances. Not a single improvement is added to the play so that it becomes more glorious when the curtain goes up on opening night than it was at the dress rehearsal. What happens instead is that the glory and goodness of this play now extends outward from the stage to the general public; now the cast's joy, the anticipation of which has been driving them to work feverishly to perfect the play, becomes greatly increased as night after night audiences keep calling them back on stage for encores.

In the same way God has willed to be the perfect God not only because he could delight in nothing less but because he looked forward to the greater blessing that would be his as his glory and goodness met real needs in the lives of people whom he would create, who would depend on him for joy and fulfillment. As Jesus himself said, "It is more blessed to give than to receive" (Acts 20:35). God's ultimate purpose is to increase his joy by sharing the blessing of the Trinity in creation. And while it constitutes a desirable goal that he took steps to attain, it is also his *free* act in that he finds so much joy just in transmitting his blessings to those who appreciate them that he wants nothing more. Simply to do his people good gives him complete satisfaction.

But just because creation gives God great delight, we cannot say that he is worshiping it; rather, he is worshiping himself as he sees his goodness bringing such blessing to people that they give their heartfelt thanks and praise to him for the benefits he imparts.[9] And here we should emphasize again Edwards' point quoted above that in understanding God's purpose in creating and redeeming, it is obvious that both he and his creation receive the fullest possible benefit.

In that his goodness and mercy pursue after his people every day of their lives (see Ps. 23:6), God himself is modeling the benevolent love of 1 Corinthians 10:24: "Nobody should seek his own good, but the good of others." But this seeking the welfare of the creature does not contradict the oft-stated affirmation in Scripture that "to [God] be the glory forever! Amen" (e.g., Rom. 11:36), for the blessing of knowing God enjoyed by believing people as his mercy and goodness pursue them daily causes their hearts to well up constantly in praise to him. Thus while the motto on God's wall would read, "The chief end of God is to serve _____ [the reader should put his or her own name here]," yet this affirmation does not deny that "the Lord alone will be exalted in that [final judgment] day" (Isa. 2:11), for he will not yield his glory to another (48:11).

Now the basic thrust of God's whole purpose in creation and redemption has become clear. It is that the earth might be filled with the glory of his desire to service people and, calling upon all his omniscience and omnipotence, to do them good with his whole heart and soul. But men and women do not become the beneficiaries of this glorious purpose unless they are willing to undergo that radical change in their lives whereby they align themselves with this great purpose. Nor can they remain neutral; they must either serve God's purpose, as David did during his lifetime (Acts 13:36), or they must reject it, as did the Pharisees and experts in the law (Luke 7:30).

Review Questions

1. Explain how God's greatest desire, which is to show mercy and benevolence to needy people, was satisfied before he actually created the world, even though it was impossible for the Father and the Son to show mercy to each other in the Trinity.

2. Why is Barth unable to account for God's attribute of mercy or grace before creation?

3. How does Edwards' explanation of God's motive for creation and redemption keep the world from becoming a "fourth member" of the Trinity, or a work essential to God's being fully God?

4. Why does knowing that God did not create a world out of need-love help you sleep better?

5. Explain how God's love for us is fundamentally different from our love for him.

6. Explain how our love for God is fundamentally different from our love for others.

7. What desirable goal did God achieve in creating the world?

NOTES

[1] Karl Barth, *Church Dogmatics,* trans. Geoffrey W. Bromiley et al. (Edinburgh: T. & T. Clark, 1936–75), II/2:121, II/1:499.

[2] The newly coined term "need-love" was introduced in the previous chapter. It is of the utmost importance to grasp the difference between need-love and benevolence in understanding the whole counsel of God as set forth in this book. I will be referring to these two different kinds of love repeatedly; as readers follow the development of these terms, they should be able (1) to define them in their own words and (2) to cite concrete examples

for both from their own life-experiences, in this way meeting the test of understanding an author's special terminology.

[3] Barth, *Church Dogmatics,* II/1:377, italics added.

[4] It should be noted that, in my thinking, an action consisting in grace or mercy is an action of benevolent love. To be sure, being merciful or gracious very often implies being benevolent to the sinner, who does not deserve such love. At root, however, mercy or grace means meeting people's great needs that they cannot supply for themselves or obligate anyone else to help them by paying a compensation of some sort. So we must not think of mercy or grace as necessarily connected with sin. I thus agree with Barth's comment that God created the world out of mercy and grace; in the initial act of creation, mercy did not involve showing undeserved benevolence toward sinners.

[5] Edwards, *Observations,* 22.

[6] Jonathan Edwards, "Dissertation Concerning the End for Which God Created the World," in *Works,* 1:102.

[7] Ibid., 101.

[8] Calvin, *Institutes,* 20:160 (1.14.1). In saying the above, Calvin was echoing both the view of Augustine (354–430) in his *Confessions* (11.12) and the view of Irenaeus (c. 177) in *Against Heresies* (2.28.3). But theologians like Jonathan Edwards and Oscar Cullmann, for whom it is more biblical to construct theology on a timeline (see chap. 7 above), feel justified to concern themselves with the motives and goals that led God to carry out a purpose implied by events happening sequentially and building on preceding events. Calvin's reluctance to question will also be evident when we come to the last section of this book, which considers why Israel by and large remains in rebellion against God and will do so until the second coming of Christ. In this matter of seeking after God's purpose in redemptive history, I side rather with Edwards, who does not hesitate to say that God, in the time before creation, was showing mercy in having the plan that he would eventually bring to pass.

[9] Our word "worship" comes from the Old English "weorthscipe," or that which possesses great value. In worshiping himself, God thus acknowledges his inestimable value.

10

The First Step in Responding to God's Purpose

Significantly, the first of the two steps involved in submitting to God's purpose corresponds to his *necessary* work of being a truly glorious God as a Trinity; the second parallels his *free* work of extending the goodness of his glory throughout the world he created. First, then, we want to delight ourselves in God, looking to him to satisfy our *need-love*. Then we want to increase our joy by exercising *benevolent* love to all other people. We do so by using our time, treasure, and talents optimally to help them come to know God, who alone can satisfy their need-love, and then come to see how they can increase that joy by helping others to know him.

These two steps appear side by side in Mark 12:28–31, where Jesus in defining the greatest commandment declared that two were primary: "The most important one . . . is this: 'Hear, O Israel: the Lord our God, the Lord is one. Love the Lord your God with all your heart and with all your soul and with all your mind and with all your strength' [Deut. 6:4–5]. The second is this: 'Love your neighbor as yourself' [Lev. 19:18]. There is no commandment greater than these." In this chapter we consider the first commandment. In the first section I set forth the inducements for looking to God to satisfy our hearts' craving for need-love; in the second, we consider how faith in God's promises is what we must keep exercising in order to love God with all the heart, soul, mind, and strength. Then it will be clear how having God meet our

need-love lays the indispensable foundation for being benevolent toward others, which is what Jesus meant by the
second commandment to "love your neighbor as yourself,"
which we consider in chapter 11.

Why Only God Can Meet Our Need-Love

The first inducement to look to God for the contentment,
joy, and bright future that we all desire is that he alone can
give it, since we are made in his image. Although we are now
fallen, sinful people, we have not lost that image. Long after
Adam and Eve had sinned, God, in decreeing that a
murderer should be punished by death, gave the following
as the reason: "in the image of God has God made man"
(Gen. 9:6). Thus the punishment for taking the life of one
who has this unique feature should be death, for the image of
God still resides in people, despite their sin.

Clear evidence of this image was pointed out by Blaise
Pascal, who argued that only the God of the Bible can satisfy
the cry for security and contentment. (See his Thought 250,
quoted above in chap. 6.) Pascal's "empty outline" or
"infinite abyss," made evident by the universal failure to
find happiness, is palpable evidence that people are made in
God's image. And if nothing in this world ever succeeds in
filling the God-shaped vacuum that necessarily exists because we are made in his image, then we all should seek
wholeheartedly to know God in order to experience the
contentment and joy that we crave.

A second inducement for loving God in the sense of
delighting in him is that he longs to share with each of us this
greatest possible joy, namely, the very joy that he has in
being the triune God. In chapter 8 we saw how the Father
and Son find such complete delight in each other that the
"spirit" of their community is a person, the Holy Spirit, the
third person of the Trinity. We also saw that "God has
poured out his love into our hearts by the Holy Spirit, whom
he has given us" (Rom. 5:5). The Holy Spirit is the
embodiment of the joy the Father and the Son have in each
other, and God wants to satisfy the need-love of people's
hearts by giving them this same Holy Spirit. We can receive

this gift because, unlike the animals, we have a God-shaped receptacle in our hearts that the Holy Spirit is specially designed to fill. Clearly, then, the opportunity to share God's own joy should induce each of us to seek him wholeheartedly and persistently in order to gain and retain the only joy and hope for the future that will eternally satisfy us. Thus Paul closed his letter to the church at Rome with the following benediction: "May the God of hope fill you with all *joy and peace* as you trust in him, so that you may *overflow with hope* by the power of the Holy Spirit" (Rom. 15:13; cf. Gal. 5:22).

The same note is struck by the psalmist, for he found fellowship with God so delightful he declared, "One thing I ask of the Lord, this is what I seek: that I may dwell in the house of the Lord all the days of my life, to gaze upon the beauty of the Lord and to seek him in his temple" (Ps. 27:4).[1] This was the experience of Moses and Joshua too (Ex. 33:7–11). They would pitch the tent of meeting outside the encampment of the Israelites, and after they entered it, the fiery cloud of God's presence and glory would come down and hover over it. Because of his many responsibilities Moses had limited time to spend there in communion with God, and so "he . . . would return to the camp, but his young aide Joshua son of Nun did not leave the tent" (v. 11). This verse implies that Joshua found fellowship with God so satisfying that his greatest desire was to feast on the joy of having communion with God.

Words cannot convey the superlative nature of this joy. But something of its nature can be known even before experiencing it by realizing that it is like the joy the disciples knew during the three years they followed Jesus around Palestine. John declared that Jesus, "the One and Only [of God], who is at the Father's side, had made [God the Father fully] known" (John 1:18). This uniqueness of Jesus is well illustrated by a former seminary student raised in the Near East by a Muslim father. He found no satisfaction in Islam, nor did he find meaning in Hinduism, which he studied for months under a famed guru in India. One day, however, he came across a New Testament, and as he read about Jesus, his reaction was, "This Jesus was surely some person!" That sense, along with his seeing genuine love for the first time among Christian young people at a Bible college, were the main causes for him to become a Christian and enter seminary to prepare for the ministry.

As the disciples, then, had the privilege of actually being with Jesus, what fulfillment must have been theirs as they walked alongside *God,* whose greatest delight comes in sharing his supreme happiness with those who turn the control of their lives over to him. There is a joyful atmosphere in the Gospels' record of the things Jesus did throughout his three-year ministry that is not to be found in any other literature.

Jesus also wants very much to have rich fellowship with us today, for he declares, "Here I am! I [always] stand at the door and knock. If anyone hears my voice and opens the door, I will come in and eat with him, and he with me" (Rev. 3:20). God himself thus wants nothing so much as to have fellowship with each of us; otherwise he would not keep knocking twenty-four hours a day. It also means each of us can have extended periods in which to be with the supremely happy God and to share in his happiness. Unlike a psychiatrist who keeps an eye on the clock so as not to give patients more than their fifty-minute hour, Jesus will fellowship with us for as long as we want and are able to sustain with our limited strength and pressing responsibilities.

Once we have experienced such times of fellowship with Jesus, including devotional Bible reading, heart searching, prayer, and meditation, we will experience the filling of our God-shaped vacuum and find our outlook on life completely changed. That Jesus is indeed able to satisfy every need is well expressed by the following hymn, written by Oswald J. Smith, a great missionary-minded pastor in Toronto, Canada, during the first half of the twentieth century.

> One sat alone beside the highway begging,
>   His eyes were blind, the light he could not see;
> He clutched his rags and shivered in the shadows,
>   Then Jesus came and bade his darkness flee.
>
> *Chorus:*
> When Jesus comes, the tempter's power is broken;

When Jesus comes, the tears are wiped away.
He takes the gloom and fills the life with glory,
    For all is changed when Jesus comes to stay.

From home and friends the evil spirits drove him,
    Among the tombs he dwelt in misery;
He cut himself as demon powers possessed him,
    Then Jesus came and set the captive free.

"Unclean! Unclean!" the leper cried in torment,
    The deaf, the dumb, in helplessness stood near;
The fever raged, disease had gripped its victim,
    Then Jesus came and cast out every fear.

Their hearts were sad as in the tomb they laid him,
    For death had come and taken him away;
Their night was dark and bitter tears were falling,
    Then Jesus came and night was turned to day.

So men today have found the Saviour able,
    They could not conquer passion, lust and sin;
Their broken hearts had left them sad and lonely,
    Then Jesus came and dwelt, Himself, within.

A third inducement for turning to God as the only One who can meet our need-love is that in addition to giving us his joy in the present, he guarantees that we shall be satisfied for all time to come. To the woman at the well of Samaria, Jesus promised, "Everyone who drinks this water will be thirsty again, but whoever drinks the water I give him will never [lit., an emphatic 'never ever'] thirst. Indeed, the water I give him will become in him a spring of water welling up to eternal life" (John 4:13–14). And to the crowd who followed him Jesus declared, "I am the bread of life. He who comes to me will [never ever] go hungry, and he who believes in me will [never ever at any time] be thirsty" (6:35).

This last statement is basic for understanding what it means to believe in Jesus so as to be saved. Not only must we trust that his death on the cross enables God to forgive our sins, but to believe properly we must also, when distressed, regain contentment and peace by "[fighting] the good fight of the faith" (1 Tim. 6:12), claiming the "very great and precious promises" (2 Peter 1:4) in Scripture. "For no matter how many promises God has made, they are 'Yes' in Christ. And so through him the 'Amen' is spoken by us to the glory of God" (2 Cor. 1:20). This believing in God's promises, so essential for filling Pascal's God-shaped vacuum, is an indispensable component of genuine faith in Christ. Unless we have confidence that the joy we are presently experiencing can always be ours, the fear of its loss would haunt us and greatly diminish that joy. Moreover God will not allow the shed blood of his Son to atone for the sins of people who heap the greatest possible insult upon his glory by scorning his promises. They do so through a persistent disbelief that manifests itself in anxiety, covetousness, regret, jealousy, an unforgiving attitude, impatience, and self-adulation. Unfortunately emphasis on believing the promises is rarely heard in Protestantism; Calvin said virtually nothing about this essential futuristic component of saving faith.[2]

So, for example, we "thirst" when there seems to be no way out of the problems closing in upon us. But we can satisfy this thirst by claiming a promise such as Psalm 16:11, "You [God] *will make known* [not the NIV's past tense] to me the path of life; you will fill me with joy in your presence, with eternal pleasures at your right hand." Or Psalm 138:8, "The Lord will fulfill his purpose for me; your love, O Lord, endures forever." And Paul assures us that "God will meet all your needs according to his glorious riches in Christ Jesus" (Phil. 4:19). Therefore we can lay aside all anxiety, such as fear that there will not be enough money for the future, and be content simply with what we now have (Heb. 13:5–6).

Another example of "thirst" is when we are tempted to lust. A well-known American pastor describes thirst in this context as follows:

> Some sexual image pops into my brain and beckons me to pursue it. The way this temptation gets its power is by persuading me to believe that I will be happier if I follow it. The power of all temptation is that it will make me happier. . . .
>
> So what should I do? Some people would say, "Remember God's command to be holy (1 Peter 1:16) and exercise your

will to obey because he is God!" But something crucial is missing from this advice, namely, FAITH. A lot of people strive for moral improvement who cannot say, "The life I live I live BY FAITH" (Gal. 2:20). A lot of people try to love who don't realize that "What counts is FAITH working through love" (Gal. 5:6 [lit. trans.]).

The fight against lust (or greed or fear or any other temptation) is a fight of faith. Otherwise the result is legalism. I'll try to explain how we fight sin with faith.

When the temptation to lust comes, Romans 8:13 says, "If you kill it *by the Spirit* you will live." By the Spirit! What does that mean? Out of all the armor God gives us to fight Satan, only one piece is used for killing—the sword. It is called the sword OF THE SPIRIT (Eph. 6:17). So when Paul says, "Kill sin by the Spirit" (Rom. 8:13), I take that to mean, Depend on the Spirit, especially his sword.

What is the sword of the Spirit? It's the Word of God (Eph. 6:17). Here's where faith comes in. . . . The Word of God cuts through the fog of Satan's lies and shows me where true and lasting happiness is to be found. And so the Word helps me stop trusting in the potential of sin to make me happy, and instead entices me to trust in God's promise of joy (Psalm 16:11).

. . . This is what Jesus meant when he said, "He who BELIEVES in me shall NEVER THIRST" (John 6:35). If my thirst for joy and meaning and passion are satisfied by the presence of the promises of Christ, the power of sin is broken. We do not yield to the offer of sandwich meat when we can see the sizzling steak on the grill. . . .

At first lust begins to trick me into feeling that I would really miss out on some great satisfaction if I followed the path of purity. But then I take up the sword of the Spirit and begin to fight. . . .

And as I pray for my faith to be satisfied with God's life and peace, the sword of the Spirit carves the sugar coating off the poison of lust. . . . And by the grace of God, [lust's] alluring power is broken.[3]

Another comforting promise is Jeremiah 38:20, "Obey the Lord by doing what I tell you. Then it will go well with you, and your life will be spared." This was said to King Zedekiah by the prophet Jeremiah when Jerusalem was about to be conquered by Nebuchadnezzar, king of Babylon.

Zedekiah, confident that God would spare Jerusalem in 587 B.C. as he had saved it from the Assyrians in 721, had sinned by refusing to heed Jeremiah's constant urging to make peace with Nebuchadnezzar. Nevertheless Jeremiah's predictions about Jerusalem's downfall proved true. The Babylonian army overran the city, captured Zedekiah, and killed his sons before his eyes. Then he was blinded and dragged off in chains to Babylon, where he died in a dungeon. But none of this disaster would have happened if he had believed God's promise and submitted to him in obedient faith.

Nor was this promise for Zedekiah alone. We too can claim it even when our sins have placed us in great difficulty; all we need do is confess them, take time to find out what God wants us to do from this moment on, and then do it. Recently a former student, a Baptist pastor in California, telephoned to report how effective this verse had been in a small group that in obedience to Hebrews 3:12–13 was meeting regularly to help its members avoid an evil heart of unbelief. One member, depressed over a difficulty his sin had brought upon him, brightened visibly with hope as he was reminded of Jeremiah 38:20.[4] Today this person is rejoicing in God as he continues to fight the fight of faith.

So indeed there is every reason to seek God with all our hearts. In the words of the hymn "How Firm a Foundation," "What more can he say than to you he hath said, To you who for refuge to Jesus have fled?"

How to Get God's Love into Our Hearts

At the end of chapter 8 we saw that God's love has been poured out into our hearts through the Holy Spirit. In that the Holy Spirit is the very love that the Father and Son have for each other, the most benevolent thing God can do for us is to share this greatest of all joys. This unsurpassed blessing obviously could not be a reimbursement for some useful and valuable work we finite creatures do for the Almighty God. Rather, it comes by faith alone, as we honor God by trusting him to keep our hearts satisfied in him. When Paul asked the Galatians, "Did you receive the [Holy] Spirit by the works of the law [not 'observing the law,' as in the NIV] or by believing what you heard?" (Gal. 3:2), he was so confident his readers would respond, "By believing what we heard," that he did not even bother to answer the question. And in Galatians 3:14 Paul explicitly declared that "by faith we . . . receive . . . the [Holy] Spirit."

Therefore if we would have our hearts satisfied with the love and delight the Father and the Son have for each other, we should be careful to let the Spirit, who is resident in the hearts of those who have turned their lives over to Christ, keep us filled with all joy and peace as we trust God's promises. It is imperative to remember that joy is the barometer of one's faith. As Paul told the Philippians, his one goal when he came to see them again would be to increase "[their] progress and joy in the faith" (Phil. 1:25). This comment, as well as his affirmation that joy comes through believing God (Rom. 15:13), must mean that our faith is measured by our joy in the Lord.

When Paul realized that he had completed the tasks the Lord had given him, he characterized his whole Christian life as having fought the *good* fight of faith (2 Tim. 4:7; cf. 1 Tim. 6:12). It is a good fight, because unlike other hostile encounters, here the victors enjoy great blessings, suffer no casualties, and are a blessing to others. The way in which this good fight is to be waged is by "[taking] up the shield of faith, with which [we] can extinguish all the flaming arrows of the evil one" (Eph. 6:16). These arrows consist of all the various doubts Satan tries to lodge in our hearts to make us despair about the future and thus lose our joy. But *all* of them can be extinguished by claiming one or more of the many promises God has given us in the Bible. So, for example, if we are under stress because we do not know the decisions to make for getting through a difficulty, we fight back by claiming the promise of James 1:5–6: "If any of you lacks wisdom, he should ask God, who gives generously to all. . . . But when he asks, he must believe and not doubt." As we claim this promise by meeting its condition, the Holy Spirit will replace our fear and despair with joy, peace, and confident hope and will give us wisdom regarding the next decision to make.

Obviously, the more promises from the Bible that we can readily cite to fight off unbelief, the sooner we will be able to regain peace and joy. Therefore everyone should build up a huge stockpile of these spiritual weapons ready for immediate use. The first step in doing so is to set time aside daily for a prayerful, systematic reading of the Bible, so that within the course of every year or so we give God the opportunity of speaking to us through every verse from Genesis to Revelation. Then we should mark those passages where God has spoken most clearly. Verses useful for overcoming the ten states of an unbelieving heart should likewise be marked, as should those that speak to our special weaknesses. At least some of these verses should then be memorized with their references so that they are in "battle readiness"—available to extinguish a flaming dart of Satan right after it strikes so that the terrible pain these arrows inflict may be short-lived.

Jesus warned that "each day has enough trouble of its own" (Matt. 6:34). Thus in order not to be overcome by a day's evil, we must become proficient in wielding the "sword of the Spirit," as Paul describes Scripture, so we can be protected by the "shield of faith" (Eph. 6:16–17). For Hebrews 3:12–13 commands, "See to it, brothers [and sisters], that none of you has a sinful, unbelieving heart that turns away from the living God. But encourage one another daily, as long as it is called Today, so that none of you may be hardened by sin's deceitfulness."

For three reasons, then, we should "let the word of Christ dwell in [us] richly" (Col. 3:16). First, "battle-ready" weapons will then always be at hand to repel sin, so we will not experience its hardening effect by delaying to overcome it. Second, we will have a sufficient number and variety of weapons to handle any kind of spiritual warfare that a day may bring. Third, with such an arsenal of retaliatory weapons, the pain we suffer from Satan's flaming arrows will be brief, and the Holy Spirit's peace and joy soon restored.

We must consider other facets of faith also in order to understand adequately how to obtain, and continue to experience, God's love and joy in our hearts.

Faith and God's Promises

Note 2 above includes a quotation from one of Luther's early writings that makes clear the necessity for believing God's promises in order to experience his peace and joy.[5] Everyone can claim and enjoy this promise, for it is conditioned simply upon one's believing that God will forgive sins and completely meet our need-love. Thus after paraphrasing this verse, Luther declared,

> [Consequently] the cross and death itself are compelled to serve me and to work together with me for my salvation. This is a splendid privilege . . . , a truly omnipotent power, a spiritual dominion in which there is nothing so good and nothing so evil but that it shall work together for good to me, *if only I believe.* . . . Thus Christ has made it possible for us, *provided we believe in him,* to be . . . his brethren, co-heirs, and fellow-kings.[6]

It is clear, then, that if we believe Romans 8:28 in the manner described by Luther, we will find the God-shaped vacuum of our hearts filled by the joy of knowing God and being assured of the good things he will do for us in the future. We can therefore be confident that he will take circumstances that now seem like extremely hurtful stumbling blocks and work so that, in time, we will see them as key stepping-stones to the happy future God wants us to have. So "in all these things we are more than [!] conquerors through him who loved us" (Rom. 8:37). For as he assures us in Jeremiah 29:11, "I know the plans I have for you . . . plans to prosper you and not to harm you, plans to give you hope and a future." According to this promise, the delight of our hearts will lie in something very different from the things in which people ordinarily find joy. Such a different focus in turn requires radically shifting our hope from things in the created world to God and his many promises. Therefore it is time now to see how repentance relates to faith.

Repentance and Faith

In Scripture repentance comes first when it is spoken of in connection with faith (Mark 1:15; Acts 20:21), but for the sake of clarity we have considered faith first, emphasizing the futuristic dimension so prominent in Scripture. Now with this dimension in mind, we understand why in the Bible repentance precedes faith. Before people find their need-love met in God, they are looking to other things, often money, for satisfaction. So believing in God has to involve a 180° turn away (that is, repentance) from the love of money to find contentment and confidence for the future simply in knowing God and depending on his promises.

The love for money, so deeply embedded in our nature, is totally incompatible with a love for God and for the future he promises. As Jesus said, "No one can serve two masters. . . . You cannot serve both God and Money" (Matt. 6:24). Yet so much a part of us is this love for money that when the disciples heard that it had to be replaced by a love for God, they objected, "Who then can be saved?" Jesus' answer was, "With men [and their innate desire for money] this is impossible, but with God [and his power to change the heart] all things are possible" (Matt. 19:25–26). It is only, however, as God answers for us the first petition of the Lord's prayer, "Hallowed [i.e., treasured] be your name" (Matt. 6:9), that we will look to him to satisfy our need-love and thus be able to "keep [our] lives free from the love of money and be content with what [we] have" (Heb. 13:5).

Something is "hallowed," or sanctified in our hearts, to the extent that we place great value on it. There is, however, no natural inclination in any of us to love and delight in God, and so we need continually to pray, "Lord, enable me to value [in my heart] your name [representing your integrity to keep your promises]." Only when we regard God himself and his promises as of the greatest value will we truly acknowledge him in our hearts as Lord, so that people will then ask us to explain the hope that we have (1 Peter 3:15).

The Obedience of Faith

It has often been observed that what people hope in for a happy future, that they worship; and what they worship, that they inevitably serve. Thus Jesus, when tempted by the Devil in the wilderness, fought back by saying, "Away from me, Satan! For it is written, 'Worship the Lord your God, and serve him only'" (Matt. 4:10). We worship God when we bank our hope for an eternally happy future both on the prospect of always being able to share with him his joy and on his integrity to keep his great and priceless promises. In this way we render the greatest possible honor to him, as did Abraham, who "gave glory to God, being fully persuaded that God had power to do what he had promised" (Rom. 4:20–21).[7] So when our hearts are full of joy as we believe God, we will not engage in any thinking or conduct that is inconsistent with our hope being in him. And then the worship of God will inevitably lead to serving him in the sense of obeying his commandments as laws of faith.

This obedience that stems from faith in God's promises is the way we serve God. Therefore when Jesus said we cannot serve God and Money, he was not talking about the way a worker serves an employer, a *client lord,* but the way a client serves a benefactor, or a *patron lord.*[8] People can in fact work for many employers. A physician, for example, may have two hundred employers (i.e., patients), all of whom the physician serves or works for without necessarily hating some and loving others. But the service Jesus was speaking about is the service we render to what we worship as promising hope for a happy future. And experience confirms that we cannot worship and serve two patron lords. We can go to only one doctor, or team of doctors, for help regarding a single health problem; we can have only one lawyer or team of lawyers representing us in a lawsuit. And it is crucial to note that we serve patron lords (in distinction to a client lord—an employer) first of all by trusting their expertise to meet some need in our lives. Then because we trust them, we follow the instructions they give for helping our need to be met. Thus, for example, we "serve" a doctor by following his or her prescriptions for restoring our health. This service is therefore an "obedience that comes from faith" (Rom. 1:5). Jesus was talking about this kind of obedience when he said, "You cannot serve God and Money."

How, then, do people "serve" money? A little reflection will make it clear that money is never like an employer, whose benefit we enhance by performing some task it needs done. Money, like God, has no needs. But people do serve money, and they do so in the same way they serve a lawyer or physician, by trying to position themselves so as to receive the greatest benefit such patron lords can give. People serving money therefore avidly read such financial guides as the *Wall Street Journal* ("the Diary of the American Dream") or *Barron's*. Often too they depend on the advice of an investment counselor or stockbroker on how to maximize their funds for the greatest future benefit. But people who serve God study the Bible, memorizing key verses and references, in order to let Christ's word dwell in them richly (Col. 3:16).

Though money can provide many things, God can do infinitely more for us than money ever could. Therefore we would be much wiser to let him satisfy our need-love, for "with skillful hands God leads [us]" (Ps. 78:72) through the unknown things that lie before us each day—something no amount of money could ever provide. Only God knows us well enough to guide us into our proper niche in life, which money can never do. Indeed, money does have value in that it enables us to command the labor of people whose skills can supply certain needs in our lives. But God also works for those who wait for him with hope and trust. There are three great advantages to the work he does for us, in comparison with that of money: (1) he will always be totally reliable in carrying out his promises, whereas money's continued value is ever uncertain; (2) he has all wisdom and therefore all skill to work for us and help us in ways that no amount of money could ever command; (3) unlike money, which will no longer benefit us at death, God will for all eternity continue to be our God and to "act on behalf of those who wait for him." As God said to Moses four hundred years after Abraham's death, "I am the God of your father, the God of Abraham" (Ex. 3:6), a declaration Jesus used to affirm that "[God] is not the God of the dead but of the living" (Matt. 22:32).

In the commands and wise sayings of the Bible, we who have seen the wisdom of serving God rather than money find sketched out the profile to which our lives are to conform. Since we have now made fellowship with God and his promises, guaranteed by Jesus, our hope for a happy future, and since we have turned over to him the responsibility for running our lives, we will, for example, obey the commandment not to steal, because we believe God's promise to meet all our needs (Phil. 4:19). An auto mechanic who is serving God in order to get the full benefit of his promises therefore will not take advantage of people's often-insufficient knowledge of how an automobile works to tell them they need an $800 repair job, when all that is wrong is a loose connection to a spark plug. Likewise a man who is a defense contractor and who believes God's promise to supply all his needs will reject the temptation to employ devious accounting methods to inflate the price he charges the government for a contract. Because his patron lord is God rather than money, he will be scrupulously honest in all his financial dealings.

Conclusion

By now it should be clear how the glory of God on earth is extended by the response of faith to his promises to be benevolent toward those he created. Again we quote from Luther's "Freedom of a Christian" to help us gain insight on how trusting God is the ultimate way to fill the earth with his glory.

> Faith honors him whom it trusts with the most reverent and highest regard since it considers him truthful and trustworthy. There is no other honor equal to the estimate of truthfulness and righteousness with which we honor him whom we trust. Could we ascribe to a man anything greater than truthfulness and righteousness and perfect goodness? On the other hand, there is no way in which we can show greater contempt for a man than to regard him as false and wicked and to be suspicious of him, as we do when we do not trust him. So when the soul firmly trusts God's promises, it regards Him as truthful and righteous. Nothing more excellent than this can be ascribed to God. The very highest worship of God is this that we ascribe to him truthfulness, righteousness, and whatever else should be ascribed to one who is trusted. When this is done, the soul consents to his will. Then it hallows his name and allows itself to be treated according to God's good pleasure for, clinging to God's promises, it does not doubt that

he who is true, just, and wise will do, dispose, and provide all things well. . . . On the other hand, what greater rebellion against God, what greater wickedness, what greater contempt of God is there than not believing his promise? For what is this but to make God a liar or to doubt that he is truthful?[9]

By now it should also be clear that obedience to the first commandment of Mark 12:28–31, to love God with all our being, lays the foundation for obedience to the second commandment, to be as benevolent toward all others as we are to ourselves. In speaking of the auto mechanic and defense contractor, we have given examples of how the worship of money could cause people to serve it (that is, to behave) in ways that hurt others. But there are also many examples of people who have made money their god during their lives and yet have contributed large sums of it to benefit humanity in many ways. Are they loving their neighbors as themselves? In the next chapter we will examine carefully what loving one's neighbor as oneself necessarily entails, for the benevolence God requires can be produced only on the foundation of having one's need-love satisfied in him.

Review Questions

1. How would you explain in a way relevant to junior high young people that they were made in the image of God?

2. In what does the belief essential for salvation consist?

3. Since the most proper objects of faith are promises concerning what God will do in the future, explain why joy will be the barometer of faith. Be able to cite a promise or two to illustrate how faith increases joy.

4. Emphasizing the fact that faith is basically directed toward God's promises, explain why faith must necessarily imply repentance (whose meaning you should explain in your own words). Then be able to show why repentance must necessarily imply faith.

5. Cite an instance from everyday life showing that despite Matthew 6:24, it is perfectly possible to serve more than two lords (employers).

6. Cite an instance from everyday life where it is impossible to serve more than one benefactor, or patron lord.

7. Understanding that Isaiah 64:4 describes the unique quality of the God of the Bible, in contrast to all other religions and philosophies of religion, explain why exercising faith in God necessarily means submitting to him as a patron lord, rather than as a client lord.

8. Why is there no other way to glorify God than to trust him?

9. Explain why the basis of each and every sin is unbelief. Be able to give a concrete example from everyday life to illustrate this abstract concept.

10. Note Luther's concept in the quotation in the section "Faith and God's Promises" and then explain why believing in Jesus must include believing the promise of Romans 8:28.

NOTES

[1] The arguments for saying that the Holy Spirit *in*dwelt people in the Old Testament, just as in the days since Christ came, appear in chapter 15 below.

[2] Often Luther spoke only of the need for faith in the atonement. But in his essay "The Freedom of a Christian," he made it explicit that to be saved, one must believe not only the atonement but also the promise of Rom. 8:28 that for one who is seated with Jesus, the ascended Lord of all, God works all things together for good. "He, however, who does not believe [Rom. 8:28] is not served by anything. On the contrary, nothing works for his good . . . and all things turn out badly for him. . . . So he is . . . a wicked man whose prayer becomes sin and who never comes into the presence of God because God does not hear sinners (John 9:31)" (in *Martin Luther: Selections from His Writings*, ed. John Dillenberger [New York: Doubleday, 1961], 64).

[3] Taken from the original text for the article in *Decision*, January 1990, "How Redeemed People Do Battle with Sin," by John Piper.

[4] See chapter 18 below for a listing of some staple biblical promises for overcoming each of the ten states of mind that constitute the evil heart of unbelief mentioned in Heb. 3:12. I will argue that, according to Scripture, the primary objective for

meeting in small groups is to help one another fight the fight of faith by claiming specific promises that speak to the unbelieving states of mind.

[5] It is noteworthy that the early Luther stressed the promise-believing aspect of saving faith. But apparently his emphasis was not well enough woven into his thinking so that it was properly stressed in his later writings.

[6] Luther, "Freedom of a Christian," 64, italics added.

[7] Conversely, we render to God the greatest insult and we sin in the most grievous way against him when we allow ourselves to be unhappy by not believing the promises that answer to our unhappiness. That is why Jesus said the Holy Spirit would "convict the world . . . in regard to sin, because men do not believe in me" (John 16:8–9). It is most important to understand that sin is essentially unbelief in God's promises.

[8] "Patron lord" is my term for best understanding the meaning of "master" in Jesus' statement in Matt. 6:24: "You cannot serve two masters [i.e., patron lords]." This term appears frequently in the remainder of the book.

[9] Luther, "Freedom of a Christian," 59.

11

The Second Step in
Responding to God's Purpose

The preceding chapter described two of the ways in which
people whose need-love was met by God were no longer
motivated to do hurtful things to others. Many more examples too could be given to show how letting God satisfy one's
need-love provides the indispensable foundation for not
doing to others what one would not want done to oneself, the
negative sense of the second commandment (Mark 12:31).
Indeed, Christianity does stress love toward others nega-
tively when it says, "Love does no wrong to a neighbor"
(Rom. 13:10), but this is nothing more than the "silver rule"
stated by Confucius (551–479 B.C.), whose ethical system is a
vital component of Chinese culture.

The Bible, however, is unique in that it also states the
command to love others in the ultimately positive sense of
the so-called Golden Rule: "Therefore all things, whatever
you wish that others would do for you, you likewise should
do for them" (Matt. 7:12, lit. trans.). While other religions
and philosophies do command love for others, only the
Bible's Golden Rule requires the apparently impossible task
of doing *everything* for *everyone else* that one would like *all*
others to do for them. How can this apparently impossible
command be fulfilled?

Before answering this question, we consider in this first
section how keeping the first commandment of letting God
meet all our need-love creates within us the positive desire,
like his, not only to want our own happiness but also to

increase it by extending our blessings to as many others as possible. Then in the second section we consider Matthew 7:7–11, which shows how it is possible to keep the Golden Rule.

Why the Knowledge of God Urges Us to Extend This Knowledge

What impels those whose need-love has been met by God to share this great joy with others is a sense of necessity. Paul said in Romans 1:14–15, "I am obligated both to Greeks and non-Greeks, both to the wise and the foolish. That is why I am so eager to preach the gospel also to you who are at Rome."

But how did Paul become indebted to all other people? Here it helps to realize that there are two ways of going into debt. The first is the usual way of borrowing a sum of money from another. Such people place themselves under the necessity of amortizing the debt by regular payments on the principle with interest. Now a necessity is something that people must have for life to be bearable, such as food, clothing, and shelter. Deprived of any of these things, we either die or find life so full of misery that death often seems preferable.

It is also a necessity to retain one's good name, which we do as long as people feel they can trust us. The regular servicing of a debt maintains our credit rating, but defaulting on it tells others that we are not trustworthy, and then we lose our reputation. As Shakespeare said in *Othello,*

Good name in man and woman . . .
Is the immediate [most valuable] jewel of their souls.
Who steals my purse steals trash—'tis something, nothing,
'Twas mine, 'tis his, and has been the slave to thousands—
But he that filches from me my good name
Robs me of that which not enriches him
And makes me poor indeed. (3.3.154–61)

Avoiding such poverty thus is likewise a necessity, for those who have lost their good name become social outcasts.

The second way we incur a debt and place ourselves under the necessity of maintaining our trustworthiness is when we learn about something that would bring great benefit to others. An illustration comes from the story of four lepers in the city of Samaria, besieged so long by Syrians that its people were about to die of starvation (2 Kings 7:3–9). Therefore these lepers decided to cross over to the Syrian camp after nightfall, for there was a possibility that the enemy would spare them and give them food. When they reached the enemy camp, however, they found to their amazement that the Syrians had deserted their tents, which were stocked with food, clothing, silver, and gold. God had caused the Syrians to hear what they thought was a great army coming to the aid of Samaria, and so they had fled in panic (vv. 6–7). After eating and drinking their fill, the lepers began to hide the rest of the food and treasure for their future use. But as the night wore on, they said to one another, "We're not doing right. This is a day of good news, and we are keeping it to ourselves. If we wait until daylight, punishment will overtake us. Let's go at once and report this to the royal palace [in Samaria]" (v. 9). The lepers then stopped trying to hoard all this food and treasure, and returning to Samaria, they made known the glad tidings of the well-provisioned Syrian tents, there for the taking.

The realization that in the deserted camp there was enough food and clothing for the whole city of Samaria made the lepers debtors, under the necessity of telling the whole populace about the blessings that could be theirs. Not to have reported their find would have been to say in effect, "You can all starve as far as we are concerned." But to have acted that way would have meant the loss of all respect from others, and to avoid this terrible humiliation the lepers reported their find to Samaria before daybreak.

Though both these situations involve indebtedness, there is a crucial difference. While making monthly payments on borrowed money is generally an irksome task, to announce good tidings such as the lepers brought is a most rewarding experience. In their case, in addition to now having all the food, clothing, gold, and silver they could want, the lepers became celebrities because of the discovery they had made and the deliverance this brought to Samaria. In the same way Paul sounds a note of profound joy as he declares that he is a debtor to all. What was his good news? He had learned that Christ has made it possible for God to forgive sins so that he could work all things together for good for those who love him. He would also work so they would become more than conquerors in that even stumbling blocks would turn out to be stepping-stones (Rom. 8:28, 37). Because this is such good news Paul was so eager to share it with the church at Rome. Here he was living out the truth of Jesus' observation that "it is more blessed to give than to receive" (Acts 20:35).

There is, however, a negative side to the discharge of this second kind of indebtedness. Just as the lepers knew they faced punishment if they failed to inform Samaria of their find, so Paul declared, "I am compelled to preach. *Woe* to me if I do not preach the gospel!" (1 Cor. 9:16). In Paul's language convention, "woe" meant the pangs of hell. And for all of us, as for Paul, it should be unthinkable to keep to ourselves the knowledge that God's ultimate delight is to do the greatest good for others by letting them share in the supreme joy he has in himself. How could any of us enjoy heaven unless we had mobilized our time, talents, and treasure to do our utmost to get the good news to the rest of the world? Sadly, many professing Christians do not feel this imperative demand because they, through unbelief, are themselves not experiencing God's great joy and peace.

But Paul was filled with this joy and was so enthusiastic about the gospel that for years he had been chafing at the bit to come and preach it at Rome (Rom. 1:8–15). To be sure, he had gone through terrible sufferings in his efforts to tell the good news far and wide. In the course of discharging his debt, he was

> in prison . . . [and] exposed to death again and again. Five times I received from the Jews the forty lashes minus one. Three times I was beaten with rods, once I was stoned, three times I was shipwrecked, I spent a night and a day in the open sea. . . . I have been in danger from rivers . . . from my own countrymen . . . from Gentiles; in danger in the city . . . in the country . . . at sea . . . and in danger from false brothers. . . . I

have known hunger and thirst. . . . I have been cold and naked." (2 Cor. 11:23–27)

And when he finally arrived at Rome, he had been a prisoner and shackled by a chain for well over two years (Acts 24:27–28:31). Yet his joy in extending abroad the "good news of great joy that will be for all the people" (Luke 2:10) more than compensated for the sufferings he endured. Writing to the Philippian church from prison, he reported how God had used even his imprisonment to spread the gospel at Rome (Phil. 1:12–18). As for the difficulties of his situation, his reaction was, "What does it matter? The important thing is that . . . Christ is preached. And because of this I rejoice" (v. 18). Paul's fundamental point in the first two chapters of Philippians is that only as Christians make the spread of the gospel their number-one priority will they have fullness of joy.

We have seen how complete was God's joy in himself as a Trinity, but we have also seen that he increased this joy by creating a world where he could share it with others. So it was with Paul, and should be with all other Christians as they find how admirably God satisfies their need-love. They surely want to maintain this joy through being thankful in every circumstance (1 Thess. 5:18) because they are convinced that in all things God is rejoicing finally to do them great good. But they are not satisfied just to bask in God's blessings. Rather, they want to extend the joy of what he does for them as far and wide as possible, for they sense the truth of Jesus' statement that their joy in God will be increased as they share it with others. The German poet Christoph A. Tiedge (1752–1803) expressed this principle well in his poem "Urania": "Joy that we share is doubly joyous."[1] And Christians surely should not deprive themselves of half the joy that is rightfully theirs by keeping the knowledge of God's great love to themselves. So as people are filled with all joy and peace as they trust God, they will want to double this happiness by using every available means to extend the glad tidings of the gospel as far as possible.

This extension can be done in many ways. Those whom

God does not call into active gospel ministry but who are experiencing how Jesus "takes the gloom and fills the life with glory" will want to devote *time* to interceding in prayer for a number of missionaries and Christian workers with whom they keep in contact. And they will want to pray for the state of the churches in all parts of the world.[2] They will also want to take time regularly and prayerfully to read and reread the Bible to learn God's whole counsel so that they can witness for Christ both to their own families and to the people with whom they come in contact. The only conclusion that can be drawn from people who have no desire to express themselves in this way is that they themselves are not yet sharing in God's own joy.

Laypeople will also want to use their *treasure* to support their own church, the parachurch organizations that carry out vital ministries, and the missionaries whom God has called to plant churches in twelve thousand of the people-groups of earth. Thus to discharge their indebtedness to extend the blessings of the gospel to the 2.2 billion people in the unreached people-groups and the 2.3 billion non-Christians in the twelve thousand reached groups, Christians will want to heed John Wesley's exhortations to use their particular *talent,* or vocation, to "gain all [the money] they can" by working industriously and wisely.[3] But overwork must be avoided, for sickness may result and thus limit their earning power. Second, people should then "economize all [they] can." Money must not be wasted on luxuries, although a reasonable amount of recreation maintains health and thus earning power. A certain amount should also be laid up for one's retirement and for one's children and their education, so that they in turn will be able to earn all they can with their particular talents. Then third, after people have economized in various ways to save as much as possible, they should "give all [they] can." Otherwise Christians will be as guilty as the lepers would have been had they not reported their find to the city of Samaria.

Jonathan Edwards, in his widely acclaimed essay "The Nature of True Virtue," defines virtue as the desire to extend and spread the very best to as many people as possible without playing favorites to one's self, family, or group of preferred people. The essence of vice is to do the opposite.[4] The reality of these definitions of virtue and vice is driven home by asking ourselves, How could we enjoy heaven if we had been guilty of vice, if during our lifetimes we had used most of our time, treasure, and talents for ourselves and our select group? But if we repent of this sin now, we will be forgiven. "If a wicked man turns away from all the sins he has committed and keeps all my decrees and does what is just and right, he will surely live; he will not die. None of the offenses he has committed [in being stingy or prayerless in the past] will be remembered against him. Because of the righteous things he has done [since becoming virtuous], he will live" (Ezek. 18:21–22).

But I should also stress the positive motivation for helping to advance the gospel: the joy of knowing that the money one has given—after diligent and wise work, and after carefully distinguishing between necessities, conveniences, and entertainments—has been and is being used to help bring the blessings of Christ to the rest of humankind. God's complete joy in himself as a Trinity led him to want to double that joy by extending it beyond himself to the human beings he created. Likewise, we will want to double our joy by seeing how adequate God is to meet our need-love as we use our resources to perform the greatest service to others—helping them to experience the joy of believing God's wonderful promises, guaranteed by the finished work of Christ. Such joy, like that of Paul, overcomes even the threat of death: "I eagerly expect and hope that I will in no way be ashamed, but will have sufficient courage so that now as always Christ will be exalted in my body, whether by life or by death" (Phil. 1:20).

World Evangelization and the Golden Rule

We now want to show how this evangelism enables us to love our neighbors as ourselves (Mark 12:31), or in terms of the Golden Rule, to do everything for others that we would want done for ourselves. In Matthew 7:7–11, the verses preceding the Golden Rule, Jesus was teaching people about prayer.

Ask and it will be given to you; seek and you will find; knock
and the door will be opened to you. . . . Which of you, if his
son asks for bread, will give him a stone? Or if he asks for a
fish, will give him a snake? If you, then, though you are evil,
know how to give good gifts to your children, how much more
will your Father in heaven give good gifts to those who ask
him! [Then comes the Golden Rule:] So in everything, do to
others what you would have them do to you.

Two objections to this plain assertion that God always
answers prayer are often heard. The first is that the God who
"works out everything in conformity with the purpose of his
will" (Eph. 1:11) has already determined everything that
will happen. Therefore he will not make any modifications of
his plans when we direct a request to him in prayer. In his
sermon entitled "The Most High a Prayer-Hearing God,"
Edwards showed the role our prayers play in God's sovereign plan to display his glory and goodness in the world.
Citing Ezekiel 36:37, "Once again I will yield to the plea of
the house of Israel and [thus] do this for them," Edwards
explained, "God has been pleased to constitute prayer to be
antecedent to the bestowment of mercy. . . . Hereby [i.e., by
prayer] is excited a sense of our need, and of the value of the
mercy which we seek . . . whereby the mind is more
prepared to prize it [than if we had not prayed], and to
rejoice in it when bestowed, and to be thankful for it."[5]

So part of God's will is that his people should ask him to
meet their needs as children ask their parents for things, and
then God provides in answer to their prayers. He is more
glorified when prayer precedes a work in which he blesses
people than he would be if he simply performed the work.
For example, when Peter was imprisoned by Herod, who
had just executed James (Acts 12:1–4), "the church was
earnestly praying to God for him" (v. 5). Thus when he was
miraculously escorted out of prison by an angel and went to
the house of John Mark, "where many people had gathered
and were praying" (v. 12), these people expressed an
amazement and joy that would not have been nearly so great
without this antecedent prayer. For this reason James taught
that "you do not have, because you do not ask God" (James
4:2). God is not so disposed to bless people when they do not

pray, because without the antecedent prayer the blessing would not glorify him as greatly. So he has ordained people's prayers along with his answers to them. This teaching gives no encouragement to be lax in prayer. To the contrary, simply understanding why God has ordained our prayers is a powerful incentive for us to go ahead and "in everything, by prayer and petition, with thanksgiving, present [our] requests to God" (Phil. 4:6).

A second objection to prayer is that although people have prayed, God has done nothing (as yet!) to answer their prayers. But in the same sermon Edwards answered this objection:

> It is fit that [God] should answer prayer, and as an infinitely wise God, in the exercise of his own wisdom, and not ours. God will deal as a father with us, in answering our requests. But a child is not to expect that the father's wisdom be subject to his; nor ought he to desire it, but should esteem it a privilege, that the parent will provide for him according to his *own* wisdom. . . . God can answer prayer, though he bestow not the very thing for which we pray. He can sometimes better answer the lawful desires and good end we have in prayer another way. If our end be our own good and happiness, God can perhaps better answer that end in bestowing something else than in the bestowment of the very thing which we ask. And if the main good we aim at in our prayers be attained, our prayer is answered.[6]

So we ought to rejoice that in God's great wisdom and love he does in fact answer all of our requests, though to be sure, he says no to some things because our having them would hurt us in the long run. We also ought to rejoice that in his wisdom he gives us what we ask at the best time, rather than at an earlier time when our very limited judgment thinks it would be best. And finally, we ought to rejoice that God's love and wisdom give us what often turns out to be far better than the precise thing for which we had asked. To use the imagery of Matthew 7:7–11, if we ask for bread, God may well give us cake, and if we ask for a fish, he may well give us caviar, for he "is able to do for us immeasurably more than all we ask or imagine" (Eph. 3:20).

In viewing Jesus' teaching on prayer with this broader

perspective in mind, we thus can understand in what sense everyone who asks will receive. As God blesses us in response to prayer, there is an increase in the display of his glory upon the earth as he shows himself to be the God who works for us by doing all manner of good things, with far more wisdom and loving concern than any human parents could have for their children.

At this point two things should be observed: (1) the Golden Rule of Matthew 7:12 comes right after verse 11, where Jesus argues that God will answer our prayers far better than is possible for earthly parents; (2) this rule is attached to what precedes by the inferential conjunction "so," or "therefore." These facts should help us see why it is not impossible to comply with the Golden Rule, which requires us to do everything for everybody that we would want done for ourselves. To comply, all we need to do is tell as many as possible that God wants to "rejoice in doing them good . . . with all [his] heart and soul" (Jer. 32:41). He does this by meeting all their need-love, doing all the vast array of things that they would really want done, had they the wisdom to know what was truly best for them. Therefore we fulfill the Golden Rule by encouraging others to trust God, so they can receive "the Spirit of sonship" (Rom. 8:15) and realize that since God loves them as his children, he will answer every prayer with wisdom and love. Then in that they are now children of the loving, almighty, and all-wise God, they will indeed have everything they could possibly want done for them as they pray.

The words of the hymn "What a Friend" indicate eloquently how much blessing we impart to people when we are instrumental in turning them from serving the creature to worshiping and serving the Creator:

> What a Friend we have in Jesus,
>   All our sins and griefs to bear!
> What a privilege to carry
>   Ev'rything to God in prayer!
> O what peace we often forfeit,
>   O what needless pain we bear,
> All because we do not carry
>   Ev'rything to God in prayer.

> Have we trials and temptations?
> Is there trouble anywhere?
> We should never be discouraged:
> Take it to the Lord in prayer!
> Can we find a friend so faithful,
> Who will all our sorrows share?
> Jesus knows our ev'ry weakness—
> Take it to the Lord in prayer!
>
> Are we weak and heavy laden,
> Cumbered with a load of care?
> Precious Saviour, still our refuge—
> Take it to the Lord in prayer!
> Do thy friends despise, forsake thee?
> Take it to the Lord in prayer!
> In his arms he'll take and shield thee,
> Thou wilt find a solace there.

We ourselves will also seek to perform specific acts of benevolence toward others in obedience to Galatians 6:10: "Therefore, as we have opportunity, let us do good to all people, and especially to those who belong to the family of believers." This command to be especially loving toward Christians does not necessarily imply playing favorites. The proper meaning, I believe, is that in seeking to do good particularly to believers, we strengthen them so that they in turn can be more benevolent to more of humankind. Only Christians will tell others of how God wants to bless them as a father blesses his children, and so when one believer strengthens another by some loving act, he or she increases the potential for all humankind to become beneficiaries of the Golden Rule. But Christians will certainly also want to be benevolent toward non-Christians in doing all kinds of thoughtful and loving things for them.

But what of non-Christians who are benevolent? At the end of the last chapter I mentioned that some people who worshiped and served money were also generous in using it for the welfare of others. This happens mostly where large sums of money have been amassed, more than the owners or their heirs and dependents will ever need. Such people may then build an art museum or establish a foundation for the support of a wide variety of worthy causes. Indeed, they do so to extend the blessings of their money for the benefit of humanity in general. But there is nothing in such gifts, as there is in the Christian benevolence we have just discussed, that aims at doing the most loving thing for others, which is to enable them to become beneficiaries of God's love, constantly pursuing after them to do them good.

Can we say, then, that non-Christians who give sacrificially for good causes show true benevolence? The answer is no, for such people are simply trying to satisfy their need-love, and a most promising way to remove discontent is to win praise from others by being benevolent. People are admired by others when they appear to be so inwardly self-sufficient that they can dispense with the amenities of life most people require. For this reason, then, many non-Christians do give sacrificially to aid good causes. And some adherents of other religions, all of which urge in some way that people work hard for God or the highest value, will sacrifice even life itself for the praiseworthiness they hope to attain thereby.

Paul was aware of this possibility, but he did not count such acts to gain approval as truly benevolent: "If I give all I possess to the poor and surrender my body to the flames [as a martyr in a presumably good cause], but have not love, I gain nothing" (1 Cor. 13:3). In his thinking, an essential ingredient of genuine love was an absence of boasting in one's prowess (v. 4) and having a hopeful demeanor (v. 7), which could exist only in those who had come to rely on God's promises as guaranteed in Christ. Therefore in biblical thinking, genuine love exists only when good works are done in a context where God rather than the doer gets the credit.

So far we have spoken primarily of Christians' desire to extend God's glory by loving acts directed toward non-Christians. But if there must always be non-Christians in order for us to double our joy, then our existence in heaven would be less happy than our present life on earth, for in heaven "nothing impure will ever enter it, nor will anyone who does what is shameful or deceitful, but only those whose names are written in the Lamb's book of life" (Rev. 21:27). And according to Jeremiah 31:34, "No longer will a man teach his neighbor, or a man his brother, saying 'Know the Lord,' because they will all know me, from the least of them to the greatest." Paul however, affirmed that his existence with Christ in heaven would be far more desirable even than being a most successful evangelist on earth (Phil. 1:23; 2 Cor. 5:8). But how could he still find such great joy in the new heavens and earth, where there would be no purpose in preaching Christ? And how can we continue to double our joy in the world to come where everyone is like Jesus Christ?

Doubling Our Joy Where Only the Righteous Exist

The answer, I believe, is found in 1 John, for here the author shows how Christians can double their joy with other Christians. He states his purpose in writing as follows: "We proclaim to you the eternal life, which was with the Father and has appeared to us. We proclaim to you what we have seen and heard, so that you also may have fellowship with us. And our fellowship is with the Father and with his Son, Jesus Christ. We write this [epistle] to make our joy complete" (1:2–4). Two things in this statement are noteworthy. First, in using "we," the apostle John was affirming that all the apostles agreed on their objective in preaching (which constitutes another piece of evidence that the final revelatory spokespersons regarded themselves as speaking in concert).[7] Second, in this introduction to his epistle John explicitly states that the aim of apostolic preaching was the accomplishment of God's purpose to enable people whom he created to share in the fullness of joy that the Father and Son have in each other (see chapter 9): "This is the message we have heard from him and declare to you: God is light, and in him there is no darkness at all. If we claim to have fellowship with him yet walk in the darkness, we lie and do not live by the truth. But if we walk in the light, as he is in the light, we have fellowship with one another" (vv. 5–7). While the fellowship spoken of here clearly includes that enjoyed with other Christians, it also involves fellowship with God.

So 1 John 1:3 and 1:5–7 set forth what we have been regarding as the first *necessary* step in responding to the whole counsel of God, which is to share in the joy of the fellowship between the Father and the Son. John also indicates that final *free* step that people are to take in order to double their joy: "We write this to make our joy complete" (v. 4). Many scribes who later copied this verse, however, felt assured that the "our" should be "your," so that the verse should read, "And we are writing this that *your* joy might be full." They reasoned that it would be nonsense for John to say that he was writing this for his own joy. What seemed more likely, then, was that the author wrote this epistle to straighten out some spiritual problem its first readers had, so they might regain their experience of full joy in the Lord. But several of the oldest texts have "our" rather than "your," and one of textual criticism's maxims is that the harder of two readings is preferable. So virtually all authorities today agree that 1:4 affirms that the author's motive in writing was to make his own joy full.

Confirmation comes from 1 John 2:12–14, where the writer regards his readers not as having some spiritual problem but as being very mature Christians: their sins have been forgiven; they have known him who is from the beginning; they have overcome the evil one; they are strong; and the word of God lives in them. But what is so unexpected is that all of these statements regarding the readers' spiritual maturity are given as *reasons* for John's writing. This connection makes sense, however, when it is understood that he wanted to increase his joy of fellowshiping with the Father and the Son by writing a letter to a group of Christians who were of sufficient spiritual maturity to share this joy.

So 1 John 1:4 and 2:12–14 support the conclusion reached in the preceding chapters, that a proper response to God's whole counsel is (1) to find one's need-love met in sharing with him, through the Holy Spirit, the joy he has in the fellowship between the Father and the Son, and then (2) to make that joy full by talking about it with other people. This step surely includes the evangelistic purpose of telling people how they too can share with God his joy. But as 1 John 1:4 indicates, we will also want to "double our joy" by discussing with fellow Christians the implications of

God's great purpose for the world. So even though there will be no more evangelizing to do in the new heavens and earth, yet we Christians can continue to have the increased joy of talking about God's love with others.

These same two passages are also helpful in answering the question of what we will be doing in the new heavens and earth throughout the eternal ages to come. Since teaching and knowledge will then be things of the past (1 Cor. 13:9, 12), there will be no need to spend time improving one another's knowledge. But we will never be bored, for we can all do as John did in this epistle: remind each other of the wonders of God's wisdom and goodness in the way he set up the created world and managed redemptive history to glorify himself in it.

Review Questions

1. Explain why for us to love God is a necessary work, but for us to love others (define your terms!) is a free work.
2. Explain why we who have believed the gospel should, like Paul, feel that we are debtors to everyone in the world.
3. Discharging a debt incurred by borrowing money involves the negative reason for wanting to be virtuous, namely, not to harm the party from whom we have borrowed. (See Edwards' comments on virtue in the first section.) What is the positive inducement for being virtuous expressed in Acts 20:35?
4. Explain how you would tell people who are engaged in one of the twenty-four thousand secular vocations that they nevertheless can be as virtuous (again note Edwards' comments on virtue) as a missionary working with a stone-age tribe in New Guinea.
5. Explain why the Golden Rule (Matt. 7:12) is completely impossible to fulfill by depending just on our own resources.
6. How does the inferential "so" or "therefore" at the beginning of Matthew 7:12 indicate to us how we can nevertheless fulfill the Golden Rule without paring

down either the number of things we want or the total world population (5.2 billion as of 1991), toward whom we are to be benevolent?

7. Why is prayer essential for getting blessings from God, even though he has already foreordained whatever comes to pass (Eph. 1:11)?

8. Explain in what sense God always answers our prayers with a yes, even though sometimes he refuses to give us what we ask.

9. Though Galatians 6:10 commands us to give first priority in being benevolent to fellow Christians, how does this verse not contradict Edwards' theory regarding what virtue is?

10. Explain how 1 Corinthians 13 (known as the love chapter) can make the apparently contradictory statements that the person showing genuine love gains (v. 3), yet "[love] is not self-seeking" (v. 5).

11. How does 1 John 1:3 confirm the thesis of this book that God created us that we might share the joy he experiences in the Trinity?

12. How do 1 John 1:4 and 2:12–14 help us understand what we will be doing in heaven throughout eternity, without ever being bored?

13. What light does this chapter shed on the reason for the declaration in Genesis 2:18 that is it not good for a person to be alone?

NOTES

[1]*Dictionary of German Quotations*, ed. Lilian Dalbiac (New York: Frederick Ungar, n.d.), 179.

[2]Patrick Johnstone's *Operation World: A Day-to-Day Guide to Praying for the World*, 4th ed. (Pasadena, Calif.: William Carey Library, 1986), 501 pp., has been updated about every four years since 1974 as to the situation of the church in the more than 220 nations and territories of the earth. Altogether some twenty-four thousand ethnic groups exist, of which about half still need to be reached in the sense of having churches founded in them that can sustain and propagate themselves (Ralph D. Winter, "The Dimin-

ishing Task: The Field and the Force," *Mission Frontiers* 13, 1 [1991]: 6). Using Johnstone's book is a must for all those who regard themselves as debtors (in the second sense) to all humanity.

³John Wesley, "The Use of Money," *The Works of John Wesley*, 2 vols., ed. A. C. Outler (Nashville: Abingdon, 1984–85), 2:266–80.

⁴Edwards, *Works*, 1:122–42.

⁵Ibid., 2:116.

⁶Ibid., 117.

⁷See chapter 1 above, where I argued that Acts 20:27, Gal. 1:8, and Jude 3 imply that the final revelatory spokespersons regarded themselves as speaking in harmony.

12

The Fall (Genesis 2:4–3:24)

In the previous four chapters we have considered the implications of God's necessary work in being the Trinity, which then led to his free work of creating the world, where he would double his joy by doing good things for those who trusted him. Now it is time to resume our movement forward in redemptive history by commencing an inductive study of Genesis 2:4–3:24. Here is the story of sin's entry into the world and of how God as a result either punished the impenitent for their sins or, on the basis of the future death of Christ, forgave those who honored him by entrusting their future to his mercy.

Our first task as we return to an inductive study of the early chapters of Genesis is to find where the segment beginning with 2:4 ends. Chapter 2 is often thought of as the "second account of creation," for whereas in 1:1–2:3 the author speaks of the creation of the man and the woman together, in 2:4–25 he speaks first of the man's creation (vv. 4–17) and then of the woman's (vv. 18–25). This second account does not mean, however, that the author was drawing on two distinct creation traditions; rather, his putting the woman's creation subsequent to the man's was intended to make an important point, which I hope to elucidate presently. Furthermore, remembering how the repetition of the sequence of days indicated that 2:3 was the end of the first segment, those following the inductive method of Bible study will be open to the possibility that the author's compositional unit beginning at 2:4 may go beyond chapter 2, for we have stressed how we must ignore the Bible's chapter and verse divisions in our effort to grasp the intended meanings of the author's actual compositional units.

So as Bereans read on into chapter 3, they will notice how the theme contained in the words "nakedness," "clothing," and "shame" appears not only in the emphatic summary of 2:25 but again at 3:7 and finally in 3:21, where God provides Adam and Eve with more adequate clothing from animal skins. They will also notice that God, Adam, Eve, and the animals appear in 2:4–25, but that only Adam, Eve, and one of the animals, the serpent, appear in 3:1–7. God then reenters the scene at 3:8 and continues to take the initiative down through 3:24. This is an important observation, because inductive Bible students have noticed how the exit or entrance of one or more of the persons figuring in a scenario is always a signal of a unit-break in narration. Hence 3:1–7, distinguished from 2:4–25 and 3:8–24 by the absence of God, would then stand out as a smaller unit on a par with 2:4–25, which also ends on the nakedness-shame theme. And 3:8–24 would also be regarded as on a par with these two preceding units, because each of the three has a nakedness-shame-clothing theme at or near the end. Even though this theme appears in 3:21 rather than 3:24, we count verse 24 as the end of the third unit of the 2:4–3:24 segment because a new theme begins at 4:1, commencing another segment-sized unit, which we will consider in chapter 15. (See fig. 2.)

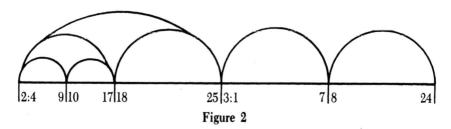

| 2:4 | 9|10 | 17|18 | 25|3:1 | 7|8 | 24 |

Figure 2

We will now carefully observe and analyze 2:4–25, the first of the three smaller units of 2:4–3:24. Our effort will be to read this passage as though we had never seen it before, setting aside any interpretations that we may have arrived at previously.

Why Nakedness Originally Produced No Shame (2:4–25)

The title for 2:4–4:24 is found in 2:4, which reads literally, "These are the bringings forth of the heavens and the earth." I regard this title as belonging to what follows rather than as a summary of 1:1–2:3, chiefly because of the frequent repetition of "out of the ground" in 2:5 (implied), 6, 7, 8 (implied), 9, and 19. In 2:6–9 there is a sequence of what comes "out of the ground": water (v. 6), the man (v. 7— "from the dust of the ground"), the garden (v. 8), and trees, both the tree of life and the tree of the knowledge of good and evil (v. 9). The placing of man's creation near the beginning of this sequence implies that those other things that come out of the ground are essential for humankind's well-being.

Then 2:10–17 repeats this sequence: water (vv. 10–14), man (v. 15a), garden (v. 15b), trees (v. 16), and the tree of the knowledge of good and evil (v. 17). "Out of the ground" does not appear in this second sequence; rather, the emphasis is on the superlative location of the Garden of Eden, where Adam will live—it lies at the head of four rivers important for the lands they touch. The sequence then ends with a command to obey God so that the man may avoid death and the loss of all this goodness. Thus whereas the first sequence (2:6–9) shows the goodness of the vertical axis from the ground upward to the man, the second sequence (2:10–17) extends this vertical axis upward from the man to God and the condition he gives Adam (and ultimately also Eve) to fulfill in order to avoid death. Because the author regards the death spoken of in 2:17 as the opposite of all the good things that God has given them to enjoy, it evidently represents a state of misery and deprivation that Adam and Eve will experience if they disobey the command not to eat of the tree of the knowledge of good and evil.

One might think that the vertical axis, consisting of Adam's sustenance from the ground upward to God and life and conditioned on obedience, would be sufficient to make a person content. But in 2:18–25 the author emphasizes that for Adam to find fulfillment, he also needed a horizontal axis as well suited for his happiness as the vertical one of 2:6–17. And we have just seen a parallel to this in 1 John. Here John had a perfect vertical axis in enjoying fellowship with the Father and the Son. But he needed a horizontal one to complete his joy (1:4), so he wrote that epistle as a way of enjoying fellowship with other mature Christians (2:12–14) in the things of God. (Life itself teaches that loneliness can be overcome and fellowship with others enjoyed only when each has an interest in some one valuable entity.)

Genesis 2:18–20 goes on to tell how Adam had become well enough acquainted with the animals (made from the ground) to give each a characterizing name. No doubt he also saw how each could be of help to him in some way. But none of the birds or the animals qualified as a "helper suitable for him," and the reader infers from 1:26–27 that this was because none was made in the image of God. God therefore proceeded to make a woman, not from the ground as with the animals, but from a part of Adam's body. The woman was created in the image of God as much as the man, for Genesis 1:27 says, "So God created man in his own image, in the image of God he created him; male and female he created them." So the woman, unlike the animals, had that compatibility after which Adam sought. Now both were content in that they could have a fellowship with each other (horizontal axis) that consisted in God (vertical axis), who walked with them each day at dusk (see 3:8). To emphasize this perfect compatibility the author quotes Adam's response on beholding his wife: "This is now bone of my bones and flesh of my flesh; she shall be called 'woman,' for she was taken out of man" (2:23). And so Adam and Eve were able to fulfill the first commandment and maintain the vertical axis by delighting in God, and the second commandment (Mark 12:31) in extending benevolence horizontally to each other by talking about God and his great goodness to them.

The author's striking way of emphasizing this total harmony is his statement in 2:25 that Adam and Eve felt no shame in being together without clothing. Since they both had complete contentment in their ability to have fellowship with each other in God, neither felt any deficiency in themselves and their situation. Therefore they had no need of clothing to make themselves more presentable. And they realized that as they remained obedient to God, he would continue this fullness of life for them. Since people inevitably serve and obey what they worship, their obedience or service to God was an expression of how much he was worth to them.[1] Thus because this first section (2:4–25) shows the greatness of God's worth to them in the care he provided as they obeyed, we may conclude that its point is that God's glory was being extended on earth by the distinctive behavior of people who delighted in his goodness, which is the chief aspect of his glory.

How Nakedness Came to Produce Shame (3:1–7)

The second unit, Genesis 3:1–7, ends on a note completely opposite from that of 2:25: "The eyes of both of them were opened, and they realized they were naked; so they sewed fig leaves together and made coverings for themselves" (v. 7). Between 2:25 and 3:7 they had somehow ceased to display God's glory and goodness on the earth by their complete contentment, for each now feels a great deficiency and a desire to cover it by making clothing.[2] Later revelation (e.g., Gen. 3:15 with Rom. 16:20) tells us that Satan, the Devil, was working through the serpent to woo first Eve's heart and then Adam's away from the worship of God, so that their behavior blasphemed rather than honored him. Here, however, we consider only the immediate way in which the serpent beguiled Eve and Adam to sin.

The serpent's strategy was to foster a "sinful, unbelieving heart" (Heb. 3:12) in Eve, so that she and her husband would doubt that God had really made himself a means to the end of doing only the greatest good for them. As a result she now began to entertain the outrageous notion that she and her husband were, after all, nothing more than pawns on God's chessboard, a means toward his attaining some goal very desirable for him but not necessarily to their liking.

To see this strategy at work it is necessary to compare carefully both the serpent's and Eve's restatements of what

God had said in 2:16–17. In 3:1 the serpent misquotes 2:16 to read as though God had said, "You cannot eat of *any* of these good trees I have provided for you," when he had actually said, "You are *free* to eat from *any* tree [but one]." In her reply Eve corrects the serpent but then herself makes three or four small but significant changes in the wording of 2:9 and 17. In 3:2 she says, "We are [word omitted] to eat of the fruit of [word omitted] the trees of the garden,"—leaving out "free" and "any." The author thus shows us that Eve no longer believed that God found his full delight just in blessing her and her husband. Then she continued (v. 3), "But God did say, 'You must not eat fruit from the tree that is in the middle of the garden [said only of the tree of life in 2:9—see Hebrew word order], and you must not touch it' [not found at all in 2:17]." By now locating the tree of the knowledge of good and evil in the middle, or most important part, of the garden, where the tree of life actually stood, and by declaring that they could not even touch this tree of knowledge, the author is telling his readers that Eve felt that God was not being fully benevolent toward her and Adam; rather, he was holding back the best things for himself.

But in thus disbelieving God's mercy, Eve and Adam utterly scorned his glory, whose apex is his disposition to be merciful and benevolent. Eve, and later Adam, said in effect, "God has created us not to bless us but to (ab)use us to fulfill some need in himself." This was the same as saying that God was really not all-glorious in himself and thus had to create human beings as a means for finding more happiness. So now the serpent, sensing that Eve no longer trusted God to be fully benevolent, made this thought explicit by declaring that the only reason God had forbidden them to eat of the tree of the knowledge of good and evil was that he did not want them to share in the joy that he had in being God (3:5). In other words, the serpent would deny that God gives "[people] drink from [his] river of delights."

NOTE. An inductive study of the dialogue between Eve and the serpent clearly indicates that the author of Genesis understood the fall of Adam and Eve to consist in the sin of unbelief. That sin basically is unbelief is stated explicitly by Jesus in John 16:9. But for Calvin, the primary spokesperson for Reformed theology, this first sin was instead a failure to live up to God's standard of meritorious works. In commenting on Genesis 2:17 in his *Institutes,* Calvin said, "These words [of this command] are so far from establishing faith that they can do nothing but shake it."[3] I argue, however, that there is much reason for regarding these words as well suited to elicit and strengthen Adam and Eve's faith. The implicit promise of life and the joy of immediate fellowship with God would provide the strongest of incentives to fulfill the condition of simply avoiding this tree and partaking of the luscious fruits of all the other trees. The explicit threat of death and all its misery would in turn furnish a powerful negative inducement to shun the tree and thus continue to enjoy all the blessings God had promised and himself guaranteed.

In Calvin's thinking, however, the promise made in Genesis 2:17 could never encourage faith and confidence in God, for its conditionality could encourage only meritorious works: "Faith properly begins with the promise, rests in it, and ends in it. For in God faith seeks life: a life that is not found in commandments or declarations of penalties, but in the promise of mercy, and only in a freely [unconditionally] given promise. *For a conditional promise that sends us back to our own works does not promise life.*"[4] So he and his followers, who down to the present advocate what is often called covenant theology, have regarded Adam and Eve as under what is called a "covenant of works."[5] According to this system, when Jesus came to earth, he fulfilled the covenant of meritorious works that Adam and Eve broke. Consequently, the gospel by which we are saved is then a "covenant of grace," made such by Jesus' having merited it for us by his perfect fulfillment of the covenant of works. Reformed theology declares that the covenant of grace is thus "unconditional," though I have yet to find anywhere in Scripture a gospel promise that is unconditional. Sometimes repentance, but always faith, is the explicit condition a person must meet in order to receive the forgiveness of sins made possible by Jesus' finished work in his incarnation and death on the cross.

In my opinion, this idea of Calvin's has introduced great confusion into the understanding of Scripture. Since his thinking is so widespread in Protestantism, I will keep stressing how all obedience to God is an "obedience that comes from faith," and never an obedience of works, for "God is not served by human hands, as if he needed anything" (Acts 17:25).

It is important to grasp what the idiom "knowledge of good and evil" meant in the language convention of the original readers of Genesis and to the Hebrew people of the Old Testament. By no means does it necessarily represent evil, for God himself possesses such knowledge (Gen. 3:22); angels have it (2 Sam. 14:17); and God gladly gave it to Solomon in answer to his prayer (1 Kings 3:9). But young children do not have this knowledge (Deut. 1:39; Isa. 7:15), and the very old have lost it (2 Sam. 19:35); hence it is adults in their prime who in some sense do have it. So when the original readers of the Old Testament encountered the expression "to know good and evil," they understood such knowledge to be what mature adults possess—a maturity in which they were independent and therefore responsible for the decisions they made.

Understanding this term in Genesis 3:5 in this way coheres well with the way Genesis 2:4–3:24 has been expounded thus far. The command not to eat of the tree of the knowledge of good and evil would then mean that Adam and Eve were not to aspire to the maturity possessed only by God, whereby they might consider themselves to be independent of him and able to enjoy a fulfilled life by taking matters into their own hands and making their own decisions for their future welfare. Genesis 3:6 indicates that the author construed the idiom in this way, for it says that Eve regarded the fruit of the tree as being able to make her wise in herself and therefore able to shape a fully happy destiny without any need for God's help. A contemporary scholar agrees with this interpretation. "[Here] man takes upon himself the responsibility of trying apart from God to determine whether something is good for himself or not."[6]

So Eve and her husband cast off all dependence on God, thinking they would then have the wisdom and power in their pathetically finite state to provide for themselves a permanently happy life. No longer worshiping him, they now broke his command and ate of the fruit of the forbidden tree.

But how very different the result that ensued! Suddenly Adam and Eve felt the horror of being cut off from God's loving care for them and found themselves left only to their greatly limited, distorted wisdom and power to provide for themselves an eternally happy future. Now they saw themselves as no more qualified for this task than are little children to fend for themselves in society. This sense of total inadequacy then aroused an overwhelming sense of shame, and so they tried to cover up their obvious limitations by making a patchwork of clothing out of fig leaves—something to help them project the personage of independence they had hoped to gain by ceasing to be dependent on God. They, like all their sinful posterity, wanted to cover up, even to themselves, how very much they were in need of God to find the happiness their God-shaped vacuum craved.[7]

NOTE. Such an interpretation of the tree of the knowledge of good and evil links up with Christ's command to "change and become like little children" in order to enter the kingdom of God (Matt. 18:3). It indicates that the essential way in which people are rebelling against God is that they are assuming that, like him, they can make the decisions necessary for enjoying a fulfilled and happy future. The folly of this rebellion is that people think that they love themselves more, are wiser, and thus better able than the all-loving, omniscient, omnipotent God to provide for themselves the fulfillment they crave. Thus conversion, according to Jesus, reverses the act of the Fall and makes a declaration, not of independence from God, but of dependence upon him. Converts thus become little children, who gladly confess that only their heavenly Father knows the niche into which they should fit in order to enjoy permanent fulfillment.

God's Response of Punishment and Mercy (3:8–24)

Verses 8–12 show how sinful Adam responded to the God who can never be indifferent to those who scorn the glory of his goodness. Though he and Eve tried to hide themselves when they heard him calling (v. 9), there was no escape. Realizing his situation, Adam replied, "I heard you in the garden, and I was afraid because I was naked; so I hid" (v. 10). God then asked, "Have you eaten from the tree that I commanded you not to eat from?" (v. 11). Rather than answer this question directly, Adam said, "The woman you put here with me—she gave me some fruit from the tree, and I ate it" (v. 12). God then asked Eve, "What is this you have done?" She likewise gave an evasive reply: "The serpent deceived me, and I ate" (v. 13).

Because of love for his own glory, God had to punish and oppose these who had scorned his benevolence. Postponing until a later chapter the punishment of the serpent, we note that in Genesis 3:16 God imposed on Eve and then on Adam a part of the miseries involved in the death warned of in 2:17. Eve's pain in childbearing would be greatly increased, and now she must subordinate her desires to those of her husband.[8] As for Adam, because he had listened to Eve eaten the forbidden fruit, he must henceforth toil to get food from ground that now preferred to grow thistles; in the end he would die, and his body would return to the ground. God then expelled Adam and Eve from the garden (vv. 22–24); verse 24 concludes the segment commencing back at Genesis 2:4.

These are all instances of God's upholding his righteousness by punishing Adam and Eve for the contempt they showed for his benevolence and glory. But amazingly, throughout this litany of woes upon humankind, God also acted in a most merciful and gracious way. First he declared that Eve's progeny would somehow bring about a final, decisive triumph over the serpent and all the evil that he represents (Gen. 3:15). Thus the reader has every reason to believe that God's original purpose in creating the earth will be realized, despite the terrible incursion of evil. Adam in fact was so encouraged by verse 15 that he implied the triumph of life over death by calling his wife Eve, "the mother of all the living" (v. 20). Another act of mercy was God's clothing Adam and Eve in more suitable garments, this time made from animal skins (v. 21).

Because these two merciful acts appear unexpectedly right in the midst of the imposition of punishments, the reader is also given to understand that God's mercy in no way condones the sin of Adam and Eve. Yet these acts do raise the question of how God, without denigrating his glory, can be merciful to people who have so scorned his worth. How is it possible for God not to devalue the worth of his glory and goodness if he is merciful to people who have sinned against him so terribly as to question his credibility and despise his wonderful promises? In the next chapter we begin to answer this crucial question.

Review Questions

1. Why were Adam and Eve not ashamed to be naked before they sinned (Gen. 2:25)?

2. Cite four evidences in Genesis 3:2–3 that Eve was beginning to sin by not believing God. Be sure you make it clear that you understand why sin is essentially unbelief, contrary to Calvin and covenant theology, which declares that Adam and Eve's sin was a failure to render a full measure of the meritorious works God had spelled out in his "job description."

3. For a Hebrew, what would Eve's eating from the tree of the knowledge of good and evil have signified?

4. Be able to relate your answer in number 3 to Jesus' statement about the need to become like little children in order to enter the kingdom of heaven (Matt. 18:3).

5. Why was Adam and Eve's sin a rejection of God's purpose in creating us human beings?

6. Why were Adam and Eve ashamed after eating from the tree of the knowledge of good and evil (Gen. 3:7)?

NOTES

[1] See note 9 in chapter 9.

[2] I defer until later chapters discussion of the way in which an evil inclination ever entered Adam and Eve's hearts so that they disobeyed God's command stated in Gen. 2:17. Several concepts (e.g., the nature of "free" will, the answerability of people for their actions, the implications of God's sovereignty) must be developed before handling this difficult problem. In the course of describing the redemptive history occurring after the Fall, I deal with these concepts at the appropriate times. Then in chapter 26, expounding Rom. 9–11, I attempt to gather it all together to be able to understand the problem of evil.

[3] Calvin, *Institutes*, 20:550 (3.2.7).

[4] Ibid., 575 (3.2.29), italics added.

[5] According to the Westminster Confession (7.2): "The first covenant made with man was a covenant of works, wherein life was promised to Adam, and in him to his posterity, upon condition of perfect and personal obedience" (Philip Schaff, *The Creeds of Christendom, with a History and Critical Notes*, 4th ed., 3 vols. [New York: Harper, 1877], 3:616–17).

[6] W. Malcolm Clark, "A Legal Background to the Yahwist's Use of 'Good and Evil' in Genesis 2–3," *Journal of Biblical Literature* 88 (1969): 277. In the technical language of modern biblical studies, "Yahwist" represents one of the (supposed) several sources of Genesis through Deuteronomy that the final editor (author) used in composing these five books.

[7] I am indebted to Paul Tournier for the concept that people use clothing as well as houses and means of transportation (cars, yachts, and airplanes) to project the personage of being self-sustaining and to cover up the pathetic limitations of their own persons (*The Meaning of Persons*, trans. Edwin Hudson [New York: Harper & Brothers, 1957], 76–77). Tournier observes that human beings sharply distinguish themselves from the animals, who always seem content with their persons: "Every other creature [besides human beings] in nature is simply itself, without this discord [between person and personage] which is our constant lot" (83).

[8] Cultures throughout the world are rife with examples of how sinful men degrade their wives and women in general. Something of the way godly husbands are to treat their wives, however, is spelled out in Eph. 5:25–33, Col. 3:19, and 1 Peter 3:7.

13

The Justness
of an Eternal Hell

In this chapter we must again interrupt our journey along the Bible's timeline to reflect on additional biblical material that will help us understand how God can uphold his glory and yet be merciful to people who scorn it. First, we must consider why "every violation and disobedience [must receive] its just punishment" (Heb. 2:2), and why the punishment for scorning God's glory must be an eternal one in hell. Then chapter 14 will show how Jesus the Son of God repaired the injury sinners have done to God's glory, so that those who reverse the Fall by becoming like little children can receive full forgiveness for their sins and even become God's children. Through the multitudes who will thus reverse the Fall, God will realize his purpose to fill the earth with his glory as the waters cover the sea.

In chapter 12 we saw how God, to continue to be righteous in delighting in his glory, had to punish Eve and Adam for scorning that glory, revealed most clearly in the benevolent love he extended to them. The punishment consisted in an increase in pain for both: Eve would suffer great pain in childbirth, and Adam, excluded from the fruit-bearing trees of Eden, must toil unceasingly to get food from the ground until he and Eve died and decomposed into the dust from which he had been made.

Later revelation, particularly that given by Jesus Christ, makes it clear that the ultimate death promised in Genesis 2:17 for despising God's mercy is an eternal hell: "Do not be afraid of those who kill the body, but cannot kill the soul. Rather, be afraid of the One who can destroy both soul and body in hell" (Matt. 10:28). The misery suffered there is as eternal as everlasting life is for those in heaven: "Then [the wicked] will go away to eternal punishment, but the right-eous to eternal life" (Matt. 25:46).

This is indeed a sobering subject, perhaps best ap-proached by considering, one by one, the steps leading to the conclusion that an eternal hell awaits those who persist in rejecting God's mercy. In the process it will become evident that it is only because he does mete out such punishment that God can remain loving. The chapter will then conclude with a consideration of the theory, quite popular today, that God's final punishment of the wicked consists simply in his annihilating the existence of those who remain impenitent.

The Eternity of Hell and God's Love

Step 1

Our consideration begins with a point made in chapter 8: God's righteousness consists in his fully delighting in his praiseworthiness, or glory. As with people, so with God: he serves what he worships, and thus his every action is based on whether or not it will uphold, in the long run, the glory of his unsurpassed goodness. Many statements in Scripture affirm that God acts out of consideration for the integrity of his name, among them the following: God created people for his glory (Isa. 43:7); for the sake of his name he redeems people and forgives their sins (Ps. 25:11; 79:9; 1 John 2:12) and likewise guides them in the paths of righteousness (Ps. 23:3; 31:3). When the king of Assyria with his far more numerous army was about to capture Jerusalem, God de-clared, "I will defend this city and save it, for my sake" (Isa. 37:35), and when Israel sinned in wanting a king so it could be like the other nations, nevertheless "for the sake of his great name" God did not reject his people (1 Sam. 12:22). But perhaps the most striking of all the passages expressing this idea is the following: "For my own name's sake I delay my wrath; for the sake of my praise I hold it back from you [Israel], so as not to cut you off. . . . For my own sake, for my own sake, I do this. *How can I let myself be defamed?*[1] I will not yield my glory to another" (Isa. 48:9–11).

Such Scripture passages led Jonathan Edwards in his essay entitled "The End for Which God Created the World" to conclude that God's sinlessness consists chiefly in his love for his own glory: "The moral rectitude of the disposition, inclination, or affection of God, *chiefly* consist in a regard to *himself,* infinitely above his regard to all other beings; or, in other words, [God's] holiness consists in this [delight in himself]."[2]

Step 2

If God does everything for his glory, and if he expends his omnipotence in delighting in his goodness, it follows that he will also take great pleasure in those who share in this delight. Thus "[God's] pleasure is not in the strength of the horse, nor his delight in the legs of a man; the Lord delights in those who fear him, who put their hope in his unfailing love" (Ps. 147:10–11). "A horse is a vain hope for deliverance; despite all its great strength it cannot save. But the eyes of the Lord are on those who fear him, on those who hope in his unfailing love, to deliver them from death and keep them alive in famine" (33:17–19).

Step 3

If God so loves his glory that he employs his almightiness in delighting in it, then that very same power will be directed for the benefit of the people who also love his glory. So it is that God pursues after them to do them good and rejoices in blessing them with his whole heart and soul. And Paul prayed for Christians to realize God's "incomparably great power for us who believe" (Eph. 1:19). But if God uses his great power to work all things together for the good of those who delight in him, then he must direct the full force of that power against people going in the opposite direction, those who rest their hopes not in the Creator but in things in the created world that seem to promise a happy future. So Ezra 8:22 says, "The gracious hand of our God is on everyone who looks to him, but his great anger is against all who forsake him."

God cannot remain indifferent to those who are going in this opposite direction. Indeed, since he loves his glory with all his power, he cannot but oppose with all his power those scorning and thus opposing his glory. To do so only halfheartedly would imply that his glory was not sufficient to satisfy his need-love. This conclusion in turn would be tantamount to admitting that since he was unable to satisfy his own need-love, neither could he fully meet that of others. But because God could never imply such an outrageous falsehood, he most certainly does oppose those who scorn his worth, thus showing that he is indeed the fully benevolent God, desiring the people he created to share with him the complete joy he has in himself. I argue, therefore, that God could not be loving to those who seek him if he did not vent the power of his wrath against those who remain impenitent. Far from being irreconcilable opposites, God's love and his wrath are simply two ways in which he makes it clear that he himself fully honors his name.

But during people's relatively short lifetimes on earth (seventy years, according to Ps. 90:10), God shows love toward both the good and the evil: "He causes his sun to rise on the evil and the good, and sends rain on the righteous and the unrighteous" (Matt. 5:45). Romans 2:4 makes clear, however, that God takes this action, not because he is indifferent to evil people, but because his kindness seeks to bring them to repentance. To those who respond to this kindness and turn to worship and serve the Creator rather than something in the created world (Rom. 1:25), God gives the privilege of sharing with him in the fellowship between the Father and the Son (1 John 1:3). But those creature worshipers who during their lifetimes misinterpret God's many blessings as evidence that he is pleased with them succeed only in "storing up wrath against [themselves] for the day of God's wrath, when his righteous judgment will be revealed" (Rom. 2:5). Death marks the time when God's patience with evil people ends, for "[men and women are] destined to die once, and after that to face judgment" (Heb. 9:27). Then the dam holding back God's pent-up wrath will burst against those who have continued to scorn his loving entreaties, and he will oppose those who have opposed his glory with the omnipotence by which he himself delights in that glory.

An analogy to the equivalence between God's love for his glory and his severity in punishing people in an eternal hell is found in the way human governments operate. For the governed to continue to enjoy the benevolence and blessing of their government, they must honor its laws, since the aim of each law is to enhance people's freedom to pursue happiness. So when individuals violate a law and, at the expense of others' right to pursue happiness, claim for themselves a greater right, the government cannot remain indifferent to their arrogance. Instead it proceeds to apprehend, prosecute, convict, and punish lawbreakers by depriving them of an amount of happiness approximately equivalent to the amount of freedom to pursue happiness that they took from others. How much of this freedom a government takes from lawbreakers—by fines, hours spent in doing community service, imprisonment, or even death—is keyed to how serious their breaking of the law curtailed their victims' freedom to pursue happiness.

Those who park overtime lessen to some extent the freedom of others to accomplish their business in a downtown area. Therefore the loss such parking violators suffer will about equal that which they inflicted on others, which may mean forfeiting the happiness that twenty dollars or more could bring them. This enacting of parking laws expresses the government's benevolent purpose to hold open for the greatest number of people the desirable but limited parking space in a shopping area. Thus as officers are seen ticketing those who have parked overtime, the government maintains credibility in its concern for people.

Greater crimes, such as running a red light, speeding, hit and run, armed robbery, kidnapping, murder, and treason, imply in an ascending degree a deprivation of others' freedom to pursue happiness. Therefore the punishment for armed robbery may well require a ten-year loss of freedom, while intentional murder will often require life imprisonment or even death, because the victim of this crime has lost all freedom to pursue happiness in this world.

The most serious of all crimes, however, is treason. Traitors arrogate to themselves the right to acquire happiness at the expense of millions of their fellow citizens, who are then deprived by the enemy of virtually all freedom. Though Norway had abolished the death penalty in 1905, nevertheless after it was freed from German occupation in 1945, it executed the traitor Vidkun Quisling. Quisling, a Norwegian who before the war had held high positions of trust in various government posts, was executed for his role in aiding the Nazis as puppet governor of Norway from 1940 to 1945. In that role he both helped the Nazis to bleed Norway white and also to apprehend and execute many Norwegians for working with the underground resistance. Therefore after the war the government felt that his crime in inflicting such great hurt on some four million people demanded the death penalty. Only this ultimately severe punishment would befit the enormity of Quisling's crime and fully restore confidence that Norway's postwar government would again vigorously work to maintain the welfare of all.

So to maintain credibility in its benevolence, a government must match the severity of punishment to the enormity of the crime. The argument for an eternal hell therefore rests upon this correspondence between enormity and severity.

Step 4

If it can now be shown in this final step of the argument that humanity has sinned in the worst possible way against God, then our sense of justice must call for the severest punishment, and the biblical teaching of eternal misery in hell for the impenitent meets that requirement. In chapter 10 we saw how the greatest possible insult we can render a person is not to trust him or her. The greater the benefit promised and the more revered the maker of the promise, the more outrageous becomes the insult in not believing that promise. In the preceding chapters we have said that God is the most praiseworthy of all beings, because as the only all-wise and all-powerful God, he has promised to give those who depend on him the greatest blessing possible, namely, the privilege of sharing with him for eternity the joy that he has in himself. Therefore those who persist in the independence Adam and Eve exhibited in the Fall are guilty of a sin of the greatest enormity. For God to be consistent with his burning desire to be fully benevolent to people, he must punish this enormous sin with the greatest severity. Thus the biblical teaching of eternal torment in hell for rejecting God's mercy should accord fully with our sense of justice.

Jesus called people the sons [and daughters] of hell (Matt. 23:15). A passage that helps us see our total depravity is God's description of Israel as "people [who] come near to me with their mouth and honor me with their lips, but their hearts are far from me" (Isa. 29:13). We all know how much more our hearts are inclined to think about succeeding in our daily tasks and how unwilling we are each day first to spend time in prayer, seeking God's wisdom for handling the affairs of that day and also asking him to guide us that we might accomplish the purposes that he has for each of our lives. The heinousness of this rebellion against dependence on God is strikingly stated in Jeremiah 2:9–13:

> "Therefore I bring charges against you again," declares the Lord. . . . "Cross over to the coasts of Kittim and look, send to Kedar and observe closely; see if there has ever been anything like this: Has a nation ever changed its gods? (Yet they are not gods at all.) But my people have exchanged their Glory for worthless idols. Be appalled at this, O heavens, and shudder with great horror," declares the Lord. . . . "My people have committed two sins: they have forsaken me, the spring of living water, and have dug their own cisterns, broken cisterns that cannot hold water."

This, then, is the sense in which people are totally depraved: we have all treated God in the most insulting way by registering again and again a vote of no confidence in his promises.[3] How often we refuse to "give thanks in all circumstances" (1Thess. 5:18) because we do not believe that God truly is working everything out for our good. People who profess to know God but are not "joyful in hope [and] patient in affliction" (Rom. 12:12) make God ashamed that they call him their God (Heb. 11:16). Their downcast and complaining temperament dishonors him before others and discourages them from turning the controls of their lives over to "the faithful God" (Deut. 7:9).

Therefore we should understand our total depravity primarily to consist in heaping the greatest insult upon God by refusing to regard him as trustworthy. This unbelieving attitude toward God also renders great injury to other people, for it reinforces their inclination to trust in themselves rather than in God to satisfy their need-love. So the enormity of people's total depravity consists both in treating God in the worst possible way and in deterring others from knowing the unsurpassed blessing of having him work for them to do them good with his whole heart and soul. The enormity of such a crime therefore requires a punishment having a corresponding severity. And the Bible's teaching that this punishment consists in eternal torment in hell has the corresponding severity. We therefore conclude that it is just and right for God to consign the impenitent to an eternal hell.

God's Love and Wrath

The tendency exists today, however, even among Bible-believing Christians, to say very little by way of warning people that they will spend eternity in hell if they are not looking to God to give them the happy future they desire. One reason to shrink from declaring this part of the biblical message is that at first glance it seems so contrary to God's love. The explanation in the preceding section, however, makes it clear that God can remain loving only by opposing, with the full fervency of his love for his own glory, those who oppose him by scorning the opportunity he gives to enjoy that glory. Great wisdom, however, must be used in presenting this truth. Paul told Timothy to preach the word, God's whole purpose, but "with great patience and careful instruction" (2 Tim. 4:2). This highly sensitive but most important matter should therefore be set forth only when there is opportunity to show people, step by step, that the enormity of their sinfulness in being totally depraved requires God to render such a corresponding severity of punishment on the impenitent. Then ministers of the word will not risk calling in question God's love or be charged, as sometimes happens, with finding sadistic delight in teaching this sobering subject.

There is evidence in Paul's farewell address to the elders of the Ephesian church that he was thinking about judgment and hell, for just before his affirmation of faithfulness in preaching the whole gospel he said, "I am innocent of the blood of all men" (Acts 20:26). This echoes the threat God gave Ezekiel to urge him to warn Israel of the severe judgment against those who persisted in sin:

> When I say to a wicked man, "You will surely die," and you [Ezekiel] do not warn him or speak out to dissuade him from his evil ways in order to save his life, that wicked man will die for his sin, and I will hold you accountable for his blood. But if you do warn the wicked man and he does not turn from his wickedness or from his evil ways, he will die for his sin; but you will have saved yourself. (Ezek. 3:18–19; see also v. 20 and 33:7–9)

No teacher of Scripture would want to share the blame for any of their hearers who have refused to give up their independence and become like little children in trusting God. How terrible it would be at the Judgment Day to see people condemned because, while we had taught them parts of the biblical message, we had said little or nothing about hell! It should also be pointed out how the above warnings reveal God's great love for people in wanting them to be clearly confronted by every reason for worshiping and serving him rather than the creature. So we please God when we warn people about hell, even though such preaching can incur anger and ridicule. But as preachers and teachers of the word, we surely will want to please God rather than people, for as Paul said, "If I were still trying to please men, I would not be a servant of Christ" (Gal. 1:10).

Paul always wanted to lay primary emphasis on God's love and kindness: "Consider therefore the kindness and sternness of God: sternness to those who fell, but kindness to you, provided that you continue in his kindness" (Rom. 11:22). Here God's kindness is mentioned first and last to show that for Paul, this is most important. But God's sternness is also mentioned twice in between, for Paul dare not downplay his severity and thus risk its being overlooked. In this same sense we should understand such statements as "[God does not want] anyone to perish, but everyone to come to repentance" (2 Peter 3:9) and "God . . . wants all men to be saved and to come to a knowledge of the truth" (1 Tim. 2:3–4), as well as Jesus' lament over Jerusalem, "How often I have longed to gather your children together, as a hen gathers her chicks under her wings, but you were not willing!" (Luke 13:34). Here we see that God's joy comes from saving people who repent, not from punishing those who persist in sin. Of the many biblical passages that make this point explicit, consider Ezekiel 33:11, Luther's ultimately comforting verse: "As surely as I live, declares the Sovereign Lord, I take no pleasure in the death of the wicked, but rather that they turn from their ways and live. Turn! Turn from your evil ways! Why will you die, O house of Israel?"

We thus may sum up the relationship between God's love and wrath with the statement, so vital for understanding his plan in redemptive history, that God's kindness (or mercy, or benevolent love) is his free, ultimate work in which his soul finally and fully delights, whereas God's wrath in punishment is his necessary, penultimate work. Though he finds no pleasure in punishing the wicked, he nevertheless does it as something he must do, so that without devaluing his glory, he can fully rejoice in being merciful to the penitent.

Is Annihilation the Punishment for the Wicked?

Necessarily, then, the foregoing passages imply that not everyone will heed God's warning and repent, so that a part of the human race will be eternally punished.[4] But some evangelicals today, while agreeing that part of the human race will be lost, are finding it increasingly difficult to teach that these lost will suffer in an eternal hell. They believe that the Bible's statements about hell can be understood as teaching that punishment for the wicked will consist simply of annihilation as centers of consciousness.

One such evangelical is Clark Pinnock, a theology professor in Toronto, and we cite his brief, two-part argument for annihilation: (1) the "exegetical flimsiness of the traditional view of hell" and (2) "the moral horror" of that view.[5]

Pinnock argues first that annihilation, not conscious punishment, is implied by the biblical statements regarding the fate of the wicked. Pinnock sees this position, for example, in John the Baptist's reference to Christ's burning the wicked as chaff (Matt. 3:10, 12), because what is burned is consumed. Annihilation is also taught, he argues, in Jesus' warning to fear God's ability to cast both the resurrected physical body and the soul into hell (Matt. 10:28).[6] To him this verse means that both body and soul will be destroyed. As for Matthew 25:46, "[The wicked] will go away to eternal punishment, but the righteousness to eternal life," Pinnock insists that the eternal punishment of the wicked is not God's "eternal punishing" but an irrevocable punishment consisting in annihilation: "The fire of hell does not torment, but rather consumes the wicked."

Pinnock next argues that conscious torment for eternity in hell is inconsistent with the love of God. "The traditional understanding of hell is unspeakably horrible. How can one imagine for a moment that the God who would give his Son to die for sinners because of his great love for them would install a torture chamber somewhere in his new creation in order to subject those who reject him to everlasting pain?" According to Pinnock, this traditional understanding is morally flawed and "is accelerating the move toward universalism." But he wants to remain true to Scripture, and so he says, "I cannot eliminate the dark side of divine judgment from the picture. The judgment is a terrible event because God's wrath against obdurate sinners is serious and consuming." "After all," he says, "the notion of being condemned to nonexistence is pretty grim."

But here we must question Pinnock's explanation of divine judgment as "terrible" because ceasing to be a center of consciousness is "serious" and "consuming." Indeed, losing all consciousness of one's existence and being consumed would be serious rather than casual, but for many, such a prospect would be desirable rather than terrible. Shakespeare's Hamlet (3.1), for example, toys with the possibility of killing himself with a dagger so as to be free from the guilt of his misdeeds. But then he recalls how few people actually have the courage to commit suicide, because they cannot be sure that they would thus escape having to endure the pain and misery of punishment for their sins. Common experience therefore told Shakespeare that for some, annihilation would be a prospect welcomed rather than feared, a fate fervently desired, as by his Hamlet, though by no means assuredly attainable.

In fact, people hardened in wickedness could take real comfort in the thought that they would simply cease to exist at death rather than having to answer to God for their sins. What must surely have consoled Adolf Hitler as he saw the inevitability of the German defeat was the thought that he could annihilate himself as a center of consciousness by committing suicide just before the Russians overran his bunker in Berlin; he must have scoffed at the idea of ever having to answer before God for the millions he had had killed, and to be punished accordingly. His presumed certainty of annihilation must have made it easier for him to carry on his wickedness. Nor can any of us justifiably classify as "terrible" the nonexistent state in which all of us were for the countless ages before our births; though without any center of consciousness, no one remembers that time as at all undesirable.

A second problem with annihilationism is that it does not have a severity that corresponds to the enormity of our sin of heaping insult after insult upon God by failing to believe his promises. The cessation of existence is by no means a severe enough punishment to pose the sort of threat that such sin against God's credibility deserves. If "every violation and disobedience [will receive] its just punishment" (Heb. 2:2), then something more than annihilation must be in store for wicked people.

Certain Scriptures also present serious difficulties for annihilationism. Jesus said concerning Judas that it would have been better for him "if he had not been born" (Matt. 26:24), which necessarily implies that something far worse lay in store for Judas than his nonexistence before birth. Another problem is that five times in Matthew's gospel Jesus spoke of how people would weep and gnash their teeth after learning of the terrible future that lay ahead of them as outcasts from God's kingdom (8:12; 13:42; 22:13; 24:51; 25:30). Matthew 13:41–42 is particularly instructive: "The Son of man will send out his angels, and they will weed out of his kingdom everything that causes sin and all who do evil. They will throw them into the fiery furnace, where there will be weeping and gnashing of teeth." Annihilationism finds difficulty in explaining why people will weep and gnash their teeth in a fire that, according to its theory, will so quickly snuff out all consciousness.

Annihilationism also takes away the sting of Jesus' warning not to fear those who can do nothing more than kill the body, but to fear God who has power to cast both body and soul into hell (Matt. 10:28). The nub of the argument is that we are not to fear what people can do to us, for while they can end our physical lives, they cannot erase our being centers of consciousness as those who have souls. But we are to fear God, who does control the status of our souls. If as Pinnock teaches, however, all that God does with the unrepentant soul is to snuff out its existence along with that of the resurrected body, then what is there to fear in the resulting nonexistence?

Finally, annihilationism does not accord well with Paul's statement that God will "punish those who do not know God and do not obey the gospel of our Lord Jesus. They will be punished [lit. 'be recompensed'] with everlasting destruction and shut out from the presence of the Lord and from the majesty of his power" (2 Thess. 1:8–9). Understanding the wicked's continued existence as suffering eternal exclusion from God's presence fits in better with the idea of a recompense than the exclusion from his presence of those who have merely ceased to exist. Moreover the continued existence of the wicked accords better both with our sense of justice and with the thesis of this chapter, that there must be an equivalence between the enormity of the crime involved in rejecting the gospel and the severity of the punishment for this crime. Simply to lose all consciousness falls far short of the severity needed to indicate the awfulness of failing to glorify the God who longs to be gracious to people and to work for their benefit throughout eternity.

What, then, of Pinnock's argument that it is impossible to imagine for a moment that the God who would give his Son to die for sinners because of his great love for them would then install a torture chamber somewhere in his new creation in order to subject those who reject him to everlasting pain? The basic problem with Pinnock's objection is that he does not probe deeply enough into the reason why God sent his Son to die for sinners. God certainly did it because he loved them, but why did this love mean that his Son had to die for them? The scriptural answer is that Christ came to die "as the one who would turn aside [God's] wrath" (Rom. 3:25 margin). Jesus had to appease God's anger so that God would remain just when he forgave sinners and in no wise tarnish his own glory. "He [sent Christ to die] . . . so as to be just and the one who justifies those who have faith in Jesus" (v. 26).

The marvel of God's love in sending Christ to die is thus the length to which he was willing to go to forgive sinners, yet without depreciating his glory and thus becoming unjust. And we have seen that God's love to sinners consists in giving them the opportunity to share with him the joy he has in his glory. Therefore, since we will exult in God's glory through eternity to come, we should rejoice in all that he does to keep his glory from being profaned. One means to this end, as we saw in 2 Thessalonians 1:9, is his punishment of sinners in hell as a recompense they pay so that their having flouted God's glory will never succeed in profaning it. Consequently, this eternal punishment should be a satisfaction to all the saints in heaven, whose greatest delight is in sharing with God the joy of his glory.

Jonathan Edwards preached a sermon entitled "The End of the Wicked Contemplated by the Righteous; or, The Torments of the Wicked in Hell, No Occasion of Grief to the Saints in Heaven." It was based on Revelation 18:20, "Rejoice over [Babylon], O heaven! Rejoice, saints and apostles and prophets! God has judged her for the way she treated you." Edwards emphasized that this rejoicing of the saints in the punishment of the wicked

> will not be because the saints in heaven are the subjects of any ill disposition. . . . The devil delights [like the SS at Auschwitz] in the misery of men from cruelty, and from envy and revenge, and because he delights in misery, for its own sake, from a malicious disposition. But it will be from exceedingly different principles, and for quite other reasons, that the just damnation of the wicked will be an occasion of rejoicing to the saints in glory. . . . It will be no argument of want of a spirit of love in them, that they do not love the damned; for the heavenly inhabitants will know that it is not fit that they should love them, because they will know then, that God has no love to them, nor pity for them. . . . [The suffering of the wicked] will be an occasion of their rejoicing, as the *glory of God* will appear in it. . . . God glorifies himself in the eternal damnation of the ungodly men.[7]

Pinnock accordingly should take seriously God's statement in the closing verse of Isaiah: "And [the saints] will go out and look upon the dead bodies of those who rebelled against me; their worm will not die, nor will their fire be quenched, and they will be loathsome to all mankind" (66:24).

In this chapter we thus have considered the recompense impenitent sinners must pay to repair the injury their sins have inflicted on God's glory. Scripture is clear that the only way they can render that recompense is to suffer the eternal punishment of God's almighty wrath in hell. If, however, that were the only way God could maintain the integrity of his glory, then he could not realize his most cherished purpose to extend the joy of his goodness outward to many, many people in the world he had created. In the next chapter, then, we consider the outworking of this purpose of God.

Review Questions

1. Why must God exact a just recompense of punishment for every sin (remember what sin is at root) in order to remain a God who can be loving?

2. Why must God vent the full force of his omnipotence against those who persist in the sin of not trusting him?

3. How is a city showing love to people in its confines by having meter maids ticket cars parked on a busy street after 4:00 P.M. on workdays? (Those living in a culture not dominated by the automobile should rephrase this question in a way that reflects how one's local government does punish those who arrogate blessings to themselves at the expense of the rest.)

4. Why would it be wrong for a city to punish someone disobeying a parking law with a $10,000 fine? Why would it be wrong for a state to punish one guilty of first-degree murder by requiring a $100 fine?

5. Explain how the doctrine of total depravity means people cannot be any worse than they are in their sins, and yet allows that such people can be philanthropic and involved in community service.

6. Explain why God punishes people in an eternal hell, even though he says, "As I live, I have no pleasure in the death of the wicked" (Ezek. 33:11).

7. In what sense does God find no pleasure at all in the death of the wicked?

8. How does the annihilationist Clark Pinnock explain the affirmation in Matthew 25:46 that the wicked "will go away into eternal punishment"?

9. Why do I think annihilationism makes it easier for people to go on sinning?

10. How can hell's being visible to those in heaven be a source of joy to the saints there?

NOTES

[1] To force our minds to think clearly about what is being said, we should rephrase the rhetorical question (in italics) as a declarative statement: "It is impossible for me [God] to do anything that would defame my name in any way."

[2] Edwards, *Works*, 1:98.

³We have seen how this refusal to glorify God does not keep people from being benevolent toward others and even laying down their lives for a good cause (see chap. 10 above). To avoid misunderstanding when talking about people's total depravity, we must always insist that it refers to people's having the worst possible attitude toward *God*.

⁴A large percentage, however, will be saved, with many yet to be converted in the future, especially after the return of Christ to earth and before the creation of the new heavens and earth. See also Rom. 11:12 ("But if [Israel's] transgression means riches for the world, and their loss means riches for the Gentiles, how much greater riches will their fullness [their conversion—see v. 26] bring!"). The "fullness" of Israel here must mean their conversion, since it is the opposite of their impenitence spoken of earlier in this verse. Then since verse 15 is so similar to verse 12, we can say that "life from the dead" coming from God's acceptance of Israel must also be a hyperbolic way of designating the greater numbers of Gentiles on earth who will then turn to God.

⁵Clark Pinnock, "Fire, Then Nothing," *Christianity Today*, March 20, 1987, 40–41. See also David L. Edwards, *Evangelical Essentials: A Liberal-Evangelical Dialogue* (Downers Grove, Ill.: InterVarsity Press, 1988), which includes a response from John Stott. In Stott's reply to Edwards, he said, "It would be easier to hold together the awful reality of hell and the universal reign of God if hell means destruction and the impenitent are no more. I am hesitant to have written these things, partly because I have a great respect for longstanding tradition which claims to be a true interpretation of Scripture [eternal punishment in hell], and do not lightly set it aside, and partly because the unity of the worldwide Evangelical constituency has always meant much to me. . . . I do plead for frank dialogue among Evangelicals on the basis of Scripture. I also believe that the ultimate annihilation of the wicked should at least be accepted as a legitimate, biblically founded alternative to their eternal conscious torment" (319–20).

⁶Scripture teaches the future bodily resurrection of both the wicked and the just in Dan. 12:2, John 5:28–29, and Acts 24:15.

⁷Edwards, *Works*, 2:208–9.

14

The Riches of God's Mercy
From the Cross

In God's dealings with Adam and Eve, we noted that he was acting toward them not only in terms of justice for their sin of unbelief but also in terms of mercy, because his purpose to fill the earth with his glory had not changed. How God could maintain this merciful purpose, even after people had sinned, is the subject of this chapter, which tells how Jesus Christ, through his incarnation, death, and resurrection, paid to God the recompense our sin demanded.

In chapter 12 we saw how God's justice required him to deprive Adam and Eve of some of their ability to pursue happiness, for they had depreciated the value of his glory by declaring their independence. If God had not thus punished them, he would have said in effect, "My ability to make them happy is not all that valuable; they certainly can find happiness independently of me." But then God would have profaned his glory by denying its irreplaceable value, and thus he would have acted unjustly. However, in responding to their rebellion by increasing the pain of childbirth for Eve and her daughters and by making it exceedingly hard for Adam and his sons after him to grow enough food from the thistle-ridden ground, God was saying, "I love my glory because it is of ultimate worth for all people, and so I oppose those who have scorned it." In so acting, God remained righteous by upholding the worth of his goodness.

We also noted in chapter 12 that God continued to be merciful to Adam and Eve. He provided them with more durable clothing from animal skins and, most important, promised that Eve's posterity, "the seed of the woman," would deliver a fatal blow to the serpent and his seed so that life, rather than death, would finally prevail in the history of the created world. But in thus showing mercy to those who had disdained his glory and in withholding the full penalty for disobedience promised in Genesis 2:17, was not God acting unrighteously and so profaning his glory? How could he remain righteous in fully honoring the glory of his name while yet showing mercy to people who have sinned against him by scorning his glory?

God's Righteousness in the Cross of Christ

Isaiah speaks of one who was "pierced for our transgressions, [who] was crushed for our iniquities; the punishment that brought us peace was upon him, and by his wounds we are healed. We all, like sheep, have gone astray, each of us has turned to his own way; and the Lord has laid on him the iniquity of us all" (Isa. 53:5–6). Thus as we saw in the preceding chapter, God had set forth Christ as a slain sacrifice that would appease his anger. Christ's finished work on the cross enabled God to remain just while yet forgiving the sins of those who believed in Jesus (Rom. 3:24–26). "Christ died for sins once for all, the righteous for the unrighteous, to bring [us] to God" (1 Peter 3:18).

Modern theologians, however, sometimes ridicule the idea that Jesus had to die for people's sins in order for God to forgive them. The late New Testament scholar Rudolf Bultmann, famous for his attempt to "demythologize" the New Testament, scoffed, "How can the guilt of one man be expiated [appeased] by the death of another who is sinless . . . ? What a primitive mythology it is, that a divine Being should become incarnate, and atone for the sins of men through his own blood!"[1] For Leslie Weatherhead too, "Surely sin is not a debt which someone else can pay for me."[2] Indeed, there is no analogy in human jurisprudence where an innocent person bears the punishment a guilty one deserves so that the guilty one is acquitted and may go free. The Old Testament too affirms this basic principle of justice:

"Fathers shall not be put to death for their children, nor children put to death for their fathers; each is to die for his own sin" (Deut. 24:16).

Nevertheless the clear teaching of the Bible is that Jesus repaired the injury a great multitude of people have inflicted on God's glory. By the way our sinful attitudes and behavior deny that God loves us, we have desecrated his glory on earth. Therefore Jesus' dying for our sins so that God could forgive us is the foundation upon which he carries out his purpose in creation, despite the sinfulness of the people he created. In our task of preaching God's whole purpose, we must surely emphasize Jesus' shed blood on the cross as the only way totally depraved people can be forgiven and share with God his own joy. But we must do more than simply repeat these words. We must also make every effort to understand how the righteous Jesus could, by dying on a cross, appease God's wrath against us sinful people. For to the extent that we have some comprehension of how Jesus paid the penalty for our sins, we will be able to help others understand this foundational subject and thus be more persuasive in urging people to bank all their confidence for a happy future on God's promises summed up in Christ. So we now proceed with the task of gaining more insight into how Jesus made it possible for God to forgive our sins.

Two questions need to be answered in order to understand how Christ could cool down God's white-hot anger against a multitude of sinners, so that he could forgive them without degrading the glory of his name. First, *How could one person die for the sins of others?* A little reflection will show why no human government would let a mother, for example, be executed for the murder her son had committed and then acquit the son. Murder implies an ultimate contempt for the right of another to pursue happiness. To maintain this right for everyone is the glory of government. If the state remained indifferent to criminals and did not apprehend, convict, and punish them, their crimes would permanently injure the state's glory. Therefore the state must repair such injury by seeing that lawbreakers are deprived of the ability to pursue happiness to the extent that they arrogated happiness for themselves at the expense of others.

Only as the state withholds from wrongdoers themselves a proper amount of freedom to pursue happiness does it maintain people's confidence that it is working for the public good. Hence it would lose this confidence if it let a murderer's mother be executed in his place. The state's motive in permitting this substitution would be interpreted as meaning it cared more about satisfying a mother's love for her son than about upholding the sanctity of the law for the benefit of all. Thus allowing others to be punished in place of the violators themselves is tantamount to saying that restoring a criminal's good name or preserving a certain person's life is more important than the general welfare. Therefore the Bible and all systems of jurisprudence refuse to let an innocent person suffer in the place of a guilty one.

Scripture, however, makes it explicit that Jesus, the innocent One, did suffer in our place and, in so doing, repaired the injury we totally depraved sinners have done to the glory of God. His motive in dying for us was not to restore our ruined reputation but to uphold the great worth of God's glory. So as his time to die on the cross drew near, Jesus said, "Now my heart is troubled, and what shall I say? 'Father, save me from this hour'? No, it was for this very reason I came to this hour. Father, glorify your name!" (John 12:27–28). Then when Judas Iscariot had left the Last Supper to betray Jesus and the die was cast for him to be crucified, Jesus declared, "Now is the Son of Man glorified, and *God is glorified* in him" (13:31).

To be sure, Jesus' purpose was also to die for sinners in order to impart the blessing of life with God to them: "God so loved the world that he gave his one and only Son, that whoever believes in him shall not perish but have eternal life" (John 3:16). His motive in dying for sinful people was the benevolent love of wanting them to share with him his greatest joy—knowing the Father. Thus just before his death and resurrection he requested of the Father "that the love you have for me may be in [the redeemed]" (17:26).

Therefore both of the Father's goals in creating the world were accomplished by Jesus' motive in dying for sinners. First, God wanted to double his joy by sharing it with the people he had created, and Jesus helped accomplish this goal by making it possible for God to forgive sinners so they could have fellowship with him. Second, God wanted to extend his goodness outward from the Trinity by showing his ultimately glorious attribute of mercy, or grace, to needy people throughout his creation. It is this second goal that should be emphasized here: Jesus' stated concern in dying for sinners was to glorify the Father by showing that his goodness, culminating in his display of mercy, was valuable enough to die for, so that the injury sinful people had inflicted on it by questioning God's trustworthiness might be overcome and God's glory displayed in the earth. Jesus' death never implied, as a substitutionary punishment would always imply in any human government, that its concern was to repair the reputation of the lawbreaker and not the glory of the state, which is to be benevolent to everyone. Indeed, those who benefited from Christ's death, rather than having their own reputations restored, began to glorify God and uphold his integrity by exhibiting an "obedience that comes from faith," a style of behavior based on confidence in God's credit rating and an assurance that he would fulfill every word of his promises.

So, contrary to the opinion of some modern theologians, we agree with Paul that "God made [Jesus] who had no sin to be sin [but not sinful!] for us, so that in him we might become the righteousness of God" (2 Cor. 5:21). By now, therefore, it is hoped that each reader has a clearer understanding of how the innocent Jesus could bear the punishment we all deserved for our sins and thus uphold God's government of the universe.

We must answer a second question, however, if we are to be more effective in urging people to turn the controls of their lives over to Jesus. *How could one person die for the sins of many?* How could one man die for the sins of a "great multitude that no one could count" (Rev. 7:9)? How could the recompense for all our sins, which would require an eternity in hell for each of us, be paid by Jesus during a mere thirty-three years of suffering on earth, particularly during the six hours on the cross, at the end of which he said, "It [paying the penalty for people's sins] is finished" (John 19:30)? To state the problem as briefly as possible, How could one die for so many, and pay such an immense recompense in such a short time?

The answer to this question lies in realizing just how much glory Jesus lost in his incarnation and death. Only as we catch a glimpse of the severity of this loss can we begin to see how he was able to placate God's anger against the enormity of the sins of this innumerable multitude of believers.[3] The starting point for understanding this severity is to get some idea of how exalted Jesus was in heaven before coming to earth to be incarnated as a man.

As we saw back in chapter 8, Jesus was "very God of very God." It is virtually impossible for any of us to understand how transcendently high God, the Creator of the universe, is in comparison with us people on earth. But some faint idea of his grandeur can be gained from certain passages in Scripture. To Isaiah, who saw God on his throne, he was "high and exalted" (Isa. 6:1); he "sits enthroned above the circle of the earth, and its people are like grasshoppers. He stretches out the heavens like a canopy, and spreads them out like a tent to live in" (40:22). Thus to God and to Jesus, his only begotten Son, "the nations are like a drop in a bucket; they are regarded as dust on the scales," and the islands are "[weighed] as though they were fine dust" (v. 15). Before Jesus' incarnation, equality with the Father was so completely his right that he entertained no thought of grasping after it as though he might somehow lose it (Phil. 2:6–8). He is and always has been the "glorious Lord Jesus Christ" (James 2:1).

Some idea of how much glory Jesus therefore lost in his incarnation can be found in the words of a well-known hymn that speaks of his leaving the "ivory palaces" and coming into a "world of woe." A helpful picture to have in mind is that of Jesus' descending a winding staircase stretching for a very long distance from the glory of heaven above far down into a world of wretched misery. Each downward step in leaving this glory increased the pain Jesus underwent to pay for our sins, and so a good part of the severity of the punishment Jesus suffered for us consisted in coming down this staircase, whose length cannot be exaggerated, since it spanned the infinite distance between the Creator and the creature. Then when he arrived on earth and found himself in human form, "he humbled himself and became obedient to death—even death on a cross!" (Phil. 2:8), the most humiliating and excruciating form of execution ever devised. As Jesus hung on that cross, God poured out on him the wrath that the redeemed deserved. Therefore in traversing the vast distance from the ivory palaces to experiencing the omnipotent fury of God's wrath, Jesus experienced a loss of glory and a severity of anguish more than equal to the punishment that the sins of all the redeemed deserved.

Here we need to remember from the last chapter that the state must take greater glory away from criminals convicted of more serious crimes. And so when we realize what Jesus suffered in losing such an enormous amount of glory by his incarnation and finally his death on the cross, we get some insight into how one person could pay the recompense needed to repair the injury that all of the sins of the redeemed have inflicted on God's glory.

One problem that may arise at this point is that people have been accustomed to think of Jesus' atonement as being accomplished only by his death on the cross. Indeed, his suffering the wrath of God while he hung on the cross was the climax of his great loss of glory, but it was not the whole story. Just before he went to the cross, Jesus said to the Father in prayer, "I have brought you glory on earth by completing the work you gave me to do" (John 17:4). We have seen how Jesus went to the cross to glorify the Father, but this verse shows that his previous life on earth also glorified the Father. Therefore it is clear that the sufferings endured both while on earth and in leaving heaven were also a part of his atoning work. So putting the Incarnation, the sufferings of a thirty-three-year lifetime, and the death on the cross together helps solve the problem of how one person, in a limited time span, could pay the recompense of an eternity in hell that each of the redeemed would have had to pay.

An appreciation of this work is also helped by reflecting on some of the ways Jesus suffered during his years on earth. Born in a stable, his first crib was a feeding trough (Luke 2:7). No sooner was he born than the king of the land, Herod, had all the children in the area of Bethlehem killed, so that this child, regarded by wise men from the East as the rightful king of the Jews (Matt. 2:2), would not threaten Herod's throne (vv. 7–18). Therefore soon after his birth Jesus had to be taken on a hasty journey to the foreign land of Egypt (vv. 13–15). In growing up there, he no doubt felt the pain of being an outsider and was probably rebuffed as he tried to make friends with other children his age. Then when Herod finally died and it was safe for Jesus to return to Palestine, his family resumed residence in Nazareth, a Galilean village regarded as most insignificant (John 1:46; cf. 7:41). There with his earthly father Jesus calloused his hands in the hard trade of a carpenter,[4] living in total obscurity as a blue-collar laborer until he was thirty years of age. The loss of glory all this lifestyle involved was summed up by Edwards as follows: "Let us consider how great a degree of humiliation the glorious Son of God, the Creator of heaven and earth, was subject to in this, that for about thirty years he should live a private, obscure life among labouring men, and all this while be overlooked, not taken notice of in the world, more than other common labourers."[5]

Nor did his entry into public ministry bring any improvement in Jesus' condition; rather it brought far greater degradation. He was without a place to lay his head (Matt. 8:20) and was so poor that he was able to pay the required tribute only by a miracle (17:27). Throughout his ministry he was reproached as a glutton, a drunkard, a deceiver of the people, a madman, one possessed with a demon, a Samaritan, a devil, one who practiced the black arts and had communication with the Devil, and a friend of publicans, prostitutes, and sinners. He was excommunicated from the synagogue (see John 9:22) and was often threatened with stoning (John 8:59; 10:31; 11:8). The Pharisees actively sought to kill him (John 7:1; 11:53; Matt. 26:4), and even his home folks at Nazareth tried to throw him off a cliff (Luke 4:29).

But the greatest humiliation befell Jesus as he was delivered up to be crucified. One of his own disciples sold him for thirty pieces of silver, the ordinary price for a slave (Ex. 21:32). And as Jesus approached the cross, a dreadful

gloom and anguish descended upon his soul as he contemplated the awfulness of being the object of his Father's wrath
against the sins of the world. Thus while kneeling in the
Garden of Gethsemane to pray, so great was the anguish of
his soul that blood was forced through the pores of his skin
(Luke 22:44). In the meantime his disciples had so little
regard for his suffering that they fell asleep. Then Jesus was
arrested, and as he was led off, all his disciples deserted him
and fled (Matt. 26:56). To be sure, Peter turned back and
followed from a distance, having boasted of his willingness
to die for him (John 13:37; 18:15), but he succeeded only in
denying him three times with curses (Matt. 26:69–75). False
witnesses then were brought against him; he was spat upon,
blindfolded, struck in the face, ridiculed, mockingly dressed
in a king's robe, and crowned with thorns. Then he was
stripped and cruelly beaten, and an insurrectionist was
released in preference to him.

Finally he was crucified, an execution that involved the
most terrible agony ever devised. But beyond his physical
sufferings, he felt the overwhelming force of God's wrath
that would have been ours in hell. He had no sweet frame of
mind, like many martyrs, to help him endure his physical
agony; rather, his most extreme anguish was that God was
treating him like a sinner. His Father had forsaken him and
had become his enemy, pouring out the full force of his
wrath upon his Son. While Jesus thus endured the wrath of
God that his elect would otherwise have experienced for
their sins, his thoughts were also filled with the dismal
gloom of the eternal hell that they deserved. The following
quotation sums up Jesus' lifelong sufferings as they climaxed
upon the cross:

> He had no beauty or majesty to attract us to him, nothing in
> his appearance that we should desire him. He was despised
> and rejected by men, a man of sorrows and familiar with
> suffering. Like one from whom men hide their faces he was
> despised, and we esteemed him not. Surely he took up our
> infirmities and carried our sorrows, yet we considered him
> stricken by God, smitten by him, and afflicted. But he was
> pierced for our transgressions, he was crushed for our
> iniquities; the punishment that brought us peace was upon

him, and by his wounds we are healed. . . . Yet it was the Lord's will to crush him and cause him to suffer. . . . He poured out his life unto death, and was numbered with the transgressors. For he bore the sin of many, and made intercession for the transgressors. (Isa. 53:2–12)

So we may conclude that Jesus, through all these sufferings, underwent a loss of glory more than sufficient to repair the injury that his people, in their sins, had inflicted on the glory of God. "None ever stooped so low as Christ," declared Edwards, "if we consider either the infinite height that he stooped from, or the great depth to which he stooped."[6] For sinners, Jesus traversed the unimaginably long distance from being himself the manifest embodiment of the glory of God to being one who was in the most contemptible state because of suffering the full force of the wrath of God. Therefore his loss of glory in his incarnation and death was indeed adequate to atone for the sins of all the elect.

God's Mercy From the Cross of Christ

With a better understanding of how Jesus' sufferings and death on the cross allowed God to show mercy without profaning the glory of his name, we now conclude this chapter by emphasizing several ways in which Jesus' work on the cross will increase our joy in all he accomplished for us.

The Importance of Jesus' Resurrection

We have seen from John 19:28–30 how Jesus' work of forgiving our sins was completed in his death on the cross. But he rose again on the third day, and the significance this act has for our salvation must be emphasized. One important aspect of his resurrection is made clear in the course of Peter's sermon at Pentecost. After recounting how Jesus had been crucified, Peter went on to say, "But God raised him from the dead, freeing him from the agony of death, because it was impossible for death to keep its hold on him." He then supported this impossibility by quoting from Psalm 16:8–11, which shows that a righteous and holy person could not be abandoned to the power of death (Acts 2:24–28). Thus Peter emphasized how Jesus' sinlessness on earth made it impossible for him to remain under the power of death—the penalty for sin—and so he was indeed qualified to die for our sins.

This conclusion is also underscored by 2 Corinthians 5:21 and 1 Peter 3:18, already cited as teaching Jesus' substitutionary atonement. Why must he have been sinless in order to die for our sins? We have seen that Jesus could die for the sins of others only because his sole motive was to uphold God's glory, whose outward manifestation people had injured so greatly by their refusal to worship him and thank him for all his blessings. But in order for Jesus to have this motive for going to the cross, his basic purpose throughout his life on earth must have been to glorify God.

The Gospels contain abundant evidence that Jesus did live in such a way, with all his hope banked on God's promise to care for him. Thus his refusal to yield to Satan's temptation and use his omnipotence to turn stones into bread during his life-threatening fast in the wilderness was explicitly based on God's promise that "man does not live on bread alone, but on every word that comes from the mouth of God" (Matt. 4:4, citing Deut. 8:3). Accordingly, Jesus waited until God sent angels to bring him food, thereby exhibiting the obedience that comes from faith.

Therefore just as Abraham "gave glory to God, being fully persuaded that God had power to do what he had promised" (Rom. 4:20–21), so Jesus glorified God during his life by trusting in God's promises. In this way his sinlessness, defined as an obedience that comes from faith, validates his assertion that he would die to uphold the Father's veracity. His resurrection is therefore important in that it verifies his righteousness in having always glorified his Father.

Another way in which Jesus' resurrection is vital for the forgiveness of sins is made clear in Romans 4:24–25: "God will credit righteousness—for us who believe in him who raised Jesus our Lord from the dead. He was delivered over to death for our sins and was raised to life for our justification." This passage implies that we could not be confident that Jesus had paid the penalty for our sins unless he had risen from the dead. Had he remained in the tomb, the conclusion would have been that he must be punished eternally like all other people who have "sinned and [fallen] short of the glory of God" (3:23). But because he was raised, we know that we can be justified, or accounted righteous, before God.

The Salvation of Believers by God's Righteousness

A second important emphasis regarding Jesus' work on the cross is that it guarantees to believers that they have forgiveness. We read in 1 John 1:9 that "if we confess our sins, [God] is faithful and just and will forgive us our sins and purify us from all unrighteousness." This means that if God did not forgive our sins when we confessed them in faith that "the blood of Jesus, his Son, purifies us from all sin" (1 John 1:7), then he would be unrighteous, because Jesus' purpose in dying on the cross was to uphold the glory of the Father. We have seen before how God's righteousness consists in his wholehearted love for his glory (step 2 in the preceding chapter), so that if he did not honor Jesus' purpose to uphold this glory, he would be sinful. Thus we can understand why John said that God had forgiven the believer's sins "on account of his name" (1 John 2:12). God must forgive us when we believe on Jesus, because otherwise he would not be loving his own glory. This consideration strengthens our faith when Satan tries to destroy it by reminding us of our sins—for he accuses Christians day and night before God (Rev. 12:10).

This insight that we are saved by the righteousness of God opened Martin Luther's eyes to the concept of justification by faith alone and led to the Reformation, which began around 1518. Luther had been meditating on Psalm 71:2, "Rescue me and deliver [save] me in your righteousness [O God]" (cf. Ps. 31:1). But he did not understand how the psalmist could ask for salvation in God's righteousness, for he had been taught that God's righteousness signified only condemnation, not salvation, for sinners could never satisfy it. Luther was also puzzled by Romans 1:16–17, where God's power unto salvation is for every one who believes, because in the gospel is revealed a righteousness from God. How could Paul regard God's righteousness as the basis for salvation when, for Luther, that righteousness had always signified the basis of his condemnation? But in keeping with the all-too-few Berean Bible readers (in his day and ours), he did not simply pass by these statements that mystified him because they were so contrary to what he had been taught. Instead he pondered them, hoping that he could gain insight into how both the psalmist and Paul could regard their salvation as dependent on God's righteousness.

Luther's action thus confirmed the observation of the philosopher John Dewey (1859–1952) that people never think until they are faced with a problem. The essence of inductive Bible study, in fact, is to look at statements in Scripture long enough until one becomes troubled about something and then to try out various possibilities until one is found that makes things cohere. What finally did this for Luther was Paul's statement that "God presented [Jesus] as a sacrifice who would turn aside [God's] wrath, taking away sin through faith in his blood. He did it to demonstrate his justice . . . so as to be just and the one who justifies [forgives and accounts righteous] those who have faith in Jesus" (Rom. 3:25–26 margin). In a flash Luther saw that the Father had to honor Jesus' death and forgive the believing sinner, or else he would scorn his own glory by not valuing the sacrifice by which Jesus his only Son had sought to uphold it. But God found no difficulty in honoring Jesus' great sufferings and death, since they were endured out of love for the Father's glory. Jesus' death for sinners in fact gave God the right to act most gloriously and to find his fullest delight in showing mercy to helpless people, so that thereby he might carry out his plan to show the fullness of his goodness, his glory, throughout the earth.

The Riches of God's Mercy

In saving humanity on the basis of his righteousness, however, God does more than just fulfill the obligation he has to remain true to himself. Since the demands of his righteousness have been met in the death and resurrection of

Christ, God then freely imparts the riches of his mercy to his people. In Romans 5:10 Paul argued that "if, when we were God's enemies, we were reconciled to him through the death of his Son, how much more, having been reconciled, shall we be saved through his life!" In other words, two immense obstacles had to be surmounted for God to bless sinful people. First, God had to be propitiated. His white-hot anger at people's refusal to be thankful and to entrust their future happiness to him had to be cooled down, so that he could be reconciled to such sinners. This was an immense barrier, because people had continually heaped the greatest insult upon God by declaring a vote of no confidence in him. And this enmity could be overcome only at the greatest cost to the Father, namely, that his only-begotten and beloved Son should take the form of a human being, to suffer and die for people's sins as God vented against him the wrath they deserved.

The unsurpassed love of God for his Son was the second obstacle God had to overcome in saving us. In that God so loved the world that he gave his Son, we understand the tremendous barrier that he overcame in paying the terrible cost of having his beloved Son die for people's sins.

But God's delight in the freedom with which he had originally purposed to create the world led him to overcome these obstacles so that creation might represent completely the fullness of his glory in the riches of his mercy. And once they were overcome, then with far greater power and fullness of desire God bestows all the riches of his mercy on the heirs of salvation. Paul made this point in Romans 8:32: "He who did not spare his own Son, but gave him up for us all—how will he not also, along with him, graciously give us all things?" The point is that if God loved us enough to overcome his enmity against us even at the cost of the death of his Son, then once those two obstacles were overcome, how much more would his love be translated into the great blessings of mercy and grace he delights to bestow on us!

Words become inadequate as Paul describes these riches, for they are "unsearchable," or (lit.) "not capable of being traced out" (Eph. 3:8). So marvelous are these riches of mercy that Paul prayed that believers might have special enablement to "know the hope to which he has called you, the riches of his glorious inheritance in the saints" (Eph. 1:18). These riches result from God's so delighting in his mercy as the apex of his glory that all his power and wisdom are employed to do good to his people and to be a means for bringing them ultimate blessing and fulfillment. This is why Paul, according to Romans 1:16–17, was so enthused and excited about the gospel: it revealed a righteousness from God, so that God's power could now be fully unleashed in love to bring to people the "all things" of Romans 8:32.

We should note how often in Scripture these riches that believers are beginning to enjoy are linked up with God's mercy or grace (which is virtually the same as mercy). In Romans 9:23, for example, Paul speaks of the "riches of his glory known to the objects of his mercy." Ephesians 2:4–7 also tells of God being "rich in mercy" and then goes on to say how he has "raised us up with Christ and seated us with him in the heavenly realms in Christ Jesus, in order that in the coming ages he might show the incomparable riches of his grace." All the riches that come to the believer are because of God's mercy made available through Christ's work on the cross. But while mercy is undeserved favor, it is not unconditional favor, for it comes to people only if they believe (Eph. 1:19).

Review Questions

1. Be able to give an example of "propitiation" from everyday life.

2. Explain why it is possible to speak of our sins as having injured God's glory.

3. Be able to explain why the Bible and secular jurisprudence do not let anyone but the convicted criminal pay the penalty for his or her crime.

4. How does Jesus' sinlessness and his statements in John 12:27–28 and 13:31 make it possible for him to have repaired the injury our sins have done to the glory of God?

5. Explain how *all* the injury that the innumerable company of the redeemed have inflicted on God's glory could be repaired by the one person, Jesus Christ, during his mere thirty-three years on earth and six hours alive on the cross.

6. Explain why Jesus' incarnation and life on earth made a substantial contribution, along with his enduring the wrath of God on the cross, to making it possible for God to forgive our sins.

7. According to Romans 4:25, what significant point was made by Jesus' having been raised from the dead?

8. Explain why, according to 1 John 1:9, God would be untrustworthy and sinful if he did not forgive our sins when we confess them.

9. Why is it, according to Romans 5:10 and 8:32, that God must be much more benevolent toward us now that Jesus has died for us who were God's enemies in that we had insulted him so by our unbelief?

10. Be able to demonstrate that you understand a basic thesis of this book—that God's grace, in being benevolent and merciful toward people, is conditional but not merited—by saying this in your own words and by citing an illustration of conditional grace taken from everyday life.

NOTES

[1] Rudolph Bultmann, "The New Testament and Mythology," in *Kerygma and Myth*, ed. Hans Werner Bartsch, trans. Reginald H. Fuller (London: S.P.C.K., 1957), 7.

[2] Leslie Weatherhead, *The Christian Agnostic* (New York: Abingdon, 1965), 113.

[3] The question of the extent of Jesus' atonement naturally arises when we think about his paying the penalty for people's sins. If one teaches that Jesus died for the sins of everyone—even for their sins of not believing on him, then the door is open to the false teaching that everyone will finally be saved (i.e., universalism), for God would be unjust to punish people for the very sins for which Jesus already paid the recompense. But Jesus spoke of his laying down his life for his *sheep* (John 10:15), which implies that he did

not recompense the sins of those remaining impenitent, who refuse to be his sheep. Also Heb. 10:14 speaks of Jesus' sacrifice as having been made for all who are being made holy, which would exclude those who remain condemned.

Coherency on this subject is attained when we understand those verses teaching that Jesus died for all (e.g., 2 Cor. 5:15; 1 Tim. 2:6) to mean that he died for all *without respect to any special distinctives:* "There is no difference between Jew and Gentile— the same Lord is Lord of all and richly blesses all who call on him" (Rom. 10:12). Jesus said simply, "Whoever is thirsty, let him come; and whoever wishes, let him take the free gift of the water of life" (Rev. 22:17). Thus, the teaching of an atonement of limited extent should never raise the fear in anyone that Jesus did not die for his or her sins. That a person *wants* Jesus' forgiveness is evidence that he or she is one for whom Jesus died, and such people should be encouraged to repent and believe in order to be saved.

[4]The word for "carpenter" represented one who worked with wood or stone. Given the scarcity of wood around Nazareth, the likelihood is that Jesus learned the difficult and dangerous trade of shaping stones by hammer and chisel.

[5]Edwards, "History," 1:578. I am indebted to Edwards for his enumeration in this treatise of how Jesus suffered both before and during his public ministry (532–619, esp. 577–80).

[6]Ibid., 577.

15

The Near Extinction
of the Woman's Seed

We return now to the Bible's timeline, looking first at the statement of Genesis 3:15 that the seed of the woman will inflict a mortal wound on the head of the serpent. At the end of chapter 12 we noted that this verse, often called the Protoevangelium ("the first indication of the gospel"), affirmed that God's purpose in creation will be realized, in spite of the incursion of evil that took place in the Fall. In analyzing the Protoevangelium, we need to discover the referents of the pronouns in this verse.

The Protoevangelium of Genesis 3:15

In declaring the punishment that was to befall the serpent, God said, "I will put enmity between you [the serpent] and the woman [Eve], and between your [the serpent's] offspring and hers [Eve's]; [her seed][1] shall crush your [the serpent's] head, and you [the serpent] will strike [only] its heel [that of the woman's seed]." The wording of this Protoevangelium is suited to concur with later revelation for several reasons. First, the "woman's seed" can refer both to a collective group and to Jesus Christ as one member of that group. Second, it speaks of the serpent as existing long after the woman, Eve, has passed from the scene, and so can refer to Satan, a fallen angelic being who is immortal. Thus this serpent whom God will place at enmity with Eve's offspring can be equated with the one whose head at some future time

223

will be bruised. Since such a wound in comparison to a mere injury to the heel implies that it is deadly; it signifies a complete triumph over the serpent by the woman's seed. Therefore Genesis 3:15 makes room for later revelations regarding this serpent as Satan and for the woman's seed as both Jesus Christ and his people. But the Protoevangelium raises two questions that need to be answered in fully understanding the author's intended meaning.

Who Are the Serpent's Seed and the Woman's Seed?

Should we understand the "seed of the serpent" to be the progeny sired by the original serpent? Hardly, because the Bible knows nothing of literal snakes as the perpetrators of subsequent evil. Can the serpent's seed then be a group of godless people, while the woman's seed is a separate group of godly people? Surprising as it may seem, I regard this to be the proper answer. A clue to what the author regarded as the seed of the serpent comes in Genesis 4:1–10, which relates how Cain, Eve's first male child, had such animosity against his younger brother, Abel, that he murdered Abel. This emergence of a specific enmity a few verses after Genesis 3:15 is significant, for the repetition encourages the reader to understand the Cain-Abel enmity in terms of that just spoken of. People motivated like Cain would therefore be the seed of the serpent, while those with Abel's motivation would be the seed of the woman.

Further evidence that this was the author's understanding of the identity of the serpent's seed is the stark contrast, to be spelled out shortly, set forth between the kinds of people sired by Cain (Gen. 4:17–24) and Seth (4:25–5:32), who was born to replace murdered Abel. Later revelation too gives considerable encouragement to accepting this interpretation of the seeds of the serpent and the woman. Jesus, for example, drew a distinction between people who are "sons of the kingdom," likened to good seed that God had sown, and "sons of the evil one," who are weeds sown by the Devil (Matt. 13:37–39). He also told the people who had believed in him but were unwilling to persevere in obeying him, "You belong to your father, the devil" (John 8:44). Then

Revelation 12:15–17 graphically depicts the battle between Satan as the serpent, or dragon, and God's people, the seed of the woman: "the serpent spewed water like a river, to overtake the woman [and her child—v. 13]. . . . But the earth helped the woman by opening its mouth and swallowing the river that the dragon had spewed out of his mouth. Then the dragon was enraged at the woman and went off to make war against the rest of her offspring—those who obey God's commandments and hold to the testimony of Jesus."

Back in Genesis, now, we must analyze what the author said about Cain and must discern what motivated him to become so angry with his brother Abel. According to Genesis 4:2–5, "Abel kept flocks, and Cain worked the soil. In the course of time Cain brought some of the fruits of the soil as an offering to the Lord. But Abel brought *fat portions* from some of the *firstborn of his flock.* The Lord looked with favor on Abel and his offering, but on Cain and his offering he did not look with favor." In his reference to the "fat portions" and the "firstborn," there is evidence the author intended his readers to regard Abel's sacrifice as superior to Cain's. It is a mistake, however, to think that this contrast was between the blood involved in Abel's sacrifice and the bloodlessness of Cain's. This popular interpretation is to be rejected, for the original readers of Genesis knew nothing of the shedding of blood, without which there is no forgiveness (Heb. 9:22), because "the life of a creature is in the blood, and . . . it is the blood that makes atonement for one's life" (Lev. 17:11). Rather, the contrast lies in the motives that led Abel to offer the choicest products of his vocation as a herdsperson, while Cain was content merely to offer a casual evidence of his vocation as a farmer.

Thus the reader infers that God accepted Abel's sacrifice because it consisted of the best fruits of his labor. This indicated that he was expressing to God both the great fulfillment he enjoyed in having fellowship with him and also his thankfulness for all of God's providential care. But there was nothing special about Cain's offering, which strongly suggests that he had merely gone through the motions of divine worship—"any old pumpkin will do." He had taken no pains to offer his best produce, since he evidently placed little value on fellowship with God, simply taking his benefits for granted. Unlike Abel, who was banking his confidence for an eternally happy and fulfilled future upon God, Cain had placed his confidence in himself, in his energy and skill in getting the land to yield crops. So whereas for Abel God and his blessings was the source of joy, Cain's joy came from seeing what his own wisdom and efforts could produce. As we saw in chapter 13, God's love for his goodness would require him to delight in Abel and his sacrifice and to reject that of Cain.

But then a problem rises: since God meant nothing special to Cain, why did God's preference for his brother's sacrifice make Cain so angry that he murdered Abel? If God meant so little to Cain, why should he be upset over God's approval of Abel's sacrifice? A plausible answer is that Cain nonetheless regarded God as the Supreme Being, and so it hurt his pride to see his brother favored. Though ego made him desire God's praise for his wisdom and diligence in excelling as a farmer, this same ego recoiled at being like Abel, who happily acknowledged his dependence on God, blessing him for his benefits and the joy of having communion with him. But when Cain saw how happy the Supreme Being was with Abel and the joy this gave his brother, his proud rebellion against God's insistence that people give all honor to him was reflected in the unhappy expression on his face.

Cain could very quickly have become as happy as Abel simply by turning to God and trusting God's perfect wisdom and power to give him a happy future. In Genesis 4:6–7 (paraphrased here), God urged him to do exactly that.

> Cain, there's absolutely no need for you to be so miserable that it shows. All you have to do is turn away from your life purpose of exalting yourself and instead glorify me by letting me manage and care for you far better than loving parents care for their children. Then I will exult in you just as much as I do in Abel, and in enjoying my care, you will be as happy as he is. It's all to your advantage to turn away from your life-goal of trying to satisfy your ego, and turn instead toward the easily attainable goal of worshiping me for the joy of having communion with me and for the eternally glorious future I want to give you. But if you do not turn from your present

goal, a terrible future awaits you, for your present sinful inclination to exalt yourself endangers you as much as having a vicious animal crouching at your front door, waiting for a chance to lunge in and devour you. If you don't remove this threat now by changing your life-goal to that of letting me glorify myself in you, your God-insulting inclination will eventually bring you and yours to terrible misery.

But Cain's pride—his preference to glory in his own abilities and accomplishments, even though they came from God—kept him from being reasonable and adopting the life-goal for which God had created him. He did not want the joy mirrored in Abel's happy countenance at the cost of giving up his attainment of ego satisfaction. So all that Cain could do at the moment to relieve his anger against God and his jealousy of Abel was to kill his brother, burying him out in the countryside so that he and all that he represented of God's love for people might be out of sight and out of mind.

Here is a clear example of the enmity predicted in Genesis 3:15. But why should there have been such a difference between Abel's life-purpose and Cain's? The answer is found in God's declaration, "*I will put enmity* . . . between [the serpent's] offspring and [the woman's]." This distinction raises a second question.

What Was God's Role with Cain and Abel?

In the author's thinking, all descendants from Adam and Eve were totally depraved;[2] from birth their hearts were inclined toward the life-purpose the serpent had urged upon their parents in getting them to sin: "Every inclination of the thoughts of [humankind's] heart was only evil all the time" (Gen. 6:5); "every inclination of [a person's] heart is evil from childhood" (8:21). So as Abel started life, he was as totally depraved as Cain, but at some point God put enmity between him and Cain by giving Abel a new heart, one inclined to seek fellowship with God and bank all in the future on his goodness. There was no essential difference between Cain and Abel, but God sovereignly chose to regenerate Abel and not Cain: "God has mercy on whom he wants to have mercy, and he hardens whom he wants to harden" (Rom. 9:18). Consequently Abel came to treasure God and his goodness and thus turned the control of his life over to God. As a result he was able to share with God the very delight God had in himself. The joy of this worship was reflected both in the expression on Abel's face and in his sacrifice.

As for Cain, though God had counseled him to be reasonable and adopt this same life-goal, God did not work in his heart to overcome its total depravity by changing its deep intention from self-exaltation to honoring God and enjoying communion with God.[3] Consequently Cain would not accept the overwhelming reasonableness of submitting to God, and since he and his descendants continued to pursue the life-purpose the serpent had urged upon Eve and Adam, they are properly called the serpent's seed. In a moment, then, we will see the great contrast between the characteristics of Cain's posterity and those of Abel's successor, Seth.

NOTE. At this point we need to pause and consider briefly what later revelation teaches about the regeneration God gives people by causing the Holy Spirit to indwell them. In the Old Testament regeneration is figuratively termed a "circumcised heart" (Deut. 10:16; 30:6; Jer. 4:4) or a new heart of flesh rather than stone (Ezek. 11:19; 18:31; 36:26; Zech. 7:12). In the New Testament it is figuratively called being "born of God" (John 1:13), being "born again" (John 3:4–5, 7), or the "washing of rebirth and renewal by the Holy Spirit" (Titus 3:5).

Indications of this regeneration in the Old Testament occur not only in Genesis 3:15 and 4:1–10 but also with regard to Caleb and Joshua, two of the twelve spies sent to reconnoiter the land God had promised the Israelites. Only these two returned with enthusiastic confidence that the Israelites could conquer this strongly fortified land and its fearsome warriors (Num. 13:25–33; 14:4–10). According to Numbers 14:24, Caleb possessed a "different spirit" from that of the ten unbelieving and discouraged spies, while Joshua was indwelt by God's Spirit (Num. 27:18). So these two spies were members of that small remnant of regenerate people always existing in ethnic Israel (Rom. 11:2–6; cf. 1 Kings 19:10, 18) alongside the great majority of Jacob's descendants, who remain unregenerate until the second coming of Jesus (Deut. 5:29; 29:4; 30:6; Jer. 4:4; 31:31–34; Rom. 11:25–26; 1 Cor. 10:5; Heb. 3:16–4:2).

We have just considered the intensity and unreasonableness of Cain's anger against Abel. Since this enmity came as a result of the new heart God had given Abel, there is good reason to regard him as born again. The same is true of Eve (and Adam), since in Genesis 3:15 God had declared he would put enmity between Eve and her seed and the serpent. But the only way depraved people can acquire a heart attitude and behavior pleasing to God is to be indwelt by the Holy Spirit (that is, regenerated): "The mind of the sinful man is death . . . [and] hostile to God. It does not submit to God's law, nor can it do so. Those controlled by the sinful nature cannot please God. You, however, are controlled not by the sinful nature but by the Spirit, if the Spirit of God lives in you" (Rom. 8:6–9). The reason, then, that Abel offered a sacrifice that pleased God was that God had placed the Holy Spirit in him so that he no longer had the stony heart with which he was born but had instead a heart of flesh. While Genesis 3 and 4 in their immediate context do not explicitly teach regeneration, they clearly imply it, so that what Romans 8:6–9 and other passages say later fits well with the account of Cain's enmity against Abel.

Understanding that some people were regenerated from the very beginning of redemptive history makes it much easier to interpret the Old Testament (which, after all, is four-fifths of our Bible). Now we can understand how Enoch (Gen. 5:22) and Noah (6:9) could walk with God and how Abraham could be God's friend (2 Chron. 20:7): they were indwelt by the Holy Spirit, born again, regenerated. To deny that these Old Testament saints were born again, one would have to hold the incredible position that Enoch and Noah walked with God and Abraham was God's friend, even though they were hostile to him.

But the biggest objection to saying that Old Testament saints were born again comes from John 7:39, "Up to that time the Holy Spirit [was not yet], since Jesus had not yet been glorified." Many have concluded from this verse that no one was indwelt by the Holy Spirit and regenerated until after Christ came. But since there is so much evidence in the Old Testament to the contrary, we understand John's "not yet" to refer to a time when the Holy Spirit, who had been at work in people's hearts from Adam onward, was to have the additional function of glorifying Jesus. Thus his coming at Pentecost would mark his official, ceremonial, and explicit coming in order to glorify Christ, whose death on the cross and resurrection had made it possible all along for totally depraved people to find mercy with God and receive new hearts. God delayed this explicit, official coming of the Holy Spirit until just after Christ's finished work so that it would be unmistakably clear to everyone that God could be benevolent and merciful to his enemies only because of the reconciliation between God and humankind that Christ accomplished. Accordingly in his sermon at Pentecost Peter said, "Exalted to the right hand of God, [Jesus] has received from the Father the promised Holy Spirit and has poured out [the evident demonstration of the fulfillment of Joel 2:28–29] you now see and hear" (Acts 2:33).

Ever since sin entered the world through the Fall, the Holy Spirit had been performing the same work of regeneration in people's hearts that he performed after Pentecost. Even before Jesus' incarnation God could give totally depraved people his Holy Spirit without profaning his glory, because 1 Peter 1:20 speaks of Jesus as being "chosen before the creation of the world" to shed his blood for the remission of sins. Revelation 13:8 also speaks of the "Lamb that was slain from [before] the creation of the world." In view of this great future event, God could then regenerate Abel, Noah, Moses, Caleb, Joshua, and others before it took place and yet remain completely glorious.

The Descendants of Cain and Seth

Cain's Descendants

Soon after Cain buried Abel out in the countryside, God said to him, "What have you done? Listen! Your brother's blood cries out to me from the ground. Now you are under a curse and driven from the ground. . . . When you work the ground, it will no longer yield its crops for you. You will be a restless wanderer on the earth" (Gen. 4:10–12). This was not an unjust punishment, yet Cain had the audacity to complain to God: "My punishment is more than I can bear. . . . And whoever finds me will kill me" (vv. 13–14). What troubled him most about this decree was that in henceforth having to keep on the move, sooner or later he would meet up with someone who would want to avenge Abel's murder. Therefore in order to maintain the serpent's seed—for a reason that will be clearer as redemptive history unfolds—God modified his decree and took steps to protect Cain. To deter a possible avenger God put a mark on him signifying that "if anyone kills Cain, he will suffer vengeance seven times over" (v. 15).

Genesis 4:16–18 then relates how Cain left God's presence and now, not having to become a wanderer, settled in the land of Nod, east of Eden. There he married and had a son whom he named Enoch.[4] Then he and his descendants proceeded to live in a way that accorded with the declaration of independence that the serpent had urged upon Adam and Eve at the Fall.

First they built a city, a promising way for Cain to gain the self-sufficiency that he had stubbornly clung to rather than yield to God's entreaty to become like his little child. A city gathered together many people with a wide diversity of valued skills, and as each benefited from the others' abilities, they all enjoyed a much higher standard of living and felt less need to depend on God.

Another serpentlike act that Cain performed was to name the city after his son (Gen. 4:17). If this city could survive for many generations without being destroyed by pestilence, fire, earthquake, flood, or war, then people would long

remember Cain as the father of the son whose name the city
bore. In this way, then, he could retain something of
permanence, despite the death that would eventually remove him from the earth.

Five generations after Cain, Lamech became the ruler of
that city. His life too was characterized by serpentlike
behavior. Not content with one wife, he married another
woman and thereby became a polygamist (Gen. 4:19). This
desire for two wives, rather than taking the single spouse
ordained by God (2:23–24), indicates a failure to find the
contentment Adam had found, first in fellowship with God,
and then in being able to share that fellowship with a
"suitable helper" for him (v. 20). In marrying a second wife,
Lamech was trying to fill the still-empty place that God
should have occupied in his heart as one made in his image.
According to God's plan a spouse made it possible to double
the joy one shared with God. But Lamech saw no future in
seeking joy in God. Rather, not finding full satisfaction in
one wife, he hoped to achieve it by acquiring a second. Thus
he regarded his wives not as ends, with whom to share his
joy in God, but as means to satisfy his need-love. He thus
had to subjugate them to the role of servicing him, a role that
only the infinite God can fulfill.

Lamech's city did indeed bring together those possessing
useful and enjoyable skills (Gen. 4:20–22). Of his offspring,
Jabal was skilled in animal husbandry; Tubal-Cain was
skilled in metallurgy. And Jubal, enjoying the higher living
standard and leisure time made possible by a city's concentration of many separate skills, could devote himself to
music. Delighting in the glory made possible by this power
to control so many things to subserve his needs and those of
others, Lamech then ordered his wives to listen to a song
extolling his glory—getting praise from others helps one
forget the harsh truth that creatures depending on themselves can never become self-sufficient like God and have
anything like his joy and rest. As the lyrics of this song
indicate (vv. 23–24), whereas Cain was able to found a city
because those hurting him would be avenged sevenfold,
Lamech now enjoyed so much power and honor that he
decreed, without divine authorization, far greater retribu-

tion. A person who merely injured him was to be killed, and Lamech's palace guard had standing instructions to punish anyone plotting his death by executing seventy-seven people—a fitting climax to the behavior profile of the serpent's seed.

Seth's Descendants

Next the author turns the readers' attention to the people who compose the woman's seed. The birth of Seth (Gen. 4:25) resumes the seed of the woman temporarily discontinued by Abel's murder. This progression is evident at the birth of Seth's son, Enosh, for the author states that now "men began to call on the name of the Lord" (v. 26). Thus through Seth's leadership a community was formed to strengthen the purpose of its members, through regular, organized public worship, to continue to satisfy their need-love in God and then in turn to love others. Further evidence that these people are to be regarded as the woman's seed is that in introducing Seth's birth, the author recalls how God made man in his likeness (5:1). Then in recounting Seth's actual birth, the author stresses that Adam "had a son in his own likeness, in his own image; and he named him Seth" (v. 3).

Seth's genealogy is then set forth (Gen. 5:4–32), sharply contrasting with Cain's in that the seventh-generation Enoch "walked with God." This description means that he so purposed to share in God's own joy that they had the full fellowship that results when two are fully taken up with the same goal. He fit in so well with God's purpose in creating people made in his image that God permitted him to bypass death so that he could have even closer fellowship with him, and that forever (v. 24). Enoch's deep intention and the profile of his behavior was obviously very different from those belonging to the seed of the serpent.

Likewise, the fact that Enoch's grandson Lamech (same name as in Gen. 4:19–24 but a different person) looked forward expectantly to what God would do with his son, Noah, in finally delivering the earth from the curse (5:29) indicates that his hope for the future was banked not on humankind's abilities but on what God would do. Thus he too fit the profile of the woman's seed, as did his son Noah, who "walked with God" (6:9).

With the passage of time the numbers both of the Cainites and Sethites increased, and their contacts became more frequent. In light of the enmity that had existed between these two groups from the beginning, the question therefore arises as to how they got along with each other. The answer is found in Genesis 6, which implies that the evil of the Cainites overwhelmed and all but eradicated the godliness of the Sethites. To understand this development, we must attempt to interpret Genesis 6:1–4, a difficult passage.

The Cainites Against the Sethites

Genesis 6:5 speaks of "how great man's wickedness on the earth had become," and verse 11 declares that the "earth was corrupt in God's sight and was full of violence." But how did such violence come to dwell on the face of the earth? Here we need to identify the "sons of God" mentioned in Genesis 6:1–2: "When men began to increase in number on the face of the earth and daughters were born to them, the sons of God saw that the daughters of men were beautiful, and they married any of them they chose." Were these "sons of God" angelic beings, or were they the godly Sethites?

The following arguments have been advanced for understanding them as angels. First, the "men" in the term "daughters of men" (Gen. 6:2) must include all men, since the "men who increased in number" in verse 1 refers to all; therefore the "sons of God" who married the daughters of men must be a separate, nonhuman group, who would then be angels. Second, the ancient expositors of this passage understood "sons of God" to refer to angels rather than Sethites. Finally, the term "sons of God" refers more often in the Old Testament to angels than to godly people (Job 1:6 and 38:7, margin; Dan. 3:25; Pss. 29:1[?]; 89:6[?]).

The following arguments, however, support understanding the "sons of God" as male Sethites. First, there has been no mention of angels thus far in Genesis, whereas we have seen how the author in 5:1 and 3 stressed that Seth was in the likeness of God and Adam. Hence the original readers, who to this point had heard nothing of angels, would naturally use this emphasis to identify the "sons of God" as Sethites. Second, in a number of places in the Old Testament godly people are called God's sons or children (Ex. 4:22; Deut. 32:5; Ps. 73:15; Hos. 1:10), so that "sons of God" could be a designation for godly people. Third, only in the poetical books (e.g., Job 1:6) but nowhere in the historical books of the Old Testament (such as Genesis) are angels called sons of God. Fourth, the godly Sethites could thus be understood as the righteous part of the "men" of 6:1, who nevertheless chose wives from the "daughters of men" (v. 2) without being too concerned whether these attractive women had Cainite or Sethite backgrounds. Hence Sethite-Cainite marriages were frequent. Possibly the Sethite men entertained the unlikely hope that their Cainite wives-to-be would soon learn nonviolent Sethite ways and raise their children in this tradition. Fifth, understanding the "sons of God" as Sethites would then harmonize with Jesus' teaching that the angels do not marry (Matt. 22:30). Finally, God's threatened punitive action in verse 3 in saying, "My Spirit will not contend with man forever," would be just if Sethite males were so naive as to think they could quickly teach Sethite ways to wives who had been immersed in violent Cainite ways from earliest childhood. But this punishment is manifestly unjust if imposed because women were overpowered by superhuman angels.

This line of Berean reasoning leads to the conclusion that the "sons of God" were the Sethites, because the arguments supporting this meaning are superior, and none of those opposing it are insurmountable. Then too, if the "sons of God" are Sethites, the whole narrative from 3:15 to the Flood in chapter 7 attains coherency, for it gives a believable account of how godly behavior vanished except for the family of Noah.

NOTE. A wise interpretational policy is always to assume an author is coherent, concluding otherwise only when the pertinent literary-historical data make incoherency the higher probability. Interpreters who assume coherency until proven wrong will get through to the intended meanings of authors more often than one who quickly concludes that strange language implies that authors have allowed something alien to their purpose to appear in their writing. The interpretation of texts, especially ancient ones, inevitably involves encountering wordings and concepts alien to our ways of thinking. So we must be willing to give sufficient time and energy to understand the sometimes strange statements found in texts. The interpreter ought to take the advice of a Mr. Hazelfoot, a teacher of the late British historian Arnold Toynbee, "to take it for granted a passage of Greek or Latin must make sense, so that to recognize that, so long as it did not seem to make sense, one had certainly not yet got on the right track."[5] Other minds, shaped by historical circumstances different from our own, are going to talk about things in ways quite different from our ways of speaking. Therefore we need to exercise our imagination to see if sense cannot be made out of things that, at first sight, seem ambiguous.

Counting "sons of God" as Sethites also yields a coherent understanding of the Nephilim spoken of in Genesis 6:4. According to this verse a group of men with this name were on the earth before the Sethites ("the sons of God") began to marry the "daughters of men," some of whom, at least, were women of Cainite descent. A people bearing the same name appear later in the disheartening report of the ten unbelieving spies: "The land we explored devours those living in it. All the people we saw there are of great size. We saw the Nephilim there. . . . We seemed like grasshoppers in our own eyes, and we looked the same to them" (Num. 13:32–33). Their name closely resembles the Hebrew verb for "fall" or "fall upon," and therefore it is natural to surmise that they acquired this name from their reputation for plundering peaceful people during sudden and violent raids.

It is also logical that people with the same name back in Genesis 6:4 would be the Lamech-types who threatened seventy-seven-fold vengeance on any who considered doing them harm (4:23–24). Perhaps the reputation that these Cainite descendants had earned made it expedient for the sons in Sethite families to try to protect themselves by making marriage alliances. But Genesis 6:4 implies that the children of these marriages had the qualities of their Cainite mothers and grandfathers: "The Nephilim [Cainites] were on the earth in those days—and also afterward—when the sons of God [Sethite men] went to the daughters of men [Cainites] and had children by [the Cainite women]. They [the offspring] were the heroes of old, [violent Cainite] men of renown."

These mixed marriages therefore greatly increased the number of Cainite-types in the earth at the expense of the godly Sethites. Such a conclusion would then explain Genesis 6:11–14: "Now the earth was corrupt in God's sight and was full of violence. God saw how corrupt the earth had become, for all the people on earth had corrupted their ways. So God said to Noah, 'I am going to put an end to all people, for the earth is filled with violence because of them. I am surely going to destroy both them and the earth. So [Noah] make yourself an ark.'"

Proceeding by the methods of inductive Bible study, we note how opposite this filling of the earth with violence was from God's purpose in creating it. He had intended to fill the earth with his glory by having people made in his image "fill" the earth and by having them rule over the fishes, birds, and animals so that the earth would fully reflect his glory and goodness. But the children resulting from the intermarriage of Sethite men and Cainite women learned violent Cainite ways, since mothers normally have more contact with their children than do fathers. As a result the violent Cainites soon far outnumbered the Sethites.

But since God expends all his energy in delighting in his glory, he could not be indifferent to this virtual overwhelming of the earth with violence. Thus the author emphasizes God's displeasure: "The Lord was grieved that he had made man on the earth, and his heart was filled with pain. So the Lord said, 'I will wipe mankind, whom I have created, from the face of the earth . . . for I am grieved I have made them.' But Noah [and his family] found favor in the eyes of the Lord" (Gen. 6:6–8).

NOTE. The Hebrew word for "grieve" in Genesis 6:6 is *nāḥam,* and its use here and elsewhere creates some difficulty in understanding how God, who foreordains all things and thus knows what will happen, can ever "grieve" or "mourn"over what he has done. A consideration of three other passages in the Old Testament that speak of this phenomenon is helpful in grasping how the God who "works out everything in conformity with the purpose of his will" (Eph. 1:11) is yet repelled by the evil that comes to pass. (In each case, the English translation that corresponds to Hebrew *nāḥam* appears in italics.) In Numbers 23:19 Balaam, the diviner, said, "God is not a man, that he should lie, nor a son of man, that he should *change his mind.* Does he speak and then not act? Does he promise and not fulfill?" This was Balaam's answer to Balak, the king of Moab, who wanted Balaam to curse Israel so it would be unable to conquer Moab. But Balaam replied that God would not "repent of" or "go back on" his promise to Abraham that he would bless his descendants and give them the Promised Land.

A similar passage is 1 Samuel 15:29, where Samuel told Saul that God would not *change his mind* in rejecting him as king over Israel. But then the writer says, "The Lord was *grieved* that he had made Saul king over Israel" (v. 35), and as a result God made David king instead. So in Numbers 23:19 and 1 Samuel 15:29 this word indicates that God's ultimate purpose remains unchanged. But in 1 Samuel 15:35 it is used to convey the idea that God was so repelled at Saul's wicked ways that he appointed David to replace him. The Hebrew word in Genesis 6:6 is used in the same way, to represent God's revulsion at the violence that had filled the earth and his resulting purpose to destroy it with the Flood. But despite this "grieving," or "repenting" as some versions have it, in neither case did God's purpose change. He went ahead with the steps necessary to fill the earth with his glory by saving Noah and his family from the flood that destroyed all the violent Cainites. And though God grieved that he had made Saul king, he proceeded with his purpose to keep the kingship alive in Israel by appointing David king in Saul's place.

These references to God's grieving thus help us readers understand how distressed God becomes over evil, but the use of this same word in Numbers 23:19 and 1 Samuel 15:29 shows that, despite his vexation over evil, God does not change his mind but continues on with his original purpose unaltered. It is comforting to know that the God who so hates evil nevertheless retains control of all things so that his purpose is carried out.

Because Noah was "a righteous man, blameless among the people of his time, and he walked with God" (Gen. 6:9), he was ordered to build an ark large enough to accommodate both his family and a pair of each of the animals God had created (vv. 14–21). Then just before the flood commenced, Noah's righteousness is stressed again: "Go into the ark, you and your whole family, because I have found you righteous in this generation" (7:1). And the chronology in Genesis 5 confirms that Noah was a Sethite. So in God's sparing righteous Noah, the sole remaining seed of the woman, while destroying all the Cainites, we see the first act designed to carry out his promise in Genesis 3:15.

Review Questions

1. What are the steps of the argument leading to the conclusion that the woman's seed is the regenerated people of God and that the serpent's seed is the unregenerate?

2. What is the ultimate explanation for the enmity between Cain and Abel?

3. What evidence is there that from Abel onward, people like him were regenerated?

4. How is one to handle the objection based on John 7:39 that people were not regenerated until after Pentecost?

5. What indications can you cite that Cain's posterity were serpentlike in their behavior?

6. What are the arguments for saying that Seth and his descendants were the seed of the woman?

7. Why did Sethite men's marrying Cainite women fill the earth with violence?

8. What point are biblical writers making when they speak of God's being grieved that he has done something, and yet carries on with a somewhat modified version of his plan?

NOTES

[1] In the Hebrew the subject of the verb "shall crush" in this third clause is a masculine pronoun meaning "he" or (if the referent is not a person) "it." The pronoun refers to the nearest preceding masculine substantive, which is "[the woman's] *seed*" at the end of the second clause. (I use the NIV's marginal reading "seed" both here and later in talking about "Abraham's seed" [see chap. 20 below] because it has the elasticity required to represent the special meaning these two terms come to have in biblical theology.) Many translations in fact use "he" for the pronoun because later revelation sees Jesus Christ as destroying Satan, who was animating the serpent ("that ancient serpent called the devil" [Rev. 12:9; 20:2]; "the God of peace will soon crush Satan under your feet" [Rom. 16:20]; "the Son of God appeared . . . to destroy the devil's work" [1 John 3:8]). The pronoun should be translated "it," however, since it refers to the just-mentioned woman's seed understood in a collective sense, the natural meaning that would have occurred to the first readers of Genesis.

[2] See note 3 in chapter 13 above.

[3] God's leaving Cain in an unregenerate state was not a final goal, which would mean that he loved the evil of Cain's behavior. Rather, he did it for an ultimate good—that of providing a context of wickedness in earth's pre-flood popoulation so that his grace in saving Noah and his family from his wrath against Cainite behavior might stand out more prominently. To make it clear that this love of the good is uppermost in God's mind even in not regenerating Cain, God remonstrated with him for his refusal to worship. In setting forth all the reasons why he should worship, he also increased Cain's guilt for his unreasonable behavior.

[4] Where did Cain get his wife? Although the author paid no special attention to Adam's daughters, they nonetheless existed (Gen. 5:4); Cain no doubt married one of them.

[5] A. J. Toynbee, "How and Why I Work," *Saturday Review*, April 5, 1969, 22.

16

Protection for
the Woman's Seed

When the flood waters subsided, the first thing Noah did upon leaving the ark was to build an altar and worship God (Gen. 8:20). God delighted so much in Noah's worshiping him for his mercy that he made a covenant with Noah and Noah's posterity: never again would he bring such destruction upon the earth, even though Noah's descendants, until regeneration, would be totally depraved. This meaning is made clear in that the preflood statement regarding the evil of humankind's heart (6:5) is repeated after the Flood as well (8:21). So the enmity between the two seeds would continue throughout redemptive history, until God's plan for the world was realized in the final triumph of the woman's seed over the serpent. Now, however, God introduced changes in society that would deter the serpent and his seed from ever again threatening to overwhelm that of the woman. Genesis 8:13–9:19 describes the first deterrent.

The Institution of the Noachic Covenant

The terms of the Noachic covenant are found in Genesis 8:21–9:17; it is concerned to a great extent with God's promise never again to destroy the earth as he had in the great flood. But now the provision is also made for a central authority, government officials with the right to punish wrongdoing, even to the extent of executing those guilty of murder: "Whoever sheds the blood of man, by man shall his

blood be shed; for in the image of God has God made man"
(9:6). To be sure, there would be unregenerate serpent-types
among Noah's posterity, but such would be deterred from
violent acts by knowing that duly authorized governmental
officials now had the power of the sword to punish their
wrongdoing. Thus never again would Cainite-minded people be able to overwhelm the godly.

What a blessing to the seed of the woman was this
authorization of government to punish evildoers! No longer
would these people, in order to have some hope of safety,
have to resort to the desperate measure of making marriage
alliances with serpent-types at the cost of having offspring
who would copy their violent lifestyle. The power of the
sword in the hand of government officials would now
provide considerable protection for the seed of the woman.

To be sure, there have been many instances in history
where the power of the sword in a nation has been abused to
suppress one religion in favor of another, and the seed of the
woman has been virtually annihilated in such situations.
One such example is the persecution of French Protestants
during the counter-Reformation of the sixteenth century; its
most terrible episode was St. Bartholomew's massacre, when
during the night of August 24–25, 1572, thirty thousand
Protestants in Paris were murdered. Consequently churches
in each nation should take seriously the command in
1 Timothy 2:1–2 to make prayer for those in authority the
first order of business at each worship service: "I urge, then,
first of all, that requests, prayers, intercessions and thanksgiving be made for everyone—for kings and all those in
authority, that we may live peaceful and quiet lives in all
godliness and holiness." Hence as governments continue to
punish the evil and thus protect the good (Rom. 13:1–7), the
people of God can live in a context where they may flourish.

Along with this new protection given to the people of God
is the repeated command of Genesis 1:28 to Noah's children:
"Be fruitful and increase in number and fill the earth" (9:1,
7). Thus we infer that God's purpose to fill the earth with the
knowledge of his glory (Hab. 2:14) remained unaltered.

The Fragmentizing of Humankind

A second deterrent was also needed in order to preserve the seed of the woman from destruction by the serpent and his seed. That protective step was the fragmentizing of humankind. Genesis 10 gives a table of the nations that stemmed from Noah's three sons, Shem, Ham, and Japheth, and "spread out over the earth after the flood" (v. 32). Verse 5 indicates the cause for this dispersion in remarking that Japheth's descendants through Javan "spread out into their territories by their clans within their nations, *each with its own language.*" But it is not until chapter 11:1–9 that details of this event—the confusion of languages at the Tower of Babel—are spelled out.

From analyzing the genealogy and chronology of Genesis 11:10–32, we may deduce that this fragmentizing of Noah's progeny into many nations took place during the life of Peleg, Shem's great-grandson, who was born 110 years after the Flood. So the many nations listed in chapter 10 resulted from the confusion of tongues at the Tower of Babel some 150 years after the Flood.

Those having developed the instincts of inductive Bible study will ask why the Genesis author chose to break chronology by first listing the many nations throughout the earth, separated by language barriers (chap. 10), and then recounting the situation that made it necessary for God to bring this about (11:1–9). A plausible answer is that this arrangement emphasized the importance of God's command for people to fill the earth. Thus the author put 9:18–10:32, climaxing with its emphasis on many nations spreading out over the earth, right after the Noachic covenant. Had he followed chronology and, after recounting the Flood, told how for a century and a half Noah's descendants congregated at just one spot instead of filling the earth, he would have weakened the significance of God's command. But by locating chapter 10 with its table of the now-dispersed nations right after the end of the Flood, the author effectively emphasized the importance of this command. Then without detracting from it in any way, he could recount how Noah's posterity, through the confusion of languages at the Tower of

Babel, became nations that were dispersed through the earth.

Thus we read in Genesis 11:1–9 how Noah's progeny rebelled against God's command to fill the earth. Instead they gathered at a single location, saying, "Come, let us build ourselves a city, with a tower that reaches to the heavens, so that we may make a name for ourselves and not be scattered over the face of the whole earth" (v. 4). This gathering of people into a city, whose greatness was to be represented by a tower, echoed the proud aspirations of the serpent's seed to exalt themselves by showing how much progress they could make on their own in overcoming finitude, needing no help from God. Consequently the Lord said, "Come, let us go down and confuse their language so they will not understand each other." The Lord then "scattered them from there over all the earth, and they stopped building the city. That is why it was called Babel— because there the Lord confused the language of the whole world. From there the Lord scattered them over the face of the whole earth" (vv. 7–9).

This second check on the powers of evil was crucial to the survival and eventual triumph of the seed of the woman. By itself the power of the sword was a mixed blessing. While it deterred wicked people from acts of violence, it also made it possible to organize and maintain a supersociety under one government. So something more was needed to counteract humankind's inbred tendency to be serpent-types independent of God. For as we have seen, these descendants of Noah had rebelled against God's command to fill the earth, choosing instead to remain congregated together in order to increase their security (Gen. 11:4).

Thus evil could still have triumphed over the woman's seed. In a supersociety held together by the sanction of the power of the sword, people with various skills could organize to provide for themselves a standard of living that could delude them into thinking they could meet all their needs, and therefore they could declare themselves independent of God. Thus people like Seth who called upon the name of the Lord (Gen. 4:26) would be completely out of step with such a demonic supersociety; they would be pressured from every side not to look to God for contentment but to contribute to the exaltation of humankind's attainment of self-sufficiency. Those who refused to join in this anti-God purpose would obviously be hated by the serpent-types, who could then use the power of the sword to eradicate them.

So in order to make it possible for the woman's seed to survive and multiply in a world filled with many unregenerated people, God fragmentized this potential supersociety into the many nations listed in Genesis 10. With a maze of language barriers now existing, the people of each language group were forced to move away from the Tower of Babel to find separate places to live. Many people in these now-separated nations would still want to become great by depending on themselves rather than God. But if one nation tried to capitalize on this inclination by gaining control of other nations, those in these nations with similar desires would resist strenuously. Thus no one nation could create an empire that would last for very long.

This second deterrent after the Flood therefore established societies in which each one's demonic tendencies would, generally speaking, be held in check by similar tendencies in neighboring nations. And with these evil inclinations under control, the people of God would be able to call upon him without arousing the fierce resistance to such dependence that would characterize a single supersociety. So by giving humankind the power of the sword and by fragmentizing them into nations, God made it possible for the seed of the women to increase in a world where they were surrounded by serpent-types.

But since even in this tolerable context demonic power from time to time finds ways to persecute the seed of the woman, the people of God have suffered martyrdom from Old Testament times up to the present. And this fact accords with the statement in Genesis 3:15 that the serpent will succeed in giving the people of God a wound in the heel, hurtful but not lethal. A good example is the Roman empire, an anti-God supersociety in that it required its subjects to regard the emperor as the supreme lord of all. But when the Jewish people refused to comply, no matter how viciously they were persecuted, Rome relented and affirmed Judaism as a "legal religion" *(religio licita)*. This concession later provided the door by which Paul was able to move Christianity out from Judaism into the Gentile world, by rightly affirming that Christianity as the natural extension of Judaism was also a *religiolicita*. As Christians became more and more numerous, however, Rome again felt threatened, and persecutions continued to break out periodically until finally the Edict of Constantine in A.D. 313 made Christianity the official religion of the Roman empire.

This development did not, however, end the persecution of the woman's seed, for history is filled with such reports. And the Bible predicts that a time will come, just before Christ's return, when the opposition of the serpent's seed will reach epic proportions in the evil Antichrist, who will reign over the whole earth (Dan. 7:23; 8:24–25; 11:36; 2 Thess. 2:3–12; Rev. 13). Even today we see how language barriers are progressively falling, for English is rapidly becoming the trade language of our global village. Such a common language, along with the tremendous power of mass communications, where through satellites and television everyone on earth can see and hear a single individual, will make possible the rise of the Antichrist. Appearing on the scene during the great tribulation (Matt. 24:21, 29; Dan. 12:1), he will make it impossible for anyone to buy or sell without having received his mark as a sign of willingness to worship him (Rev. 13:12, 16–17; 14:9)—no longer an impossibility in this day of laser identifiers, data processing, information banks, and computer networks. The Antichrist's purpose will be to destroy the seed of the woman (Rev. 12:17), and that may well be the reason why Jesus said that during his reign there would be days of such great tribulation that unless they were shortened, not even the elect could be saved (Matt. 24:21–22). In 2 Thessalonians 2:7 we read that the Antichrist is being restrained now, and it is plausible to regard this restraining force as the language barriers God set up at the Tower of Babel.

So as a result of the confusion of languages at the Tower of Babel, nations have been dispersed throughout the world. This fact, along with the power of the sword, has made it possible for the people of God to survive and for God, through them, to begin to fill the earth with his glory.

Review Questions

1. Explain why what God did in the Noachic covenant made it impossible for violence to fill the earth again.
2. Why should praying for earthly rulers be the first order of business in a Christian gathering?
3. How was the Genesis author helped in realizing his purpose by listing the nations spread throughout the earth *before* telling of the Tower of Babel incident that caused their spread?
4. What repetition occurs in Genesis 9–11 that picks up on an earlier emphasis and indicates what the Genesis author's purpose is?
5. Explain why God's work at the Tower of Babel was every bit as important for preserving the seed of the woman as was the Noachic covenant?

PART 3

ISRAEL, THE LESSON
BOOK FOR THE NATIONS

17

The Forgiveness
of Abraham's Sins

In part 2 we explored the foundational themes of redemptive history as taught or intimated in Genesis 1–11. Here in part 3 we consider God's next step toward fulfilling his great purpose—his call of Abraham to found a new nation. According to the genealogy in 11:10–26, Abraham was the son of Terah, a descendant of Shem, the first of Noah's three sons. Abraham was born in Chaldea, one of the nations separated by the language barriers erected four generations before his birth. While living in the city of Ur, his father, Terah, had thought of moving from that land to Canaan but settled instead in Haran, another Chaldaic city, where he died. God then commanded Abraham to leave Chaldea for a land he would show him: "Leave your country, your people and your father's household and go to the land I will show you. I will make you into a great nation and I will bless you; I will make your name great,[1] and you will be a blessing. I will bless those who bless you, and whoever curses you I will curse; and all peoples of the earth will be blessed through you" (12:1–3).

In line with the great redemptive promise of Genesis 3:15, this is a first, partial listing of the blessings of God's covenant of mercy, a covenant doubly sure because it was based not only upon his promise but also upon an oath. God repeated this promise with an oath in Genesis 22:16–18, which Hebrews 6:18 comments upon by saying, "God did this so that, by two unchangeable things in which it is impossible

for God to lie, we who have fled to take hold of the hope
offered to us may be greatly encouraged." It should be noted
that this covenant is not unconditional. In order to receive
the blessings promised in verses 2 and 3, Abraham had to
obey the commands of verse 1 to leave his homeland and
settle in a foreign land. But these actions were not works in
the sense of being services rendered to God. Rather, they
were evidences of the "obedience that comes from faith," an
obedience motivated by Abraham's confidence that what
God had promised, he would do. And in such obedience God
receives all the glory.[2]

In order to enjoy these immense blessings, Abraham
obeyed God and moved his family out from Haran and the
Chaldean nation to go toward the land of Canaan. God did
not tell him just where he was to settle, but he must have
designated the direction for him to take, because Genesis
12:5 says that "they set out for the land of Canaan." Abraham
would thus have followed the Fertile Crescent, extending
northwestward from Haran and then around southwestward.
When they reached their destination, God promised Abraham, "To your offspring I will give this land," even though
the Canaanites were then occupying it (vv. 6–7).

Here we should pause and note what a remarkable step
this was for God to take in carrying out his plan for the world.
One might think that after dividing the descendants of Noah
into the many nations of Genesis 10, God would then
inaugurate the "great commission" (cf. Matt. 28:18–20),
sending preachers into each of these nations urging all
people to become like the woman's seed instead of the
serpent's, or words to that effect. In this way the fatal blow
against the serpent, predicted in Genesis 3:15, could soon be
delivered. But instead, surprisingly, God took just one family
out of Chaldea and guided it into the land occupied by the
Canaanite nation. Later this family would become a new
nation occupying that land, and in some way it would then
be the means by which all other nations would eventually be
blessed.[3]

God's dealings with Abraham become even more remarkable when we observe that throughout the Old Testament
and up to the time of Christ—about two thousand years—he

is concerned almost exclusively with Israel, the nation comprising Abraham's descendants through his grandson, Jacob. As for the rest of the nations during this time, God "let all [of them] go their own way" (Acts 14:16; cf. 17:30). Then when Jesus came, as recorded in the four Gospels, he commanded his small number of Jewish disciples to go to every people-group in the world and teach them so they also could enjoy the universal blessings of the covenant God had made with Abraham.[4] The rest of the New Testament then tells how the good news of the covenant of mercy, the gospel, was freed from the cultural bonds of the Israelite nation so it could be readily received by the many people-groups throughout the earth, without their having to undergo unnecessary cultural changes—an important matter when one considers the great diversity of customs to be found in the various ethnic groups of earth.

But why the two-thousand-year delay in implementing this plan? In the following chapters we will seek to show the Bible's own reason for this surprising action, and why it was better for God during this period to deal almost exclusively with the Jewish people than to have the gospel go out immediately to all the nations separated at the Tower of Babel. Something of the same problem is evident earlier, too, for the question arises as to why God did not, immediately after the Fall, give people the power of the sword and institute human government. Then wrongdoers would have been punished by duly-constituted authorities, and violence would not have so filled the earth that God had to destroy all but Noah's family in order to keep the seed of the woman alive. Geerhardus Vos (1862–1949), a revered student of Scripture, answers this earlier question as follows:

> Had God permitted grace freely to flow out into the world and to gather great strength within a short period, then the true nature and consequences of sin would have been very imperfectly disclosed. Man would have ascribed to his own relative goodness what was in reality a product of the grace of God. Hence, before the work of redemption is further carried out, the downward tendency of sin is clearly illustrated [by the Flood] in order that subsequently in the light of this

downgrade movement the true divine cause of *the upward course of redemption might be appreciated.*[5]

Before we can decide whether or not this answer is in keeping with the Bible's own explanation, we must consider further biblical data, as must also be done before we can explain the two-millennia delay. But for now we turn our attention to the event that is so foundational for the remainder of redemptive history, namely, the calling out of Abraham to found the Jewish nation, whose history provides the baseline along which God brings to pass the crucial steps in completing his plan for the world.

To understand Abraham's importance for subsequent redemptive history, we begin with the way he received the forgiveness of sins. This is an appropriate starting place because Genesis 15:6 ("[Abraham] believed the Lord, and he credited [his faith] to him as righteousness"), the one explicit mention of his forgiveness, is referred to four times in the New Testament (Rom. 4:3, 23; Gal. 3:6; James 2:23). Abraham's forgiveness received such emphasis because it was the basis for all the other blessings God promised and gave to him.

The New Testament makes it abundantly clear that by imitating Abraham's faith, others too enjoy the blessings that come to those who are forgiven. Thus Paul reminded the erring Galatians that all the benefits they had enjoyed so far had come simply through believing God. Then he enforced this point by saying, "Consider Abraham: 'He believed God, and it was credited to him as righteousness'" (Gal. 3:5–6). And to the church at Rome he wrote, "Therefore, the promise comes by faith, so that it may be by grace and may be guaranteed to all Abraham's offspring. . . . He is the father of us all. As it is written, 'I have made you a father of many nations' [Gen. 17:5]. He is our father in the sight of God, in whom he believed—the God who gives life to the dead and calls things that are not as though they were" (Rom. 4:16–17).

In this chapter we thus consider the nature of Abraham's forgiveness, and then in chapters 18 and 19 we examine the essentials of this faith that brings both forgiveness and God's blessings. Chapter 20 then investigates the identity of the "offspring" or "seed" of Abraham who come from all the nations and are to enjoy the blessings of Genesis 12:3.

Abraham's Forgiveness According to Genesis 15:6

Abraham came from a family of idolaters: "This is what the Lord, the God of Israel, says: 'Long ago your forefathers, including Terah the father of Abraham and Nahor, lived beyond the River and worshiped other gods'" (Josh. 24:2). But Abraham turned from idols to serve the living God when he obeyed the call to leave Chaldea and become an exile in the Canaanites' land. Nevertheless as Genesis 12–22 make clear, he did not become sinlessly perfect upon responding to this call, for from time to time he lapsed into great sins, the most notable of which were his twice selling his wife into a harem (12:11–15; 20:2).

Yet Abraham was forgiven, credited as righteous. On the occasion when this declaration was made, "[God] took [Abraham] outside [his tent] and said, 'Look up at the heavens and count the stars—if indeed you can count them.' Then he said to him, 'So [numerous] shall your offspring be'" (Gen. 15:5). Then comes the declaration of forgiveness in verse 6.

Paul's Interpretation of Genesis 15:6

Paul interprets this verse for us in Romans 4. "For what does the scripture say? 'Abraham believed God, and it was credited to him as righteousness.' Now when a man works, his wages are not credited as a gift but as an obligation. However, to the man [like Abraham] who does not work but trusts God who justifies the wicked, his faith is credited as righteousness" (vv. 3–5).

Verse 4 alludes to a common Jewish interpretation of verse 3, which Paul explicitly rejected. According to that view Abraham's being accounted righteous, or forgiven, came as a wage that God as an employer paid to him the worker, in compensation for needful service rendered. But in verse 5 Paul gave what he regarded as the correct interpretation: far from being an employee earning wages from God, Abraham did not work but trusted God to work for him in forgiving all his ungodliness. When Paul spoke here of God's justifying the wicked, he implied that Abraham was forgiven both for all his past sins and also for present evil tendencies that would produce future sins. Or to say it positively, God credited him as righteous while he was still sinful so that God could proceed with the work of imparting the great blessings he had promised to Abraham and his "seed" (Gen. 12:2–3). The condition Abraham met in order to be forgiven and thus be blessed was simply to believe the promise that his posterity would constitute a large nation that would be protected by God and eventually impart its divine blessings to all other nations.

Romans 4:6–8 leaves no doubt about the meaning Paul gave to the word "credited" as he quoted Genesis 15:6: "David says the same thing when he speaks of the blessedness of the man to whom God credits righteousness apart from works: 'Blessed are they whose iniquities are forgiven, whose sins are covered. Blessed is the man whose sin the Lord will never count against him' [Ps. 32:1–2]." By citing these verses, Paul emphasized that Abraham was forgiven, despite his still falling far short of sinlessness. This interpretation, however, is quite opposite from the Jewish view of Genesis 15:6 as represented in verse 4.

A Common Jewish Interpretation of Genesis 15:6

We know a Jewish understanding of this verse from various noncanonical Jewish writings written before, during, and even after Paul's day. These are (1) the Apocrypha and pseudepigrapha, books for the most part dated between 200 B.C. and A.D. 200;[6] (2) the Mishnah, the codification of oral tradition, first put into writing soon after A.D. 200; (3) expositions and applications of the Mishnah called Midrashim, and (4) commentaries on the Old Testament called Gemara. The Mishnah and Gemara together compose the Talmud, which is an immense body of literature. As groups of Jews were scattered to many countries after the destruction of Jerusalem in A.D. 70, they carried with them at least portions of the Talmud, which to the present day has enabled them to maintain their cultural distinctives.

These writings contain a number of references to the Jewish concept of faith in relation to works. Fourth Ezra, written in the first century A.D., declares, "And it shall be that everyone who will be saved, and will be able to escape on account of his works, *or* on account of the faith by which he has believed . . ." (9:7). Here there was nothing of the contrast between faith and works such as Paul drew in Romans 4:4–5. Likewise a midrash on Exodus 14:31, which speaks of the Israelites' believing God after their deliverance from Pharaoh's pursuing army, affirms, "So you find that our father Abraham became heir of this and of the coming world simply by *the merit of faith* with which he believed in the Lord, as it is written, 'He believed in the Lord, and He counted it to him for righteousness.'" Early in the twentieth century a German authority on rabbinic literature concluded that in this passage "faith was not the opposite of works [as in Rom. 4:4–5], but was itself a work, which could, when the occasion arose, be credited by God to man as a merit, just as fulfilling any other commandment. This was how the rabbis interpreted Genesis 15:6. . . . Abraham had exercised faith . . . and therefore God could count that act of faith as righteousness, that is, as a meritorious act."[7]

Reasons for Accepting Paul's Interpretation of Genesis 15:6

One fact a Berean interpreter will note in seeking to decide whether Paul's or the rabbis' interpretation of Genesis 15:6 is correct is that in reckoning faith as righteousness, God was doing something essential for solving a great problem facing Abraham. He had now been a nomad in Canaan for ten years (16:3), but as yet he and his wife Sarah had had no children. How, then, was he going to become the father of the great nation God had promised him? If in lieu of a son his heritage was to go to Eliezer, his chief servant (v. 2), then Eliezer's posterity, not Abraham's, would be the great nation God had promised.

But God encouraged Abraham by declaring, "[Eliezer]

will not be your heir, but a son coming from your own body will be your heir" (Gen. 15:4). God then led Abraham outside his tent, promising him that the descendants from his own son would be as numerous as the stars they could now see overhead. At this word Abraham's fears were finally laid to rest, for he *believed* God, "and [God] credited [his faith] to him as righteousness."

The problem that had been troubling Abraham was immense. And this factor points up a serious difficulty with the Jewish interpretation of Genesis 15:6, namely, that Abraham's faith was merely one more righteous act adding a tiny amount of merit to that already amassed by his many other good works. Something that in the Jewish view is so small is poorly suited to evoke the magnificent response of God in promising a child after so many years of barrenness. Such a recompense is far too great to be commensurate with just one act of faith.

But Genesis 15:6 affirms—contrary to the Jewish interpretation—that this one act of faith counted for far more than what one bit of merit could do for an already illustriously righteous man. Abraham's faith that night played a vital role in completely changing his status from that of a sinner to one credited as a righteous person before God. In receiving such forgiveness from God, something sufficiently important had transpired to provide the answer to Abraham's problem of childlessness. This is Paul's emphasis in Romans 4:5, where he speaks of how Abraham's faith justified him, even though he was a wicked person. In this act God cleared away all his anger against Abraham for his sins, so that without profaning his glory, he could now fully bless Abraham and thus employ his creative power to fulfill the promises enunciated in Genesis 12:2–3. So Paul's interpretation that Abraham received the forgiveness of sins for his one act of faith answers adequately to the immense problem confronting him.

A second line of argument in favor of Paul is that Genesis, in recounting some of Abraham's sins, supports Paul's statement that Abraham was a wicked person (Rom. 4:5). This Jewish view of Abraham, to the contrary, tends to ignore his sins, despite their being specifically recounted in the Genesis narrative. Thus the pseudepigraphical *Jubilees*, written in the second century B.C., affirms that "Abraham was perfect in all of his actions with the Lord and was pleasing through righteousness all the days of his life" (23:10). Since some of God's promises to Abraham cite his descendants as likewise recipients, Judaism has thought that the more righteous Abraham was seen to be, the more secure would be their future blessings. Thus particularly comforting to them is God's response to Abraham's triumph over the ultimate test of obedience—being willing to sacrifice Isaac: "I swear by myself . . . because you [Abraham] have done this and have not withheld your son, your only son, I will surely bless you and . . . *your descendants* will take possession of the cities of their enemies" (Gen. 22:16–17).

But this failure to acknowledge Abraham's sinfulness argues against this Jewish interpretation of Genesis 15:6, for Genesis clearly portrays Abraham as a wicked man who needed forgiveness. First, he said that Sarah was his sister so that Pharaoh would not murder him in order to get Sarah into his harem (12:11–16). That this falsehood was in God's sight a great sin is evident both from the punishments he inflicted on the royal household and from Pharaoh's great fear in learning that Sarah was Abraham's wife. Another great sin was Abraham's attempt to have a son by Hagar, his wife's chief servant (16:1–16), for this was an act contrary to God's promise that he would have a son by Sarah (17:16). Abraham also sinned in telling Abimelech, the Canaanite king of Gerar, that Sarah was his sister (20:2); both God's message to Abimelech that he was as good as dead for taking Sarah (v. 3) and Abimelech's anger at Abraham (vv. 4–18) show how much Abraham's lie displeased God.

In recounting these sins, the author wanted to make it clear that Abraham was a fallible person. He learned to fear God only gradually over a span of twenty-five years (Gen. 22:12; cf. 12:4 and 21:5). This reference to Abraham's sins coheres with understanding the reckoning of righteousness in 15:6 as a forgiveness that gave him the status of a righteous man. Thus since God regarded the sinful Abraham as now forgiven, the way was clear to carry out his promises without profaning his holy name by greatly blessing one prone to rebel against him.[8] So we conclude that Paul's interpretation of Genesis 15:6 in Romans 4:3–5 is to be accepted rather than this Jewish one, based both on the demands of the immediate context, which addresses Abraham's immense problem, and on the demands of the larger context, which candidly details Abraham's sins.

A third support for Paul's interpretation is that he explicitly negates any idea of Abraham's being a patron performing useful services for God in order to be recompensed with wages. Genesis 15:1–6 makes it clear that God is the Patron, and Abraham the client. That Abraham has this understanding is evident in that he tells God of his urgent need to have a child by Sarah so that he could father the great nation promised him. Moreover God, in responding to Abraham, is behaving like a patron in promising to do something that is indispensable for the fulfillment of the promises of 12:2–3.

Indeed, any thought that the almighty and all-sufficient God could ever be the client of Abraham—or anyone else, for that matter—is appalling, for it implies that he would then be dependent on finite people to perform useful services for him. But nothing could be further from the truth, for God needs nothing from those he has created. Therefore contrary to this Jewish view of Abraham as the patron, Paul followed Genesis 15:1–6 in seeing Abraham as God's client: "To [Abraham] who does not work but trusts God who justifies the wicked, his faith is credited as righteousness" (Rom. 4:5). Thus like all clients, Abraham trusted God the Patron to use his resources and skills to meet his needs.

Life is full of instances demonstrating that for a client to receive the services of a patron, he or she must have complete assurance that the patron is abundantly qualified to impart a sought-after benefit. Physicians expect their patients to trust their expertise in handling health problems by following the regimen they prescribe. Thus if a patient persistently fails to follow it, before long the physician is apt to say, "I think you had better see some other physician, one whom you do trust. So do not bother to make any further appointments to see me."

Another example of the necessity for clients to trust patrons comes from the way Japan and other Asian nations have recently outproduced the United States. Management in America has too often regarded itself as superior and its employees inferior. But a moment's reflection makes clear that a company's management is completely dependent on its skilled employees in order to be successful and remain competitive with similar companies. For some strange reason, however, American management has often ignored this fact, maintaining instead an adversarial relationship with its employees, voting large salaries and perquisites for its executives but giving employees meager wages and fringe benefits. Therefore labor has had to organize itself into unions, resorting to costly and sometimes deadly strikes in order to force management to give it a fair recompense for its work. And it was inevitable that employees, receiving so little trust and honor from management, have frequently failed to perform their tasks well. It was no wonder, then, that customers gradually realized that Japanese automobiles, without costing more, were much better quality than many made in America.

Such developments have forced American management to take a hard look at itself. In studying the reasons why Americans preferred to buy Japanese cars, it soon became apparent that the Japanese managers' view of their work force differed markedly from that generally held by their American counterparts. The former did not vote themselves the much higher salaries that American management did, nor did they remain aloof from their workers. In fact they often ate with them in order to hear, firsthand, how certain procedures might be changed so that better cars could be built. American managers, on the other hand, frequently feeling vastly superior to those on the assembly line, would eat in a plush executive dining room on the top floor of their building. Japanese managers likewise encouraged their workers to submit suggestions as to how any step in constructing a car might be speeded up and done less expensively without sacrificing quality. Such an attitude demonstrated to the workers that management saw itself as their client and was therefore rendering them the greatest honor by trusting them as patrons. But Americans are just beginning to learn to trust their work force as patrons, and the automobile industry is struggling to regain its share of the market.

A confirmation of how ill-advised American management's attitude toward labor has been became evident recently when Japan built a Nissan factory in Tennessee; this plant was to employ American labor but to be managed by the Japanese. The United Auto Workers, the labor union that had organized the Ford and General Motors work forces and fought through many a bitter strike with both companies for more than half a century, tried to persuade the Nissan workers to join their union. But these workers had already felt themselves so honored and valued as patrons by Nissan's management that they voted overwhelmingly not to join.

Further light is cast on the dynamics of the management-labor relationship by the well-known author Studs Terkel, who in 1972 published a book entitled *Working*. It consisted of tape-recorded reports of some fifty people in various vocations as to what they liked and disliked about their jobs as patrons. Wages were surely an important consideration. But Terkel discovered that people seek a satisfaction from work that is far beyond what money can give. A supermarket checker, for example, said,

> The pay is terrific. I automatically get a raise because of the union. Retail Clerks. Right now I'm ready for retirement as far as the union goes. I have enough years. I'm as high up as I can go. I make $189 gross pay [1972]. When I retire I'll make close to five hundred dollars a month. This is because of the union. Full benefits. . . . The young kids don't stop and think what good the union's done (377).[9]

But this checker did not want to stop working and live off her pension, because she found so much satisfaction in using her abilities as a checker. "When I'm on a vacation, I can't wait to go, but two or three days away, I start to get fidgety. I can't stand around and do nothin'. I have to be busy at all times. I look forward to comin' to work. It's a great feelin'. I enjoy it somethin' terrible" (380).

What made her enjoy her work so? It was not that management honored her—her union had to fight for decent wages. Rather, what gave her satisfaction was the honor and appreciation that her client customers showed her for her expertise in her job. "I know the price of every [item]. . . . On the register is a list of some prices, that's for the part-time girls. I never look at it" (375). The basic reason she enjoyed her work was the opportunity it gave her to exercise her skill as a checker in rendering speedy service to her customers. She also appreciated being regarded as trustworthy. As to ringing up prices on the cash register, she said, "I catch [mistakes] right then and there. I tell my customers, 'I overcharged you two pennies on this. I will take it off of your next item.' So my customers don't watch me when I ring up. They trust me" (378).

She also found joy in giving each customer the fullest service. "What irritates me is when customers get very cocky with me. 'Hurry up,' or 'Cash my check quick.' I don't think this is right. You wait your time and I'll give you my full, undivided attention. You rush [me] and you're gonna get nothin'" (378). From such recordings of people in many vocations, Terkel concluded that satisfactions from work involved "a meaning . . . well over and beyond the reward of the paycheck" (xiv).

Hence we conclude that work's ultimate satisfaction is taking a skill that meets a genuine need others have, extending it so as to benefit as many as possible, and then being trusted, honored, and appreciated for meeting that need. Skilled workpersons are therefore patron lords in that they are trusted to perform a needed service for others. And they are lords in that they can refuse to supply this service if their would-be clients do not honor them by rendering an obedient trust to them. In chapter 9 we saw that God's reason for creating the world and planning redemptive history was to know the joy of being a patron lord who would be worshiped by his creatures for meeting their needs. We also need to recall Isaiah 64:4, a passage that makes clear what is unique about the religion of the Bible: "Since ancient times no one has heard, no ear has perceived, no eye has seen any God besides you, who acts on behalf of those who wait for him."

Such illustrations from everyday life therefore effectively counter ever seeing Abraham as the workperson a Jewish interpretation saw him to be. Rather, he is the client, dependent on God, the Patron Lord, to work for him and accomplish things so desirable that to receive them he left his homeland and lived the rest of his life as a foreigner in Canaan. Thus Paul's interpretation of Genesis 15:6 is further confirmed.

> NOTE. In concluding this consideration of Paul's interpretation, something should be said about the important biblical word "grace" in Romans 4:4: "Now when a man works, his wages are not credited to him as a gift [lit. 'not according to grace'] but as an obligation." This verse means that the services, or "works," performed by a patron for a client make the client a debtor who must reimburse the patron with a commensurate wage. So there is nothing of grace in the recompenses that clients give patrons for their services (e.g., what patients pay doctors). But what motivates the patrons to want to use their skills to meet the needs of clients? The above examples of the Nissan assembly-line worker and the supermarket checker make it clear that while reimbursement plays an important role, what matters most is the delight in seeing that one is valued by a client for having a skill to meet that client's need. This delight that causes a patron to give "full and undivided attention" to appreciative and trusting clients is grace.
>
> It is clear that the motive that led God, the Patron Lord, to bless Abraham was free from any sense of discharging an obligation to him for any services that he had rendered. Instead, what led God to account Abraham righteous when he believed him was delight in his ability to forgive sins and to use his great power and wisdom to fulfill the promises he had made. Thus God worked out of a motive of grace to save Abraham, and it should be noted that this was the same motive that led God to create the world in the first place.
>
> In the discussion of grace it has been emphasized that patrons will do their very best for clients who honor them by trusting them. How then, it may be asked, did God create the world out of grace before there were people in it

to render him praise? The answer is that he created the world in the joy of the praise he knew he would receive from redeemed people for all the benefits he would provide for them.

Review Questions

1. Why did God postpone giving the power of the sword and fragmentizing the nations until after the Flood, thus permitting the seed of the woman to become almost extinct?

2. Why is it necessary to regard God's counting Abraham's faith as righteousness (forgiveness) first before understanding anything else about Abraham?

3. Drawing upon Romans 4:4 and quotations from Jewish literature, explain a common Jewish interpretation of Genesis 15:6. Then cite four reasons leading inescapably to the conclusion that Paul's interpretation in Romans 4:5, and not this Jewish one, is correct.

4. From the illustrations given of workers and management, be able to explain (1) why an assembly-line worker is, vis-à-vis management, a patron lord, and (2) why the management of, say General Motors, are client lords.

5. In what way is God's reason for creating and redeeming the world identical with the deepest reason anyone has for pursuing his or her vocation?

NOTES

[1] It is noteworthy that Noah's posterity had sought to make a name for themselves (Gen. 11:4) by *rebelling* against God's command to spread throughout the earth, seeking instead to organize themselves into a supersociety around the Tower of Babel. Abraham and his descendants, however, would receive a great name by *complying* with God's command, through the confidence that he would then fulfill the great promises of Gen. 12:2-3.

[2] The precise meaning of the terms "obedience that comes from faith" and "descendants of Abraham" will be better grasped after

additional material is presented in chapters 18–20 below. These key phrases are crucial for understanding the *covenant* aspect of redemptive history, which becomes explicit for the first time with Abraham.

[3] God's promises to Abraham in Gen. 12–22 are concerned almost entirely with things he would do to found the Jewish nation. Though scattered throughout many nations during the past four thousand years, dwelling in the former Canaanite area for less than half that time, the nation retains its identity to this day. Chapters 17–20 in this book draw attention to the way later revelation builds on statements in the Genesis narrative to give the full picture of how foundational this covenant was for the good news of the gospel that later would go to all the nations of the earth.

[4] Obviously the promises regarding the land and the numerous progeny, so prominent in the Genesis narrative of Abraham, do not have any direct relevance to the other nations, who will be receiving Abraham's blessing. In chapter 20 below we consider the particular content of the "blessing of Abraham" promised to believers in all nations (Rom. 4:16–18; Gal. 3:8, 14).

[5] Geerhardus Vos, *Biblical Theology* (Grand Rapids: Eerdmans, 1961, reprint), 56, italics added.

[6] The Old Testament Apocrypha are the books appearing alongside the Jewish canonical books in Jerome's Latin Old Testament (the Vulgate), completed in A.D. 405. Except for 4 Ezra (= 2 Esdras), these same books appear in the Greek Old Testament, called the Septuagint (the LXX, completed in the late second century B.C.). In all probability they are a part of the "hidden" books (see n. 4 in chap. 2 above) spoken of in 4 Ezra 14:23–48. The latter passage tells the story of how Ezra and five secretaries in the fifth century B.C. were able to restore ninety-four sacred books lost when Jerusalem and the temple were destroyed in 587 B.C. Of these books twenty-four were regarded as canonical and available for all to read. The remaining seventy, however, were considered hidden and less accessible, "in order to give them [only] to the wise among your people" (v. 46). In the earliest extant texts of the LXX, however, extracanonical books such as 1–2 Maccabees, Tobit, Judith, and Ecclesiasticus did appear alongside the canonical ones and therefore were no longer "hidden."

Only a part of the fifty-two writings of the "pseudepigrapha," or books attributed to ideal figures featured in the Old Testament, are properly characterized by this word. See *The Old Testament Pseudepigrapha*, ed. James H. Charlesworth, 2 vols. (New York:

Doubleday, 1983–85). The term "pseudepigrapha" has now become the name for books representing various Jewish points of view from 200 B.C. to A.D. 200 that belong neither to the rabbinic tradition nor to the Dead Sea Scrolls of the Qumran community. Some of them have only recently been published or even discovered.

[7] Hermann L. Strack and Paul Billerbeck. *Kommentar zum Neuen Testament aus Talmud und Midrasch*, 3d ed., 6 vols. (Munich: C. H. Beck'sche, 1966), 3:188–89.

[8] In chapter 14 we considered how Jesus' work made it possible for the righteous and holy God to remain just and yet justify a wicked person like Abraham. There is no evidence, however, that Abraham knew anything about this reasoning; he did not understand how God could forgive a sinner like him without profaning his glory. But since he was convinced that "the Judge of all the earth [will] do right" (Gen. 18:25), he simply believed God's declaration that he was forgiven, without knowing anything about Christ's incarnation or work on the cross. The reason God could forgive wicked Abraham was because God's plan to have Jesus atone for sins was so certain to take place that he was regarded as "the Lamb that was slain from the creation of the world"(Rev. 13:8). Today we must surely emphasize that our sins are forgiven by Christ's having died for them on the cross and that sinful people should never presume to come directly to God, trying to bypass Jesus' atoning work. Jesus said, after all, "I am the way and the truth and the life. No one comes to the Father except through me" (John 14:6). And Peter declared that "salvation is found in no one else [than Jesus], for there is no other name under heaven given to men by which we must be saved" (Acts 4:12).

[9] Studs Terkel, *Working* (New York: Avon Books, 1972), copyright by Pantheon Books, a division of Random House, Inc. Permission to use quotations from this checker was kindly granted by the publisher. Page numbers follow the quotations in parentheses.

18

Abraham's Faith
in God's Promises

The preceding chapter spoke of Abraham's faith as the essential condition for his being justified. Once his sins had been forgiven, God, without profaning his glory, could bless him by fulfilling the great promises he had made. Though Genesis 15:6 is the only place in the Abraham narrative that explicitly refers to his having faith or believing in God, the New Testament in interpreting Abraham sees faith as operating throughout his life.

This trust is evident first in his leaving Haran to become a sojourner in another land: "By faith Abraham, when called to go to a place he would later receive as his inheritance, obeyed and went, even though he did not know where he was going" (Heb. 11:8). He also acted in faith when he resolved to remain in Canaan, the land where God had told him to reside and which someday would be occupied by the great nation he would found (Gen. 12:7; cf. 13:14–18): "By faith he made his home in the promised land like a stranger in a foreign country" (Heb. 11:9).

Genesis relates, however, that soon after arriving in Canaan, Abraham went on to Egypt to find relief from a famine. There he became ensnared in a difficulty that apart from divine intervention, would have made the fulfillment of God's promises impossible. The Pharaoh ruling Egypt, hearing of Sarah's beauty, took her into his harem. Had she remained there, Abraham could never have had the child through whom the great nation was to come. God, however, remarkably delivered him by inflicting illness on Pharaoh's household, informing Pharaoh that the cause was the new arrival in his harem, who was in fact Abraham's wife. Pharaoh then scolded Abraham severely for lying to him and commanded his soldiers to escort Abraham, Sarah, and all they had out of Egypt (Gen. 12:18–20).

Thus Abraham returned to Canaan, settling at the same place where he had originally built an altar, and there he again called upon God (Gen. 13:1–4). Apparently his amazing deliverance from Egypt resulted in Abraham's resolve to remain in Canaan for the rest of his life, for Hebrews speaks of how he had every opportunity to return to Chaldea but never did, "for he was looking forward to the city with foundations, whose architect and builder is God" (Heb. 11:10, 15).

The New Testament therefore characterizes Abraham's life as one of faith and portrays him as an example that all God's people are to follow (Rom. 4:12). Thus Paul used the single reference to Abraham's faith in Genesis 15:6 to urge the Galatians not to start trying to earn God's blessings as though he were their client, but simply to go on trusting him as their Patron Lord. Reminding them that it was through faith alone that the great blessings they had already received had come, he admonished them to "consider Abraham: 'He believed God, and it was credited to him as righteousness' [Gen. 15:6]" (Gal. 3:5–6). This passage makes it clear that Paul regarded the faith Abraham exercised in being forgiven as likewise essential in continuing to receive God's promised blessings. Thus the Galatian churches would continue to enjoy the blessings of Abraham only if they would go on trusting God as clients trust a patron.

This faith that we are to exercise comprises three essential elements. In this chapter and the next we consider them in order to know better how to trust God and receive the blessings he wants so much to impart to us. These elements are (1) faith's futuristic orientation, (2) its power to motivate obedience to God, and (3) its demand for perseverance. This chapter emphasizes faith's futuristic component, but in so doing it also shows how such faith is strengthened for

Christians today by its past component of remembering what Christ accomplished for us in his death and resurrection.

Faith's Futuristic Orientation

Romans 4:18–25 makes both the futuristic and the past orientation of faith very clear, first by showing the futuristic component of Abraham's faith, which Christians must also have, and then by showing how the faith of Christians is strengthened by the work Christ accomplished for his people in his death and resurrection.

> Against all hope [the unpromising visible circumstances of his life], Abraham in hope believed [God's unseen but heard promises] and so became the father of many nations, just as it had been said to him, "So shall your offspring be" [Gen. 15:5]. Without weakening in his faith, he faced the fact that his body was as good as dead—since he was about a hundred years old—and that Sarah's womb was also dead. Yet he did not waver through unbelief regarding the promise of God, but was strengthened in his faith and gave glory to God, being fully persuaded that God had power to do what he had promised. This is why "[his faith] was credited to him as righteousness" [Gen. 15:6]. The words "it was credited to him" were not written for him alone, but also for us, to whom God will credit righteousness—for us who believe in him who raised Jesus our Lord from the dead. He was delivered over to death for our sins and was raised to life for our justification.

One striking feature of this passage is Paul's use of Genesis 15:6 to apply to the later time in Abraham's life when God told him that he and Sarah would have a son in their old age and he responded with a laugh of faith (17:17). To be sure, a few verses later we read of Sarah's laughing to herself over the apparent impossibility of this promise and of God's rebuking her for this evidence of unbelief (18:10–15). There is a similarity between these two incidents in that Abraham and Sarah were speaking to themselves in laughter. But I argue that Abraham's falling on his face and laughing as he says to himself, "Shall a child be born to a man who is a hundred years old?" was an act of worship, and therefore his question should not be construed as an expression of doubt but one of wonder and of faith. This interpretation is confirmed by Abraham's resolve, that very day, obediently to submit himself and all the males in his household to circumcision (17:23–27).

Paul also interpreted Genesis 17:17 in this way. His use of Genesis 15:6 in Romans 4:22 shows not only that God fulfills his promises and blesses people on the basis of the forgiveness of their sins but also that they go on enjoying this forgiveness so essential for receiving God's blessings only as they persevere in believing him.[1] Then in verses 23–24 Paul emphasized that this futuristic component of faith must also exist for Christians today in order to enjoy forgiveness.

One difference between Abraham's faith and ours today, however, is that our futuristic faith in God's promises is strengthened by looking back to what Christ did for us in the past in his death for our sins and his resurrection for our justification (forgiveness): "God will [also] credit righteousness—for us who believe in him who raised Jesus our Lord from the dead. He was delivered over to death for our sins and was raised to life for our justification." Here the necessity for our faith to have a past component is unmistakably clear. But a faith that only looks back to Christ's death and resurrection is not sufficient, for Paul has just implied in verse 23 that forgiveness for the Christian also depends on having, like Abraham, a futuristic faith in God's promises. Thus we cannot regard justifying faith as sufficient if it honors only the past fact of Christ's death and resurrection but does not honor the future promises of God, thus mocking his character and integrity.

Two obstacles occur in the text following Romans 4:24–25 that have often hindered Christians from seeing the need for a futuristic component in saving faith. The first comes from the start of a new chapter division after Romans 4:25. Placing the division between chapters 4 and 5 at this point was unfortunate, for it has encouraged people to regard Paul's train of thought as ending with verse 25, so that 5:1 and following commence a new line of thought. Some have therefore come to the conclusion that forgiveness (justification) comes simply from believing in Christ's death and resurrection and that the Christian emulates the faith of

Abraham simply by believing in the promise of the forgiveness of sins certified by Jesus' resurrection. Thus Charles Hodge in expounding Romans 4:23–24 in his commentary on Romans put it as follows:

> [Abraham] believed in God as quickening from the dead, that is, as able to raise up one as good as dead, the promised Redeemer. Therefore those to whom faith shall now be imputed for righteousness are described as *those who believed that God hath raised up Jesus from the dead.* By thus raising him from the dead, he declared him to be his Son, and the seed of Abraham, in whom all the nations of the earth were to be blessed. The object of the Christian's faith, therefore, is the same as the object of the faith of Abraham. Both believe the promise of redemption through the promised seed, which is Christ.[2]

Hodge had to put much "theological exegesis" into this interpretation, for he wanted to regard Abraham's faith that he would have a son by Sarah to mean that he would receive forgiveness by believing that from the son's posterity would come the future Redeemer of the world. In this way he sees Abraham as believing in the promise of a redeemer. According to this view the Christian today is not believing a promise of something yet future, but in the fact of what God has already accomplished in the past. Thus nothing is left of the futuristic orientation of Abraham's faith. But such difficulties begin to vanish if we ignore the chapter break after verse 25.

The second obstacle arises from the preference of expositors of Romans to regard the "have" in Romans 5:1 (in the phrase "have peace with God") as an indicative statement of fact rather than as a command to be fulfilled as one believes God's promises. Indeed, some copiers of handwritten manuscripts of Romans during the fourteen hundred years before the printing press felt that this word should be spelled so the verse would read, "Therefore, since we have been justified by faith, we are having [present indicative] peace with God." Then since there is an obvious parallelism between verse 1 and verses 2 and 3, the verbs of these latter verses would also be indicative. (Their spelling in Greek permits them to be understood either as indicatives or imperatives.) Hence, to regard the "have" in verse 1 as an indicative commits one to regard the main verbs in verses 2 and 3 as also being indicatives and excludes any possibility for these verses to require faith that has a futuristic aspect in believing God's promise.

But according to the best textual evidence, the Greek word for "have" in verse 1 is *echōmen* ("let us have," a so-called hortatory subjunctive), not *echomen* ("we have," an indicative). Romans 5:1 accordingly should be translated, "Therefore, since we have been justified by faith, *let us keep on having [or enjoying]* peace with God." The next two verses would then read as the margin of the NIV acknowledges: "And let us [keep on rejoicing] in the hope of the glory of God. Not only so, but let us also [keep on rejoicing] in our sufferings." But only those who believe the promise that "in all things God works for the good of those that love him" (Rom. 8:28) will be able to enjoy peace with God through all of life's adversities and to glory in their sufferings.

Unfortunately, however, the committee responsible for the textual criticism of the Greek New Testament published by the United Bible Societies in 1966 chose to retain the indicative spelling for the main verb of verse 1 and thus also for the main verbs of verses 2 and 3. Bruce Metzger, the chairperson for the committee, explained its decision as follows:

> Although the [hortatory] subjunctive *echōmen* ["let us have"]. . . has far better external support [textual evidence] than the indicative *echomen* ["we have"] . . . a majority of the Committee judged that internal evidence must here take precedence. Since in this passage it appears that Paul is not exhorting but stating facts ("peace" is the possession of those who have been justified), only the indicative is consonant with the apostle's argument.[3]

I contend, however, that in addition to the "far better" textual evidence for the hortatory subjunctive, there are three reasons for saying that the internal evidence also strongly supports the imperative idea. First, if we translate the "have" of Romans 5:1 as an indicative, then the causal clause of this verse, "because we have been justified by faith," and the main clause, "we have peace with God," are saying the same thing. Justification *is* to have peace with God in the sense that one has the forgiveness of sins. But a causal clause must always say something different from the main clause it supports. Romans 5:1 is speaking nonsense if it is saying, "Since we have the peace with God that justification brings, we have peace with God." But if the "have" in the main clause is a hortatory subjunctive, then the causal clause is saying something different: "Since we have the forgiveness of sins and God is no longer our enemy but our Father, let us then allow his peace to rule in our hearts experientially, despite life's sufferings."

Second, if the main-clause verbs of Romans 5:1–3 are in the indicative mood, then verse 3 is making a statement that is not generally true. We who claim justification by faith do not, as a matter of fact, consistently glory in sufferings. To the contrary, only as we are reminded that "in all things God works for the good of those who love him" are we able to rejoice in how the present stumbling blocks of suffering will become stepping-stones leading to far greater future blessings than would have been possible without the suffering. Thus Romans 5:3 becomes much more relevant and applicable when its main verb is seen as a command rather than a statement of fact.

Third, since we are able to obey the commands of verses 1–3 only by crediting God's promises, we then see how our faith, like Abraham's, must have a future component. Thus we need to emulate this man who, against the darkness of visible circumstances, nevertheless rejoiced in the way God would glorify himself by fulfilling his promise to him (Rom. 4:18–22).

I therefore argue that the main verbs of Romans 5:1–3 should be regarded as imperatives because of both the superior internal evidence and the superior external, textual evidence. Christian faith thus must have the futuristic component that Abraham's faith had or it will not be reckoned to us for righteousness, as Abraham's confidence in God's promises was. But since it is faith's past component— Christ's death and resurrection—that makes possible our justification, we have an even stronger reason to believe God's promises than Abraham had.

Faith's Past Orientation

It is comforting to realize that Romans 4:18–5:3, which teaches that faith today, like Abraham's yesterday, must have a futuristic orientation, also speaks pointedly about the basis upon which the holy God finds it possible to forgive people who have failed to trust him. Thus Christians today, who know the significance of Jesus' death and resurrection, have a much greater encouragement to trust in God's promises than did Abraham, who accepted God's forgiveness in Genesis 15:6 with no idea at all of how this offer was possible.

Another passage like Romans 4:23–25 that is often cited to prove that Christian faith has only a past component is 1 Corinthians 15:3–4. Here Paul listed the essential features of the gospel—"that Christ died for our sins according to the [Old Testament] Scriptures, that he was buried, that he was raised on the third day according to the Scriptures"—but said nothing about the significance of his death and resurrection for one's future. It should be noted, however, that this passage has the style of a creed, and as such it is necessarily brief. It states only the foundational facts of Christian doctrine, leaving it then to the Christian teacher to spell out the necessary futuristic implications.

Romans 10:9 also has a creedal sound in pinpointing as essential to salvation the need to confess with the lips Christ as Lord and to believe in one's heart that God raised him from the dead. This phrase unmistakably indicates that genuine faith must be more than mere intellectual assent to the past historical fact of Jesus' resurrection. One must assent also to the significance it should have for the future, and when a person becomes convinced of the difference Jesus' resurrection makes for his or her future, then the heart attitude and outlook will be radically changed.

One vital implication of believing "in your heart" that God raised Jesus from the dead is spelled out in Romans 10:9–10. In the preceding verses (6–8) Paul cited Deuteronomy

30:14, which has the order "mouth . . . heart." To follow this order Paul said in Romans 10:9, "If you confess with your mouth, 'Jesus is Lord,' and believe in your heart that God raised him from the dead, you will be saved." But obviously an inward faith must precede a verbal confession, and so in verse 10 Paul reversed things: "For it is with your heart that you believe and are justified, and it is with your mouth that you confess and so are saved."

The kind of outward confession Paul had in mind in this passage was not confessing Jesus before other people, as is required for salvation according to Matthew 10:32 and Luke 12:8. The immediately following sentences force the reader to understand the "confession" with the lips as a calling upon God to impart the blessings sorely needed to cope with the many hardships through which we must go to enter the kingdom of God (see Acts 14:22). Here the necessity to believe on Jesus as one's Patron Lord and to call upon him for help becomes clear, for Romans 10:12 says, "There is no difference between Jew and Gentile—the same Lord is Lord of all and richly blesses all who call upon him." So in order to be saved and enjoy the blessings God wants to impart to us who are forgiven, we must believe in Jesus' death and resurrection in such a way that we regard God as our Patron Lord—our benefactor—in freely giving us all things needed both now and in the future.

The confidence that Christians today have in the bright future God has for them is greater than that of Abraham, for Abraham knew nothing of the implications of the Christ-event for one's future—for example, that "if, when we were God's enemies, we were reconciled to him through the death of his Son, how much more, having been reconciled, shall we be saved through his life!" (Rom. 5:10). Here Paul was resorting to what is called an a fortiori argument, one leading to a conclusion that firmly stands, because it has prevailed over greater obstacles. The two stronger obstacles are cited in the "if" clause of this verse: (1) we were God's enemies, and (2) God had to subject his Son to the cruelest of deaths and the full force of his wrath in order to reconcile us to himself without profaning his glory. But formidable as these obstacles were, he surmounted them. Therefore God will most certainly overcome the lesser problems posed by our need to be redeemed from the sinfulness and adversity that climax in the death of the body. Thus goodness and love will assuredly pursue us all the days of our lives, and we can confidently anticipate dwelling in the house of the Lord forever. Likewise when faith realizes what obstacles God has already overcome in reconciling us to himself, we will be all the more persuaded to believe him when he promises, "I will rejoice in doing [you] good . . . with all my heart and soul" (Jer. 32:41).

This a fortiori argument occurs again in Romans 8:31–32. In summarizing what he has said thus far in Romans, Paul here emphasizes that if God is for us, no one can be against us. "He who did not spare his own Son, but gave him up for us all—how will he not also, along with him, graciously give us all things?" In other words, now that the far greater obstacles of our enmity with God and the pain he suffered in Christ's death for our sins have been surmounted, whatever barrier may stand in the way of God's giving us all things will easily be overcome.

Faith in the past facts of what God did for us through Christ's death and resurrection thus offers a powerful persuasion also to have a faith oriented to the future, to trust that we can always enjoy fellowship with God and that he will bounteously supply our needs henceforth. We exercise such faith by claiming God's promises often during each day to fight back anxiety, bitterness, covetousness, regret, and other attitudes of unbelief that will be dealt with in the next section. Thus we continue to enjoy peace in fellowshiping with God (Rom. 5:1). And as we learn to rejoice in hope of the glory of God (5:2; 12:12), we will be able to obey the seemingly impossible command to rejoice in life's tribulations as they come, because we have the certain knowledge that in everything God is working for our good. Likewise we will have the confidence that "in all these things we are more than conquerors through him who loved us" (Rom. 8:37), and we will understand that this means God will work so that apparent stumbling blocks will eventually become stepping-stones to enjoying God's glory in all its fullness.

Fighting Ten Specific Attitudes of Unbelief

Hebrews 3:12–13 exhorts us, "See to it, brothers, that none of you has a sinful, unbelieving heart that turns away from the living God. But encourage one another daily, as long as it is called Today, so that none of you may be hardened by sin's deceitfulness." The way to persevere to the end and "keep [ourselves] in God's love" (Jude 21), that is, in the place where we experience the joy of his fellowship and benefit from his actions on our behalf, is to take vigorous steps to fight the fight of faith the moment we detect any symptoms of unbelief. Such symptoms will often be evident in a loss of joy and peace. But unbelief can also manifest itself in a very deceptive and sinful elation as we rejoice in some triumph we have exerienced or savor some wise or heroic thing we foolishly take credit for having done (see "Self-Adulation" below). Temptation to sin will also allure us by the promise of pleasures that nevertheless prove to be unfulfilling and short-lived (see "Indulgent Desires" below).

It is vital to know how to identify each of these ten specific states of mind, any one of which constitutes an evil heart of unbelief. After identifying it, we should fight against it by (1) prayerfully meditating on and claiming several promises from the "faithful God" (Deut. 7:9) that are directly and explicitly pertinent, and also by (2) considering the threats indicating the severity with which God will deal with those who allow unbelief to remain by not taking immediate steps—"as long as it is called Today" (Heb. 3:13)—to overcome it. Such perseverance in fighting unbelief is essential, for we "come to share in Christ *if* we hold firmly till the end the confidence we had at first" (v. 14). We must therefore heed Paul's words that "now [God] has reconciled [us] by Christ's physical body through death to present [us] holy in his sight . . . *if* [we] continue in [our] faith, established and firm, not moved from the hope held out in the gospel" (Col. 1:22–23). To encourage such perseverance, we begin now to consider each of these ten evidences of unbelief, citing Scripture passages urging an opposite, believing state of mind, along with promises and threats that will motivate us to fight unbelief until victory comes.

Many more verses than those cited below should be added as weapons in the fight of faith. But those cited will give one a good start in getting rid of an evil heart of unbelief in any of its several forms. Jesus fought back against Satan in his wilderness temptation by quoting short statements of Scripture and refusing to credit the Devil's lies (Matt. 4:1–10). How much more, then, must we rely upon Scripture to withstand satanic attack, preferably on our knees in prayer with a Bible and a hymnbook at hand. According to Ephesians 6:17, we should use the "sword of the Spirit, which is the word of God" in carrying on this spiritual warfare. A sword is not something unwieldy or indefinite, and so in using the sword of the Spirit, we should fight back against Satan with specific promises that strike to the core of the lie by which he is trying to destroy our faith. Having certain key verses memorized along with their references will help to stop unbelief quickly, before it gets into our hearts.

When Paul heard at Athens that the recently converted Thessalonians were encountering much persecution, he reacted with great anxiety: "For this reason," he wrote, "when I could stand it no longer, I sent to find out about your *faith*. I was afraid that in some way the tempter might have tempted you and our efforts might have been useless" (1 Thess. 3:5). This passage clearly implies that Satan's whole strategy against believers is to destroy their faith, understood as their confidence in God and his promises. So the way to fight back is by citing prayerfully a few verses pertinent to the way we are being tempted not to believe God. Since nothing wounds Satan more than to have his lies countered by promises from the Scriptures of the faithful God, the best way to resist him is by "standing firm in the faith" (1 Peter 5:9). As we "resist the devil, he will flee from [us]" (James 4:7). In fighting unbelief and getting back to the place where we are once more filled with joy and peace, we are pitted against satanic forces, and so we must depend upon the divine resources of the Word of God and prayer.

It is helpful to realize that the key element in the Christian life is faith: Satan, our adversary, is trying to destroy our faith, and our one job as Christians is to "fight the good fight of the faith" (1 Tim. 6:12). Since faith's natural object is

God's promises, we should note especially those passages in
the Bible where promises are made, and also the threats of
the misery that we will experience if we do not believe.

Singing an appropriate hymn is also very helpful in
battling unbelief, for singing implies praise. In 2 Chronicles
20:19–22 the people of God became victorious by believing
and praising God:

> Then some Levites . . . stood up and praised the Lord, the
> God of Israel, with very loud voice. Early in the morning they
> left for the Desert of Tekoa. As they set out, Jehoshaphat stood
> and said, "Listen to me, Judah and people of Jerusalem! Have
> faith in the Lord your God and you will be upheld; have faith
> in his prophets and you will be successful." After consulting
> the people, Jehoshaphat appointed men to sing to the Lord
> and to praise him for the splendor of his holiness as they went
> out at the head of the army, saying, "Give thanks to the Lord,
> for his love endures forever." As they began to sing and
> praise, the Lord set ambushes against the men of Ammon and
> Moab and Mount Seir who were invading Judah, and they
> were defeated.

False Guilt

The first of the ten specific states of mind that constitute an
evil heart of unbelief is a false guilt. According to Revelation
12:10 Satan is the "accuser of our brothers, who accuses
them before our God day and night." Some think that this
accusation goes on in heaven, with the Christian who is
being accused knowing nothing about it, much as Job, for
example, was unaware of Satan's accusations against him
(Job 1:9–11; 2:4–5). But consider also Zechariah 3:1, which
mentions "Joshua the high priest standing before the angel
of the Lord, and Satan standing at his right side to accuse
him." So Joshua surely felt the sting of these accusations.
And Christians do feel condemned from time to time for
foolish things they have done in the past. Such an accusation
can come at one with a force so overwhelming that it surely
seems to be satanic, for Satan does try to destroy Christians'
confidence by accusing them of their supposed sins.

These "sins" that Satan accuses us of, however, never

include our failures to carry out the obedience of faith. If he did that, he would be preaching the gospel by reprimanding us for not believing God's promises! He would in fact be augmenting the work of the Holy Spirit, which is to convict the world of the sin of unbelief (John 16:8–9). So his accusations are never for sins understood as disobedience, or works of unbelief. Satan indeed generally has grounds for his accusations, since all sins have elements of foolishness, ignobility, shame, and weakness. Far from showing their root to be a failure to believe God, however, Satan's strategy is to attack our egos, taunting us for not sufficiently employing our own wisdom and strength in coping with some situation. Since his one objective is to destroy our faith, his accusations always carry with them an implicit demand to trust in ourselves rather than in God (cf. 2 Cor. 1:9); as he did, we want to be "like the most High" (Isa. 14:14).

The problem is complicated because with our inherent pride, we naturally hate the idea that our sin consists in a failure to acknowledge that we are clients deserving only mercy from God as our Patron Lord. Nor are our consciences, distorted by sin, always able to give us accurate readings on the quality of our actions. Our hearts are "deceitful above all things and beyond cure [when left to our own understanding]. Who [by oneself] can understand it?" (Jer. 17:9). "It is not for man to direct his steps" (10:23). Like the psalmist, we must therefore pray, "Search me, O God, and know my heart; test me and know my anxious thoughts. See if there is any offensive way in me, and lead me in the way everlasting" (Ps. 139:23–24).

Thus as the Holy Spirit works through the Scriptures, God will show how opposed our basic attitudes are to resting in his promises (Heb. 4:12). Then we will feel true guilt and sorrow at how our unbelief has dishonored God's glorious name. Such grief, however, will not be a worldly sorrow that leads to discouragement and death, which would happen if we accept the poor self-image Satan tries to give us and conclude that we are worthless and that there is thus no use trying to go on. Instead, the grief for sin that comes from God's convicting work carries with it the promise of forgiveness, so that it "brings repentance that leads to salvation and leaves no regret" (2 Cor. 7:10). We are comforted, for example, by remembering Exodus 34:6–7, which speaks of God as compassionate and gracious, "slow to anger, abounding in love and faithfulness, . . . forgiving wickedness, rebellion and sin." That God is slow to anger means that we do not lose forgiveness as soon as an evil heart of unbelief has gained the ascendancy. But if we persist in letting unbelief go unchecked, God will become angry with us and eventually take our forgiveness away. Exodus 34:7, for example, thus ends by saying, "Yet he does not leave the guilty unpunished." For that reason also Psalm 103:9, immediately after citing Exodus 34:6–7, goes on to say, "[God] will not always accuse [or seek to convict us of unbelief], nor will he harbor his anger for ever [but will vent it after protracted unbelief]."

What we must do to be forgiven is confess our sin to God and turn away from it: "If we confess our sins, he is faithful and just and will forgive us our sins and purify us from all unrighteousness" (1 John 1:9). This verse is especially effective in resisting the Devil so that he will soon stop accusing us and flee, because it declares that God would become sinful were he not to forgive a Christian's sin, when he or she confesses and turns away from it. The reasoning behind this truth comes from the immediate context: "If we walk in the light, as he is in the light, we have fellowship with one another, and the blood of Jesus, his Son, purifies us from all sin" (v. 7). In other words, as we have seen in chapter 14 above, if God did not forgive the Christian who confesses and turns away from sin, God would become unrighteous by holding in contempt Christ's atoning work, whose purpose was to uphold God's glory.

In Mark 3:28 Jesus said, "I tell you the truth, all the sins and blasphemies of men will be forgiven them." Indeed, the next verse does talk of the unforgivable sin of blaspheming the Holy Spirit, but such sin occurs only after a person has persisted in refusing to believe God's great desire to be merciful and to forgive sins. Consequently, the threat of Mark 3:29 drives the Christian to take confidence in the promise of the preceding verse. These, then, are some basic weapons to use when Satan condemns us for not being the wise, courageous, mature, and strong people that our egos would like us to be.

Anxiety

Satan tries to get believers to credit some dark scenario that might plausibly follow from problems presently confronting them. Then the anxiety syndrome gains ascendancy in the heart as the Christian runs through the bleak scenario again and again, thus failing to "demolish arguments and every pretension that sets itself up against the knowledge of God" (2 Cor. 10:5). In this state of mind the Christian has ceased to believe God and "rejoice in [him] always" (Phil. 4:4) because of the confident hope the Christian is to derive from God's promises (Rom. 12:12).

To fight against anxiety and recover the joy of the Lord, the Christian must resist Satan with verses such as the following: 1 Peter 5:7: "Cast all your anxiety on him, for everything that concerns you concerns him as well [lit. trans.]"; Matthew 6:25, 33: "Therefore I tell you, do not worry. . . . But seek first God's kingdom, for then all life's necessities will be added to the blessings you are already enjoying by laying hold of the promises" [authors own translation and exposition]; Isaiah 51:12: "I, even I, am he who comforts you. Who are you that you fear mortal men, the sons of men, who are but grass, that you forget the Lord your Maker, who stretched out the heavens and laid the foundations of the earth?" Note how our being fearful is regarded by God as arrogance in not trusting him as children look to loving parents to care for them. See also Isaiah 7:9: "If you do not stand firm in your faith, you will not stand at all"; 2 Chronicles 20:20: "Have faith in the Lord your God and you will be upheld . . . [and] be successful."

Regret

When hindsight shows us that we should have zigged rather than zagged in making some decision in the past, Satan loves to tell us the lie that we have thus irretrievably lost a very substantial portion of future happiness. We are predisposed to believe this lie, for the irreversible nature of a past decision, now so obviously foolish, seems to make the bleakness of the future as certain as the foolishness of the past. All too easily do the words of the poet John G. Whittier resonate within us:

> For of all sad words of tongue or pen,
> The saddest are these: "It might have been!"

Such words, however, do not mesh at all with the burning love that God has for those who will trust him. So we must use verses such as the following to expose this lie for what it is and overcome our inclination to believe it.

Jeremiah 38:20 was the prophet's assurance to King Zedekiah, who had persistently disobeyed God in refusing to surrender Jerusalem to the Babylonian armies, whose battering rams even then could be heard breaking through the walls of the city. Here was a person who, because of his sin and the imminence of destruction, surely seemed to have no possibility of any happy tomorrows. But Jeremiah declared, "Obey the Lord by doing what I tell you. Then it will go well with you, and your life will be spared." So Jeremiah provided a positive incentive for this obedience of faith with the promise of a happy future—something that Zedekiah, like everyone, wants above all else. But there was a negative incentive as well: "If you will not surrender to the officers of the king of Babylon, this city will be handed over to the Babylonians and they will burn it down; you yourself will not escape from their hands" (v. 18). Zedekiah, however, credited neither the promise nor the threat, and as a consequence the city did fall. His sons were killed before his eyes, after which he was blinded and carried off in chains to Babylon (39:5–7).

First Samuel 12:20–21 was Samuel's reply to Israel when the nation ruefully realized its great sin in insisting on a king: "Do not be afraid. . . . You have done all this evil; yet do not turn away from the Lord, but serve the Lord with all your heart. Do not turn away after useless idols. They can do you no good, nor can they rescue you, because they are useless.[4] For the sake of his great name the Lord will not reject his people, because the Lord was pleased to make you his own."

See also Romans 8:28: "And we know that in all things God works for the good of those who love him"; Romans 8:37: "In all these things [the misfortunes of life—see vv. 35–36] we are more than conquerors through him who loved us." In chapter 10 we noted that the way we more than conquer a misfortune is for God to cause it, in retrospect, to become a stepping-stone rather than a stumbling block, so that its aftermath brings about something better than would have been the case had it not happened. God acts in exactly this manner, according to Romans 8:28, read in the light of verse 37. See also Genesis 50:20 for a concrete, biblical example of how such a divine use of a misfortune happened for Jacob and his family. To fight the fight of faith successfully we have to learn to commit not only the future but also the past to the Lord.

Covetousness

This form of unbelief comes when we are dissatisfied with what we possess or with our station and circumstances in life. A threat to help us work out our salvation with fear and trembling by not letting this state of mind get the ascendancy comes from Ephesians 5:5: "Of this you can be sure: No immoral, impure or greedy [covetous] person—such a man is an idolater—has any inheritance in the kingdom of Christ and of God." 1 Timothy 6:6–12 offers a combination of promises and threats to motivate us:

> Godliness with contentment is great gain. For we brought nothing into the world, and we can take nothing out of it. But if we have food and clothing, we will be content with that. People who want to get rich fall into temptation and a trap and into many foolish and harmful desires that plunge men into ruin and destruction. For the love of money is a root of all kinds of evil. Some people, eager for money, have wandered from the faith and pierced themselves with many griefs. But you, man of God, flee from all this, and pursue righteousness, godliness, faith, love, endurance, and gentleness. Fight the

good fight of the faith. Take hold of the eternal life to which you were called.

Other key verses to use against covetousness include Proverbs 30:7–8: "Give me neither poverty nor riches, but give me only my daily bread. Otherwise, I may have too much and disown you and say, 'Who is the Lord?' Or I may become poor and steal, and so dishonor the name of my God"; Proverbs 23:4: "Do not wear yourself out to get rich; have the wisdom to show restraint"; Philippians 4:11–13: "I have learned to be content whatever the circumstances. I know what it is to be in need, and I know what it is to have plenty. I have learned the secret of being content in any and every situation, whether well fed or hungry, whether living in plenty or in want. I can do everything through him who gives me strength"; Hebrews 13:5–6: "Keep your lives free from the love of money and be content with what you have, because God has said, 'Never will I leave you; never will I forsake you.' So we say with confidence, 'The Lord is my helper; I will not be afraid. What can man do to me?'"

Bitterness

Bitterness exists when a person harbors a grudge or an unforgiving spirit against another for a wrong done to one. A parable in Matthew 18:23–35 tells how a master, after auditing his accounts, discovered that one of his servants owed him ten thousand talents. A talent was a large sum of money in that culture, for it took more than fifteen years for a person doing ordinary manual labor to earn just one talent. So the master's first response was to try to recoup some of this immense debt by selling the servant, his wife, and children as slaves. But when that servant fell on his knees and implored the master to give him time to repay his debt, the master "took pity on him, canceled the debt and let him go" (v. 27). Now another servant owed one hundred denarii—the earnings of one hundred days' labor—to the servant who had just been forgiven his debt. But that forgiven servant, instead of forgiving in turn such a small debt, demanded immediate repayment and, turning a deaf ear to the servant's pleas for time to repay, had him thrown into the debtor's prison.

When the master of these servants heard how harshly the forgiven servant had treated his fellow servant, the master withdrew his forgiveness: "'You wicked servant,' he said. 'I canceled all that debt of yours because you begged me to. Shouldn't you have had mercy on your fellow servant just as I had on you?' In anger his master turned him over to the jailers to be tortured, until he should pay back all he owed" (Matt. 18:32–34). Then Jesus said, "This is how my heavenly Father will [also] treat each of you unless you forgive your brother from your heart" (v. 35). Such a threat should surely make everyone fear the unbelief that lies behind bitterness and an unforgiving spirit.

According to Romans 12:19 God declares that vengeance against all wrongdoing is exclusively his prerogative, and he therefore promises, "I will repay." So those who persist in harboring an unforgiving spirit toward others who have wronged them are guilty of not believing God's promise to see to matters himself. On the basis of this promise we therefore ought to render a work of faith by feeding our enemy if he or she is hungry (Rom. 12:20), thus heeding the command, "Do not be overcome by evil, but overcome evil with good" (v. 21).

A similar command is found in Exodus 23:4–5: "If you come across your enemy's ox or donkey wandering off, be sure to take it back to him. If you see the donkey of someone who hates you fallen down under its load, do not leave it there; be sure you help him with it." We should note that in these admonitions to return good for evil, God is not asking us to regard the evil that our enemies may have committed against us as no longer evil (note Isa. 5:20: "Woe to those who call evil good and good evil"). But we are to forgive in the sense of leaving to God the whole responsibility for seeing that the wrongdoer gets his or her comeuppance, in the meantime being benevolently inclined toward our enemies, as taught in Matthew 6:12: "Forgive us our debts, as we also have forgiven our debtors." God will not apply the propitiation accomplished by the shed blood of his Son to those who try to exact vengeance on their own, thus implying that God is a liar in saying that "every violation and disobedience [will receive] its just punishment" (Heb. 2:2). Therefore we must fight the good fight of faith not to let bitterness or an unforgiving spirit remain in our hearts. We must go to our knees and, with these commands, enforced by such promises and threats, preach to ourselves and supplicate God's help until the bitterness melts away and we again have joy and peace as we trust in him.

Jealousy and Envy

This common evidence of an evil heart of unbelief arises when we see another person succeed in getting some desirable thing that we wish we could have. In John 21:18–19 Jesus told Peter that he would die as a martyr. Peter then asked how John's life would end, but in verse 22 Jesus replied, "If I want [John] to remain alive until I return [and thus avoid martyrdom], what is that to you? You must follow me." Jesus' point is that he alone, as the Bread of Life, is able to satisfy our hearts, despite circumstances. So when others find themselves in better circumstances than are presently coming our way, it matters not, if we are believing Jesus in such a way that we do not hunger and thirst (John 4:13–14; 6:35).

See Psalm 73:25–26: "Whom have I in heaven but you? And earth has nothing I desire besides you. My flesh and my heart may fail, but God is the strength of my heart and my portion forever"; Psalm 37:7–8: "Do not fret when men succeed in their ways, when they carry out their wicked schemes. Refrain from anger and turn from wrath; do not fret—it leads only to evil. For evil men will be cut off, but those who hope in the Lord will inherit the land"; Galatians 5:19–21: "The acts of the sinful nature are obvious: sexual immorality, impurity and debauchery; idolatry and witchcraft; hatred, discord, jealousy, fits of rage, selfish ambition, dissensions, factions and envy; drunkenness, orgies, and the like. I warn you, as I did before, that those who live like this will not inherit the kingdom of God"; 1 Thessalonians 5:18: "Give thanks in all circumstances, for this is God's will for you in Christ Jesus"; Romans 8:32: "He who did not spare his own Son but gave him up for us all—how will he not also, along with him, graciously give us all things?"

Impatience

The pride that remains in us who are still only in the process of ceasing to be sons and daughters of hell (Matt. 23:15) and becoming like Jesus (Gal. 4:19) often causes us to feel that we should be getting on faster with some project and that we are not well advised simply to let God work for and through us in his own time and way as we wait for him. Even though Ephesians 2:10 says that we are God's workmanship and that he has prepared in advance the good works that we are to do, and even though God has mapped out the particular course each one of us is to follow through life (2 Tim. 4:7), yet our desire to be great is so strong that it can cause us to leave off waiting on God to work in us according to his good purpose (Phil. 2:13); in impatience we may try to marshal our resources to accomplish some task that seems to be all-important.

But Isaiah 50:10–11 provides a strong negative motivation to fear this particular form of an unbelieving heart: "Who among you fears the Lord and obeys the word of his servant? Let him who walks in the dark, who has no light, trust in the name of the Lord and rely on his God. But now, all you who light fires [by dreaming up plausible ways in which to get ahead] and provide yourselves with flaming torches, go, walk in the light of your fires and of the torches you have set ablaze [note the sarcasm]. This is what you shall receive from my hand: You will lie down in torment."

Isaiah 40:28–31 gives the positive side to encourage us to wait for God's guidance in doing the good works he has foreordained for us: "Do you not know? Have you not heard? The Lord is the everlasting God, the Creator of the ends of the earth. He will not grow tired or weary.... He gives strength to the weary and increases the power of the weak. Even youths grow tired and weary, and young men stumble and fall; but those who hope in the Lord will renew their strength. They will soar on wings like eagles; they will run and not grow weary, they will walk and not be faint."

In Numbers 9:15–23, the way God led Israel in the wilderness provides the ultimate incentive to overcome impatience and wait willingly for God.

> On the day the tabernacle, the Tent of the Testimony, was set up, the cloud covered it. From evening till morning the cloud above the tabernacle looked like fire. That is how it continued to be; the cloud covered it, and at night it looked like fire. Whenever the cloud lifted from above the Tent, the Israelites set out; wherever the cloud settled, the Israelites encamped. At the Lord's command the Israelites set out, and at his command they encamped. As long as the cloud stayed over the tabernacle, they remained in camp. When the cloud remained over the tabernacle a long time, the Israelites obeyed the Lord's order and did not set out. Sometimes the cloud was over the tabernacle only a few days. . . . Whether the cloud stayed over the tabernacle for two days or a month or a year, the Israelites would remain in camp and not set out; but when it lifted, they would set out. At the Lord's command they encamped, and at the Lord's command they set out. They obeyed the Lord's order, in accordance with his command through Moses.

This cloud consisted of the glorious presence of God, the experience of which alone will fill the God-shaped vacuum that Blaise Pascal described (see chap. 10 above). Note also Exodus 33:7–11:

> Now Moses used to take a tent and pitch it outside the camp. . . . Anyone inquiring of the Lord would go to the tent of meeting. . . . As Moses went into the tent, the pillar of cloud would come down and stay at the entrance, while the Lord spoke with Moses. . . . The Lord would speak to Moses face to face, as a man speaks with his friend. Then Moses would return to the camp, but his young aide Joshua son of Nun did not leave the tent.

Clearly, the presence of the Lord was Joshua's greatest delight. And this was true for Moses as well, for when God promised him, "My Presence will go with you, and I will give you rest," Moses' response was, "If your Presence does not go with us, do not send us up from here" (Ex. 33:14–15). The psalmist displayed the same attitude: "I love the house where you live, O Lord, the place where your glory dwells" (Ps. 26:8).

So the problem of an evil heart of impatience makes us face up squarely to the question of whether we love God or the world. According to 1 John 2:15–17 we will do God's will only if we love fellowship with him more than what the world has to offer, for we will always serve what we worship: "Do not love the world or anything in the world. If anyone loves the world, the love of the Father is not in him. . . . The world and its desires pass away, but the man who does the will of God lives forever." Surely the good fight of faith will frequently need to be fought at this point of the object of our love—whether fellowship with God or the world's rewards.

This passage in 1 John is important in that it provides the key for each person to find the particular way God wants him or her to go. In order to know God's will, a person must prefer God to the world, and so when one's heart is unhappy, he or she should prayerfully wait for God to show the next course of action to be taken in order to maintain the love of the Father in the heart. People who do this in the little and big decisions of life are loving and trusting God. So Jesus said, "Not everyone who says to me, 'Lord, Lord,' will enter the kingdom of heaven, but only he who does the will of my Father who is in heaven" (Matt. 7:21).

Listlessness and Despondency

These tendencies are the direct opposite of impatience. Sometimes the Devil tries to destroy our confidence by saying that we are at a dead end and that there is no way out. Or perhaps we get that burned-out sense in which we feel that we just cannot carry on our responsibilities. At such a time Psalm 16:11 (margin) brings comfort with its promise, "You [God] will make known to me the path of life; you will fill me with joy in your presence, with eternal pleasures at your right hand." As we wait upon God during such times, he will show us the next step to take that will bring us life. Perhaps he will show us how to make our way through a seemingly impossible schedule and give us the strength for each task that lies before us. Or he may arrange circumstances to make it clear that we should "come with [him] . . . to a quiet place and get some rest" (Mark 6:31). Another verse to use as the sword of the Spirit to make the Devil flee from us when we feel like giving up is Psalm 23:2–3, "[The Lord] makes me lie down in green pastures, he leads me beside quiet waters, he restores my soul. He [then] guides me in paths of righteousness for his name's sake." We cannot expect to know the way God wants us to go until we first find rest for our souls by learning from him. See also Matthew 11:28–30.

In addition to such promises we must also consider the severity of God's threats against a tendency to want to give up. Hebrews 10:35–38: "So do not throw away your confidence; it will be richly rewarded. You need to persevere so that when you have done the will of God, you will receive what he has promised. . . . My righteous one will live by faith. And if he shrinks back, I will not be pleased with him."

Self-Adulation

Sometimes an evil heart of unbelief takes the form of elation for some triumph we have enjoyed or for some clever, creative, or well-advised thing we think we have done. Then the pride that gains ascendancy in the heart must be rooted out quickly. Perhaps the most cogent statement of pride's unreasonableness is 1 Corinthians 4:7: "What do you have that you did not receive [as a gift]? And if you did [thus] receive it, why do you boast as though you did not?" A concrete elaboration is provided by Deuteronomy 8:17–18: "You may say to yourself, 'My power and the strength of my hands have produced this wealth for me.' But remember the Lord your God, for it is he who gives you the ability to produce wealth."

Only God, who is the cause of his own existence, has the right to glory in himself, as 1 Corinthians 1:27–31 makes clear:

> [God] chose the foolish things of the world to shame the wise;
> God chose the weak things of the world to shame the strong.
> He chose the lowly things of this world and the despised

things—and the things that are not—to nullify the things that are, so that no one may boast before him. It is because of him that you are in Christ Jesus, who has become for us wisdom from God—that is, our righteousness, holiness and redemption. Therefore, as it is written, "Let him who boasts boast in the Lord!" [Jer. 9:24].

The following promises and threats therefore help us to fight with the resolution necessary to win out over this manifestation of unbelief: James 4:6: "God opposes the proud but gives grace to the humble [Prov. 3:34]"; Isaiah 57:15: "For this is what the high and lofty One says—he who lives forever, whose name is holy: 'I live in a high and holy place, but also with him who is contrite and lowly in spirit, to revive the spirit of the lowly and to revive the heart of the contrite'"; Psalm 138:6:"Though the Lord is on high, he looks upon the lowly, but the proud he knows from afar"; Proverbs 11:2: "When pride comes, then comes disgrace, but with humility comes wisdom"; Proverbs 16:18: "Pride goes before destruction, a haughty spirit before a fall"; Proverbs 29:23: "A man's pride brings him low, but a man of lowly spirit gains honor"; Isaiah 2:11–12: "The eyes of the arrogant man will be humbled and the pride of men brought low; the Lord alone will be exalted in that day. The Lord Almighty has a day in store for all the proud and lofty, for all that is exalted (and they will be humbled)."

That his desire for his people to be humble is simply for their welfare is stated strikingly in Jeremiah 13:15–17:

Hear and pay attention, do not be arrogant, for the Lord has spoken. Give glory to the Lord your God before he brings the darkness, before your feet stumble on the darkening hills. You hope for light, but he will turn it to thick darkness. [This is a strong threat to make us zealous to flee from pride.] But if you do not listen, I will weep in secret because of your pride; my eyes will weep bitterly, overflowing with tears, because the Lord's flock will be taken captive.

Here is a strong inducement to avoid pride, for it shows how much God desires our humility so we will be in the place where he can have the joy of doing beneficial things for us. This remarkable passage also shows how God does indeed delight more in being merciful than in meting out punishment.

See also Matthew 23:12: "Whoever exalts himself will be humbled, and whoever humbles himself will be exalted"; Philippians 2:3: "Do nothing out of selfish ambition or vain conceit, but in humility consider others better than yourselves" (even the most gifted people can always find some ways in which others are superior to them); 1 Peter 5:5–6: "All of you, clothe yourselves with humility toward one another, because 'God opposes the proud but gives grace to the humble' [Prov. 3:34]. Humble yourselves, therefore, under God's mighty hand, that he may lift you up in due time."

Indulgent Desires

In Romans 6:12 Paul commanded, "Do not let sin reign in your mortal body so that you obey its evil desires." He stressed the urgency of obeying this command by saying, "If you live according to the sinful nature, you will die; but if by the Spirit you put to death the misdeeds of the body, you will live" (Rom. 8:13). Although born again and indwelt by the Holy Spirit, each of us still has a sinful nature at work in our bodies and minds that frequently causes us to have desires— much stronger than our actual needs—for food, sexual gratification, sleep, and many others things to which we easily become addicted. We saw in chapter 10 above how such desires carry with them the lie that only by satisfying them will we be able to carry on the tasks before us.

When we yield to one of these desires, our confidence in Christ falters, and we deny Jesus' promise in John 6:35 that "he who believes in me will never be thirsty." We forget the promise that if we set the Lord before us, he will make known to us the path of life so that we have eternal joy from God (Ps. 16:8, 11). But if we believe these great and precious promises, a sense of joy will rise in our hearts. God will then indicate to us the next step to take in doing his will, and then we will experience what Jesus was talking about when he said, "My food . . . is to do the will of him that sent me and to finish his work" (John 4:34). The joy of knowing that one is doing God's will is far more satisfying than overeating. Also, as the hymnwriter put it,

> When evil thoughts molest,
> With this I shield my breast:
> May Jesus Christ be praised.

Contemplating what Jesus Christ has promised to do for us in the future will lift our hearts to a joy that abides and replaces the impure and fleeting pleasure evil desires might bring.

The passages cited for fighting against these ten states of an unbelieving heart are what make up the "sword of the Spirit, which is the word of God" (Eph. 6:17). As we fight to believe God's promises and to avoid his threats, we will find that this word is "living and active" (Heb. 4:12) because Jesus himself through the indwelling Holy Spirit works in our hearts to cause the Devil to flee from us. God alone has the power to subdue what Paul called the law of sin and death "at work in the members of my body, waging war against the law of my mind and making me a prisoner of the law of sin at work within my members. What a wretched man I am! Who [a person, and not some formula!] will rescue me from this body of death? Thanks be to God—[I will be delivered] through Jesus Christ our Lord!" (Rom. 7:23–25). God, however, will accomplish this deliverance only for those who by their zeal show that they love nothing so much as his loving care and that they fear nothing so much as the consequences of unbelief. Romans 11:19–22 sums up the situation well:

> You [Gentiles] will say then, "[Jewish] Branches were broken off so that I could be grafted in [to the olive tree of God's people]." Granted. But they were broken off because of unbelief, and you stand [only] by faith. Do not be arrogant, but be afraid [of unbelief]. For if God did not spare the natural branches, he will not spare you either. Consider therefore the kindness and sternness of God: sternness to those who fell, but kindness to you, provided that you continue in his kindness [by believing God's promises]. Otherwise, you also will be cut off.

Thus God works in us both to will and to act according to his good purpose (Phil. 2:13)—in two ways. He motivates us positively through blessings far beyond imagining for those who trust him. But he also sets forth clearly the reality of the threats for unbelief that represent his sternness (Rom. 11:22). When we value his promises and fear his threats, then we will diligently work out our salvation by overcoming an evil heart of unbelief. To be sure, at times our hearts are indifferent to these promises and threats, but we can change our motivation if we want to. If we take time prayerfully to consider God's kindness in his promises and his sternness in his threats, our desire for obedient fellowship with him will become stronger.

It is also helpful to have a small group of believers who meet for an evening each fortnight to share experiences in fighting the fight of faith. In fact the warning of Hebrews 3:12–13 to beware lest there be in any of us an evil heart of unbelief implies that the readers would be small groups that met in each other's nearby homes—the main meeting places of Christians for at least the first three centuries of the church. Today the automobile and the telephone have released us from those near us that used to supply members for these small groups. So to obey Hebrews 3:12–13 (and 10:24–25), we must take special pains to gather a small group willing to meet regularly. The agenda during these meetings should be to update one another on how successful we have been in carrying on the fight of faith. Reports of victories in certain adverse circumstances will help others see how to use Scripture when faced with similar problems. Defeats should also be reported so that special encouragement can be given. Then praise for victories and requests for help in failures should be offered during a closing time of prayer.

Review Questions

1. Be able to state 5:1 in a way that (1) translates the participle into a causal clause, and (2) takes the finite verb of the main clause as a first person plural imperative (a hortatory subjunctive).

2. What are the arguments for saying that Romans 5:1–3 implies having a futuristic faith like Abraham's?

3. What is the argument for understanding 5:3 as an imperative command rather than an indicative statement?

4. Explain why, with our past orientation of faith in Jesus' death and resurrection, we should be more strongly motivated to believe God's promises for the future than Abraham was.

5. With two exceptions joy is the barometer of faith (hope, or confidence in God). Cite verses to show this to be so. What are the two sorts of unbelief that bring a pseudo-joy?

6. What passage of Scripture shows the basic aim of Satan and his cohorts? Given this aim, what should be our basic task in living our own Christian lives and in encouraging others in theirs?

7. When Satan accuses Christians (Rev. 12:10), what is the one sin he never taunts us for having?

8. What is a good verse to show that when an attitude of unbelief has gained ascendancy in our hearts, we have not lost forgiveness, so that if we should be killed suddenly before gaining victory over this sinful attitude we would still go to heaven?

9. According to Isaiah 51:12, why does God regard our fearfulness and anxiety as an insult against him?

10. How can a person know the particular will of God for his or her life (it is different for each of us)? What are the key verses on which the answer is to be built?

11. How do Hebrews 3:12–13 and 10:24–25 argue that we must assemble regularly in small groups in order to obey these passages?

NOTES

[1]Reference to faith's perseverance raises questions as to how sin could then remain in Abraham's life—and ours—and how one can nevertheless have full assurance of final forgiveness when that

forgiveness depends on persevering faith. I attempt to answer these difficult questions in chapter 19.

[2] Charles Hodge, *Commentary on the Epistle to the Romans,* rev. ed. of 1886 (Reprint, Grand Rapids: Eerdmans, 1953), 128.

[3] Bruce M. Metzger, *A Textual Commentary on the Greek New Testament: A Companion Volume to the United Bible Societies' Greek New Testament (third edition)* (London: United Bible Societies, 1973), 511.

[4] Note that God's purpose for his people, even after they have made a grave mistake, is for them to profit in the true sense of being "rich toward God" (Luke 12:21).

19

Abraham's Persevering Faith

The preceding chapter showed how Abraham's faith was grounded in God's promises, so that its futuristic dimension was altogether prominent. Now in this chapter we consider the significance of the second and third elements of Abraham's faith, namely, his obedience of faith and his consequent perseverance in faith. Thus far we have considered two instances of Abraham's faith in God's promises: (1) his belief that a son born from his own body would be his heir (Gen. 15:1–6), and (2) his faith upon the reassurance that this heir would be born to Sarah, although she was now ninety years of age (17:15–17). His faith in this second instance produced an obedience and work of faith in that he had himself and the males of his household circumcised (17:23–27).

This chapter reflects on further instances where Abraham's trust led to an obedience of faith that produced a work of faith. Then having in mind all of his acts of faith over the major portion of his adult life, we will consider his perseverance in faith as we attempt to answer certain questions this third aspect raises.

Abraham's Obedience of Faith

While faith must necessarily obey God, it is important to understand from the outset that growth in a life of faith does not mean sinless perfection, even though as we shall see,

301

God's enablement—regeneration—made Abraham's obedience possible. We must therefore ask why this divine
enablement was not always effectual, for Abraham did have
lapses of faith at various times. The answer to this question
will then give us a better understanding of how justification
depends on persevering faith, the second theme of this
chapter.

The First Act of Faith

Abraham's first obedience of faith was his resolve, on the
basis of promises received from God, to move from Chaldea
to Canaan: "By faith Abraham, when called to go to a place
he would later receive as his inheritance, obeyed and went,
even though he did not know where he was going" (Heb.
11:8). It is not hard to imagine the difficulties he encountered when it became known that he was preparing to move
his large household and possessions to a foreign land. People
for miles around must have been scandalized to hear that he
was exchanging his comfortable home for a tent (Gen. 12:8),
and his many friends and relatives for foreign neighbors,
who in all probability would resent his cattle and possessions, so extensive that more than three hundred bond-
servants were needed to manage everything (v. 5; cf. 14:14).
Some must have regarded him as mentally unbalanced when
he explained that he was leaving because God, the Creator of
heaven and earth, was going to show him a land now
belonging to another nation but that would one day belong to
his own posterity. Moreover God had promised that these
descendants would be the means for transmitting his unsurpassed blessings to all of earth's ethnic groups.

But Abraham endured the continued din of this ridicule,
and when all was in readiness, his caravan left the city
because he was "certain of what [he did not yet] see" (Heb.
11:1). He obeyed because he believed God, and as he thus
fulfilled the condition for receiving God's blessings, he had
complete assurance that he would indeed enjoy them.

The most vital concern for each of us is to have a joyful and
fulfilled future. Someone has observed that whatever people
hope for in the future, that is what they worship, and

whatever people worship, that is what they inevitably serve. So when our faith has the vital futuristic component explained in the last chapter, we are assured that God's goodness and love will pursue us throughout our lives. And when our heart's treasure lies with such a God instead of with the treasures of earth, then we will serve him and do as he commands (Matt. 6:19–21, 24). Thus Abraham must have had this hope, this certainty regarding the future, when on the basis of the promises of Genesis 12:2–3, he carried out the commands of verse 1: "Leave your country, your people and your father's household and go to the land I will show you. I will make you into a great nation and I will bless you; I will make your name great, and you will be a blessing. I will bless those who bless you, and whoever curses you I will curse, and all peoples on earth will be blessed through you."

The objection may be raised that it is arbitrary to understand the commands of Genesis 12:1 as calling for an obedience that comes from faith. Some may argue that since the blessings of verses 2 and 3 will come only by meeting the conditions of verse 1, these blessings should be understood as elements in a job description that employees agree to fulfill for commensurate wages; they are not like blessings sick people will receive as they, on the basis of faith in their physician, obediently submit to whatever health regimens are prescribed.

This objection is not valid, however, because there was none of the equivalence that must exist between wages earned and the value of the service rendered the client. The magnificent promises of Genesis 12:2–3 far surpassed the faith required for Abraham to leave his homeland. Indeed, they were like the priceless good health a patient (a client) regains simply by following the prescriptions of the doctor (a patron).

Thus if we could have conversed with Abraham as he was organizing his caravan to leave Chaldea, we would have sensed that he regarded himself as a client receiving benefits far in excess of any sacrifice he was making. Any thought of his doing something heroic for God—as though Abraham were the patron and God the client—would therefore be banished from our minds. In obeying God, Abraham was simply doing what would make his life and that of his posterity fully blessed and significant for the whole of world history. It becomes clear, then, that in his work of leaving Chaldea, Abraham was the client who, instead of priding himself on what he was doing, was giving all praise to his Patron Lord for his great love in promising to do such wonderful things for him.

Abraham's Regeneration

In considering Abraham's faith thus far, we might think that it was nothing more than acting reasonably—doing what was required to receive God's unmatched blessings. But in previous chapters I have emphasized the Bible's teaching that people are totally depraved, unwilling in their pride and self-confidence to be reasonable in surrendering the control of their lives to God. So in describing Abraham's obedience of faith in leaving Chaldea, God's work of regeneration must also be stressed.

Apart from regeneration, people are inclined to hate every evidence affirming that they should humbly acknowledge themselves to be clients, very much in need of the Patron God who is sufficiently wise, strong, and loving to give their lives fulfillment for the future. "Light has come into the world, but men loved darkness instead of light because their deeds were evil. Everyone who does evil hates the light, and will not come to the light for fear that his deeds will be exposed" (John 3:19–20). Here we see how light and reason clearly tell people that they need Someone far wiser and stronger than themselves, and very loving, to plot out the course that each should take in order to have an eternity of happy and fulfilled tomorrows. But only those whose hearts God has regenerated will be reasonable and entrust their lives to him and his promises: "Whoever lives by the truth comes into the light, so that it may be seen plainly that what he has done has been done through God" (v. 21). In other words, people see clearly enough to turn the controls of their lives over to God only after he has given them a new heart that desires to act reasonably.[1]

So Abraham was able to entrust his future to the great promises of God only because God had already worked in his heart to put enmity between him and the serpent's seed, causing him, like Abel, to want to trust and glory in God rather than in himself. Several verses in Genesis hint at this decision, the most striking being Genesis 18:19: "I have chosen [Abraham], so that he will direct his children and his household after him to keep the way of the Lord by doing what is right and just, so that the Lord will bring about for Abraham what he has promised him." Elsewhere too this theme is echoed: "I am the Lord, who *brought* you out of Ur of the Chaldeans to give you this land to take possession of it" (15:7); "God *had me wander* from my father's household" (20:13); "The Lord, the God of heaven, who *brought me out* of my father's household . . ." (24:7). Each of these passages stresses the divine initiative: behind Abraham's decision to obey was God's regenerative activity, so that all credit goes to him.

The language of these verses is very similar to that found in Ezekiel: "I will give you a new heart and put a new spirit in you; I will remove from you your heart of stone and give you a heart of flesh. And I will put my Spirit in you and move you to follow my decrees and be careful to keep my laws" (Ezek. 36:26–27; cf. 11:19–20). Jeremiah 32:40 makes the same point: "I will inspire them to fear me, so that they will never turn away from me." With verses like these in the Old Testament, it is no wonder Jesus marveled that Nicodemus, the leading teacher in Israel, knew nothing of regeneration (John 3:10).

Abraham's Lapses of Faith

Regeneration does not mean sinless perfection, and we have already mentioned how the Genesis account emphasizes Abraham's several lapses of faith. Abraham's first lapse may have been taking his nephew Lot with him, when God had commanded him to "leave his people. . . and go the land I will show you" (Gen. 12:1). According to Genesis 12:4, "[Abraham] left, as the Lord had told him," but "Lot went with him." Lot had many flocks, possessions, and servants

(13:5–6), and having these along would provide greater security for Abraham, a stranger in a foreign land. Such vast flocks, however, needed grass, and Abraham, who had been used to the fertile river-bottom land of Ur, was uneasy about the drier highlands of Judea. When God appeared to him there, he did commemorate the occasion by building an altar (12:7), although apparently he was restless and so moved on southward. Then when famine struck, the only apparent way to keep his and Lot's flocks alive was to go to Egypt, where food and provender were usually abundant.

His desire for a security guaranteed by large possessions and plenty of food was indeed satisfied in the land of Egypt—but at the terrible expense of being out of the land God had promised and separated from the wife through whom the great nation God had promised would come. Now the joy he had had in the promises of God had been superseded by his desire for earthly security, and as a result he was in an experience not unlike that of Paul: "What I do is not the good I want to do; no, the evil I do not want to do— this I keep on doing" (Rom. 7:19).

Abraham had so desired to be in the place where God's great promises would be fulfilled that he had suffered all the difficulty of leaving Chaldea, but now he was in Egypt— without Sarah. He had painted himself into a corner. There was no possibility from a human vantage point for getting out of Egypt to the place where God would fulfill his promise, for how could Sarah ever be extricated from Pharaoh's harem? So desperate was Abraham's plight that he could have known of no formula by which he could escape. Again like Paul, he could only say, "What a wretched man I am! *Who* will rescue me?" (Rom. 7:24).

But as with Paul, so with Abraham: God was the one who could and did deliver. Miraculously, Sarah was returned to Abraham, who in the meantime had become "very wealthy in livestock and in silver and gold" (Gen. 13:2). So impressed was he at this great deliverance that he returned "to the place between Bethel and Ai where his tent had been earlier and where he had first built an altar. There [Abraham] called on the name of the Lord" (vv. 3–4). This experience of being delivered out of Egypt greatly encouraged him to believe that God would indeed keep his promises.

One evidence of his increased confidence in God was that he was now less dependent upon possessions. Now he was willing to let Lot take the best part of the land, while he himself moved to Hebron, a settlement in the hills above the Jordan valley. There he built another altar to God (Gen. 13:18). In these benevolent and worshipful acts he was walking in the many footsteps of faith that according to Romans 4:12 are normative for all the people of God. It should be noted, however, that just as God had originally caused him to wander from his father's house (20:13), so this later step of obedience came about in part because of how remarkably God had rescued him from the difficulties incurred by his sin, and not because Abraham was in any sense a religious hero.

His next great step of obedience was taken when he believed God's promise to give him a son by Sarah, even though she was ninety years old and so far had been barren. In the preceding chapter I argued that Abraham's laughter in Genesis 17:17 was a laughter of faith and not mocking, unlike Sarah's in Genesis 18:12. We also saw how Paul regarded this laugh of faith as evidence of Abraham's belief in God, who gives life to the dead and calls into existence what had not existed. Such faith was possible because, as Paul accurately observed, Abraham had been "strengthened [by God] in his faith" (Rom. 4:20).

But between these two expressions of faith Abraham had another lapse. The fear that Sarah could not bear him a son had gained the ascendancy in his heart, and so at her suggestion he fathered a child by Hagar, Sarah's chief maidservant (Gen. 16:1–4). Hagar then became so unbearably proud that Abraham permitted Sarah to send the pregnant Hagar away. Though this decision must have been very painful for him, God worked remarkably by appearing to Hagar through an angel. Telling her to return to Sarah and humbly submit, he then promised that from her son Ishmael a large nation would be established (vv. 9–10). But lest Abraham think that Ishmael would indeed be the seed that had been promised, God predicted that instead of being a blessing to people, "He will be a wild donkey of a man; his hand will be against everyone, and everyone's hand against him" (v. 12).

As a result Abraham, seeing how God took care of Hagar and what God would do with Ishmael, even though not the son through whom the nation would be built, became the more deeply convinced that God was with him and would keep his promises. So in the aftermath of Abraham's disobedience and unbelief in fathering a child by Hagar, God strengthened his faith so that when he was told that he and Sarah would have Isaac, he laughed the laugh of faith (Gen. 17:17).

But before Sarah bore Isaac, unbelief prevailed again in Abraham's heart. Having now moved south to Gerar, he began to fear that Abimelech, the local chieftain, would kill him in order to get Sarah as a wife. Therefore he told Abimelech that she was his sister, and Abimelech took her. Soon after, God warned Abimelech in a dream that she was Abraham's wife and that he would die if he kept her (Gen. 20:3–7). So Abimelech immediately returned Sarah to Abraham, along with cattle and servants as a gift, and invited him to dwell wherever he wanted in Abimelech's territory (vv. 8–16). Abimelech had become convinced that God was with Abraham in all that he did, and so Abimelech also made a treaty with him, wanting to remain on good terms with one so blessed by God (21:22–34). In the meantime Sarah gave birth to Isaac (vv. 1–7).

Thus in the aftermath of another time when Abraham was in unbelief, God marvelously worked to sustain him, and this additional experience of God's desire and ability to keep his promises further strengthened his faith. Therefore after concluding his treaty with Abimelech, "Abraham planted a tamarisk tree in Beersheba, and there he called upon the name of the Lord, the Eternal God" (Gen. 21:33).

At a later time, when God commanded him to slay his only son, Isaac, as a sacrifice, Abraham now had such confidence in God that he forthwith made preparations to kill the one through whom God had promised that he would father a great nation. He was convinced that God would even raise Isaac from the dead in order to make good his promise.

Accordingly Abraham told his servants as he and Isaac left to go to the place of sacrifice, "Stay here with the donkey while I and the boy go over there. *We* will worship, and then *we* will come back to you" (Gen. 22:5). Thus the writer of Hebrews properly interprets this incident when he says, "By faith Abraham . . . was about to sacrifice his one and only son. . . . [He] reasoned that God could raise the dead" (Heb. 11:17–19). And when God saw Abraham's faith he said, "Do not lay a hand on the boy. . . . Now I know that you fear God, because you have not withheld from me your son, your only son" (Gen. 22:12). God also declared, "I swear by myself . . . that because you have done this . . . I will surely bless you." Then he repeated almost verbatim the promises he had initially made to Abraham in Genesis 12:2–3, which proves that God's blessings are dependent on a faith that obeys and finally prevails over unbelief, not just on the first act of faith.[2] So Abraham's life climaxed with an obedience that implied strong confidence in God's ability to work supernaturally in order to remain true to his promise.

In recounting these parts of Abraham's life, we thus see concrete examples of how faith in God's promises causes a person to obey God and produce works of faith. Abraham's lapses into sin show that such faith is not perfect and unwavering but grows progressively in strength, especially as God works to overcome apparently hopeless situations brought on by the sin of unbelief. So we are led to understand Abraham's persevering obedience of faith as a divine work in which God's glory became manifest precisely against the backdrop of Abraham's imperfection. Indeed, growth in grace surely comes as a person obeys God and does not yield to temptation. But growth also comes from the chastenings God inflicts on people for falling into the sin of unbelief, a thesis confirmed by Hebrews 12:5–6: "My son, do not . . . lose heart when [the Lord] rebukes you, because [he] disciplines those he loves, and he punishes everyone he accepts as a son [Prov. 3:11–12]"; "No discipline seems pleasant at the time, but painful. Later on, however, it produces a harvest of righteousness and peace for those who have been trained by it" (Heb. 12:11).

The life of Abraham therefore is not to be understood as

the development of a religious hero, but as the story of one who developed faith and godliness as a beneficiary of God's mercy. Such a life fits well into God's purpose in creating the world: to show forth his glory in his merciful goodness.

Abraham's Persevering Faith

At this point we must answer several questions regarding the relationship of obedient, persevering faith such as Abraham demonstrated to the all-important subject of justification, the indispensable foundation that must be in place for God to show blessings to sinners.

When Did Abraham Become Justified?

According to Genesis 15:6, his faith was credited to him for righteousness when, after being in Canaan for ten years, his confidence that he would have an heir was rekindled as God promised that his progeny would one day be as numerous as the stars in the night sky. But what about Abraham's first act of faith, when he obeyed God and left Chaldea? If he was not declared forgiven until ten years later, was he still a guilty sinner when he responded positively to God's promises in Genesis 12:2–3, and also during the following years up until 15:6? No, for I argue that he most certainly was justified from the very first time he believed God in Chaldea because his confidence in God's promise then was not essentially different from the confidence he regained from God's repeated promise in 15:4–5.

These two facts from Abraham's life thus lead to the thesis that *the condition for justification is persevering faith*. This view is supported not only by the virtual impossibility of supposing he was God's enemy even after his first act of faith in leaving Chaldea, but also by Paul's use of Genesis 15:6 for Abraham's act of faith twenty-four years later (discussed in the preceding chapter), when at the age of almost one hundred he was told that he would have a son by Sarah, then ninety and barren all her life (Gen. 17; Rom. 4:17–22).

A final consideration strengthening the thesis that justification depends on persevering faith is James's use of

Genesis 15:6 to affirm that Abraham was justified by faith "some time later" when he showed his willingness to offer up Isaac (Gen. 22:1–19).

> Was not our ancestor Abraham considered righteous [justified] for what he did [by works] when he offered his son Isaac on the altar? You see that his faith and his actions were working together, and his faith was made complete by what he did [by works]. And the scripture was fulfilled that says, "Abraham believed God, and it was credited to him as righteousness" [Gen. 15:6]. . . . You see that a person is justified by what he does [works] and not by faith alone. (James 2:21–24)

In the sixteenth century Protestantism's founders, Luther and Calvin, found difficulty in harmonizing this passage with Paul's emphasis that people are saved by faith and not by works (Eph. 2:8–9). Luther affirmed that "many sweat hard at reconciling James with Paul . . . but unsuccessfully. 'Faith [alone] justifies' [Paul, in Rom. 3:28] stands in flat contradiction to 'Faith [alone] does not justify' [James 2:24]. If anyone can harmonize these sayings, I'll put my doctor's cap on him and let him call me a fool."[3] But Luther (and Calvin) did not enjoy the benefits of the rather recent movement in biblical theology and so were apparently unaware that Paul used "works" in two very different senses.[4] Thus Luther unfortunately repudiated James as subcanonical.

Calvin, for his part, gave a meaning to James's use of "justification" that is not supported by the text. A second-generation leader of the Reformation after Luther, Calvin was fearful of weakening the Bible's authority over the church in any way, and so, unlike his predecessor, he refused to discount the authority of James's epistle. Trying to keep James on a par with the other canonical books, he argued that his epistle and Paul could be reconciled by realizing that for James, "justify" meant the "declaration" rather than the "imputation" of righteousness.

> How, then, shall we say that [Abraham] obtained righteousness by an obedience that followed long after [Gen. 15:6]? Therefore either James wrongly inverted [faith and obedience]—unlawful even to imagine!—or he did not mean to call him justified, as if he deserved to be reckoned righteous. What

then? Surely it is clear that he himself is speaking of *the declaration, not the imputation,* of righteousness. It is as if he said: "Those who by true faith are righteous [justified] prove their righteousness [justification, forgiveness] by obedience and good works, not by a bare and imaginary mask of faith." . . . As Paul contends that we are justified apart from the help of works, so James does not allow those who lack good works [that always accompany genuine faith] to be reckoned righteous. (20:816 [3.17.12], italics added)

Calvin was surely aware that one of James's concerns was to strip away all validity from a faith understood simply as assent to some theological doctrine, for James noted that even the demons assent to the doctrine that there is only one God (James 2:19). But unlike mere professing Christians, whose outlook and attitude are unaffected by this fact, the demons cannot even begin to think about it without shuddering at its terrible implications for their future as rebels against God. And since they tremble when thinking about God's oneness, the demons are actually closer to genuine faith than professing Christians who readily affirm God's oneness but do not grasp its far-reaching implications. Although such professors are feverishly seeking the many good things the one God has lovingly made available for them in the world he created, they never once bother to worship and glorify him for these benefits, and so they store up for themselves the full force of God's wrath against them at the future day of judgment (Rom. 1:21; 2:4–5).

Therefore in James's thinking genuine faith must go beyond mere intellectual assent concerning biblical doctrines. People must let the implications of these doctrines radically affect their hearts so that they respond positively to God with the obedience and works of faith. Thus in James 2:18 he recounts the objection to be raised against those who regard faith as simply mental assent: "You [say you] have faith; [but] I have deeds. [Try to] show me your [genuine] faith without deeds [which you will find impossible], and I will [easily] show you my [genuine] faith by what I do." So the apparent contradiction between James and Paul vanishes when one understands that James was advocating, in his own way, Paul's affirmation that "in Christ Jesus . . . the only thing that counts is faith expressing itself through [the works of] love" (Gal. 5:6). Paul therefore wanted to say the same thing as James: genuine faith carries with it the power to do righteous works.

Paul would also have agreed with James that Abraham's work of preparing to sacrifice Isaac was an obedience of faith because it demonstrated his confidence in God's promises. But he would have disagreed strongly with Calvin, who saw obedience and works as only accompanying, and not stemming from, genuine faith. Back in chapter 12 we noted the key statement in Calvin's *Institutes* (3.2.29) showing that in his thinking, faith could have nothing directly to do either with God's commandments or with the conditions for receiving his promises.[5] Thus in speaking of God's repeating his promises to Abraham and undergirding them with an oath "because you [Abraham] have obeyed my voice [in preparing to sacrifice Isaac]" (Gen. 22:18), Calvin asked, "Did Abraham merit by his obedience the blessing whose promise he had received before the commandment was given? Here, surely, we have shown without ambiguity that the Lord rewards the works of believers with the same benefits as he had given them before they contemplated any works, as he does not yet have any reason to benefit them except in his own mercy" (20:823 [3.18.2]).

But in saying this, Calvin went against the precise wording of Genesis 22, which explicitly affirms that the promise was undergirded by an oath because Abraham obeyed God's voice. But Calvin could not bring himself to say that any of God's blessings are ever given because of an obedience of faith.

> Those whom the Lord has destined by his mercy for the inheritance of eternal life he leads into possession of it . . . by means of good works. What goes before [obedience and good works] in the order of the dispensation he calls the cause of what comes after [eternal life]. In this way he sometimes derives eternal life from works [e.g., Rom. 2:6–10; see 20:821 (3.18.1)], not intending [eternal life] to be ascribed to [good works]; but because he justifies those whom he has chosen in order at last to glorify them [Rom. 8:30], he makes the prior grace [of doing good works and being obedient], which is a

step to that which follows, *as it were the cause.* But whenever the *true* cause is to be assigned, he does not enjoin us to take refuge in works but keeps us solely to the contemplation of his mercy. (20:787 [3.14.21], italics added)

Had Calvin realized that Paul spoke of works in the two sharply different senses noted above (see n. 4), he would not have had to explain why he changed what Scripture calls a cause (e.g., Gen. 22:18) into a "step," "as it were." This is not Berean docility to Scripture but a forcing of Scripture to fit a theological system deemed absolutely indispensable. Calvin should have honored the affirmation of Galatians 5:6 that faith expresses itself [reflexive!] in the works of love. Likewise, he should have taken seriously Paul's speaking of a "work produced by faith" (1 Thess. 1:3) and an "act prompted by [one's] faith" (2 Thess. 1:11).

Calvin's attempt to harmonize James and Paul contains other problems. In declaring that James in 2:24 meant to point out how Abraham's faith was publicly declared as genuine but was not imputed to him for righteousness in the sense of full forgiveness, he was going against the intended meaning of Genesis 15:6 (see chap. 17 above), which James cited to affirm his assertion. Furthermore, James's concern in 2:14–26 was to urge a faith that saves a person (v. 14), not simply to tell people how they could demonstrate their saving faith. Another problem, which relates to perseverance, is Calvin's concession that Abraham had been justified by faith long before the incident of Genesis 15:6: "For Abraham [the Lord] reckoned faith as righteousness . . . after he had for many years excelled in holiness of life. . . . Yet he still had a righteousness set in faith [during the years from Gen. 12:1 to 15:5]. From this we infer, according to Paul's reasoning, that [Abraham's justification] was not of works [Eph. 2:9]" (20:778 [3.14.11]). So Calvin affirmed that Abraham was justified by his first act of faith "many years" before Genesis 15:6 (cf. Heb. 11:8 and the section "The First Act of Faith" above).

But if Calvin agreed that God had already counted Abraham's first act of faith (Gen. 12:4) for righteousness and then said the same in response to his act of faith ten years later (15:6), then he should have been willing to let James apply Genesis 15:6 to Abraham's faith in being willing to offer up Isaac, especially when Paul applied this verse to Abraham's act of faith in Genesis 17 (Rom. 4:17–22). Thus Calvin too should have taught that justification depends on a persevering faith, since he regarded Abraham as already justified when Genesis 15:6 occurred. But inconsistent with his last statement quoted just above, he insisted that "Abraham had been justified by his faith when Ishmael was as yet not conceived, who had already reached adolescence before Isaac was born. How, then, shall we say that he obtained [imputed] righteousness by an obedience that followed long after [Gen. 15:6]?" (20:816 [3.17.12]). These several inconsistencies in his attempt to harmonize James and Paul regarding Abraham's justification therefore confirm our thesis that justification does depend on persevering faith.

Several further reasons also support this affirmation regarding justification. Whenever a client retains a patron of some sort (lawyer, doctor, coach, etc.), the implication is that the client is going to remain committed to the patron for as long a time as it takes to receive the desired benefit. So just as it would be a travesty for sick patients to have confidence in their doctors only during the first consultation and thereafter to ignore their advice, so it is unthinkable that people could receive forgiveness from God just at their first act of faith and after that see no further need to believe and obey him.

Furthermore, faith is the way God's glory and goodness become externalized in the world he created and the history that he ordained. Therefore a single act of faith, followed by years of unrighteous living because one never again believed and acted on any of God's promises, would go completely contrary to his whole purpose in creation. But this situation would be intolerable. Thus it is people like Abraham, whose faith caused him to become a permanent sojourner in a foreign land because his whole desire was concentrated on the fulfillment of God's promises, who, with such persevering works of faith, are the ones God is not ashamed to have call him their God (Heb. 11:15–16).

Here Jonathan Edwards has a most helpful remark in his

"Concerning the Perseverance of Saints."[6] He took issue with Calvin for regarding perseverance as part of Christ's blessing of sanctification rather than as part of the faith that brings justification. Indeed, for Calvin perseverance is essential to receiving eternal life, but only as a part of the sanctification that must exist alongside of, but not because of, justifying faith. Edwards argued, however, that perseverance is an essential part of justifying faith:

> But [contrary to Calvin] we are really saved by perseverance. . . . Faith is the great condition of salvation: it is that by which we are justified and saved, as [faith] is what renders it congruous that we should be looked upon as having a title to salvation. But in this faith on which salvation thus depends, the perseverance that belongs to it is one thing that is really a fundamental ground of the congruity that faith gives to salvation. . . . Without [perseverance], it would not be fit that a sinner should be accepted to salvation. . . . For, though a sinner is justified in his first act of faith; yet even then, in that act of justification, God has respect to perseverance as being virtually [implied] in the first act. And it is looked upon as if it were a property of that faith by which the sinner is then justified . . . because by divine establishment [perseverance] shall follow [i.e., God has promised it]; and so [perseverance] is accepted, as if it were a property contained in the faith that is then seen [at the first act]. . . . Without this [acceptance of perseverance as virtually in the first act of faith], it would not be congruous that a sinner should be justified at his first believing; but it would be needful that the act of justification should be suspended till the sinner had persevered in faith.

It is noteworthy that Edwards stays far away from the Roman Catholic position that no one can be assured of forgiveness until life's end, when one could prove perseverance. To the contrary, he insisted that a person is justified at his first act of believing. This line of thought leads to the second question that basing justification on persevering faith raises.

Can Believers Always Have the Assurance of Going to Heaven?

How can believers always have the assurance of going to heaven when death might suddenly overtake them during one of their lapses of faith? As applied to Abraham, this question would ask, "Were Abraham's sins forgiven when he was stranded in Egypt and Sarah had been taken into Pharaoh's harem?" Or, "Were his sins forgiven when he tried to raise up the promised offspring by Hagar, Sarah's chief maidservant?" The answer to both is yes, for on the basis of an act of faith, God continues to be the "compassionate and gracious God, *slow to anger*, abounding in love and faithfulness, maintaining love to thousands, and forgiving wickedness, rebellion and sin" (Ex. 34:6–7). Exodus 20:5–6 enlarges on this point by quoting God as saying, "I, the Lord your God . . . [show] love to a thousand generations of those who love me and keep my commandments [but not without lapses]."

Since God is slow to anger, he maintains forgiveness for the person who lapses from faith for a period of time. God's people do have their experiences of defeat, times described by Paul in Romans 7:13–25. In such times they learn the power of their inbred sin and become more aware that only God through Christ has the power to break its grip on their lives. The lessons Abraham learned of God's deliverance during his lapses of faith were, as we have seen, vital for its strengthening. Therefore a person would not be lost during such a lapse if death overtook that person. God maintains forgiveness during such times, since he has permitted these lapses in believers in order to strengthen their faith.

Another reason why forgiveness is maintained during such lapses is that one of the promises people believe when they turn to God as their Patron Lord is that he will work to enable them to persevere to the end: "[Jesus] is able to save forever those who come to God through him, because he always lives to intercede for them" (Heb. 7:25 margin). So those in a Romans 7 experience have the confidence described in Psalm 40:1–3: "I waited patiently for the Lord; he turned to me and heard my cry. He lifted me out of the slimy pit, out of the mud and mire; he set my feet on a rock and gave me a firm place to stand. He put a new song in my mouth, a hymn of praise to our God." This promise is one of the mainstays of those who discover that an evil heart of unbelief has gained the ascendancy; it provides powerful encouragement to believe that they still have the forgiveness of sins, and that on the basis of this confidence they can carry on the fight of faith described in chapter 18.

Scripture, however, does speak of those who once had faith and then made shipwreck of it (1 Tim. 1:18–20). Likewise the second and third soils in the parable of the sower (Matt. 13:3–9, 18–23, and parallels) represent people who at one time committed themselves to God as their Patron Lord but then allowed trouble, persecution, the worries of this world, the deceitfulness of wealth, and the desires for the pleasures of life to choke the implanted word, so that it died out. Only the people represented by the fourth soil, who hear the word and hold it fast in a noble and good heart and bear fruit in patience, persevere to the end and are saved.

This last paragraph, however, seems to contradict our assertion that people are justified in their first act of faith, an affirmation made to do justice to the biblical teaching that people are justified through believing. For example, Romans 1:17 declares that in the gospel "a righteousness from God [forgiveness] is revealed . . . that is by faith," and John 3:18 says, "Whoever believes in [Jesus] is not condemned." The necessary implication of these and many similar statements is that a person's sins are forgiven the moment he or she believes, that is, the moment the future is committed to God as Patron Lord.

But other Scriptures warn that a person's faith may not endure or be genuine. John tells us that though many believed on Jesus because of his many miracles, "[he] would not entrust himself to them, for he knew all men [and] . . . what was in a man"(John 2:23–25). On another occasion "even as [Jesus] spoke, many put their faith in him. To the Jews who had believed him, Jesus said, 'If you hold to my teaching, you are really my disciples'" (8:30–31). But later these same Jews said to Jesus, "Aren't we right in saying that you are . . . demon possessed?" (8:48). And John 12:42–43 says, "Yet at the same time many even among the [Jewish] leaders believed in [Jesus]. But because of the Pharisees they would not confess their faith for fear they would be put out of the synagogue; for they loved praise from men more than praise from God."

So the test of the genuineness of one's first act of faith is its ability to persevere and, despite temporary setbacks, to fill one again with all joy and peace in believing. Paul accordingly said, "By this gospel you are saved, if you hold firmly to the word I preached to you. Otherwise, you have believed in vain" (1 Cor. 15:2; cf. Rom. 11:19–22).

This necessity for faith to persevere is why Paul told the Philippians to "continue to work out your salvation with fear and trembling [lest unbelief overtake you]" (Phil. 2:12). He applied this rule to his own life as well, for in 1 Corinthians 9:22–23 he related how he had "become all things to all men so that by all possible means [he] might save some." What is significant here is his reason: "I do all this for the sake of the gospel, that I may share in its blessings." Just a few verses later this idea is found again: "I beat my body and make it my slave so that after I have preached to others, I myself will not be disqualified [from sharing the gospel's blessings]" (v. 27). These considerations, however, lead to a third question.

Can Believers Have the Assurance of Sins Forgiven When They First Believe?

If perseverance in faith is the test of its genuineness, how can we have the assurance of sins forgiven when we first believe? When we are in the deep and slimy pit described by the psalmist in 40:1–3, it is well-nigh impossible to recall our first act of faith and determine that it was truly saving faith. So what we should do in these "Romans 7 experiences" is to look again to the cross of Jesus and let his finished work assure us of sins forgiven. This does not mean we are getting converted again; it is simply to erase any lingering question about our first act of faith by making sure that we are trusting in Christ for the forgiveness of sins here and now. Then after determining which of the ten states of unbelief have plunged us into this slimy pit, we should start to lay hold on promises assuring us that God will work to replace our bleak outlook with all joy and peace as we trust him.

These New Testament threats directed at Christians often raise the related question as to how one can presently be assured of salvation when some who now show every evidence of being genuine Christians may nevertheless make shipwreck of faith in the future. The answer is that these threats drive the elect to exercise great care daily to maintain full assurance, so that unbelief will not harden their hearts (Heb. 3:12) and thus cause shipwreck to occur. We are explicitly commanded to exercise diligence "in realizing the full assurance of hope until the end, so that [we] may not be sluggish, but imitators of those who through faith and patience inherit the promises" (Heb. 6:11–12, lit. trans.). Hebrews 10:22–23 makes the same point: "Let us draw near to God with a sincere heart in full assurance of faith. . . . Let us hold unswervingly to the hope we profess, for he who promised is faithful." We make our "calling and election sure" (2 Peter 1:10) by exercising diligence to keep our assurance fervently alive.

There are other encouraging promises as well, such as Paul's confidence that "the Lord will rescue me from every evil attack and will bring me safely to his heavenly kingdom" (2 Tim. 4:18); "God is faithful; he will not let you be tempted beyond what you can bear. But when you are tempted, he will also provide a way out, so that you can stand up under it" (1 Cor. 10:13). There is also the confidence that Jesus "is able to save forever those who come to God through him, because he always lives to intercede for them" (Heb. 7:25). A specific illustration is Jesus' statement to Peter before Peter had denied him three times with curses: "Simon, Simon, Satan has asked to sift you as wheat. But I have prayed for you, Simon, that your faith may not fail. And when you have turned back, strengthen your brothers [with this confidence in my power to keep you from falling]" (Luke 22:31).

So the threats of Scripture need not make us unsure of our persevering to the end. Rather, if we take them seriously, we will understand that they are threats of what will befall people who persist in not believing God. If we work out our salvation in the fear of what unbelief will do (Rom. 11:20), then we will exercise diligence to have full assurance by claiming God's promises. Hence the threats will motivate us to keep on fighting the fight of faith, so that we experience joy and confidence from the promises rather than the fear that such threats can create. Even if we should become lazy or sluggish for a time, as had the readers of Hebrews, we are encouraged to renew the battle, since "the Lord [is] the compassionate and gracious God, *slow to anger,* abounding in love and faithfulness, maintaining love to thousands, forgiving wickedness, rebellion and sin" (Ex. 34:6–7).

But if we fail to respond to God and his promises in this way, there will come a time when the duration of our sluggishness will wear out even God's slowness to anger; thus Exodus 34:7, right after speaking about God's disposition to forgive, suddenly warns that nonetheless he "does not leave the guilty unpunished." So all Christians must be aware that if they allow an evil heart of unbelief to maintain the ascendancy long enough, the time will come when their sinfulness will cause them to "[crucify] the Son of God all over again and [subject] him to public disgrace." Such people cannot be restored again to repentance (Heb. 6:4–6); for them "no sacrifice for sins is left, but only a fearful expectation of judgment and of raging fire that will consume the enemies of God" (10:26–27). The elect take such threats seriously, and they take pains to overcome their evil heart of unbelief as soon as possible. So by taking the Bible's threats seriously and exercising diligence to maintain full assurance, they will make their calling and election sure (2 Peter 1:10).

A good summary of this matter of assurance is found in a sermon often preached by John Wesley: "That assurance of faith which [believers] enjoy excludes all kinds of doubt and fear. It excludes all kinds of doubt and fear concerning their future perseverance; though it is not properly . . . an assurance of what is future but only of what now is."[7] An illustration of "an assurance of what is future" is the certainty of death and taxes. We know that without our meeting any conditions, the tax man and the mortician will be collecting money from us or our estate. But "an assurance of what now is" can be illustrated by the fact that only as we diligently maintain dental hygiene do we have, from day to day, the assurance we will never wear dentures.

In other words, as we are diligent in fighting the good fight of the faith, we have full assurance that Christ will enable us to persevere to the end. Even if we should fail to exercise this diligence for a time, we can resume it and thus again have the full assurance about which Wesley spoke. And we can go on enjoying it as we keep ourselves "in God's love" (Jude 21) and "[continue] in his kindness" (Rom. 11:22).

Review Questions

1. Why is an act of faith coming ten years after Abraham's first act of faith when he left Ur of the Chaldees nevertheless just as essential for his justification?

2. How does one argue that the commands of Genesis 12:1 called for an obedience of faith from Abraham and not works in which he could boast?

3. How does Galatians 5:6 help us see that James was not contradicting Paul when he said that "a person is justified by works and not by faith alone"?

4. Cite two reasons why the condition for forgiveness is persevering faith.

5. How does this insistence avoid the Roman Catholic trap of having no assurance of salvation in this life?

6. In your own words, to be sure you clearly understand Wesley, explain his statement of how we are to have assurance without believing in eternal security.

NOTES

[1]As long as people have access to the knowledge of how they should respond to God, they are responsible to obey, for such access provides people with *physical ability* to obey. Totally depraved people are therefore still held responsible to obey, for though they do not want to and thus lack *moral ability*, they have physical ability to worship God and to be thankful for, all the blessings they enjoy from him through creation (Rom. 1:18–23, esp. v. 20). Likewise in human affairs physical ability makes

people responsible to obey the laws of the land, and an unwillingness to keep these laws (i.e., a lack of moral ability) does not excuse them. For example, the government holds people responsible to pay their taxes as long as information on how to compute them, determined by the latest legislation, is within reach; access to this information makes them responsible. The government will not regard lack of moral ability ("I can't bear to part with this money" or "I want to give my tax money to charity instead") as excusing a person from paying the taxes required by law.

2A lifetime of persevering faith is not always essential to justification. An act of faith made near death will save a person. Thus in response to the faith of one of the criminals crucified with him, Jesus said, "I tell you the truth, today you will be with me in paradise" (Luke 23:43).

3Werner Georg Kümmel, *The New Testament: The History of the Investigation of Its Problems,* trans. S. MacLean Gilmour and Howard Clark Kee (New York: Abingdon, 1972), 26, cited from Luther's preface to the Revelation of John in his German translation of the New Testament, first published in 1522.

4Paul used it pejoratively for works in which people thought they could boast before God (Rom. 3:27–28, lit. trans.; 4:6; 9:32; Eph. 2:9; Titus 3:4–5, lit. trans.). But he also spoke of works that were viewed as honoring God because they proceeded from faith (1 Thess. 1:3; also Gal. 5:6 and 2 Thess 1:11 in the Greek). See Georg Bertram's article on "work": "Ergon," in *Theological Dictionary of the New Testament,* 2:649–52.

5For Calvin, only assurance based on God's supposedly *unconditional* gratuitous promises of mercy could remove fear from the heart and replace it with a sense of being God's child. This assurance made obeying the Bible's commands easier. "[Justification] is the main hinge on which religion turns. . . . For unless you first of all grasp what your relationship to God is, and the nature of his judgment concerning you, you have neither a foundation on which to establish your salvation [forgiveness] nor one on which to build piety toward God" (*Institutes,* 20:726 [3.11.1]).

6This citation is taken from the 1858 edition of Edwards's *Works* (3:515–16; see n. 3 in chap. 7 above), since for some reason certain key statements in this passage have been omitted from the Banner of Truth version.

7John Wesley, "On Free Grace: Rom. 8:32," in *The Works of the Rev. John Wesley, A.M.,* 7 vols., 3d ed. (New York: Eaton & Mains, 1896), 1:485.

20

The Blessings
for Abraham's Seed

Since God's people are all to "walk in the footsteps of [Abraham's] faith," in the last two chapters we have been concerned with the essentials of that faith—futurity, obedience, and perseverance. For Abraham the blessings based on this faith were mainly a land and a posterity that would one day occupy that land as a great nation. But while his faith is normative for all of God's people, these blessings of a land and a posterity are not. What is normative for his seed is learned from incidental happenings and statements throughout the Genesis narrative. Our first task in this chapter is thus to spotlight these incidental remarks, and then to see what further light is cast on them by later revelation. Our second task is to discover the identity of the seed of Abraham who are to inherit these blessings.

The Blessings of Abraham for All Peoples

We saw how Abraham's justification, though made explicit only in Genesis 15:6, was foundational for all the blessings bestowed on him. This same forgiveness also underlies the three blessings all peoples will receive as they persevere in fighting the fight of faith.

To Have God as One's God

Before God told Abraham that circumcision was to be the sign of the covenant that he was making with him and all those who would comprise his seed, he said, "I will make you very fruitful; I will make nations of you, and kings will come from you. I will establish my covenant as an everlasting covenant between me and you and your descendants after for the generations to come, to be your God and the God of your descendants after you. . . . And I will be their God" (Gen. 17:6–8). The promise "I will be your God" continues to be affirmed throughout the remainder of redemptive history (e.g., Lev. 26:12; Ps. 48:14; Jer. 31:33; 32:38; John 20:17; Rev. 21:3, 7). This is clearly the greatest of God's blessings to his people.

To be sure, in seeking for the significance of God as "my" God, there must be no thought of possession so as to control him, as would be the case with "my" bicycle, which is mine to do with as I wish. No, God acts sovereignly: "Our God is in heaven; he does whatever pleases him" (Ps. 115:3). But the statement still conveys much of the idea of possession. Just as owning a car means that all its parts are for the owner's benefit, so the promise "I will be your God" means that all that God is as God, he is for the benefit of those who, like Abraham, are believing in him. Great encouragement to expect a happy future comes from knowing that God finds his full delight in summoning all his omniscience and omnipotence to pursue after his people to do them good. Jeremiah 32:38–41 helps us see this intent as the apex of God's covenant of grace:

> They will be my people, and I will be their God. I will give them singleness of heart and action, so that they will always fear me for their own good and the good of their children after them. I will make an everlasting covenant with them: I will never stop doing good to them, and I will inspire them to fear me, so that they will never turn away from me. I will rejoice in doing them good and will assuredly plant them in this land with all my heart and soul.

As noted in chapter 10 above, the greatest good God does for his people, "the seed of Abraham," is to have them share with him, through the Holy Spirit, the joy that the Father and the Son have in each other.

To Gain Eternal Life

If God loves his people by allowing them to share with him everything that the Creator can share with a creature, then a part of the blessing of Abraham would be eternal life. God gave a hint of this to Abraham when he said, "All the land that you see I will give to you and your offspring forever" (Gen. 13:15). Never during his lifetime did the land become his, and he knew that several generations of his seed must come and go before they would possess it (15:13–16). Nevertheless God had said, "I will give to you [sing.] all the land that you see." It would seem that such a statement could be made only if Abraham survived death.

And survive it he did, because four hundred years after Abraham's death God declared to Moses that he was still Abraham's God (Ex. 3:6), a statement upon which Jesus based his argument for the resurrection from the dead: "In the account of the [burning] bush, even Moses showed that the dead rise, for he calls the Lord, 'the God of Abraham.' . . . He is not the God of the dead, but of the living, for to him all are alive" (Luke 20:37–38). Paul too was convinced of the resurrection, for he spoke of his "hope in what God has promised to our fathers . . . that God raises the dead" (Acts 26:6, 8). Consequently, those who have God as their God must likewise have the eternal life that is his, since having God as one's God means enjoying all that God is for one's benefit. How could anyone on earth not greatly value sharing for all eternity God's own joy in himself!

To Receive Mercy

Abraham's servant used the word *hesed* ("mercy; kindness") to sum up the way God had blessed his master throughout his life. As that life was nearing its end, this mercy climaxed in a most remarkable manner. Isaac needed a wife, but Abraham did not want him to marry a Canaanite woman. Therefore he sent his trusted chief servant back to Chaldea to find a bride for his son (Gen. 24:1–4). Upon arriving at Nahor, a city in Chaldea, the servant prayed,

O Lord, God of my master Abraham, give me success today, and show kindness [*hesed*] to my master Abraham. See, I am standing beside this spring, and the daughters of the towns-people are coming out to draw water. May it be that when I say to a girl, "Please let down your jar that I may have a drink," and she says, "Drink, and I'll water your camels too"—let her be the one you have chosen for your servant Isaac. By this I will know that you have shown kindness [*hesed*] to my master. (Gen. 24:12–14)

Even before he finished praying, Rebekah, a distant cousin of Abraham, arrived at the spring and, filling her jar, began to water her camels. When the servant asked for a drink, she gave it to him and then said, "I'll draw water for your camels too" (v. 19). Marveling at this wonderful answer to prayer, the servant bowed his head and worshiped, saying, "Praise be to the Lord, the God of my master Abraham, who has not abandoned his kindness [*hesed*] and faithfulness to my master" (Gen. 24:26–27).

The Hebrew *hesed* is a very important term in the vocabulary of the Old Testament. Many have understood this word as a necessary implication of *berit* ("covenant"),[1] and so the old ASV and the RSV regard it as signifying "covenant-keeping love," or "steadfast love." In a more recent article, however, H. J. Stoebe argues that *hesed* should rather be understood as that attitude in God that led him to enter into a covenant with Israel.[2] Stoebe's basic argument comes from Deuteronomy 7:7–9, where God's *hesed* to undeserving Israel was what led God to make a covenant with Abraham and his seed. "It was because the Lord loved you and kept the oath [covenant] he swore to your forefathers that he brought you out with a mighty hand and redeemed you from the land of slavery" (v. 8). For Stoebe, then, *hesed* was God's love that led him to make a covenant with Israel. Verse 9 then says, "Know therefore that the Lord your God is God; he is the faithful God, keeping his covenant and love [lit. trans. here of *hesed*] to a thousand generations of those who love him and keep his commands." To be sure, God's basic stance toward Israel was controlled by his covenant. But it did not control all of God's actions. The *hesed* that had initiated the covenant also determined how the covenant should be administered in new situations.

An instance of the nontheological use of this word casts light on its meaning. According to Genesis 20:13 Abraham had said to Sarah as they left Chaldea and embarked into foreign lands, "This is how you can show your *hesed* to me: Everywhere we go, say of me, 'He is my brother'" (according to v. 12, Abraham was actually her half-brother). For Sarah to say this and thus become vulnerable to Pharaoh and later Abimelech was obviously more than should be expected of a wife. From this and other nontheological passages in the Old Testament, we can see that *hesed* represented an action far beyond what one would be obligated or expected to do, thus conveying the idea of performing a benefit that is merciful and wonderful beyond all that is customary or even imaginable. This word occurs most often in the Psalms, where it is used to represent how God will do abundantly above and beyond all that his people expect of him. So, for example, Psalm 33:18–19 says, "But the eyes of the Lord are on those who fear him, on those whose hope is in his *hesed*, to deliver them from death and keep them alive in famine." This promise comforts the saints by assuring them that in dire circumstances God will do "immeasurably more than all we ask or imagine" (Eph. 3:20) as his goodness and *hesed* follow them throughout their lives. So to have the blessing of Abraham is to have God not only working in surprisingly wonderful ways for his people as they trust him but pursuing relentlessly after them to do them such good eternally, as David said in a literal rendering of Psalm 23:6.

Thus the blessing of Abraham for all his seed consists fundamentally in having their sins forgiven, having God as their God, gaining eternal life, and seeing God do wonderfully surprising things for them in keeping his covenant of mercy. But having enumerated such valuable blessings, we now have the greatest interest in knowing just who the seed of Abraham are who will enjoy these blessings that compose the inheritance (Gal. 3:29).

The Identity of the Seed of Abraham

According to Jewish thinking in New Testament times, actual physical descent from Abraham was the best qualification for regarding oneself as the seed of Abraham. This understanding is clearly reflected in what John the Baptist said to the Jewish multitude who came out to be baptized: "Produce fruit in keeping with repentance. And do not begin to say to yourselves, 'We have Abraham as our father.' For I tell you that out of these stones God can raise up children for Abraham" (Luke 3:8). Even Gentiles who became full proselytes by submitting to circumcision, proselyte baptism, and the presentation of an offering could never lay claim to the merit that a physical descendant of Abraham had by virtue of that fact. "Participation in Abraham's merit was contingent upon being his physical descendant; proselytes had to forgo all such participation simply because they were not physically descendants."[3]

Although the Christian Justin Martyr (c. A.D. 130) may have overstated the Jewish point of view somewhat in his *Dialogue with Trypho*, he nevertheless affirmed the importance a Jew attached to physical descent from Abraham when he said to Trypho, "[Your teachers] beguile you . . . supposing that the everlasting kingdom will be assuredly given to those who are of Abraham after the flesh, although they be sinners, and faithless, and disobedient towards God."[4]

Several New Testament passages that mention the seed of Abraham, however, unequivocally deny that physical descent is essential for enjoying the benefits of the covenant God made with him and his seed. We saw in preceding paragraphs what John the Baptist said to the Jews. Jesus warned them similarly: "I know you are Abraham's descendants. Yet you are ready to kill me. . . . If you were Abraham's children . . . then you would do the things Abraham did. As it is, you are determined to kill me, a man who has told you the truth. . . . Abraham did not do such things" (John 8:37–40). Paul too, in writing to the Gentile Galatians, declared, "Understand, then, that those who believe are children of Abraham" (Gal. 3:7). But does the Old Testament itself agree with such a view, or is this New Testament view a radical reinterpretation?

An examination of the Abrahamic narrative, Genesis 17 in particular, reveals that the seed of Abraham, to whom the covenant blessings were promised, was not coextensive with his physical descendants. For one thing, these blessings applied only to one of Abraham's several children. Both Ishmael and the six sons Abraham had by Keturah (Gen. 25:1–2) were excluded, for God had said explicitly, "My covenant I will establish with Isaac" (17:21). Then as the covenant blessings were passed on from Isaac, they went to Jacob and not to his twin, Esau (chaps. 25, 27).

There is also evidence that the "seed of Abraham" extended beyond the boundaries of his physical descendants. According to Genesis 17:5, Abraham would become "a father of a *multitude of nations* [lit. trans.]." In addition to the Jews, only two nations—the Arabians through Ishmael and the Edomites through Esau—came from Abraham's physical posterity. But since the author sees all the peoples of earth as someday blessed through Abraham's seed (12:3), it would seem that the *multitude* of nations and the kings that Abraham would father are in fact to be equated with these worldwide "peoples." Consequently, the writer of Genesis 17 was clearing the way for Abraham to become the father of those from "every tribe and language and people and nation" (Rev. 5:9) who would receive blessings as the "seed of Abraham" without actually being his offspring through Jacob.

Another indication that the seed to whom the promises apply is greater than Abraham's physical descendants is that servants within his household were also to receive circumcision as a sign of the covenant (Gen. 17:10–14). This is not to say that everyone who received circumcision enjoyed the blessings of the covenant, for Ishmael, though excluded from it, was circumcised (v. 23). But it does leave open the possibility that at least some of those who became attached to Abraham's household or, in later years, to the nation of Israel, could enjoy the covenant blessings without having a genealogy that traced back through Jacob and Isaac to Abraham.

Beyond these indications that discourage equating the seed of Abraham with his physical posterity, there are in Genesis certain pointers as to the essential element of the seed of Abraham. The one thing that Isaac and Jacob had in common was the express lack of anything in themselves that presumably would have qualified them to be heirs of Abraham's blessings. As for Isaac, his birth would never have occurred, had things been left up to forces already resident in the world. He was born only because God worked in fulfillment of his promise, "Is anything too hard for the Lord? I will return . . . at the appointed time next year and Sarah will have a son" (Gen. 18:14). As for Jacob, since he was born after his twin brother, Esau, he should not have received the birthright and thus been the one through whom the covenantal promises to Abraham continued to be dispensed. But he became the heir simply because God so ordered it (25:23). In short, just as there was nothing in Abraham himself that qualified him to be called out to found a new nation, so with those who take over his covenantal blessings after him: they are qualified for blessing not because of any quality inherent in themselves but only by virtue of a sovereign act of God.

Thus Paul's doctrine that the seed of Abraham were simply those who trusted God as Abraham did arose from understanding that the most important thing about Isaac and Jacob was God's sovereign working. So in talking about God's choice of Isaac rather than Ishmael, Paul says, "In other words, it is not the natural children [e.g., Ishmael] who are God's children, but it is the children of the promise [e.g., Isaac] who are regarded as Abraham's offspring" (Rom. 9:8). Then in describing Jacob's choice over Esau, Paul declared, "Not only that, but Rebekah's children had one and the same father, our father Isaac. Yet, before the twins were born or had done anything good or bad—in order that God's purpose in election might stand: not by works but by him who calls— she was told, 'The older will serve the younger.' Just as it is written, 'Jacob I loved, but Esau I hated'" (vv. 10–13).

Here it becomes evident that what is decisive in making men and women the true seed of Abraham is God's work. People may think they can obligate him to bless them by supposedly praiseworthy "works," done by recourse to the powers and distinctives ("the flesh") that lie at their disposal. But as Paul points out, the Genesis narrative clearly shows that neither "flesh" nor "works" helps one become Abraham's heir. The attainment of this great blessing comes not through the flesh but through God's promise; not through works but through God's purpose and calling.

Nevertheless the emphasis that this blessing comes through God's working and not through human effort does not imply that people should just helplessly sit by and wonder if God chose them to be children of Abraham. The doctrine of unconditional election, which Paul stresses in Romans 9:6–24, in fact opens to everyone the door of the blessing of salvation because it discourages once and for all any appeal to some distinctive that one possesses or could produce. If salvation depended on producing a certain distinctive, then all those who could not produce it would be automatically excluded. But while there are always some who cannot be this or do that, yet everyone can call out for mercy and help.

We must not overlook how Paul argues from unconditional election to the fact that God proffers salvation to everyone (Rom. 9:30–10:21). In Romans 10:12–13 he puts the argument in a nutshell: "There is no difference between Jew and Gentile—the same Lord is Lord of all and richly blesses all who call on him, for, 'Everyone who calls on the name of the Lord will be saved' [Joel 2:32]." The idea is that since no one possesses any distinctive that can alter God's estimate of him or her as pitiable and undeserving, therefore God's indefinably great riches are available to anyone who calls upon him for mercy. Those who feel the need of God's mercy and are willing to trust him rather than themselves for salvation and its blessings may rightfully regard themselves as the elect and may accept Jesus' offer that "if anyone is thirsty, let him come to me and drink" (John 7:37; cf. Rev. 22:17). Thus people concluding from the doctrine of unconditional election that they could not be saved because they might not be among the elect could do so only by visualizing themselves as needing some special distinctive in order to be elect. Such a conclusion, however, is impossible, for it denies the doctrine itself. But to affirm this doctrine is to know that everyone can be saved who calls upon God and also to rule out finding any encouragement in what an individual is or might be able to do.

So in Romans 4:16 Paul says, "Therefore, the promise [to the seed of Abraham] comes by faith, so that it may be by grace and may be guaranteed to all Abraham's offspring— not only to those who are of the law but also to those who are of the faith of Abraham. He is the father of us all." A person must believe in order to be saved, but since in believing, people look away from what they are or do to what Another is and does, God therefore is ready to save everyone who is willing to come to him as a supplicant of mercy.

Indeed, a faith that is willing to obey is the only qualification for belonging to Abraham's seed. But such faith, if arising long enough before death, will inevitably result in good works. We have already seen how faith in future promises will produce righteous deeds, a truth affirmed by passages declaring that those who are Abraham's seed do the works of love. Thus Jesus taught that an essential characteristic of this seed is that it does good works; in John 8:39–40, for example, he emphasized that the true children of Abraham would reveal themselves because "[they] would do the things Abraham did," and not attempt to kill those who had told them the truth. Far from being a murderer like his physical descendants, who killed the prophets and finally Jesus himself, Abraham was a loving man. As he and Lot stood looking at the lush Jordan valley on the one hand and the drier Judean highlands on the other, Abraham gave Lot complete freedom to choose whichever he preferred, though by rights the choice should have been Abraham's. But Lot selfishly chose the well-watered valley and settled near the city of Sodom (Gen. 13:5–9).

It was not long, however, until four powerful kings raided that valley and carried off not only its material possessions but Lot as well. Again Abraham demonstrated his love in his willingness to "lay down his life for his [brother]" (John 15:13), for supported by only 318 servants, he attacked these four kings to save his nephew. His efforts were successful, and the recaptured wealth of Sodom and Gomorrah then fell into his hands. But as a man who simply wanted to love others and owe no one anything, Abraham took only one-tenth of these goods as a tithe to give to Melchizedek, priest of God Most High, and gave the rest back to the king of Sodom (Gen. 14). Because Abraham was a man of faith, who was blessed by God Most High, his own needs were entirely met, and consequently he was free to give himself to others in a love that was not self-seeking (1 Cor. 13:5). In short, as a man of faith, he produced the works of love.

Hence the essential element of the seed of Abraham is trust in God. He is worth so much to them that they keep his commandments and serve him, since people cannot but serve what they worship. The faith that is their essential characteristic is therefore never a faith separate from the works of love (Gal. 5:6; James 2:14–17). Thus works that stem from faith—that is, from confidence and joy in what God will do for us, enforced by the love he has already shown us—are often spoken of as the condition for salvation (e.g., Gen. 22:16–18; 26:3–5; Ps. 15; Matt. 19:18–21; 25:34–36, 41–43; Luke 10:26–28; 19:1–10; John 5:28–29; Rom. 2:7; 1 Cor. 7:19; Gal. 5:6; 6:8–10; Col. 3:23–24; James 2:24). But as we saw in the preceding chapter, such works are very different from those done to boast in what we are in ourselves. "For it is by grace you have been saved, through faith—and this not from yourselves, it is the gift of God—not by works, so that no one can boast" (Eph. 2:8–9).

How Can God's People Really Be Abraham's Seed?

But against what has been said, the objection could surely be raised that to call people who are not physical descendants of Abraham his "seed" is to violate language conventions. Paul, however, indicated how believers from all peoples of earth—those not Abraham's descendants—can rightly be called his seed. It is because of their union with Christ: "If you belong to Christ, then you are Abraham's seed, and heirs according to the promise" (Gal. 3:29). Paul could say this because "the promises were spoken to Abraham and to his seed. The Scripture does not say 'and to seeds,' meaning many people, but 'and to your seed' [Gen.

17:7], meaning one person, who is Christ" (v. 16). In other words, Jesus Christ was himself a descendant of Abraham both through his physical mother, Mary, and through his legal father, Joseph. So all who have become united to him through the indwelling Holy Spirit are also, in a sense that does not violate language conventions, Abraham's offspring.

Many have felt that Paul's argument here is weak because it all seems to hinge on the fact that the word "seed" in the passage he cited from Genesis is singular rather than plural. But "seed" in the singular is a collective noun, and therefore a historical-grammatical reading of Genesis 17:7, "I will establish my covenant . . . [with] you and your descendants [lit. 'seed']," certainly does not have to mean that the promises God made to Abraham were really for the one individual, Jesus Christ. But is not Paul then guilty of a drastic reinterpretation of this verse and similar passages in the Genesis narrative when he makes "seed" refer to Jesus Christ? Here E. Earle Ellis makes some helpful observations:

> The true significance of Paul's usage lies in the argument running throughout the chapter [Gal. 3]. It is whether the "faith" descendants or the "law" descendants are the true seed; Paul argues that it is only to the former class of posterity that the promises belong. The Jews employ the same restricted use of "seed" with regard to Isaac and Ishmael [i.e., Jews would contend, contrary to Paul, that the singular seed referred to in Gen. 12:7 is not the Messiah but Abraham's posterity through Jacob, for they must exclude Ishmael and also Esau]; Paul takes the collective character of the word to imply a class restriction of a different kind. "A plural substantive . . . if it admits of plurality (as it is interpreted by Paul himself, Rom. 4:18; 9: 7), at the same time . . . involves the idea of unity" [Lightfoot]. . . . It was to the faith-seed that the promises belonged, and this class was determined not by physical descent but by faith-union with Messiah.[5]

The faith of Abraham, Isaac, and Jacob is, as we have seen, the response that answers appropriately to God's blessing people without reference to any distinctive they might inherently possess. Thus Ellis's statement "It was to the faith-seed that the promises belonged" is yielded by the historical-grammatical exegesis of Genesis itself, and Paul's allusion to "seed" in the singular in the Genesis text is appropriate for emphasizing that the seed of Abraham is one sort of people, whose primary characteristic is to regard themselves as clients who look to what God, the loving Patron Lord, will do for them. Setting forth the seed of Abraham in this light, Genesis is open to supplementation by knowledge coming from later revelation regarding the One who makes it possible to bless this class of people. Such a One would be, as it were, their Head, inasmuch as it is through his work that promises to bless them can be made. Thus Paul's argument in Galatians 3:16 is that just as the promises in Genesis are made to those who have faith in what God does, so Genesis holds open the door to the possibility that later revelation will make these promises apply in a particular way to the One whose work enabled God to be righteous in blessing sinners with such promises. Paul's argument, then, is simply another case of the historical-grammatical data of an Old Testament passage forcing the meaning of that passage to remain open and receptive to later revelation.

Therefore since the seed of Abraham, constituted by faith, naturally join with the One who makes that faith possible and thus becomes their Head, and since that Head was himself a physical descendant of Abraham, the term "seed of Abraham" is an appropriate title for all the people of God. As people are *united* to Christ by faith (Gal. 3:7, 29), they become Abraham's seed because Jesus Christ was his physical descendant. "Even Abraham's heirship rested in this faith-union [with the Messiah]," Ellis remarks.[6] That is, Abraham himself is the "seed of Abraham" by virtue of union with Christ, even though the revelation he received told him nothing about Christ. We can even say that Abel, Enoch, and Noah were likewise the seed of Abraham, though Abraham was their seed in the sense of being their physical posterity.

The Status of Abraham's Physical Descendants

As we have seen, the Abrahamic narrative in Genesis predicted that his descendants would be a large nation and occupy the land of Canaan. By the time of Solomon a millennium later (c. 1000–900 B.C.), they had occupied not only Canaan but also land from Egypt to the Euphrates River (1 Kings 4:21). Solomon's reign was oppressive, however, and the ten northern tribes broke away from Judah and Benjamin and made Samaria their capital. But in 721 these northern tribes were defeated by the Assyrians and lost their identity as Jews. The southern kingdom lasted until 587, when it too met disaster and its people were carried off captive to Babylon. When the Babylonians were defeated by Persia, however, some of the Jews were permitted to return to Jerusalem to rebuild a smaller temple (in 538 B.C.). Israel then remained in the former land of Canaan, though almost always under foreign rule, until A.D. 135. At that time, following a third revolt against Rome, all Jews were forbidden to set foot in the territory around Jerusalem, and most of them were soon dispersed to nations throughout the world. Nonetheless with the help of the traditions recorded in their Talmud, they kept their cultural distinctives and so retained their identity as Jews.

Then with the rise of the Zionist movement during the first half of the twentieth century, many Jews returned to Palestine, becoming a nation in 1948. But wars and strained relations between them and the Palestinians and other Arab peoples have characterized their history ever since. Nor have many of them as yet found their Messiah.

But to understand the "seed of Abraham" as consisting only of those who are united by faith to Jesus Christ before his second coming would give an incomplete picture, for Paul cautioned,

> I do not want you to be ignorant of this mystery, brothers . . . [that] Israel has experienced a hardening in part [excluding the ever-present but small remnant] until the full number of the Gentiles has come in. And so all Israel will be saved, as it is written, "The deliverer will come from Zion; he will turn godlessness away from Jacob [Isa. 59:20–21], and this is my covenant with them, when I take away their sins [Jer. 31:33– 34]" (Rom. 11:25–27; cf. vv. 12, 15).

The preceding verses have been talking about the Jewish people's impenitence, and in this passage itself ethnic Israel and the believing Gentiles are distinguished. So here Paul is definitely talking about the future conversion of all ethnic Israel.

Paul saw the fulfillment of God's promises to the seed of Abraham,[7] understood in the more obvious sense as his physical posterity (through Jacob) alive at some future time, as of the greatest importance, "for God's gifts and his call are irrevocable"(Rom. 11:29). Thus there will come a time when the nation of Israel as a whole will become the true seed of Abraham, in the same way as the rest of his seed—through God's special working in their hearts.

God pictures this regeneration in Zechariah 12:10: "I will pour out on the house of David and the inhabitants of Jerusalem a spirit of grace and supplication. They will look on me, the one they have pierced, and they will mourn for him, as one mourns for an only child." At that time Israel will be cleansed from their sins (Zech. 13:1) and all will know the Lord, from the least of them to the greatest (Jer. 31:34). I believe this means that every ethnic Israelite alive at the time of Jesus' second coming will be converted by his appearance, so that the identifiable descendants of Abraham will then also become the "seed of Abraham." In this way the promises to Abraham's descendants will be kept. But we must also remember that throughout history there have always been ethnic Jews who belonged to Abraham's spiritual seed, and we need to understand who they were. First we look at who they were not.

The Disobedient Majority

Our concern here is not with Ishmael and Esau, whom even Jewish exegesis excludes from consideration, but with Abraham's physical descendants through Jacob. What status do they enjoy by virtue of this physical descent? Did the Old Testament give them any encouragement to believe, as the Jews in Jesus' day did, that this lineage itself would make them acceptable, even though they personally were unbelieving and disobedient?

Paul stated that "not all who are descended from Israel are Israel. Nor because they are his descendants are they all Abraham's children" (Rom. 9:6–7). He also pointed out that Jacob's descendants "were all under the cloud and that they all passed through the sea. They were all baptized into Moses in the cloud and in the sea. They all ate the same spiritual food and drank the same spiritual drink. . . . Nevertheless, God was not pleased with most of them; their bodies were scattered over the desert" (1 Cor. 10:1–5). The writer of Hebrews also paints a dark picture of the majority of Israelites: "Who were they who heard and rebelled? Were they not all those Moses led out of Egypt? And with whom was he angry for forty years? Was it not with those who sinned, whose bodies fell in the desert? And to whom did God swear that they would never enter his rest if not to those who disobeyed? So we see that they were not able to enter, because of their unbelief" (Heb. 3:16–19). Stephen too, after summarizing the history of the physical descendants of Jacob, said, "You stiff-necked people, with uncircumcised hearts and ears! You are just like your fathers: You always resist the Holy Spirit! Was there ever a prophet your fathers did not persecute? They even killed those who predicted the coming of the Righteous One. And now you have betrayed and murdered him" (Acts 7:51–52).

Are these statements simply the Christian reaction against Judaism, or do they coincide with what the Old Testament itself teaches about the physical descendants of Abraham through Jacob? According to Ezekiel, God said,

> On that day I swore to them that I would bring them out of Egypt into a land I had searched out for them, a land flowing with milk and honey, the most beautiful of all lands. And I said to them, "Each of you, get rid of the vile images you have set your eyes on, and do not defile yourselves with the idols of Egypt. I am the Lord your God." But they rebelled against me and would not listen to me; they did not get rid of the vile images they had set their eyes on, nor did they forsake the idols of Egypt (20:6–8).

Thus Stephen's view of Israel's past was no Christian reinterpretation of the Old Testament but reflected natural meanings found in the Old Testament itself. The record of Exodus likewise bears out how Israel, shortly after confidently promising at Sinai to "do everything the Lord has said" (Ex. 19:8), constructed a golden calf, danced around it, and in defiance of the second commandment (20:3: "You shall have no other gods before me"), said, "These are your gods, O Israel, who brought you up out of Egypt" (32:4). As a consequence, God pronounced them a "stiff-necked people" (v. 9) and would have destroyed them then and there had it not been for Moses' reminder that such an action would be interpreted by the Egyptians to mean that God had an evil intent in bringing the people out of Egypt (v. 12). As Moses also argued that God had made a covenant with Abraham, Isaac, and Jacob to give their descendants the land of Canaan (v. 13), God relented, and Israel was spared.

A few months later, however, God again determined to destroy them, this time for failure to believe that he would enable them to conquer the inhabitants of Canaan. Again Moses intervened, objecting that if God now destroyed the people just as they were about to enter the land of Canaan, the nations would conclude that God was not able to keep his oath to give his people the land by overcoming its inhabitants (Num. 14:16). Moses also reminded God that he was typically slow to anger and that through his love (again, *ḥesed*) he forgave sin (vv. 17–19). So once more God withheld judgment from Israel (v. 20), although he did condemn them to wander in the wilderness for forty years (vv. 33–34).

Then as the forty years neared completion, Moses gathered the Israelites together and commanded, "Circumcise your hearts, therefore, and do not be stiff-necked any longer" (Deut. 10:16). According to Deuteronomy 30:6 a "circumcised heart" is able to love God; this phrase, then, or a "new heart" (Ezek. 18:31; 36:26; cf. 11:19), is the Old Testament way of expressing regeneration. It is clear, therefore, that for the most part Israel was stiff-necked and uncircumcised in heart, hence unbelievers whom God had to destroy.

The Faithful Remnant

While the New Testament, following the Old Testament, pictures the majority of Israelites in the wilderness as disobedient, it also implies that there was a faithful remnant in their midst. Paul's saying that God was displeased with *most* of those in the wilderness (1 Cor. 10:5) implied that some did please him. The Pentateuch indicates that two of these were Caleb and Joshua. These men represented the minority opinion of the contingent of spies sent to feel out the land of Canaan. Whereas ten declared it was impossible to conquer the land, Caleb insisted that they were well able to do it (Num. 13:30). Together he and Joshua pled with the disbelieving people: "The land we passed through and explored is exceedingly good. If the Lord is pleased with us, he will lead us into that land, a land flowing with milk and honey, and will give it to us. Only do not rebel against the Lord. And do not be afraid of the people of the land, because we will swallow them up. Their protection is gone, but the Lord is with us. Do not be afraid of them" (14:7–9).

The people, however, sided with the majority and even tried to stone Caleb and Joshua. As a result God consigned all except these two (and no doubt a few others) to die in the wilderness. But, said the Lord, "because my servant Caleb has a different spirit and follows me wholeheartedly, I will bring him into the land" (Num. 14:24). Joshua too was a man "in whom is the spirit" (27:18).

It is understandable, then, why Caleb and Joshua, possessing these qualities, so aroused the anger of unregenerate Israel that they wanted to stone them. Here is another instance of God's placing enmity between his people and the seed of the serpent by giving these men circumcised hearts in the midst of those whose hearts remained uncircumcised. Thus we may conclude that Caleb and Joshua were a part of the few "survivors" (Isa. 1:9), the remnant who continued to exist in Israel down through its history.[8] This remnant constituted the seed of Abraham, who enjoyed the blessings described at the beginning of this chapter. These are the people who through Israel's history could genuinely say, "Oh, how I love your law! I meditate on it all day long" (Ps.

119:97), because they were the seed of the woman, her "offspring ... who obey God's commandments" (Rev. 12:17).

"All Israel Will Be Saved"

As was noted above, this event of nationwide salvation will take place at Jesus' second coming. At that time all ethnic Israel alive at that time will be regenerated and join with Gentile believers from many nations under the headship of Christ.

Review Questions

1. Explain the great promise of the gospel, "I will be your God," in other words so that (1) the marvel of it becomes apparent, and (2) the implied danger of this statement is averted.

2. Explain why the promise of God's *hesed* is so great. Draw upon what the word meant to a Hebrew.

3. How does the Genesis text, which a Jew would accept as true, show that being the seed of Abraham is not a matter of physical descent?

4. How does unconditional election encourage everyone to be saved?

5. Explain how Abraham himself was Abraham's seed.

NOTES

[1] E.g., Nelson Glueck, *Hesed in the Bible* (Cincinnati: Hebrew Union College Press, 1967); Rudolf Bultmann, "Eleos," in *Theological Dictionary of the New Testament*, 2:479–80; Norman H. Snaith, *The Distinctive Ideas of the Old Testament* (London: Epworth Press, 1950), 94–130.

[2] H. J. Stoebe, "Hesed," in *Theologisches Handwörterbuch zum Alten Testament*, 2 vols., ed. Ernst Jenni and Claus Westermann (Munich: Chr. Kaiser, 1971–76), 1:599–621.

[3] Strack and Billerbeck, *Kommentar*, 1:119.

[4]Justin Martyr, *Dialogue with Trypho,* ed. and trans. Alexander Roberts and James Donaldson, The Ante-Nicene Fathers, vol. 1 (Grand Rapids: Eerdmans, n.d.), 269.

[5]E. Earle Ellis, *Paul's Use of the Old Testament* (Grand Rapids: Eerdmans, 1957), 71–72.

[6]Ibid., 72.

[7]E.g., Gen. 13:15; 15:5; 17:7–16; 21:12–13; 22:17–18.

[8]God assured Elijah that he was not the only believer left but that there were seven thousand in Israel who had not bowed the knee to Baal (1 Kings 19:18; cf. 18:22). In Paul's day there was also a "remnant [of Israelites] chosen by grace" (Rom. 11:5), and no doubt Paul regarded himself and the other believing Jews as belonging to it.

21

What Was the Purpose of the Law?

After considering the nature of the seed of Abraham and a brief history of the Jewish people, we now turn to the next major event on the timeline of redemptive history: the giving of the Mosaic law to Israel some 430 years after Abraham's time (see Gal. 3:17). In answer to the question of the purpose of the law, Paul answered, "It was added [for the sake of] transgressions until the Seed [Christ] to whom the promise had referred should come" (Gal. 3:19). He spoke similarly in Romans: "The law was added so that the trespass might increase" (5:20), and "In order that sin might be recognized as sin, [the law] produced death in me through [the law] which was good, so that through the [good] commandment sin might become utterly sinful" (7:13).[1] Such an assessment of the law, however, raises several questions that we consider in this chapter.

How Does the Good Law Increase Israel's Sinfulness?

In Galatians 3:21 Paul asked, "Is the law, therefore, opposed to the promises of God?" He answered, "Absolutely not! For if a law had been given that could impart life, then righteousness would certainly have come by the law." The law's inability to impart life was its deficiency, as other verses indicate (e.g., Rom. 8:3); it generally was not accompanied by God's power to dethrone the ego so that people would become supplicants of mercy. Thus, as Paul's answer

implied, there was nothing in the thought structure of the
law itself that kept it from imparting life. As we have seen,
the merciful promises made to Abraham and his seed were
conditioned upon responding to God's commands with an
obedience of faith rather than with service supposedly
deserving recompense. Therefore its work of increasing
Israel's trespass did not come from the law itself but from
sin. And "the Scripture declares that the whole world is a
prisoner of sin, so that what was promised, being given
through faith in Jesus Christ, might be given to those who
believe" (Gal. 3:22). In other words, trespasses increased
because of God's purpose, set forth in Scripture, to put all
things under sin's dominion for the time being. He used the
law to carry out this purpose: "Before this faith [in Christ]
came, we [Jews] were held prisoner by the law, locked up
until [that] faith should be revealed" (v. 23).

Thus the law given through Moses at Sinai kept Israel
locked up, as it were, in a sinful condition, because God's
regenerative power for the most part did not accompany that
law so that the Israelites would humbly submit to it as a law
of faith. It is therefore clear that in placing outside the law
the reason for its inability to make people good, Paul was
necessarily implying that the law itself, both in its content
and its thought structure, was as capable of making people
righteous as was the gospel.

Further discussion of why God used the good law to
increase Israel's sinfulness and consequent punishment will
be aided if we first consider five matters concerning the law's
similarity to the gospel that are not dealt with in the
Appendix below.

Paul Denied That the Law Was Sin

Consider Paul's question and answer in Romans 7:7–8:
"Is the law sin? Certainly not! Indeed I would not have
known what sin was [after conversion] except through the
law. For I would not have known what coveting really was if
the law had not said, 'Do not covet' [Ex. 20:17]. But sin,
seizing the opportunity afforded by the commandment,
produced in me every kind of covetous desire." Paul

concluded, "So then, the law is holy, and the commandment is holy, righteous and good" (v. 12)—as well as "spiritual" (v. 14). This passage makes the same point as Galatians 3:19–23 considered above: the power of sin makes use of the good and righteous law to stir up the sinful tendencies in people.

Some argue, however, that sin comes from the nature of the law itself. On the basis of 2 Corinthians 3:6, "[God] has made us competent as ministers of a new covenant—not of the letter but of the Spirit, for the letter kills, but the Spirit gives life," Dunn has inferred that "the 'letter/Spirit' antithesis [here] is . . . between the law and the Holy Spirit, the regulating principles of the old and new covenants respectively."[2] In other words, it is the verbalized rules of law that encourage legalism and sinfulness, whereas righteousness comes from the new motivation given by the Holy Spirit.

The problem with this understanding, however, is in the way Paul contrasts the "Spirit" and the "letter" in Romans 2:27–29 and 7:6. These two passages make evident that this contrast consists not in the nature of the law in comparison with the Spirit but in whether or not a person has an inward heart desire to obey the law's intended meaning rather than simply to display some visibly observable modes of conduct regarded as evidence of one's compliance with the law. Thus Romans 2:29 says, "A man is a Jew if he is one inwardly; and circumcision is circumcision of the heart, by the Spirit, not by the written code. Such a man's praise is not from men, but from God." In regard to Romans 7:6, Thomas Provence has pointed out that after Paul speaks of Christians as having been released from the law so that they serve in the new way of the Spirit and not in the old way of the written code,

> he immediately launches into a defense of the law which he characterizes as "holy, just and good" (vii 12) and even "spiritual" (vii 14). Since it is impossible to give the law any higher commendation than this, the law of [Rom. 7:]12 and 14 cannot be the same as the "letter" of [2 Cor. 3:6]. The law, or "letter" from which we are released (Rom. 7:6) is the one without the Spirit . . . and thus [is] the very opposite of the "spiritual" law of v. 14.[3]

C. E. B. Cranfield's comment on Romans 7:6 makes the same point:

> [Here Paul] does not use "letter" as a simple equivalent of "the law." "Letter" is rather what the legalist is left with as a result of his misunderstanding and misuse of the law. It is the letter of the law in separation from the Spirit. But since "the law is spiritual" (v. 14), the letter of the law in isolation from the Spirit is not the law in its true character, but the law as it were denatured. It is this which is opposed to the Spirit whose presence is the true establishment of the law.[4]

Romans 8:3 also makes clear that the law by itself is "weakened by the sinful nature" in that it lacks the power of the Holy Spirit. But there is nothing about this law that puts it in conflict with the Spirit, for Paul immediately added that through Christ "the righteous requirements of the law [can] be fully met in us, who do not live according to the sinful nature but according to the Spirit" (v. 4). Then he spoke of how "the sinful mind is hostile to God. It does not submit to God's law, nor can it do so. Those controlled by the sinful nature cannot please God" (vv. 7–8). Thus everything depends on the inward attitude of the heart, with the great contrast lying between the unregenerated flesh and the indwelling, regenerating Spirit. Those indwelt by the Spirit are disposed to comply with the spiritual law of faith, just as they will respond positively to the gospel.

Paul Never Belittled the Law

The similarity between the law and the gospel is further supported by the fact that Paul never belittled the law. He asked, "Do we then nullify the law by this faith? Not at all! Rather, we uphold the law" (Rom. 3:31). This positive stance toward the law is borne out in Paul's three statements that begin by denying that either "circumcision or uncircumcision have any value." In the first he continues, "The only thing that counts is faith expressing itself through love" (Gal. 5:6). The second gives the positive counterpart by saying, "What counts is a new creation" (6:15). For the third, what is important is "keeping God's commands" (1 Cor. 7:19). In

Paul's thinking, therefore, "faith expressing itself in love," "the new creation," and "keeping God's commands" were all in the same category. So the law, or God's commandments, was not regarded as something inferior to faith and the new creation.

The New Covenant Added Only Regeneration of the Heart

A third reason for regarding the law and the gospel as similar is that in those passages speaking of the new covenant as replacing the old, the only change that occurs is that the heart is regenerated by the Holy Spirit. Jeremiah 31:31–33 is the classic passage that makes this difference clear:

> "The time is coming," declares the Lord, "when I will make a new covenant with the house of Israel and with the house of Judah. It will not be like the covenant I made with their forefathers when I took them by the hand to lead them out of Egypt, because they broke my covenant, though I was a husband to them," declares the Lord. "This is the covenant I will make with the house of Israel after that time," declares the Lord. "I will put my law in their minds and write it on their hearts. I will be their God, and they will be my people."

Ezekiel makes the same point:

> I will give them an undivided heart and put a new spirit in them; I will remove from them their heart of stone and give them a heart of flesh. Then they will follow my decrees and be careful to keep my laws (11:19–20).

> I will give you a new heart and put a new spirit in you; I will remove from you your heart of stone and give you a heart of flesh. And I will put my spirit in you and move you to follow my decrees and be careful to keep my laws (36:26–27).

The Old Testament Faithful Loved the Law

The similarity of the law with the gospel is also evident from the attitude that the tiny minority in Israel who were regenerated had toward the law. Moses enjoined Israel to "observe [God's decrees and laws] carefully, for this will show your wisdom and understanding to the nations, who will hear about all these decrees and say, 'Surely this great nation is a wise and understanding people.' ... And what other nation is so great as to have such righteous decrees and laws as this body of laws I am setting before you today?" (Deut. 4:6, 8).

And according to the psalmist, the "delight [of the blessed man] is in the law of the Lord, and on his law he meditates day and night" (Ps. 1:2). Another declared that "the law of the Lord is perfect, reviving the soul. . . . The precepts of the Lord are right, giving joy to the heart. The commands of the Lord are radiant, giving light to the eyes. . . . The ordinances of the Lord are sure and altogether righteous" (19:7–9). Psalm 119:97 exults, "Oh, how I love your law! I meditate on it all day long."

The Law at Sinai Was a Law of Faith

The final evidence for the similarity of the law with the gospel comes from Hebrews 4:2, where the writer declares that "we also have had the gospel preached to us [in today's church], just as they did [the Israelites who came' out of Egypt]; but the message they heard was of no value to them because those who heard it did not combine it with faith." This comparison of law and gospel necessarily implies that the law presented at Sinai was one of faith, with essentially the same content needed for salvation as the message people received in New Testament times. But people today, like the Israelites in the wilderness, are just as liable to God's wrath if they do not, in faith, turn the control of their lives over to the God who yearns to be benevolent to them.

The passages examined in this section make it evident that the law is indeed a spiritual law and similar to the gospel. This conclusion leads naturally to the next question.

Why Give a Spiritual Law to an Unregenerated People?

Moses made it very clear that he regarded the great majority of the Israelites who came out of Egypt as a "stiff-necked people" (Deut. 9:6). To be sure, when they received the law at Sinai, the people had confidently assured Moses that they would obey all of God's commandments. Yet near the end of Moses' life he declared, "To this day the Lord has not given you a mind that understands or eyes that see or ears that hear" (29:4).

As we have seen in chapter 20, however, there were always a few who were regenerated (1 Kings 19:18 mentions seven thousand in Elijah's day), though this group from the time of Abraham onward was always small in comparison to the whole of Israel. Romans 9:32, for example, says that the majority of Israel did not comply with the law, "because they pursued it not by faith but as if it were by works." And according to Romans 11:7,

> What Israel sought so earnestly [forgiveness and compliance with the law] it did not obtain, but the elect [among them] did. The others were hardened, as it is written, "God gave them a spirit of stupor, eyes so that they could not see and ears so that they could not hear, to this very day" [Isa. 29:10]. And David says, "May their table become a snare and a trap, a stumbling block and a retribution for them. May their eyes be darkened so they cannot see, and their backs be bent forever" [Ps. 69:22–23].

Why, then, did God find it desirable to give the law to Israel, when the great majority had no inclination to take the humble stance of those who could only plead for mercy? The answer is that by giving proud, self-confident people a law of faith, they would commit the ultimate sin of standing it on its head, changing it into a law of works. This perversion involved the great cosmic role-reversal in which finite human beings regarded themselves as patron benefactors who served God as the needy client. Thus Paul declared that "the law was added so that the trespass might increase" (Rom. 5:20). Then in Romans 7:13 he asked, "Did [the law] which is good, then, become death to me? By no means! But in order that sin might be recognized as sin, it produced death in me through [the law that] was good, so that through the commandment sin might become utterly sinful."[5]

In Paul's thinking, the law gave the sinful heart the

foothold it needed in order to rise up to the heights of committing the most outrageous sin. In his own case, he spoke of how sin, "seizing the opportunity afforded by the commandment," worked all kinds of evil desire in him, so that he became utterly sinful (Rom. 7:8, 11). From this vantage point, then, we understand how he could say that "the power of sin is the law" (1 Cor. 15:56). The proud, self-reliant ego finds nothing so promising for achieving its goal of being great than to take God's law of faith, which is like a doctor's prescription, and turn it upside down into a law of works, or a kind of job description. Proud people then think of themselves as benevolent patrons performing services for the Almighty but very needy God, and this attitude enables their pride to soar to demonic limits. After his conversion, Paul saw that his pride had indeed soared to these ultimate heights, making him in the process "the worst of sinners" (1 Tim. 1:16). What was true for him as a leading Israelite was therefore at least implicitly true of every other unregenerated Israelite.

Why Did God Want to Make Israel's Guilt So Utterly Apparent?

Now we can see why the presence of the law brings God's wrath (Rom. 4:15). It is because totally depraved people take this law of faith and distort it into a law of works, a job description showing how they can help the needy God. Such cosmic blasphemy deserves the utmost wrath. By the same token, people who have not been given the law based on faith are also without sin's best opportunity for fully realizing itself and so, relatively speaking, are less sinful. Thus Paul declared that "apart from law, sin is dead" (7:8).

Nevertheless all humankind, Gentile as well as Jew, have sinned and "[fallen] short of the glory of God" (Rom. 3:23), so that apart from conversion they have "[stored] up wrath against [themselves] for the day of God's wrath" (2:5). But "Jesus redeemed us from the curse of the law by becoming a curse for us" (Gal. 3:13). Thus our transgression of the law, which consisted in our refusal to trust and glorify God, has been forgiven. And now that we are joined with Jesus, we have his desire, so evident while he was on this earth, to comply with the law as a law of faith, and thus to glorify God.

So while all humankind sin against God by refusing to trust and glorify him, yet Israel stands out in history as the concrete and explicit example of "ultimate sin." For this reason Moses said, "Take this Book of the Law and place it beside the ark of the covenant of the Lord your God. There it will remain as a witness against you" (Deut. 31:26). It has indeed performed this witness: because Israel turned the law into a law of works, God has poured out fearful punishments on them.

The Old Testament itself declares this perversion to be the reason for the disasters that have befallen Israel, especially since her land was taken from her in 587 B.C. When Jeremiah predicted such punishment, the people asked, "Why has the Lord decreed such a great disaster against us? What wrong have we done? What sin have we committed against the Lord our God?" Jeremiah's answer, quoting God, was, "It is because your fathers forsook me . . . and followed other gods and . . . did not keep my law" (Jer. 16:10–11). Then as the Babylonian battering rams were smashing through Jerusalem's walls, Jeremiah acknowledged to God that "[Israel] did not obey you or follow your law; they did not do what you commanded them to do. So you brought all this disaster upon them" (32:23).

The law clearly states that it is not a law of works but of faith. Near the beginning of the Ten Commandments God is quoted as saying, "I, the Lord your God . . . [show] love [*hesed* ('mercy')] to a thousand generations of those who love me and keep my commandments" (Exod. 20:5, 6). Since the blessings coming from such obedience are those of mercy, they can never be regarded as a recompense for obedience and works done for God as a client lord. Rather they are benefits coming from a trustful obedience to him as a patron Lord. So this statement teaches that the Ten Commandments (and any commandment God would ever make) must be understood in terms of a law of faith and never as a law of works.

Paul said Israel transgressed the law because "they purused it not by faith but as if it were by works" (Rom.

9:32). And Isaiah would have agreed with this, for he spoke
of Israel's rejection of the law as part of their unwillingness
to bank their hope on God.

> These are rebellious people, deceitful children, children
> unwilling to listen to the Lord's instruction [*tôrâ*, torah, or
> "law"]. They say . . . to prophets, ". . . give us no more visions
> of what is right! Tell us pleasant things, prophesy illusions.
> Leave this way, get off this path, and stop confronting us with
> the Holy One of Israel!" Therefore this is what the Holy One
> of Israel says, "Because you have rejected this message, relied
> on oppression and depended on deceit, this sin will become
> for you like a high wall, cracked and bulging, that collapses
> suddenly, in an instant. . . ." This is what the Sovereign Lord,
> the Holy One of Israel says, "In repentance and rest is your
> salvation, in quietness and trust is your strength, but you
> would have none of it." . . . Yet the Lord longs to be gracious
> to you; he rises to show you compassion. For the Lord is a
> God of justice. Blessed are all who wait for him (Isa. 30:9–13,
> 15, 18).

Except for the small remnant of regenerated Israelites that
always existed, the great majority of Israel never welcomed
God's gracious entreaties. consequently the nation as a
whole was severely punished for rejecting the law as a law of
faith.

But Israel's punishment was not because it was different
from the other nations nor was it inflicted solely to help
Israel understand its sin. The nations of earth also needed to
understand that these calamities befell Israel because it had
failed to obey God's law of faith. The following passages
make this failure very clear.

> Your children who follow you in later generations and
> foreigners who come from distant lands will see the calamities
> that have fallen on the land and the diseases with which the
> Lord has afflicted it. The whole land will be a burning waste
> of salt and sulfur—nothing planted, nothing sprouting, no
> vegetation growing on it. It will be like the destruction of
> Sodom and Gomorrah, Admah and Zeboiim, which the Lord
> overthrew in fierce anger. *All* the nations will ask: "Why has
> the Lord done this to this land? Why this fierce, burning
> anger?" And the answer will be: "It is because this people

abandoned the covenant of the Lord, the God of their fathers, the covenant he made with them when he brought them out of Egypt. They went off and worshiped other gods and bowed down to them, gods they did not know, gods he had not given them. Therefore the Lord's anger burned against this land, so that he brought on it all the curses written in this book. In furious anger and in great wrath the Lord uprooted them from their land and thrust them into another land, as it is now" (Deut. 29:22–28; cf. Jer. 22:8–9; 2 Chron. 7:19–22).

Ezekiel 5:5–15 is another passage that helps us understand why God gave a spiritual law to a carnal people. As Israel occupied the center ring among the nations, God, the ringmaster, describes the nation's behavior, saying,

> This is Jerusalem, which I have set in the center of the nations, with countries all around her. Yet in her wickedness she has rebelled against my laws and decrees more than the nations and countries around her. . . . Therefore this is what the Sovereign Lord says: I myself am against you, Jerusalem, and I will inflict punishment on you in the sight of the nations. Because of all your detestable idols, I will do to you what I have never done before and will never do again. Therefore in your midst fathers will eat their children, and children will eat their fathers. I will inflict punishment on you and will scatter all your survivors to the winds. Therefore as surely as I live, declares the Sovereign Lord, because you have defiled my sanctuary with all your vile images and detestable practices, I myself will withdraw my favor; I will not look on you with pity or spare you. A third of your people will die of the plague or perish by famine inside you; a third will fall by the sword outside your walls; and a third I will scatter to the winds and pursue with drawn sword. . . .
>
> I will make you a ruin and a reproach among the nations around you, in the sight of all who pass by. You will be a reproach and a taunt, a *warning* and an object of horror to the nations around you when I inflict punishment upon you in anger and in wrath and with stinging rebuke.

But as the nations view the disaster that befell Israel, they should have no attitude of smug superiority, for God had said, "See, I am beginning to bring disaster on the city that bears my Name, and will you [nations] indeed go unpunished? You will not go unpunished, for I am calling down a sword upon all who live on the earth, declares the Lord Almighty" (Jer. 25:29).

It was on such passages that Paul based the following conclusion: "Now we know that whatever the law says, it says to those who are under the law [e.g., Jer. 16:10–11], so that every mouth may be silenced and the whole world held accountable to God" (Rom. 3:19). Clearly, as the nations of earth consider Israel's horrifying history, they should ask why this nation, which has survived so long, should be punished so severely. And in this way Israel's failure to comply with the law as a law of faith should serve as a warning to all nations not to make the same mistake.

Nevertheless every people has been like Israel. The whole of humankind, despite receiving all the benefits they have enjoyed from God, "neither glorified him as God nor gave thanks to him" (Rom. 1:21). As a result his wrath has been revealed against the entire human race by giving them the inclination to behave in unnatural, unseemly ways. Homosexuality has always been rife (vv. 24–27), as have other improper, shameful actions. People are "full of envy, murder, strife, deceit. . . . They are gossips, slanderers, . . . insolent, arrogant, . . . senseless, faithless, heartless, ruthless" (vv. 29–31). But these peoples have also been aware that "those who do such things deserve death" (v. 32). As a result they are very quick to judge others for such actions, though unwilling to face up to their also having done them. Thus all peoples have attempted to present an outward show of righteousness, concluding that because they were able to criticize others for wrongdoing, they themselves were righteous and should therefore escape the judgment of God. They have even regarded the good things God has done for them as his reward for their supposed righteousness, when actually his goodness was bestowed only to get them to repent and thus escape the coming judgment. And unless they do repent, they will receive the full force of God's wrath at the last day (2:1–5).

Yet even though the nations have ignored the warning provided by Israel, God's lesson book was there and should have convinced them both of their own guilt and of the certainty that similar calamities would befall them if they continued to scorn God's mercy. At this point, however, another question is bound to rise.

In What Sense Was Israel a Lesson Book Only Until Christ?

As we have seen, the law was intended to hold Israel in bondage until Christ came (Gal. 3:19, 24). But this expectation seems totally contrary to what actually happened, for Paul was deeply troubled that some twenty years after Christ had ascended and returned to heaven, Israel for the most part still did not believe in him (Rom. 9:1–5; 11:5). Yet with the coming of Christ enough calamities had now befallen unbelieving Israel (calamities recorded in the Old Testament Scriptures) to qualify it as a lesson book for the nations. Hence as Jewish believers went out from Jerusalem preaching Jesus, they were able to hold up Israel as the warning that Isaiah, Jeremiah, and Ezekiel had spoken about and thus help the peoples of earth come to the Lord by the humility of faith.

Therefore Paul declared that the period of time required for Israel to become a lesson book for the nations had ended: "The law was put in charge to lead us to Christ that we might be justified by faith. Now that faith has come, we are no longer under the supervision of the law" (Gal. 3:24). Thus people who now responded to the lesson book, both believing Jews like himself and also believing Gentiles, were released from the bondage brought about by sin's power to distort the law (vv. 22–23).

Another aspect of the law's imprisoning effect was removed when Jesus taught in such a way as to make all meats clean (Mark 7:19). Israel's dietary laws had helped make her the lesson book for the nations by separating her from other peoples so that she would be conspicuous. But now that this book was available to aid those preaching Christ to all nations, he abolished the law's dietary rules, which otherwise would have made it unnecessarily difficult for other peoples to accept the gospel. The same thing occurred in having baptism replace circumcision as the sign of the covenant, a development discussed further in the next chapter. These two facets of Jewish law that had kept Israel isolated from other nations—a kosher diet and circumcision—were now removed by Christ so that the lesson book could be used with maximum effectiveness to further the gospel.

But while many in these nations have come to faith in Christ, for the most part the Jewish people have remained in unbelief, tragically hardened even more in it by the inhuman way alleged Christians have so often treated them. They have been forced to live in ghettos; thousands were slaughtered by Crusaders moving down the Rhine valley on their way to wrest the Holy Land from Islam; pogroms have been commonplace. But Paul taught that Israel's continued unbelief since Christ and the calamities that keep befalling this nation should be a strong incentive for people to put their trust in God and for believers to persevere in faith. Nor should Gentiles feel any sense of smugness as they come to enjoy the blessings of Abraham:

> If some of the [Jewish] branches have been broken off [the olive tree of Israel], and you, though a wild olive shoot, have been grafted in among the others and now share in the nourishing sap from the olive root, do not boast over those branches [now lying on the ground]. If you do, consider this: You do not support the root, but the root supports you. You will say then, "Branches were broken off so that I could be grafted in." Granted. But they were broken off because of unbelief, and you stand [only] by faith. Do not be arrogant, but be afraid [of unbelief]. For if God did not spare the natural branches, he will not spare you either. Consider therefore the kindness and sternness of God: sternness to those who fell [through unbelief], but kindness to you, *provided* that you continue in his kindness. Otherwise, you also will be cut off [for unbelief]. (Rom. 11:17–22)

Review Questions

1. How does Jeremiah 31:31–34 prove that the law and the gospel are the same in thought structure and content?

2. How does Hebrews 4:2 show that the way to be saved today is the same as it was for Israel in the wilderness?

3. How does God's having given the law to Israel without the regenerative power to keep it help the gospel to get to people, when the Great Commission is given?

4. What do Deuteronomy 29:22–28 and Ezekiel 5:5–15 tell us as to why God dealt only with Israel for about two thousand years and allowed the nations of earth to go their own ways (Acts 14:17)?

5. In what sense was the law given to Israel only until Christ (Gal. 3:19, 24)?

6. Explain how, according to Romans 11:17–22, the law is still writing a lesson book from Israel for people today.

7. How will you interpret "in the fullness of times God sent forth his Son" (Gal. 4:4) when you preach or teach this verse?

8. Musing on Romans 11:17–22, explain how Israel's continued rebellion spurs you on today to keep persevering in fighting the fight of faith.

NOTES

[1]An inquiry into the nature of the law is helpful for understanding its purpose. Since such an inquiry involves some rather detailed exegesis of Gal. 3:10–12, 17–24, and Rom. 9:30–10:10, it seems best to place this discussion below in the Appendix, entitled "The Nature of the Mosaic Law." The conclusion of this exegetical study is that the law is a law of faith telling supplicants of mercy how they may receive God's unmatched blessings.

[2]James D. G. Dunn, "2 Corinthians III.17—'The Lord Is the Spirit,'" *Journal of Theological Studies*, n.s., 21, 2 (1970): 310 n. 2.

[3]Thomas E. Provence, "'Who Is Sufficient for These Things?' An Exegesis of 2 Corinthians ii 15–iii 18," *Novum Testamentum* 24, 1 (1982): 64–65.

[4]C. E. B. Cranfield, *A Critical and Exegetical Commentary on the Epistle to the Romans*, 2 vols., International Critical Commentary (Edinburgh: T. & T. Clark, 1975–79), 1:339–40.

[5]This passage, by the way, probably reflects Paul's meaning when, in responding to the question "What, then, was the purpose of the law?" (Gal. 3:19), he answered that it was given for the sake of trespasses. He meant that it was given to increase the enormity of Israel's sin.

22

The Jewish Ceremonial Law

Now we have moved a good way through redemptive history and have presented a solution to the problem that arose from God's singling out Abraham and dealing only with the Jewish nation for two thousand years before inaugurating the Great Commission (Matt. 28:20; Mark 16:15). And I believe that a solution has also been provided for the biggest problem in seeing the unity of the Bible, namely, Paul's apparent contrasting of law and gospel. Our next step, then, is to gain a better understanding of the law's role in preparing the lesson book by looking at its ceremonial aspects.

In chapter 21 we considered how Israel has been and is a "lesson book for the nations" because of the punishments God has been meting out for its refusal to comply with the law as a law of faith. In dealing with God's commands, however, we have disregarded until now what is often called the ceremonial law. Here are found liturgical regulations for the Levitical priesthood and the sacrificial system it was to administer, dietary regulations regarding Israel's foods and their preparation, and a miscellaneous number of regulations that did not build a more loving society so much as they kept Israel separate from other nations. An example of such a regulation is Leviticus 19:19, "Do not wear clothing woven of two kinds of material," which immediately follows the important moral law, "Love your neighbor as yourself" (v. 18). The terms "ceremonial law" and "moral law" do not appear in the Bible. But just as the church has had to invent the term "Trinity" to do justice to scriptural data making it clear that God is three persons, so it has had to invent these terms to do justice to the two sorts of commands found in Exodus through Deuteronomy.

As has been indicated, one purpose of the ceremonial law was to enable Israel to fulfill its crucial role in world history. God kept the nation separate during the two millennia from Abraham to Christ so that when it came time for the gospel to go out to the nations, they could see Israel clearly and learn from the terrible punishments that befell it not to scorn God's mercy in unbelief and proud self-reliance.

The record of Jesus' commission to his apostles, predicted in God's promises to Abraham (Gen. 12:3; 17:4–7), is found in Matthew 28:18–20, Mark 16:15, Luke 24:46–49, and Acts 1:8.[1] It is also implied in Jesus' command to Peter to "feed my sheep" (John 21:17), understood in conjunction with his saying, "I have other sheep that are not of this sheep pen. I must bring them also . . . and there shall be one flock and one shepherd" (John 10:16).

But since the function of the ceremonial laws had been to keep Israel separate, with the giving of the Great Commission, they obviously had to be set aside. The principle upon which these ceremonial laws were based is made explicit: "You are to be my holy people. So do not eat the meat of an animal torn by wild beasts" (Ex. 22:31; cf. Lev. 11). Thus Moses introduced the dietary laws of Deuteronomy 14:3–21 by saying, "You are a people holy to the Lord your God. Out of all the peoples on the face of the earth, the Lord has chosen you to be his treasured possession." But at the end there is a hint that these laws were not universally applicable, for verse 21 commands, "Do not eat anything you find already dead. You may give it to an alien living in any of your towns, and he may eat it, or you may sell it to a foreigner. But you are a people holy to the Lord your God." Here was an example of one law for Israel and another for the foreigner. Therefore such ceremonial laws were set aside when the gospel went from Israel to the other peoples of earth, for requirements such as "Do not wear clothing woven of two kinds of material" (Lev. 19:19) or "You are not to eat . . . the camel and the rabbit" (Deut. 14:7) would be nothing but a vexing hindrance to getting out the gospel.

The command preceding this verse, however, "Love your neighbor as yourself" (Lev. 19:18), was essential for bringing the gospel's blessings to the world, and therefore it was emphasized (Rom. 13:9; Gal. 5:14; James 2:8). In connection with the moral laws, which enhance people's living together in a loving society, the Old Testament was emphatic that what applied to Israel applied also to the foreigner. Israel had been given laws such as "If anyone takes the life of a human being, he must be put to death. Anyone who takes the life of someone's animal must make restitution—life for life. If anyone injures his neighbor, whatever he has done must be done to him: fracture for fracture, eye for eye, tooth for tooth" (Lev. 24:17–20). But these are followed by the Lord's command to Moses, "You are to have the same law for the alien and the native-born. I am the Lord your God" (v. 22). The same phenomenon occurs in Leviticus 19, which contains orders such as "Do not steal. Do not lie. Do not deceive one another" (v. 11); "Do not hate your brother in your heart" (v. 17); "Do not practice divination or sorcery" (v. 26); "Do not turn to mediums or seek out spiritists" (v. 31); "Rise in the presence of the aged, show respect for the elderly" (v. 32). At the end, then, there is the summary command, "When an alien lives with you in your land, do not mistreat him. The alien living among you must be treated as one of your native-born. Love him as yourself" (v. 33).

So when Mark interpreted Jesus' teaching that people were not defiled by what they ate to mean that he "declared all foods 'clean'" (Mark 7:19), he was not contradicting Jesus' statement in Matthew 5:17–19: "Do not think that I have come to abolish the Law or the Prophets; I have not come to abolish them but to fulfill them. . . . Anyone who breaks one of the least of these commandments and teaches others to do the same will be called least in the kingdom of heaven, but whoever practices and teaches these commands will be called great in the kingdom of heaven." Jesus was well aware of the Old Testament law's implication that the ceremonial law was valid only during the time Israel was to be kept separate from the nations. Therefore when he made all foods clean, he was not breaking the law but simply annulling commands that, if kept, would have made it virtually impossible for other nations to accept the gospel.

Neither did he break the law when, after his resurrection and ascension, he explicitly told Peter, the chief apostle, that he and the other apostles were to eat any and all foods the Gentiles ate as they were about to take the gospel to them. This instruction occurred when Peter, staying at a home in Joppa, had a vision of something like a sheet let down from heaven filled with various animals and birds the Old Testament law had forbidden Jews to eat.

> It contained all kinds of four-footed animals, as well as reptiles of the earth and birds of the air. Then a voice told him, "Get up, Peter. Kill and eat." "Surely not, Lord!" Peter replied. "I have never eaten anything impure or unclean." The voice spoke to him a second time, "Do not call anything impure that God has made clean." This happened three times, and immediately the sheet was taken back to heaven. (Acts 10:12–16)

A few minutes later emissaries arrived from Cornelius, a Roman centurion at Caesarea, who in a vision had been commanded to summon Peter from Joppa (Acts 10:3–6). The Holy Spirit told Peter to return with these messengers, and when he arrived, he said to Cornelius and his guests, "You are well aware that it is against our law for a Jew to associate with a Gentile or visit him. But God has shown me that I should not call any man impure or unclean. So when I was sent for, I came without raising any objection. May I ask why you sent for me?" (vv. 28–29).

Cornelius then told Peter about his vision, mentioning that all his friends had now assembled in his house to "listen to everything the Lord has commanded you to tell us" (Acts 10:33). Peter then began to preach (vv. 34–43), and while he "was still speaking these words [that forgiveness of sins comes through Jesus' name], the Holy Spirit came on all who heard the message" (v. 44). When Peter saw this event, he "ordered that they be baptized in the name of Jesus Christ" (v. 48).[2]

So until the time came to give the Great Commission,

these ceremonial laws kept Israel separate so that her history could be a lesson book for the world that would help the spread of the gospel to all peoples. In this regard two additional parts of the ceremonial law are of particular importance: (1) circumcision as the sign of the covenant given during Abraham's lifetime and (2) the sacrificial liturgy administered by the Levitical priesthood, which was ordained following the Exodus.

Circumcision as the Sign of the Covenant

God's words to Abraham regarding circumcision are as follows:

> This is my covenant with you and your descendants after you, the covenant you are to keep: Every male among you shall be circumcised. You are to undergo circumcision, and it will be the sign of the covenant between me and you. For the generations to come every male among you who is eight days old must be circumcised, including those born in your household or bought with money from a foreigner—those who are not your offspring. Whether born in your household or bought with your money, they must be circumcised. My covenant in your flesh is to be an everlasting covenant. Any uncircumcised male, who has not been circumcised in the flesh, will be cut off from his people; he has broken my covenant. (Gen. 17:10–14)

The Initial Meaning of Circumcision

In the passage just quoted, note that circumcision was required of every male who would henceforth belong to the society centered around Abraham. Not blood ties but association with Abraham was the determining factor; so long as a male was a part of Abraham's society, he was to have the sign of circumcision. Apparently, then, circumcision was a mark that would give this new nation cohesion, a sense of identity and distinctiveness. Since only males bore the sign and since this was a patriarchal society, the meaning conveyed by circumcision would not be so much what was true for individuals as what was true for the corporate entity of the nation as a whole.

From early on, the term "circumcised" was used figuratively to denote what was pure, just as its opposite, "uncircumcised," signified what was impure or imperfect. Thus when Moses balked at God's commission to lead Israel out of Egypt because he was not a good public speaker, he objected that he was a man of "uncircumcised lips" (Ex. 6:12, 30, lit. trans.). And in chapter 21 we saw how Moses also used this figure to denote the perverse attitude Israel had. Another such passage is Leviticus 26:41–42: "Then when their uncircumcised hearts are humbled and they pay for their sin, I will remember my covenant with Jacob [Gen. 28:13–15; 35:11–12] and my covenant with Isaac [Gen. 26:2–5] and my covenant with Abraham [Gen. 17:4–8; 22:15–18]."

Since in the language conventions of Israel, circumcision could be used in this figurative way, it is natural to assume that the rite implied an ethical distinction not enjoyed by the uncircumcised. This was surely the signification that Israel later attached to its circumcision in distinguishing itself from the Gentiles. And this attitude was reflected by Paul when he spoke of those who are "Gentiles by birth and called 'uncircumcised' by those who call themselves 'the circumcision' (that done in the body by the hands of men)" (Eph. 2:11). Paul himself used the term in this ethical sense to represent the way Christ had regenerated the Gentiles: "In [Christ] you [Gentiles] were also circumcised, in the putting off of the sinful nature, not with a circumcision done by the hands of men but with the circumcision done by Christ" (Col. 2:11). Thus since circumcision had this ethical sense for Paul, he was able to regard Abraham's circumcision as a sign of the righteousness that he had received through believing God: "[Abraham] received the sign of circumcision, a seal of the righteousness that he had by faith while he was still uncircumcised" (Rom. 4:11; cf. Gen. 15:6 with Gen. 17).

Circumcision's Later Meaning

If circumcision for Abraham, however, signified the righteousness that he received through faith, what then did circumcision signify for the nation that he founded, when most did not share his righteousness? When Moses commanded Israel to "circumcise [their] hearts" as they were about to enter the Promised Land (Deut. 10:16), he was not concerned about the physical ritual, though in fact none of those born during the forty-year wilderness wanderings had as yet been circumcised.[3] Rather, he was bewailing their rebellious hearts (e.g., Deut. 9:6; 29:4; 31:27), the *inward uncircumcision* that denied the outward sign.

Neither did outward circumcision imply an inner righteousness for Israel in Jeremiah's day (c. 620 B.C.). All the males of Judah were circumcised then, but Jeremiah, speaking for God, commanded, "Circumcise yourselves to the Lord, circumcise your hearts, you men of Judah and people of Jerusalem, or my wrath will break out and burn like fire because of the evil you have done" (Jer. 4:4). Jeremiah in fact went one step beyond Moses and declared that Israel's uncircumcised behavior actually made her outward circumcision an uncircumcision: "'The days are coming,' declares the Lord, 'when I will punish all who are circumcised only in the flesh [lit. circumcised in uncircumcision]—Egypt, Judah [!], Edom, Ammon, Moab and all who live in the desert in distant places. For all these nations are really uncircumcised, and even the whole house of Israel is uncircumcised in heart'" (9:25–26).

All these nations did practice circumcision, and the Jews gloried in the ritual because it played such a crucial role in the Abrahamic covenant. So it was a great shock to hear Jeremiah classify their circumcision as no different from that of pagan peoples. It was even more shocking for him to say that Judah, along with the rest of the peoples cited, were "circumcised in uncircumcision," which meant that Judah's circumcision was really a sign of the wickedness and uncleanness that uncircumcision represented. This charge must have outraged Jeremiah's hearers, for "uncircumcised" was an epithet historically reserved for godless enemies such as the Philistines (e.g., Judg. 14:3; 1 Sam. 14:6).

Thus Israel's outward circumcision, which according to divine sanction was to represent an inward righteousness, had come to represent instead an inward *un*righteousness that should be represented by *un*circumcision. Such a statement forcefully called attention to Israel's rebellion against God, even though he had graciously singled Israel out as his people in a special sense that will become fully clear only when all Israelites alive at the second coming of Jesus are regenerated. So when God punished Israel, despite all its God-given advantages and divinely sanctioned circumcision, it should have been plain to all nations that neither would he show partiality to them because of any of their vaunted distinctives. Indeed, they would be punished just as severely unless they renounced all claims to any special preference and became simply supplicants of his mercy.

Paul too stressed Israel's sinfulness. To be sure, they considered themselves superior to Gentiles, for they were "[guides] for the blind, a light for those who are in the dark, [instructors] of the foolish . . . because [they had] in the law the embodiment of knowledge and truth" (Rom. 2:17–20). Their actions, however, belied such confidence, for though they preached against stealing, they stole; though they preached against adultery, they committed it; though they abhorred idols, they robbed pagan temples to add to their cherished idol collections (vv. 21–24). Indeed, the Jews had never been known to be such a lawless people. But because they boasted in their possession of the law (v. 23) yet failed to comply with it as a law of faith, they dishonored God so fully that they became "utterly sinful" (7:13), as evil as if they actually did steal, commit adultery, and collect idols as their hobby. Thus the Gentiles had come to blaspheme God's name on their account, for the Jews' attitude of regarding God as their client lord instead of their Patron Lord encouraged the Gentiles to do the very same thing (2:24).[4]

Therefore when Paul said, "Circumcision has value if you observe the law, but if you break the law, you have become as though you had not been circumcised" (Rom. 2:25), he was not imposing some Christian idea on the Jewish Old Testament but simply repeating what Moses implied and Jeremiah made explicit. Jewish circumcision had come to signify their cosmic blasphemy of turning the law of faith upside down into a law of works by which they supposed they were servicing the needs of the client God. But the nations of earth too are guilty of the outrage of failing to glorify and thank God as their Patron Benefactor (Rom. 1:21), a fact that Israel's catastrophic history should make unmistakably clear (see Ezek. 5:5–15).

Why Baptism Replaced Circumcision

Since circumcision had come to signify sin rather than righteousness, it could therefore no longer serve as the sign of the covenant of grace enjoyed by the people of God. John the Baptist made this fact evident when he required the Jews to prepare for the coming of the kingdom of God by exhibiting a repentance that renounced all dependence on being Abraham's children (Luke 3:8). This attitude necessarily also implied renunciation of any dependence on circumcision. Since baptism was a requirement for a proselyte (a Gentile converting to Judaism), a Jew who submitted to John's baptism was acknowledging that as far as salvation was concerned, he was in the same category; his connection with Abraham as symbolized by circumcision was of no value whatsoever. Therefore it was appropriate that the church, composed of people who, like Abraham, had a genuine righteousness from God, should have a different sign of that righteousness. It was also fitting that the church, which was in a continuity inaugurated by John the Baptist, should adopt as this sign the rite of baptism by which he had signified to disobedient Israel that it had no more favor before God than did Gentile sinners.

Since the church was to consist of peoples from all these nations, it was also important that its sign of the covenant be relatively easy for new believers to accept. In that Jewish males were circumcised when only eight days old, Israel had not found circumcision a difficult sign to adopt. But older men who wished to join themselves to the commonwealth of Israel found submission to the rite quite another matter, so that the greater number of prospective proselytes settled instead for being mere "God-fearers." If circumcision had remained as the sign of the covenant, the Great Commission would have had a virtually insurmountable obstacle to overcome in including all nations in the people of God. We sense something of this thinking when the apostles, as a result of the Jerusalem Council, agreed that Gentile Christians did not need to be circumcised. Thus they declared in their encyclical letter, "It seemed good to the Holy Spirit and to us not to burden you" (Acts 15:28), a message that caused the Gentile churches to rejoice (v. 31). Christianity could well have remained a Jewish sect had not the apostles decided forthrightly to admit the Gentiles to full standing simply on the basis of baptism.

Baptism was also far more suitable than circumcision in that it is a rite to which both male and female can submit. We have seen how circumcision was given to signify something about the corporate entity of the nation that Abraham founded, a necessity because Israel *as a nation* was to become a lesson book for all peoples. But when the lesson book was complete, it was *individuals* who were to learn the lesson. The people of God consists of individuals who through repentance and faith have come to possess new hearts through the indwelling Holy Spirit—a fact that the Old Testament made evident in its teaching regarding the remnant. Thus Peter in his first sermon, which led to the founding of the church at Pentecost, said, "Repent and be baptized, *every one of you*" (Acts 2:38). And since the people of God exist only as individuals who have received a new heart, it is therefore fitting that they receive a sign of the covenant symbolizing what is true for each one, whether male or female.[5]

So God smoothed the way for the gospel to cross cultural lines to reach the earth's thousands of ethnic entities. It was and is difficult enough for Jesus' apostles and missionaries to learn the particularities of any of these cultures so that they can formulate the essentials of the gospel in terms that communicate it accurately and effectively. But if the dietary laws of Moses and circumcision had also been essential to accept, the missionary outreach would have been quickly stopped, and Christianity would have become just a footnote regarding some obscure and short-lived Jewish sect mentioned incidentally in a few texts from the first or second century.

The Function of the Mosaic Sacrificial System

Another important part of the ceremonial law was the Jewish sacrificial system and the priesthood administering it. In the rest of this chapter we consider this system in some detail.

In A.D. 70 the Jewish rebellion against Roman rule, begun four years earlier, was crushed; at that time the temple, where the Jewish sacrificial system was practiced, was destroyed. Since the Jews who survived the fearsome slaughter were scattered in all directions, it was impractical to try to reinstitute this system set forth with such detail in the Old Testament. So for almost two thousand years the Jews have had to carry on their religion without practicing it.

God's purpose in bringing this system to an end was to make evident to everyone that Jesus Christ, in his person and work, remedied the imperfections in the Levitical priesthood, becoming himself a sacrifice to God so complete that it was accomplished "once for all" (1 Peter 3:18). When we analyze the former Levitical sacrificial system, we gain an even greater appreciation of the perfection of Jesus' priesthood and sacrifice.

The Jewish sacrificial system is therefore a substantial part of the lesson book of Israel that God wrote to facilitate the preaching of Jesus Christ to the peoples of earth. Furthermore, it was inextricably linked to the commands of the Mosaic law, so that "when there [was] a change of the priesthood [from Levi to Christ], there must also be a change of the law" (Heb. 7:12). Like Paul, Hebrews argues that the Mosaic covenant (but not the Abrahamic) had no power to bring people to God: "The former regulation is set aside because it was weak and useless (for the law made nothing perfect), and a better hope is introduced, by which we draw near to God" (vv. 18–19). The old covenant was faulty because it did not provide enablement to do the will of God (8:7–13). But Jesus, as the guarantor of the new covenant (7:22), equips believers with everything good that they may do his will, working in them what is pleasing to him (13:21).

Like Paul, Hebrews saw Jesus as replacing the imperfect and impotent Sinaitic covenant; unlike Paul, it contrasted the old sacrificial system, which shared the law's imperfection, with the perfect work of Christ. Thus the Old Testament sacrifices could not clear the conscience of the worshiper (Heb. 9:9); in contrast to the eternal redemption effected by Christ's sacrifice, the blood of goats and bulls sanctified only for an outward cleansing (v. 13); the law could never, with the same sacrifices offered year by year, make perfect those who draw nigh (10:1, 11); and it was impossible for the blood of bulls and goats to take away sins (v. 4).

Such statements raise the question whether or not they constitute a reinterpretation of the intended meaning of the Old Testament texts, especially when such statements as the following appear so often in connection with the old sacrificial system: "[the burnt offering] will be accepted on his behalf to make atonement for him [someone needing forgiveness]" (Lev. 1:4); "the priest will make atonement for them, and they will be forgiven" (4:20); "because of the uncleanness and rebellion of the Israelites, whatever their sins have been" (16:16).

Forgiveness and the Sacrificial System

In determining the nature of the forgiveness provided in the Old Testament sacrificial system, we must first gain some understanding of the strong communal bond tying Israel together. Old Testament scholar Gerhard von Rad describes this bond as follows:

> Through ties of blood and common lot the individual was regarded as being so deeply imbedded in the community that an offense on his part was not just a private matter affecting only himself and his own relationship to God. On the contrary, wherever there had been a grave offense against the divine law, what loomed largest was the incrimination which the community experienced in consequence at the hands of God, for because of the sin nothing less than the whole possibility of its cultic activity had become imperilled. The community had thus a vital interest in the restoration of order. In cases where Jahweh had not reserved to himself a special settle-

ment for good or for ill, order was restored by either the execution or the excommunication of the offender.[6]

So for Israel, evil consisted not only in an individual act but also in the forces it set in motion to bring dire consequences upon the entire community. Much of the Levitical sacrificial system functioned to avert these consequences that less serious sins would bring upon the people at large. The Mosaic scheme distinguished between two kinds of sins: those that were inadvertent or unintentional and those done "defiantly." This distinction appears, for example, in Numbers 15:27–31: "But if just one person sins unintentionally, he must bring a year-old female goat for a sin offering. The priest is to make atonement before the Lord for the one who erred by sinning unintentionally, and when atonement has been made for him, he will be forgiven.... But anyone who sins defiantly . . . blasphemes the Lord, and that person must be cut off from his people.... His guilt remains on him."

According to this passage, the only way to maintain the stability of the community when a sin had been committed defiantly was to excommunicate or execute the guilty party. Both partners to incest were to be excommunicated (Lev. 20:17–18), but adultery demanded execution, as did homosexuality (vv. 10, 13). In Exodus 21:14 premeditated murder was described as acting "deliberately," another denotation for sins whose resultant calamity can be averted from the community only by execution or excommunication. To have contempt for the verdict of a priest or a judge was also a defiant sin punishable by death (Deut. 17:12–13). And apparently to break a vow was also a sin for which no atonement could be made, for in Deuteronomy 23:21 a man bears iniquity who makes a vow null and void.

However, one who made a rash vow that might bind him or her to do evil could break the vow and yet receive atonement and be restored to the privileges of a theocratic citizen through a sin offering (Lev. 5:4–6). The unintentional defilement spoken of in verses 2–3 could also be atoned for by the sin offering. In fact, any unintentional breaking of the law could be atoned for (Lev. 5:17–19; Num. 15:22–26).

Leviticus 4 makes the same point in telling how a priest (vv. 3–12), the community (vv. 13–21), a leader (vv. 22–26), and an individual member of the community (vv. 27–35) who had committed unintentional sins could nevertheless continue to enjoy the blessings of the sacral community through bringing a sin offering. Atonement could also be attained for certain premeditated sins, such as remaining silent when one had witnessed a crime (Lev. 5:1) and having illicit relations with a slave girl (19:20–22). Robbery, fraud, extortion, and misappropriation of funds were also covered by the guilt offering if the offender, in addition to bringing the sacrifice, made 120 percent restitution (6:1–7).

In this survey of how sin could be atoned for in the Mosaic ritual, we should note first of all that the emphasis is indeed on unintentional sins, those "committed in ignorance" (Heb. 9:7), for which the Mosaic ritual could make amends. As Rowley put it, "The Law is much concerned with involuntary acts and ritual uncleanness where no ethical considerations were involved"[7] But it should be stressed that little provision was made for the more common deliberate sins; it should also be emphasized that only sins involving specific acts are considered. Nothing is said about atoning for sins of attitude, though the Mosaic law talked about these as well (e.g., Lev. 19:17–18). This emphasis upon the outward act, plus the fact that sacrifices averted calamity from the community, supports the assertion of Hebrews 9:13–14 that these sacrifices "sanctify them so that they are outwardly clean," in distinction to a cleansing of the conscience whereby one can henceforth serve God. Only those sins that, by virtue of their concrete, public nature, would impair the solidity of the sacral community were dealt with by the Old Testament sacrificial system.

In the Old Testament there was also an atoning for serious sins in the sense of postponing their punishment. According to Exodus 32:30–35 there were two levels on which God could be propitiated. After the people had sinned in constructing the golden calf, Moses returned to Sinai, saying, "Perhaps I can make atonement for your sin" (v. 30). He was even willing to have his own name blotted out of God's book if that would effect an atonement, but God replied, "Who-

ever has sinned against me I will blot out of my book. Now
go, lead the people to the place I spoke of. . . . However,
when the time comes for me to punish, I will punish them
for their sin"; then "the Lord struck the people with a plague
because of what they did with the calf Aaron had made" (vv.
32–35). Here we see that in those days God's anger against
sin could finally be satisfied only by blotting offenders out of
his book of life. But this passage also shows that he could be
placated temporarily.[8] Here the plague that God visited on
the people cooled his anger for a time so that he could
command Moses to continue to lead them on to the Promised
Land (Ex. 33:1–3). Therefore they were forgiven on the first
level, but not on the second, for Exodus 32:30–35 makes it
clear that these idolatrous people would finally be condemned. Moses, however, implied that his name is in God's
book and that he had what we might call second-level
forgiveness.

Psalm 78:38 likewise expresses this temporary, first-level
placation of God evident in the preservation of Israel in the
wilderness: "Yet he was merciful; he forgave their iniquities
and did not destroy them. Time after time he restrained his
anger and did not stir up his full wrath." Though God did
hold back his full wrath upon unregenerate Israel, this
passage, by its very reference to God's *full* wrath, shows that
the forgiveness they did receive was only the first-level sort.
In this sense, it seems, God (in Moses' words) had "par-
doned them from the time they left Egypt until now" (Num.
14:19).

It is not difficult to understand how such a pardoning can
be construed as the "outward" cleansing of Hebrews 9:13,
for it falls short of that cleansing of the conscience in which
one knows that the sin question has been settled once for all
and that one can therefore go on serving God with full
assurance. It is also understandable how forgiveness on this
first level required the repetition of sacrifices year by year, so
that the wrath of God, constantly welling up because of the
people's wickedness and rebellion (Lev. 16:21), might
thereby be held in abeyance. But this situation is completely
different from what will be true when God makes the new

covenant with them and no longer remembers their sin (Jer. 31:33–34; cf. Rom. 11:26).

This first-level placation of God made possible by the Old Testament sacrificial system was not, however, the whole story for Israel. The very fact that Moses had assurance that his name was in God's book indicates that he enjoyed second-level forgiveness. Like Abraham, Moses was not a perfect man, for he disobeyed God by striking the rock twice to get water instead of just once, thereby displaying doubt that God could bring water out of a rock without additional help from him. Therefore Moses was not allowed to enter the Promised Land (Num. 20:10–12; Deut. 1:37–38), and Joshua, his assistant, became the leader who accomplished this. In speaking of Moses and his spokesperson Aaron, Psalm 99:8 says, "O Lord our God, you answered them; you were to Israel a forgiving God, though you punished their misdeeds." So while God did chastise such remnant people for their wrongdoings, they nevertheless enjoyed second-level forgiveness.

But how was this possible when the Mosaic cult could grant only the first-level forgiveness of a delay of judgment? For example, though David had sinned "defiantly" (Num. 15:30), first in committing adultery with Bathsheba and then in trying to cover it up by having her husband, Uriah, killed in battle (2 Sam. 11:2–27), nevertheless he received second-level forgiveness. David was conscious that his iniquity was great (Ps. 25:11), an iniquity evidently consisting of a defiant or willful sin, as the parallel between "great transgression" and "willful sin" in Psalm 19:13 indicates. This could never be forgiven through the cult—but it could be forgiven on the basis of God's *ḥesed* ("mercy"). A noteworthy aspect of the Psalms is their emphasis on this term (see chap. 20 above), which appears some 120 times. Along with two other terms closely tied to it that apply to what God does for people (*ṣedeq*, "righteousness," and *'emûnâh*, "faithfulness"), *ḥesed* shows clearly that the basis of the religious life of a remnant person was the assurance of God's love, guaranteed by his righteousness and faithfulness. Thus in the great sin that occasioned Psalm 51, possibly David's adultery with Bathsheba and the murder of her husband, he did not go through cultic channels to get forgiveness. Instead he went directly to God and pled for his *hesed:* "Have mercy on me, O God, according to your unfailing love [*hesed*]; according to your great compassion blot out my transgressions" (Ps. 51:1; cf. 25:6–7). David acknowledged that burnt offerings availed nothing and that the only condition for receiving *hesed* was a broken spirit and a contrite heart (51:16–17). But when forgiveness was received and the joy of his salvation was restored (v. 12), God would be pleased to have him offer righteous sacrifices and whole burnt offerings (v. 19).

Psalm 50 makes the same point. Indeed, God was not unhappy with the sacrifices that Israel was constantly bringing (v. 8), but what he particularly wanted was their sacrifice of thank offerings, fulfillment of vows, and dependence on him in the day of trouble (vv. 14–15, 23). Thus when in Psalm 40:6 it is said, "Sacrifice and offering you did not desire, . . . burnt offerings and sin offerings you did not require," the point is certainly not that sacrifices played no part in the religious life of Israel. Rather, in accordance with the teaching of the law, they were to be offered by those who had the right heart attitude—"I delight to do your will, O my God" (v. 8)—just as today in submitting to baptism or the Lord's Supper, we are to do so as an expression of an inward heart attitude. Israel's presentation of burnt offerings (Lev. 1), grain offerings (Lev. 2), and fellowship offerings (Lev. 3) therefore was to be an outward manifestation of an inward gratitude to God.

This emphasis on one's heart attitude as one participated in the Old Testament sacrificial system appears also in the Prophets. Isaiah reports God as speaking of how in the end days he would "bring [foreigners] to my holy mountain and give them joy in my house of prayer. Their burnt offerings and sacrifices will be accepted on my altar" (Isa. 56:7). And through Jeremiah God spoke of how in the end days there "will be heard once more the sounds of joy and gladness, . . . the voices of those who bring thank offerings to the house of the Lord, saying, 'Give thanks to the Lord Almighty, for the Lord is good; his love endures forever'" (Jer. 33:10–11). Malachi too speaks of how God will purify people's hearts before they offer sacrifices: "[God] will purify the Levites and refine them like gold and silver. Then the Lord will have men who will bring offerings in righteousness" (Mal. 3:3).

This perspective of proper heart motive should be kept in mind in dealing with hyperbolic statements in the prophets that, taken by themselves, seem to say that God never commanded sacrifices and does not want Israel carrying on its sacrificial system. Hosea, for example, declared that God desires "mercy, not sacrifice, and acknowledgment of God rather than burnt offerings" (Hos. 6:6). Jeremiah 7:22–23 quotes God as saying, "When I brought [Israel] out of Egypt and spoke to them, I did not [NIV adds 'just'] give them commands about burnt offerings and sacrifices, but I gave them this command: Obey me, and I will be your God and you will be my people. Walk in all the ways I command you, that it may go well with you." And in Amos 5:21–24 God said, "I hate, I despise your religious feasts; I cannot stand your assemblies. Even though you bring me burnt offerings and grain offerings, I will not accept them. Though you bring choice fellowship offerings, I will have no regard for them. Away with the noise of your songs! I will not listen to the music of your harps. But let justice roll on like a river, righteousness like a never-failing stream!"[9] But when people did practice justice and righteousness, God was pleased with their sacrifices. While the remnant did not find second-level forgiveness in the Old Testament sacrificial system, but rather by appealing to God's *hesed,* they still used it to make offerings to express their love and thankfulness (cf. Ps. 51:16–18).

The Typological Significance of the Sacrificial System

We have now seen how the Old Testament supports the statement in Hebrews that the sacrificial offerings were incapable of providing ultimate forgiveness. But was Hebrews not reinterpreting the data according to Christian presuppositions with its insistence that the Mosaic cult had a predictive aspect indicating that better things were yet to come? When the author said that "the law is only a shadow of the good things that are coming" (10:1) and that "Christ came as high priest of the good things that are already here"

(9:11), he was definitely declaring that in the law itself there was a promise and that Christ was the fulfillment of this promise. But was there evidence of this future promise in the law itself and its concomitant promise, or was the author of Hebrews reading the Old Testament through Christian spectacles? To answer this question we need to be aware of the significance of types in the Old Testament and their antitypes in the New Testament.

NOTE. Both a type and a prophecy are predictive. A type, however, is a less explicit prediction than a prophecy. Micah 5:2 was an explicit prophecy when it predicted that the Messiah would appear in Bethlehem, for the fulfillment comes with one-to-one correspondence in Matthew 2:1: "After Jesus was born in Bethlehem. . . ." But when Isaiah told King Ahaz that a young woman would be with child and give birth to a son and that before this child reached the age of accountability the land would be deserted and taken over by Assyria (Isa. 7:14–17), this was a prophecy that was fulfilled but a short time afterward (8:3–8). This event of prophecy and its fulfillment soon after stood as a remarkable incident along the timeline of redemptive history.

Now since God is carrying out a single purpose in redemptive history, which will climax in his glory's filling the earth as the waters cover the sea, then as we go forward along that timeline, we should expect similar and increasingly remarkable things to be happening. Thus Matthew used the incident from Isaiah 7:14–8:4 as a predictive type that was fulfilled in Jesus' virgin birth. Concerning Mary's becoming pregnant, he said, "All this took place to fulfill what the Lord has said through the prophet," and then quotes Isaiah 7:14 in Matthew 1:22–23 as the antitypical fulfillment of a type and not as the fulfillment of a prophecy. Thus J. Gresham Machen said,

> One may hold that in the passage [Isa. 7:14] some immediate birth of a child is in view, but that that event is to be taken as a foreshadowing of a greater event that is to come. . . . Grammatico-historical exegesis does not demand the exclusion of all

typology from the exalted language of the Old Testament prophets; the question whether all typology is to be excluded is a question which should be settled, not by the mechanical application of modern exegetical methodology,[10] but only by patient and sympathetic research. . . . The result [of such research], we think, will be that in the dealings of God with his covenant people will be found a profound and supernatural promise of greater things to come.[11]

In the same manner, R. V. G. Tasker said concerning Matthew 1:22–23 that the evangelist's quotation is not the kind of quotation that a modern Christian would think of making; but to the evangelist there was a real analogy between the history of Israel and the experience of Him who was "the fulness of Israel"; and it is just the realization of this truth that differentiates more recent biblical scholarship from the point of view displayed by Burkitt [who regarded things as did Bultmann].[12]

In order to regard the report of antitypical fulfillments as supporting the validity of the earlier type, there must be in the Old Testament material at least a necessarily implied predictive element. The prospect for an antitypical fulfillment of the events occurring in Isaiah's time comes from Isaiah 2:11, "The eyes of the arrogant man will be humbled and the pride of men brought low; and the Lord alone will be exalted in that day" (cf. vv. 20–21). A similar prospect for the Old Testament sacrificial system comes from God's command to Moses: "Make this tabernacle and all its furnishings exactly like the pattern I will show you" (Ex. 25:9, 40). This same command is cited by the writer of Hebrews after declaring that "[the Levitical priests] serve at a sanctuary that is a copy and shadow of what is in heaven" (Heb. 8:5). Moses was shown this pattern after ascending Mount Sinai, where he, Aaron, Nadab, Abihu, and the seventy elders

saw the God of Israel. Under his feet was something like a pavement made of sapphire, clear as the sky itself. . . . When Moses went [farther] up on the mountain, the cloud covered it, and the glory of the Lord settled on Mount Sinai. For six days the cloud covered the mountain, and on the seventh day the Lord called to Moses from within the cloud. To the

Israelites the glory of the Lord looked like a consuming fire on top of the mountain. Then Moses entered the cloud as he went on up the mountain. And he stayed on the mountain forty days and forty nights" (Ex. 24:10, 15–18).

During this time God began to spell out the details of the tabernacle where the sacrificial system would be carried on (Ex. 25:1–8), and it was at the conclusion of this first set of instructions that he commanded Moses to make a tabernacle on earth corresponding to what he had seen inside the cloud of God's glory.

Thus when Moses brought the plans back down the mountain and the building of the tabernacle began, it was an earthly representation of something outside the visible, tangible world of that time. From this fact the writer of Hebrews argued that the tabernacle, the sacrificial system, and the law, which were all of a piece, were a part of this world. The tabernacle was an "earthly sanctuary" (9:1), one made by human beings "that was only a copy of the true one [in heaven]" (v. 24). As such, it had similarities with that after which it was patterned. But it also had contrasts with the heavenly reality that was fully revealed on earth in the coming of Christ. This latter reality was "not man-made, that is to say, not a part of this creation" (v. 11); it was "set up by the Lord, not by man" (8:2). But the Pentateuch itself looked forward to such a heavenly in-breaking, for in Numbers 14:21–23 God prefaced an oath regarding the destruction of the unbelieving Israelites by saying, "As surely as I live and as surely as the glory of God fills the whole earth. . . ."

Thus Moses' sacrificial system did in fact contain a promissory element that began to be fulfilled in the work Christ did on earth to redeem his people. But since the Old Testament tabernacle and sacrificial system were built from materials in this world and yet patterned after heavenly things, and since Christ revealed the Father fully (John 1:18), one is to expect both contrasts and similarities between the Old Testament tabernacle and sacrificial system, on the one hand, and the perfect revelation of God in Christ, on the other. (See Table 1.)

Because of such contrasts the writer of Hebrews spoke of

Jesus' ministry as superior to that of the old covenant (8:6). Also because of these contrasts the Mosaic sacrificial system is not a prophecy but rather a type of the work of Christ.

Table 1
Comparisons Between the Old and New Testament Sacrificial Systems

Old Testament	New Testament
Sin was remembered *year after year* (Heb 9:6; 10:1, 3).	Jesus obtained for us eternal redemption *once for all* (Heb. 7:27; 9:12, 26; 10:12).
Priests *stood*, since they must continually offer sacrifices day after day (10:11).	Jesus, after offering his once-for-all sacrifice, was *seated*, awaiting the final victory it would accomplish (10:12–13).
Priests offered sacrifices in a sanctuary *of this world*, set up *by man* (9:1).	Jesus brought his sacrifice into *heaven*, into the sanctuary set up *by the Lord* (8:2; 9:11, 24).
Priests offered *the blood of animals* (9:7, 13; 10:1).	Jesus offered *his own blood* (9:14).
No ultimate forgiveness was obtained (9:9, 13; 10:1).	Jesus' sacrifice *made his people perfect forever* (9:14–15; 10:14).
Priests were themselves *sinners* who had to offer sacrifices for their own sins (5:2–3; 7:27).	Jesus was *without sin* (2:10; 4:15; 7:26).
High priests *died* and had to be replaced (7:23, 28).	Jesus *lives forevermore* (7:25, 28).
No oath established priesthood or covenant (7:20).	Priesthood and new covenant are *founded upon an oath* (6:17–20; 7:21–22).

The question arises, however, as to why God allowed the inferior type to exist for one nation for over a thousand years before bringing in its superior antitype that would benefit all nations. If we follow the line of thought indicated by Galatians 3:22–24 (discussed in chap. 21 above), the answer is that God allowed the message of his mercy, but generally without any accompanying power, to apply to one nation, Israel, in order that from the lesson of its history, all nations might realize the sin of rejecting God's mercy and be warned of the need to submit to it. Then as God's mercy becomes manifest in Christ in a way far superior to that of the Old

Testament types, these nations have greater reason to
appreciate him than if they had not had the opportunity from
the Old Testament to see Jesus' superiority by way of
contrast.[13]

But let us look also at the continuity that exists between
type and antitype, considering how much easier it is to tell
the nations what Christ has done now that we have the
symbolism for it provided by the Mosaic sacrificial system.
How helpful it is, in getting across the idea that we can come
to God only through the propitiatory work of Christ, to depict
this work in terms of the concrete symbols of the tabernacle,
the altars, and the shedding of blood. The abstractions of
Paul such as propitiation would be well-nigh impossible to
communicate to the nations of earth—let alone to junior
highers in our churches—unless we could use the imagery
from the Old Testament, such as may be drawn from the
ritual for the Day of Atonement. Flannelgraphs are made to
order for showing that the mercy seat was above the ark of
the covenant, with the tables of the law inside the ark.
There, as we have seen in chapter 21, they were to be a
testimony against the people of Israel. But because the
people persistently failed to keep God's laws, his anger was
aroused against them. Therefore year by year the high priest
would go into the Holy of Holies, where the ark and the
mercy seat were located, to sprinkle the blood of a slain
animal on the front of the atonement cover (Lev. 16:14–15).
Thus an atonement was made for the Most Holy Place so that
despite "the uncleanness and rebellion of the Israelites,
whatever their sins have been" (Lev. 16:16), God could go
on living in their midst. In the same way he has now been
fully placated toward humankind through the blood of
Christ, so that we can approach God boldly and with full
assurance, knowing that the sin question has been settled
once and for all.

Old Testament history thus was "written to teach us"
(Rom. 15:4; cf. 1 Cor. 10:11). Without it, our understanding
of the full revelation of redemption given in the New
Testament would be impossible. How helpful for under-
standing sanctification is the graph that can be drawn of
Abraham's spiritual development (see chaps. 18 and 19

above). How could we communicate this concept to others without the Old Testament material? We thus see that for carrying out the Great Commission with its charge to *teach* all nations, the Old Testament is an absolute necessity—so essential, in fact, that God delayed giving his commission until the lesson book of Israel's history could be written. Had he sent Christ to effect redemption at Genesis 12, giving the Great Commission at that time, the command would have misfired because there would have been no Old Testament background to provide an adequate vocabulary for telling of what God had done in Christ. But since God allowed the Old Testament to be written first, many more people among the nations have been and will be brought to Christ because the Old Testament makes the message comprehensible. And since the Old Testament not only helps people understand the work of Christ better by the way it symbolizes his work but also helps them appreciate it the more by being a contrast to his work, God's purpose in creating the world is therefore closer to being realized. Perhaps, after all, a redemptive history that allows the inferior to exist first is the best of all possible histories. At least Paul thought so after concluding a survey of it (Rom. 11:33–36; see also chap. 26 below).

Review Questions

1. How do Deuteronomy 14:21 and Leviticus 24:22 provide us with the key for distinguishing between the ceremonial law and the moral law?

2. How could Jesus claim he would not break the least commandment of Moses and yet set aside the dietary laws as the gospel went to the nations?

3. How could Jews be shown that Paul's regarding the Jews' circumcision as uncircumcision was something their own Scripture teaches?

4. Give at least three reasons why water baptism replaced circumcision as the sign of the covenant.

5. Why is Hebrews not contradicting Leviticus when it says that the Old Testament cult could not forgive sins,

yet Leviticus talks about the various offerings making an atonement?

6. How did the people of the small remnant in Israel get forgiveness for a "defiant" or "presumptuous" sin?

7. What is the difference between a type and a prophecy?

8. What was there in Exodus 25–40 that makes it mandatory to regard the tabernacle in the wilderness and the sacrificial system as types?

9. How does the way a type contrasts with its antitype (i.e., its fulfillment) help realize God's goal for the history of the world?

10. How does the continuity between the Old Testament cult and Christ's work help in getting the gospel out to the nations?

NOTES

[1] Luke and Acts were written by Paul's "dear friend Luke, the doctor" (Col. 4:14) and were originally one continuous writing. They were separated, it seems, in order to include Luke's report of the life of Jesus with the other three accounts in Matthew, Mark, and John. Acts, alluding to what Jesus had begun to do while on earth (Acts 1:1), relates what he continued to do as the ascended Lord to get the church well established in the Gentile world. He achieved this result by working through the Holy Spirit and by intervening variously in earthly affairs, such as in the remarkable conversion of Paul (Acts 9:1–19; 22:4–16; 26:9–18).

[2] Furthermore, Jesus did not break the Old Testament law when, through the Holy Spirit, he signified to the Jerusalem Council and to James in particular, the leader of the Jerusalem church, that Gentile believers should not be required to be circumcised (Acts 15:1–21).

[3] This matter was taken care of as soon as they entered Canaan (Josh. 5:2–9). Circumcision had not been practiced during this period as part of Israel's punishment for not believing that God would enable them to conquer the land of Canaan (Num. 14:33–34).

[4] Remember that Jesus told the Pharisees, "You travel over land and sea to win a single convert, and when he becomes one, you make him twice as much a son of hell as you are" (Matt. 23:15).

[5]In view of what has been said about the significance of baptism's replacing circumcision as the sign of the covenant for the church, the new Israel, it is indeed mystifying to hear the late British Baptist H. H. Rowley say, "It is surely one of the unsolved mysteries of Christian scholarship why the leap should be made [from circumcision] to what is a completely different and unrelated rite [water baptism]" (*Unity of the Bible* [Cleveland, Ohio: World Publishing, Meridian Books, 1957], 137).

[6]von Rad, *Old Testament Theology*, 1:264.

[7]Rowley, *Unity of the Bible*, 51.

[8]Likewise in God's dealings with the world in general, he is propitiated to the extent of sending rain on the unrighteous (Matt. 5:45) and providing all people with good things (Acts 14:17). People should never infer from such verses, however, that God is ultimately placated toward them, for God extends such goodness only to lead people to repentance. Otherwise, their continued unrepentance treasures up wrath for them at the day of judgment (Rom. 2:4–5). Thus Christ is the atonement for the sins of all humanity (1 John 2:1–2) in the sense that he makes it possible for God to grant them time to enjoy his goodness and so repent.

[9]For further expressions of this theme, see also Isa. 1:13–17 and Mic. 6:6–8.

[10]Rudolf Bultmann, who regarded Matthew's "fulfillment" as simply Christian allegorizing, was guilty of such application. According to Bultmann, the method of allegorizing "was taken over by Hellenistic Jewry and applied to the Old Testament. Where Philo used the method of allegorizing, to derive from their reading of the Old Testament timeless truths of theology, cosmology, anthropology, and ethics, the New Testament uses it to find Messianic prophecies. In every case it is clear that what is already known [from New Testament times] is derived from reading of the [New Testament] texts. But people want to find it in the old texts so that it can count as an authoritative truth" ("Prophecy and Fulfillment," in *Essays on Old Testament Hermeneutics*, ed. Claus Westermann [Richmond: John Knox, 1963], 51).

[11]J. Gresham Machen, *The Virgin Birth of Christ* (New York: Harper & Brothers, 1930), 292–93.

[12]R. V. G. Tasker, *The Old Testament in the New Testament* (Philadelphia: Westminster, 1947), 20–21.

[13]See the quotation from Vos, *Biblical Theology* (chap. 17, n. 5).

23

The Kingdom of God in the Old Testament

To this point in tracing out God's purpose and goal in redemptive history, we have concentrated on the covenant God made with Abraham, mentioning also from time to time how it is continued in the new covenant that believers enjoy today. Such a covenant of mercy must have been operative from the moment Adam and Eve began to doubt that God really did have their best interests at heart, for they did not die as forewarned in Genesis 2:17. The reason is that the fall of Adam and Eve did not cause God to deviate in the least from his ultimate purpose in creation, which was to display there the glory of his mercy. Bible students and theologians since Luther have called this merciful or gracious work of God his *proper* work, in contrast to his *strange* work,[1] such as his allowing violence to fill the world so that, with the exception of Noah's family and the animals, it had to be destroyed.

It was also God's strange work to defer for a time the confusion of languages, which permitted the seed of the serpent to congregate around the Tower of Babel, where they again threatened the survival of the woman's seed. Another aspect of this strange work was God's confining his dealings for two millennia to Abraham and his physical descendants through Jacob. Only at the end of this period did God's only begotten Son commission his followers to go and tell the nations of earth the good news that the Almighty

God wanted nothing so much as to be gracious to those humble enough to welcome God's great mercy.

But we must remember Vos's insight (noted above in chap. 17) that these strange works of God have helped those living further along on the timeline of redemptive history to realize the great power of human sinfulness. As a result they glorify and thank God all the more for his proper works, like the Noachic covenant and the confusion of tongues at Babel, which helped preserve the seed of the woman for a final triumph over Satan. Though the Old Testament is mostly the history of Israel under God's strange work of their imprisonment by the law, its writing was an essential for taking the gospel to the nations. For in the Old Testament they could see plainly what a dreadful future awaited them if they did not profit from Israel's example, repent of their pride, and submit to God as supplicants of his mercy.

Thus the law that kept Israel imprisoned under sin's power was a covenant that functioned to perform God's strange work. Even though its terms are basically no different from God's proper work in the Abrahamic and new covenants, yet in that for the most part the law was not accompanied by his power, it made Israelites like Paul before his conversion "utterly sinful" (Rom. 7:13) in committing the cosmic blasphemy of viewing themselves as patron benefactors of a needy, client God.

Another important strand of this strange work is the events that occurred under the concept of the kingdom of God. Beginning with Saul and 1 Samuel, much of the Old Testament concerns Israel's kings. The Davidic covenant in particular, by which God promised to perpetuate the dynasty until his appointed King should reign, is an aspect of redemptive history that must now be summarized.

As there was need to determine the essential idea of the covenant as God's oath to his people (Gen. 22:16–18; Heb. 6:13–19), so there is need to grasp the fundamental idea at the basis of the term "kingdom of God." An examination of the many relevant contexts indicates that the kingdom of God is not primarily a specific realm over which God rules but rather his *right* to reign as king over a realm. George Ladd has done much to clarify this crucial idea:

If . . . the Kingdom is the *reign of* God, not merely in the human heart but dynamically active in the person of Jesus and in human history, then it becomes possible to understand how the Kingdom of God can be present and future, inward and outward, spiritual and apocalyptic. For the redemptive royal activity of God could act decisively more than once and manifest itself powerfully in more than one way in accomplishing the divine end.[2]

What constitutes this "divine end" is the salvation of his people from the power of Satan:

The kingdom of God is . . . primarily a soteriological concept. It is God acting in power and exercising his sovereignty for the defeat of Satan and the restoration of human society to its rightful place of willing subservience to the will of God. It is not the sovereignty of God as such; God is always and everywhere the sovereign God. . . . It is the action of the sovereign God of heaven by which his reign is restored in power to those areas of his creation which he has permitted in rebellion to move outside the actual acknowledgements of his rule. . . . The "history" of the kingdom of God is therefore the history of redemption.[3]

This definition of the kingdom of God shows how very close the concept is to that of the covenant of mercy, which was defined as God's commitment and oath to honor Christ's death for the salvation of people. With but little difficulty, then, it can be seen that Christ's death gave God the right to reign savingly to restore fallen people to their rightful place as his children. In fact, in discussing the covenant, we saw (in chap. 14 above) how Christ's death enabled God to be righteous in justifying the sinner, which is the same as saying that his death gave God the right to reign savingly. The covenant of mercy and the kingdom of God, then, are two closely allied aspects of redemptive history. Whereas the covenant concept in Scripture stresses God's commitment and oath to save, the kingdom concept stresses his reign whereby he actively carries out his right to save people, a right made possible by the death of Christ.

The covenant and the kingdom appear side by side in several places in Scripture. In Ezekiel 37:24–27, for example, the establishment of David as king is predicted in the same breath as the promise that God will make an eternal covenant with Israel to be their God and they his people. There is also the striking statement in Luke 22:29–30: "I confer on you a kingdom, just as my Father conferred one on me, so that you may eat and drink at my table in my kingdom."[4] And even where these terms are not found explicitly together, we may safely assume that throughout redemptive history one is never without the other, for wherever God is exercising his *right* to save, he is also carrying out his *oath* to save.

Thus the concept of the kingdom of God can be summarized in the same way as the covenant. First, there is God's exercise of his kingdom before there has been any official announcement of its establishment, just as the covenant of mercy was operative in the lives of Abel and the Sethites before its first explicit statement in the Abrahamic covenant. Then just as God's strange work was exhibited in the Mosaic covenant in imprisoning Israel under sin, so his strange work was exhibited in the kingdom, as he granted Israel's request for a king like the other nations, thereby beginning the long story of both godly and wicked rulers that terminated in the disappearance of Israel from the political scene. Finally, just as the new covenant was inaugurated officially at the Last Supper as Jesus prepared to die for his people's sins, so after his resurrection and ascension this One who had the legal right to David's throne was officially inaugurated as the supreme Ruler over God's kingdom. Therefore in concluding his sermon at Pentecost, Peter said,

> [David] was a prophet and knew that God had promised him on oath that he would place one of his descendants on his throne. Seeing what was ahead, he spoke of the resurrection of the Christ, that he was not abandoned to the grave, nor did his body see decay. God has raised this Jesus to life. . . . For David did not ascend to heaven, and yet he said, "The Lord said to my Lord: 'Sit at my right hand until I make your enemies a footstool for your feet' [Psalm 110:1]." Therefore let all Israel be assured of this: God has made this Jesus, whom you crucified, both Lord and Christ. (Acts 2:30–36)

There are three phases through which the kingdom of God goes from Genesis to the New Testament. The first phase is its early work in saving people in Old Testament times, before any official inauguration.

God's Saving Activity Throughout the Old Testament

In discussing the kingdom of God in the Old Testament, Ladd has stressed the promises for the future kingdom that are contained there: "Our main concern is with the Kingdom of God as a hope."[5] While this is surely a strong emphasis (see the section below entitled "The Glorious Kingdom to Be Established by God"), there is ample data to show that the kingdom of God was an actuality in the present as well as a promise for the future. Thus Psalm 74:12 asserts, "You, O God, are my king from of old; you bring salvation upon the earth." If the kingdom of God is his working to save people, then this verse clearly teaches that it was operative back in the Old Testament, long before Christ appeared on earth. Surely God's work in regenerating Abel so that there was enmity between him and Cain was a working of salvation in the midst of the earth, as was his work with all the seed of the woman and the remnant during Old Testament times. This meaning is likewise clear in Daniel's quotation of King Darius of Persia: "I issue a decree that in every part of my kingdom people must fear and reverence the God of Daniel. For he is the living God and he endures forever; his kingdom will not be destroyed, his dominion will never end. He rescues and he saves; he performs signs and wonders in the heavens and on the earth. He has rescued Daniel from the power of the lions" (Dan. 6:26–27).

The problem with the nonremnant majority in Israel was simply that they "did not believe in God or trust in his deliverance [salvation]" (Ps. 78:22). David, however, indicated the remnant's joy in possessing the kingdom of God when he prayed, "Restore to me the joy of your salvation, and grant me a willing spirit, to sustain me" (51:12).

The great objection to saying that the kingdom of God was a present reality in the Old Testament is that in the New Testament it is announced as making its appearance for the first time. Thus Luke 16:16 affirms that "the Law and the Prophets were proclaimed until John. Since that time, the good news of the kingdom of God is being preached, and everyone is forcing his way into it." And Jesus himself said, "I tell you the truth: Among those born of women there has not risen anyone greater than John the Baptist; yet he who is least in the kingdom of heaven is greater than he" (Matt. 11:11). This verse is not implying, however, that John as an individual was not enjoying the blessings of the kingdom of God, for Luke 13:28 declares, "There will be weeping there, and gnashing of teeth, when you see Abraham, Isaac and Jacob and all the prophets in the kingdom of God." John was therefore in the kingdom, for Jesus clearly counted John as the last and greatest of the prophets, as he said to the multitudes, "What did you go out into the desert to see? A reed swayed by the wind? If not, what did you go out to see? A man dressed in fine clothes? No, those who wear fine clothes are in kings' palaces. Then what did you go out to see? A prophet? Yes, I tell you, and more than a prophet. This is the one about whom it is written: 'I will send my messenger ahead of you, who will prepare your way before you [Mal. 3:1]'" (Matt. 11:7–10).

So as a prophet, John was enjoying the blessings of God's saving work and will be in that future realm of the kingdom with the patriarchs and the other Old Testament prophets. But he is not regarded as being in the kingdom of God when he is seen in his place in the sequence of events in redemptive history, that is, in his role as the last of the prophets and the one who introduced Jesus Christ. As the greatest of the prophets, John nevertheless still belonged to the era of promise and therefore to this inferior category, so that the very least person in the superior category of the kingdom of God in its fulfillment would be greater than he.

NOTE. Therefore just as the seed of the woman were beneficiaries of the covenant of mercy long before the inauguration of the new covenant or even the Abrahamic covenant, so the seed of the woman has benefited from the kingdom of God since the beginning of redemptive history, long before its official inauguration at the coming of Jesus. Likewise, the Holy Spirit, who is the great benefit bestowed upon redeemed people, has been enjoyed from the beginning, but his official outpouring came only at Pentecost, after Jesus has finished the work of salvation (Acts 2:33), so that no one could miss the point that the blessing of the Holy Spirit is made possible only because of what Christ accomplished. For this reason John 7:39 declares that "up to that time the Spirit had not been given [officially and with ceremony], since Jesus had not yet been glorified." But his presence was obvious, for example, in the prophet Micah (Mic. 3:8) and in Elizabeth, the mother of John the Baptist (Luke 1:41). John himself was "filled with the Holy Spirit even from birth" (Luke 1:15). And the kingdom of God and the Holy Spirit, the greatest of God's blessings, are inseparable, for "the kingdom of God is not a matter of eating and drinking, but of righteousness, peace and joy in the Holy Spirit" (Rom. 14:17).

The kingdom of God, then, working throughout Old Testament times and right up to the coming of Jesus Christ, created enmity between the seed of the serpent and the seed of the woman during the time that Israel as a nation was failing in its attempt to be the kingdom of God on earth.

Israel's Failure to Realize God's Kingdom

We come now to the second heading for understanding the biblical data regarding the kingdom. The theocracy that God established with Moses had no provision for an executive branch. Though it had priests, a law, and judges to settle disputes, God himself was to rule over the people of Israel, who were to be for him a kingdom of priests (Ex. 19:6). Therefore as Israel's king, God saved them at the Red Sea; as they stood on its shores, viewing the wreckage of the Egyptian army, they sang, "The Lord is my strength and my song; he has become my salvation" (15:2).[6] But after the people had settled in the land of Canaan, they forsook God, and "in his anger . . . the Lord handed them over to raiders who plundered them. He sold them to their enemies all around, whom they were no longer able to resist. Whenever Israel went out to fight, the hand of the Lord was against them to defeat them, just as he had sworn to them. They were in great distress" (Judg. 2:14–15). God, however, heard their cry and provided earthly rulers, "judges, who saved them out of the hands of these raiders" (v. 16). But after God had saved Israel through Gideon, the people decided they wanted him rather than God to rule over them. Gideon, being a wise man, refused, insisting, "I will not rule over you, nor will my son rule over you. The Lord will rule over you" (8:22–23).

Later, however, Samuel did the exact opposite and appointed his sons to be judges (1 Sam. 8:1–3). But they were wicked men who oppressed Israel, and so the elders asked Samuel to appoint instead a king, "to lead us, such as all the other nations have" (v. 5), "and fight our battles" (v. 20; cf. 12:12). Though it grieved Samuel to have the people reject his sons, the Lord said to him, "Listen to all that the people are saying to you; it is not you they have rejected, but they have rejected me as their king. As they have done from the day I brought them up out of Egypt until this day, forsaking me and serving other gods, so they are doing to you [in rejecting your sons]. Now listen to them; but warn them solemnly and let them know what the king who will reign over them will do" (8:7–9).[7]

So Samuel called the people together and said, "This is what the Lord, the God of Israel says: 'I brought Israel up out of Egypt, and I delivered you from the power of Egypt and all the kingdoms that oppressed you.' But you have now rejected your God, who saves you out of all your calamities and distresses. And you have said, 'No, set a king over us.' So now present yourselves before the Lord by your tribes and clans" (1 Sam. 10:18–19).

Saul was then chosen as king, but in Samuel's farewell to the people (1 Sam. 12), he emphasized both their great sin in asking for a king and the necessity for them and their king to be careful to obey God. There was encouragement too in the promise that God would not forsake his people, despite their sin.

NOTE. In all fairness it should be pointed out that there was considerable argument from expediency for setting up a dynasty of kings in Israel. Things had reached a deplorable state by the end of the book of Judges (Judg. 17–21 describes events that are about the most sordid in the Bible). Throughout these chapters the author declares, "In those days Israel had no king; everyone did as he saw fit." There was also a sense in which God ratified the decision of the people to have a king by telling Samuel to hearken to the people's request (1 Sam. 8:7–9). It would seem that in their disobedience it was more desirable for them to have a king than to be without one. Thus Deuteronomy 17:14–20 gave Israel instructions about the kind of king it should choose when the people came into the land and decided they wanted a king like the other nations had. Among other things, he must be appointed by God and should continually read the law so he would be just in ruling over Israel. Perhaps having such a king would remove any excuse for their disobedience.

But having a king did not increase Israel's compliance with God's commandments. The unity the nation thus attained simply made its disobedience more obvious, for many of its kings from Saul to the destruction of Judah in 587 B.C. openly flouted God's law. Saul himself proved to be so unruly that Samuel finally told him, "Because you have rejected the word of the Lord, he has rejected you as king" (1 Sam. 15:23). David was then selected in Saul's stead, and under his leadership Jerusalem was made the capital and the kingdom was greatly extended. Yet at the peak of his success David committed adultery with Bathsheba and had her husband killed, and in punishment God declared, "The sword will never depart from your house, because you despised me and took the wife of Uriah the Hittite to be your own" (2 Sam. 12:10).

The fulfillment of this prophecy began almost immediately, for David's son Absalom killed his brother Amnon (2 Sam. 13:28) for raping his sister Tamar. Absalom, who then had to flee for his life, encouraged a revolt against his father, which was finally put down only when Absalom was killed (18:14). And when David selected Solomon, his son by Bathsheba, to succeed him, Solomon could secure his throne only by slaying his brother Adonijah (1 Kings 2:23).

During Solomon's reign Israel achieved her greatest prosperity and territorial gains. But soon he began to exhibit the traits that were expressly forbidden to Israel's kings (Deut. 17:16–20). Though kings were not to multiply horses, Solomon had four thousand, plus twelve thousand horsemen and fourteen hundred chariots (1 Kings 4:26; 10:26). The amassing of silver and gold was forbidden too, but Solomon made silver as common as stone in Jerusalem (10:27). The king was likewise strictly commanded not to have many wives, lest they turn away his heart from God. Solomon, however, had not only seven hundred wives but three hundred concubines, who did in fact "[turn] his heart after other gods, and his heart was not fully devoted to the Lord his God, as the heart of David his father had been" (11:3–4).

Moreover Solomon's rule had become so oppressive that when his successor refused to lighten the people's load, the ten northern tribes split away from the southern two. Thereafter the two hundred years of the northern kingdom's existence was a bloody sequence of seven godless dynasties, and when it was destroyed by the Assyrians in 721 B.C., the reason was simple: the people had been idolatrous and disobedient to the law, despite the repeated warnings of the prophets (2 Kings 17:7–18).

But the southern kingdom too was rebellious: "Even Judah did not keep the commands of the Lord their God. They followed the practices Israel [the ten northern tribes] had introduced" (2 Kings 17:19). Though David's dynasty remained unbroken and several kings were godly men under whom Judah experienced revivals, evil prevailed, reaching its lowest point in Manasseh, "so that [Judah] did more evil than the nations the Lord had destroyed before the Israelites" (2 Kings 21:9).

After Manasseh seven more kings reigned in Jerusalem, including the good King Josiah. After Josiah, however, evil Jehoiakim came to the throne, and Jeremiah warned, "Hear the word of the Lord; O house of David, this is what the Lord says: 'Administer justice every morning; rescue from the hand of his oppressor the one who has been robbed, or my wrath will break out and burn like fire because of the evil you have done—burn with no one to quench it'" (Jer. 21:11–12). Jehoiakim, however, did not repent, and God therefore decreed that Judah be destroyed "because of the sins of Manasseh and all he had done, including the shedding of innocent blood. For he had filled Jerusalem with innocent blood, and the Lord was not willing to forgive" (2 Kings 24:3–4). The days of Judah's kings were now numbered: "This is what the Lord says: I am going to fill with drunkenness all who live in this land, including the kings who sit on David's throne, the priests, the prophets and all those living in Jerusalem. I will smash them one against the other, fathers and sons alike, declares the Lord. I will allow no pity or mercy or compassion to keep me from destroying them" (Jer. 13:13–14). This prediction came to pass during the reign of Zedekiah. Jerusalem was destroyed, and Zedekiah's sons were killed before his eyes, after which he was blinded and led in chains to die in Babylon.

The whole story of Israel's failure was summarized by Nehemiah in the following prayer:

> In all that has happened to us, you have been just; you have acted faithfully, while we did wrong. Our kings, our leaders, our priests and our fathers did not follow your law; they did not pay attention to your commands or the warnings you gave them. Even while they were in their kingdom, enjoying your great goodness to them in the spacious and fertile land you gave them, they did not serve you or turn from their evil ways.
>
> But see, we are slaves today, slaves in the land you gave our forefathers so they could eat its fruit and the other good things it produces. Because of our sins, its abundant harvest goes to the kings you have placed over us. They rule over our bodies and our cattle as they please. We are in great distress. (Neh. 9:33–37)

This passage clearly states that the kingdom God had given Judah was a part of his goodness, but "even while they were in their kingdom, enjoying [God's] great goodness to them," they refused to serve him and obey his laws. This failure to obey the law given at Sinai emphasized the inability of

Israel, generally lacking divine enablement, to represent a kingdom of God on earth.

The Glorious Kingdom to Be Established by God

The story of the kingdom of God in Israel does not end here, however, for the prophet Nathan, David's counselor, had predicted that David's dynasty would never cease. The prophetic writings too speak often about the third phase of God's kingdom, one to be established by his righteous King, whose people will be inclined to obey.

The first indication of this glorious kingdom came from the prophet Nathan, who, soon after David became king in Jerusalem, told him of God's promise regarding his kingdom:

> The Lord declares to you that the Lord himself will establish a house for you. When your days are over and you rest with your fathers, I will raise up your offspring to succeed you, who will come from your own body, and I will establish his kingdom. He is the one who will build a house for my Name, and I will establish the throne of his kingdom forever. I will be his father, and he will be my son. When he does wrong, I will punish him with the rod of men, with floggings inflicted by men. But my love [*hesed*] will never be taken away from him, as I took it away from Saul, whom I removed from before you. Your house and your kingdom will endure forever before me; your throne will be established forever. (2 Sam. 7:11–16)

Although the word "covenant" does not appear in this passage, it follows the pattern of the Noachic, Abrahamic, and new covenants in that the words "I will," referring to what God will do, appear several times. And later David himself referred to it as a covenant: "Is not my house right with God? Has he not made with me an everlasting covenant, arranged and secured in every part?" (2 Sam. 23:5). Likewise Jeremiah declared: "This is what the Lord says, 'If you can break my covenant with the day and my covenant with the night, so that day and night no longer come at their appointed time, then my covenant with David my servant . . . can be broken and David will no longer have a descendant to reign on this throne'" (Jer. 33:20–21). Much of Psalm 89 also designates this promise made to

David as an eternal covenant: "I will maintain my love to [David] forever, and my covenant with him will never fail. . . . I will not violate my covenant or alter what my lips have uttered. Once for all, I have sworn by my holiness— and I will not lie to David—that his line will continue forever and his throne endure before me like the sun" (vv. 28, 34–36). There is a note of conditionality in Psalm 132:11–12: "The Lord swore an oath to David, a sure oath that he will not revoke: 'One of your own descendants I will place on your throne—if your sons keep my covenant and the statutes I teach them, then their sons will sit on your throne for ever and ever.'" But the psalm's conclusion clearly indicates the permanence of the Davidic dynasty: "The Lord has chosen Zion, he has desired it for his dwelling: 'This is my resting place for ever and ever; here I will sit enthroned, for I have desired it. . . . Here I will make a horn grow for David and set up a lamp for my anointed one'" (vv. 13–14, 17).

In the history of David's line, the promise of this covenant was made good. His descendants were indeed chastened. Because Solomon was oppressive, ten tribes were given to Jeroboam, the first of the northern kings. But God said,

> I will not take the whole kingdom out of Solomon's hand; I have made him ruler all the days of his life for the sake of David my servant, whom I chose and who observed my commands and statutes. I will take the kingdom from [David's] son's hands and give you [Jereboam] ten tribes. I will give one tribe to [David's] son so that David my servant may always have a lamp before me in Jerusalem, the city where I chose to put my Name. (1 Kings 11:34–36)

David's descendants therefore continued to rule at Jerusalem, though sometimes their sins were so great that it was only for David's sake that God did not destroy the dynasty (1 Kings 15:3–4; 2 Kings 8:16–19). Finally, however, things became so bad that in 587 B.C. Jerusalem was destroyed, and the reigning king, Zedekiah, was taken captive to Babylon.

Fifty years later some of the exiles returned to Jerusalem, but since they were under Persian rule, no one could reign as king. Thereafter though their overlords changed, Israel remained a subject people, and finally in A.D. 135 any lingering hopes of regaining their sovereignty were dashed forever when Rome crushed the Jewish uprising under Bar Cochba. From that time until the fourth century, the Jews were forbidden even to enter Jerusalem, and then only for one day a year. As we have noted, Jeremiah had foretold both the destruction of David's throne (Jer. 13:13–14) and also the permanence of the covenant God had made with him (33:19–22). Ezekiel too, while predicting the dynasty's ruin, affirmed that the Davidic covenant would still hold: "This is what the sovereign Lord says: . . . 'A ruin! A ruin! I will make [the throne of David] a ruin! It will not be restored until he comes to whom it rightfully belongs; to him I will give it'" (Ezek. 21:26–27). This event would take place when God would "raise up to David a righteous Branch, a King who will reign wisely and do what is just and right in the land. In his days Judah will be saved and Israel will live in safety. This is the name by which he will be called: The Lord Our Righteousness" (Jer. 23:5–6).

But if David's throne was empty from the time of Zedekiah to some future point when this righteous Branch will be raised up, how can it still be said that the Davidic covenant was permanent? A hint is found in Jeremiah 33:17: "'David will never fail to have a man to sit on the throne of the house of Israel.'" In other words, in accordance with the root meaning of "kingdom" (*malkût* in the Old Testament, *basileia* in the New Testament), there would always be a scion of David who would have the right to rule. Even though no kings of David's line actually ruled after Zedekiah, yet the Davidic covenant remained in force because there was always someone of his posterity who had the right to take the throne, if it could have been established.

Matthew's genealogy of Jesus in 1:1–17 and Luke's in 3:23–37 both emphasize that Jesus' genealogy traces back to David through Joseph, Jesus' legal father, although they follow different paths. Matthew carries the genealogy from David back through the succession of the kings of Judah to David's son Solomon, while Luke traces his genealogy back to David's son Nathan. The differences between these two genealogies reflect different Jewish understandings regarding the ancestry of the Messiah.[8] Thus, in the Jewish thinking of that time, it was possible to relate Joseph, and thus Jesus, back to King David. And so the angel said to Mary, "The Lord God will give [Jesus] the throne of his father David" (Luke 1:32), "because [Joseph] belonged to the house and line of David" (2:4).

Jesus, then, was one who could have been the righteous Branch predicted by Jeremiah, for it was his right to rule over Israel. But was he the one the prophets had predicted? Jesus did announce the realization of the kingdom of God as having taken place, and he performed the miracles that were to accompany the fulfillment of the promised kingdom of God (Isa. 35:5–6; cf. Matt. 11:2–6). But he did not rule over Israel and free it from subservience to Rome. In fact, its people in conjunction with the Gentile rulers had him crucified as a criminal. And though his followers regarded his resurrection and ascension as the fulfillment of the Old Testament promises based on the Davidic covenant (Acts 2:30–31; 13:34), no salvation came to Israel as a nation. Instead the Roman armies destroyed Jerusalem in A.D. 70, and after the disastrous Bar Cochba revolt in 135, the people were scattered in all directions. Was the New Testament then radically reinterpreting the Old Testament to regard Jesus as the promised Messiah? In part 4 I attempt to answer this question by illumining Jesus' accomplishments in terms of the kingdom of God when he first came to earth.

Review Questions

1. What particular thing about God is being said when there is talk of his kingdom? Or, what is the *kingdom* of God, and what is the *merciful covenant* of God?

2. How do I argue that John the Baptist enjoyed the saving benefits of the kingdom, even though Matthew 11:11–14 and parallels speak of him as not belonging to it?

3. Why did God delay the ceremonial inauguration of the kingdom of God, the giving of the Holy Spirit, and the commencement of the new covenant, when these bless-

ings were being enjoyed by the seed of the woman right back to the beginning?

4. How could Jeremiah predict that a time would come when no king would sit on David's throne but at the same time say that the Davidic covenant was as certain as the Noachic covenant?

5. How does Ezekiel 21:27 show that the basic idea of the kingdom of God is the *right to rule* rather than a *realm* over which the king rules?

NOTES

[1] This terminology comes from Isa. 28:21: "The Lord will rise up as he did at Mount Perazim; he will rouse himself as in the valley of Gibeon—to do his work, his *strange* work, and perform his task, his *alien* task."

[2] George E. Ladd, *Jesus and the Kingdom* (New York: Harper & Row, 1964), 38.

[3] George E. Ladd, *Crucial Questions About the Kingdom of God* (Grand Rapids: Eerdmans, 1952), 83–84.

[4] The Greek work for "confer" is *diatithemai,* a verbal form of the substantive *diathēkē,* "covenant."

[5] Ladd, *Jesus and the Kingdom,* 42.

[6] Confirming Ladd's thesis that the kingdom of God is his saving activity, many Old Testament passages relating to the kingdom include the concept of salvation.

[7] According to 1 Sam. 8:11–18, a king would do the following: "He will take your sons and make them serve with his chariots and horses, and they will run in front of his chariots. Some he will assign to be commanders of thousands and commanders of fifties, and others to plow his ground and reap his harvest, and still others to make weapons of war and equipment for his chariots. He will take your daughters to be perfumers and cooks and bakers. He will take the best of your fields and vineyards and olive groves and give them to his attendants. . . . He will take a tenth of your flocks, and you yourselves will become his slaves. When that day comes, you will cry out for relief from the king you have chosen, and the Lord will not answer you in that day."

[8] Marshall D. Johnson, "Genealogy of Jesus," in *The International Standard Bible Encyclopedia,* 4 vols., ed. Geoffrey W. Bromiley et al. (Grand Rapids: Eerdmans, 1982), 2:428.

PART 4

THE GOSPEL GOES
TO THE WORLD

24

Jesus Presents the Kingdom of God

Part 3 was devoted to an overview of the lesson book God wrote as he dealt with Israel for the two thousand years from Abraham to Christ, a period during which he "let all nations go their own way" (Acts 14:16). But when enough of the lesson book of Israel had been written and "the time had fully come, God sent his Son" (Gal. 4:4) into the world to satisfy God's justice so sinners throughout history could receive forgiveness and be adopted into God's family. Thus when Jesus was about to ascend back to heaven to sit at the Father's right hand, he commanded those whom he had appointed as apostles to take this message of salvation out of its Jewish confines to all peoples of earth. And Acts 8:1 then tells how, because the Jewish majority mounted a great persecution against the church in Jerusalem (6:8–8:1), many Christians had to leave the city. But "those who had been scattered preached the word wherever they went" (8:4).

[They] traveled as far as Phoenicia, Cyprus and Antioch, telling the message only to Jews. Some of them, however, men from Cyprus and Cyrene, went to Antioch and began to speak to Greeks also [i.e., Gentiles], telling them the good news about the Lord Jesus. The Lord's hand was with them, and a great number of people believed and turned to the Lord. News of this reached the ears of the church at Jerusalem, and they sent Barnabas to Antioch. When he arrived and saw the evidence of the grace of God, he was glad and encouraged them all to remain true to the Lord with all their hearts. He

405

was a good man, full of the Holy Spirit and faith, and a great
number of people were brought to the Lord. Then Barnabas
went to Tarsus to look for Saul [Paul], and when he found
him, he brought him to Antioch. (Acts 11:19–26)

A year later the Holy Spirit said, "Set apart for me
Barnabas and Saul for the work to which I have called
them." Then the Christians in the church at Antioch, after
they had fasted and prayed, "placed their hands on them and
sent them off. The two of them, sent on their way by the
Holy Spirit, went down to Seleucia and sailed from there to
Cyprus. When they arrived at Salamis, they proclaimed the
word of God in the Jewish synagogues" (Acts 13:2–5).

Later they came to Antioch of Pisidia (Acts 13:14–43),
about a hundred miles in from the south coast of what is
present-day Turkey, and Paul preached in the synagogue
there also. In this sermon he rehearsed the history of the
Jews, the lesson book God had been writing, climaxing it
with reference to how they had had Christ crucified and in so
doing had fulfilled the Old Testament prophets (vv. 27–29).
Nevertheless,

> God raised him from the dead, and for many days he was seen
> by those who had traveled with him from Galilee to Jerusa-
> lem. They are now his witnesses to [the Jewish] people. We
> tell you the good news: What God promised our fathers he has
> fulfilled for us, their children, by raising up Jesus. . . .
> Therefore, my brothers, I want you to know that through Jesus
> the forgiveness of sins is proclaimed to you. Through him
> everyone who believes is justified from everything you could
> not be justified from by the law of Moses. (Acts 13:30–32,
> 38–39)[1]

The Jews urged him to preach again. Therefore

> on the next Sabbath almost the whole city gathered to hear the
> word of the Lord. When the Jews saw the crowds [of
> Gentiles], they were filled with jealousy and talked abusively
> against what Paul was saying. Then Paul and Barnabas
> answered them boldly: "We had to speak the word of God to
> you first. [But] since you reject it and do not consider
> yourselves worthy of eternal life, we now turn to the Gen-
> tiles. . . . When the Gentiles heard this, they were glad and

honored the word of the Lord; and all who were appointed for eternal life believed. The word of the Lord spread through the whole region. (Acts 13:44–49)

This scenario, which occurred repeatedly during Paul's three missionary journeys, took place again at the very end of Acts as he preached to the Jews in Rome. When he arrived there, they said, "We want to hear what your views are, for we know that people everywhere are talking against this sect" (Acts 28:22). So

[the Jews] arranged to meet Paul on a certain day, and came in even larger numbers to the place where he was staying. From morning till evening he explained and declared to them the kingdom of God and tried to convince them about Jesus from the Law of Moses and from the Prophets. Some were convinced by what he said, but others would not believe. They disagreed among themselves and began to leave after Paul had made this final statement: "The Holy Spirit spoke the truth to your forefathers when he said through Isaiah the prophet: 'Go to this people and say, "You will be ever hearing but never understanding; you will be ever seeing but never perceiving." For this people's heart has become calloused; they hardly hear with their ears, and they have closed their eyes. Otherwise they might see with their eyes, hear with their ears, understand with their hearts and turn, and I would heal them.' Therefore I want you to know that God's salvation has been sent to the Gentiles, and they will listen!" (Acts 28:23–28)

As of today the gospel has gone to thousands of people-groups, to the extent that self-sustaining churches have been established among them. In the last almost 2000 years of gospel outreach, churches have also been established in many hundreds of people-groups that have since died out or amalgamated with other peoples. Nevertheless, thousands of mostly smaller people-groups still have never had anyone with a sufficient understanding of their language, culture, and history to plant churches among them that would then spread until all those in the group could be evangelized. But Jesus said, "This gospel of the kingdom will be preached in the whole world . . . and then the end will come" (Matt. 24:14). So the worldwide mission of the church should be our primary concern, for Jesus will not return until the whole world has been evangelized.

Now, however, we need to review the public ministry of Jesus and see how preaching changed as the "time had fully come." In the last section of the previous chapter we have already seen how the Old Testament prophets spoke of the future coming of the kingdom. John the Baptist continued that emphasis in the early pages of the Gospels but declared that the fulfillment was just about to occur: "Repent, for the kingdom of heaven is near" (Matt. 3:2). Then Jesus came, as John predicted, and announced,"The time has come" (Mark 1:15). We have seen how shortly afterward, when preaching in the synagogue at Nazareth, Jesus quoted from Isaiah 61:1–2, in which the future Messiah declared, "The Spirit of the Lord is on me, because he has anointed me [Messiah means 'anointed one'] to preach good news to the poor." Then he asserted, "Today this scripture is fulfilled in your hearing" (Luke 4:16–19, 21).

This statement is an instance of what John Bright called "a tremendously significant change of tense,"[2] from the future to the present, with Jesus' declaration that Old Testament prophecy has now been fulfilled. The New Testament still looks forward to a consummation yet to come, but it regards this event as being guaranteed by the fulfillment that has already happened in Jesus Christ. As Cullmann has put it, in New Testament thought "the decisive turn of events has already occurred in Christ,"and "the future expectation is founded in faith in the 'already' "[3]

The Difference Made by the Change of Tense

George Ladd summed up the difference produced by this change of tense as follows: "The New Testament locates the Kingdom in Jesus' person and ministry."[4] A sampling of Jesus' preaching quickly leads to the conclusion that "no one ever spoke the way this man does" (John 7:46), for he "taught as one who had authority, and not as their teachers of the law" (Matt. 7:29). With but a word Jesus exorcised demons, so that people said, "What is this? A new teaching—and with authority! He even gives orders to evil spirits and they obey him" (Mark 1:27).

In line with his authority Jesus prefaced many of his statements with *amēn*, "I tell you the truth." As we have seen above in chapter 3, in the Old Testament this term was used only to affirm what another had said. Jesus himself, however, frequently used the term to affirm his own statements. An example of his usage is Mark 3:28: "I tell you the truth [*amēn*], all the sins and blasphemies of men will be forgiven them." His unique usage of this word indicates that he was so sure of the truth of what he said that he could use this word to give full authority to his own statements.

He also exercised the authority to forgive sins, which the Old Testament had said God alone could do: "I, even I, am he who blots out your transgressions, for my own sake, and remembers your sins no more" (Isa. 43:25; cf. Ps. 103:2–3). But to the paralytic lowered through the roof for healing, Jesus said, "Son, your sins are forgiven." The shocked reaction of the scribes and religious leaders was, "Why does this fellow talk like that? He's blaspheming! Who can forgive sins but God alone?" (Mark 2:5–7).

> [But] immediately Jesus knew in his spirit that this was what they were thinking in their hearts, and he said to them, "Why are you thinking these things? Which is easier: to say to the paralytic, 'Your sins are forgiven,' or to say, 'Get up, take your mat and walk'? But that you may know that the Son of Man has authority on earth to forgive sins. . . ." He said to the paralytic, "I tell you, get up, take your mat and go home." He got up, took his mat and walked out in full view of them all. This amazed everyone and they praised God, saying, "We have never seen anything like this!" (Mark 2:8–12)

So Jesus was mighty in deed as well as in word. When the imprisoned John the Baptist began to doubt that Jesus was the promised Messiah, he sent some of his disciples to Jesus to ask,

> "Are you the one who was to come, or should we expect someone else?" At that very time Jesus cured many who had diseases, sicknesses and evil spirits, and gave sight to many who were blind. So he replied to the messengers, "Go back

and report to John what you have seen and heard: the blind receive sight, the lame walk, those who have leprosy are cured, the deaf hear, the dead are raised, and the good news is preached to the poor." (Luke 7:20–22)

These were the very things that the Messiah would do, according to Isaiah (35:5–6), and such works were affirmed by Nicodemus, a leading teacher in Israel, who asserted: "Rabbi, we know you are a teacher who has come from God. For no one could perform the miraculous signs you are doing if God were not with him" (John 3:2). And Jesus' argument against those seeking to kill him for speaking as though he was God was, "Do not believe me unless I do what my Father does. But if I do it, even though you do not believe me, believe the miracles, that you may know and understand that the Father is in me, and I in the Father" (10:37–38).

In accordance with the reign of God as the fundamental idea of his kingdom, the power and authority to work salvation was indeed resident in the person of Jesus. And as he exercised these rightful powers of the kingdom, it was inevitable that a realm was established into which people entered. Some who entered were tax collectors and prostitutes (Matt. 21:31), for Jesus forgave those like the sinful woman (Luke 7:50). Likewise, to the horror of the Pharisees, Jesus declared that salvation had come even to the house of the tax collector Zacchaeus and that he too was a son of Abraham (Luke 19:9). Jesus also had table fellowship with "sinners," that is, representatives of the mass of people in Israel (the *am hā-'āreṣ,* or people of the land, "this mob that knows nothing of the law" [John 7:49]), who ignored the Pharisaic traditions. In reply to the Pharisees' objections, however, Jesus said, "I have not come to call the righteous, but sinners" (Mark 2:17).

Those who thus entered the kingdom Jesus offered had the privilege of regarding God as their Father, for they learned to pray, "Our Father in heaven . . ." (Matt. 6:9). The idea of God as a father to those who trusted him was hinted at in Psalm 103:13 ("As a father has compassion on his children, so the Lord has compassion on those who fear him"), but the sense of intimacy with him as Father that

characterized the ministry of Jesus had never before been
equaled. Thus the church, following Jesus' example, had the
audacity when talking to God to use the endearing expression "Abba, Father" (Rom. 8:15; cf. Mark 14:36). And for
Jesus so to love sinners and to teach those entering the
kingdom to regard God as their father fits perfectly with the
fact that resident in him was God's *right* to save people—
which is to say that the kingdom of God had come in his
person.

But perhaps the most significant evidence that the powers
of the kingdom of God were resident in Jesus' person was his
authority over satanic forces. The most striking passage is
Matthew 12:22–37, where in reply to the Pharisees' charge
that he cast out demons by the prince of demons, Jesus
argued that Satan would never be a party to destroying his
own kingdom. But since he, Jesus, did cast out demons,
therefore the kingdom of God "has come upon you" (v. 28).[5]
Jesus regarded Satan as having been cast down from heaven
(Luke 10:18), even though we know that he continued to
have power during Jesus' ministry (John 13:27) and will
have until the end of this age (Eph. 2:2; 6:10–12; Rev.
12:10–12; 20:10). This can only mean that while the powers
of the age to come, which will see the total defeat of Satan,
were resident in Jesus' person, yet during his incarnation he
did not use this authority to terminate completely Satan's
work, and he continues to allow Satan to function as the "god
of this age" (2 Cor. 4:4). This meaning is made quite clear
not only by Jesus' speaking of the kingdom as a present
reality (fulfillment) but also as that whose blessings would
be fully realized only in the future (consummation).[6]

The blessings to be enjoyed at the consummation of the
kingdom of God are (1) a resurrection to immortality (Luke
20:35–36; cf. 1 Cor. 15:44), (2) the ability to see God face to
face (Matt. 5:8; cf. 1 Cor. 13:12), (3) the gathering together
of all the people of God and a separation between them and
the wicked (Matt. 25:46), (4) the full joy of the Lord (Matt.
25:21), and (5) the complete reorganization of creation (Matt.
19:28; Rom. 8:20–23; Rev. 21:5). Only when Satan and the
unrepentant are completely separated from the righteous

will all of God's power be placed in the employ of his love to effect a creation that completely reflects his perfections.

Since the promise of the kingdom of God is fulfilled but not consummated during Jesus' incarnation, and since the powers of evil continue to hold a limited but nevertheless real sway on earth after his ascension, it necessarily follows that the lives of his followers, like that of the incarnate Jesus himself, will be characterized by suffering. This fact accords with his ultimate purpose in coming, which was to "give his life as a ransom for many" (Mark 10:45). Had the power resident in Jesus at his first coming been unleashed to achieve complete consummation of the kingdom, then he could not have suffered that complete loss of glory by which he repaired the injury sinners have inflicted upon God's glory (see chap. 14 above). But since only through Jesus' suffering and death could God receive the right to save sinners, Jesus set his face steadfastly toward Jerusalem to die (Luke 9:51; 13:22; 17:11; 18:31). And because he held back his divine powers and died on the cross for our sins, the powers of the kingdom could be manifested from the Fall onward and could achieve consummation in the establishment of a new heavens and earth.

Thus we are faced with the apparent paradox that only because Jesus gave up power was it possible for him to exercise the power of the kingdom of God. Nowhere was this limitation more evident than when he hung on the cross, being mocked by the rulers and soldiers, who said, "He saved others; let him save himself if he is the Christ of God, the Chosen One. . . . If you are the king of the Jews, save yourself" (Luke 23:35–37). At this point Jesus appeared as the epitome of foolishness, but in the wisdom of God, it was only because he did not save himself that he is able to save others.

Why Israel Rejected the King

A complex of issues is involved in explaining why the leaders of Israel delivered up Jesus to be crucified. To begin with, from the outset he refused to employ his power and authority to give the Jews the deliverance from Rome that they felt they deserved. No doubt something of this hope was in the thinking of the priest Zechariah when at the birth of John the Baptist he blessed God for this person who would play a crucial role in bringing "salvation from our enemies and from the hand of all who hate us" (Luke 1:68–75). The same sentiment was expressed by two of Jesus' disciples as they returned to Emmaus after the crucifixion: "We had hoped that he was the one who was going to redeem Israel" (24:21). Even John the Baptist, as he languished in Herod's dungeon, wondered why, if Jesus had brought the kingdom of God, he did not use his power to destroy the likes of an evil Herod (Matt. 11:2–6).

Indeed, Jesus had come to minister to the "lost sheep of Israel" (Matt. 15:24), and he directed his disciples not to "go among the Gentiles or enter any town of the Samaritans" (10:5). But whereas the chief interest of the average Israelite was to be free from Rome and again a sovereign nation, Jesus' main concern was to find those in Israel manifesting a genuine repentance and willingness to trust in God. Thus he found greater faith in a Gentile centurion than in Israel (8:10) and virtually no faith among his home folks in Nazareth (Mark 6:6). And because of their incredulity at the claim of this local carpenter's son to be the fulfillment of Isaiah 61:1–2, Jesus refused to perform the miracles he had done in Capernaum. Furthermore, he intimated that just as Elijah's power benefited the Gentile widow of Zarephath and the Gentile leper Naaman, so too he would be more disposed to perform miracles before the Gentiles (Luke 4:22–27). This statement so angered them that they tried to throw Jesus off a cliff. Jesus was similarly rejected when the very multitudes who had clamored to make him king became disenchanted at his refusal to become a political savior (John 6:15–42).

But it was not so much the common people who rejected Jesus (great multitudes of them followed him) as the religious leaders. Sometime after the return of Israel from the Exile, the Pharisees had become the epitome of the effort to promote legalistic adherence to the law in the erroneous belief that such behavior would rectify the mistake that had caused Israel to go into captivity. But this thinking was no solution to the problem, for it led to "religious intolerance and pride [which] is the final expression of [a person's] sinfulness."[7]

Thus Jesus regarded the Pharisees as the taproot of the unbelief he found so appalling in Israel; they were the essence of the "wicked generation" (Matt. 11 and 12, esp. 12:39, 41, 42, 45). The power they held over the nation is reflected in the shock Jesus' disciples experienced when he scolded the Pharisees for disobeying the teachings of the law, the word of God, out of preference for the tradition they had developed (Matt. 15:3–14, esp. v. 12).[8] Jesus infuriated them in other ways as well: he (1) scored them for their hypocrisy (e.g., Matt. 23), (2) flouted their customs (e.g., Mark 7:13), (3) ate with tax collectors and "sinners" (e.g., Mark 2:16), (4) remained unintimidated by their threats (Luke 13:31–33), (5) performed miracles to show up the lack of love in their rigid adherence to the law (e.g., Mark 3:1–5), (6) refused to perform the ultimate sign of Daniel 7:13 to prove that he was indeed the Christ (Matt. 12:38; cf. John 10:24), and (7) outwitted them in public debate when they tried to trip him up (Mark 11:27–12:34).

In the final contest, to put Jesus to death the Pharisees joined hands with the chief priests, many of whom were even unorthodox Sadducees, who denied a future resurrection from the dead. These priests stirred up the multitude to demand that Jesus be crucified by Pilate (Mark 15:11–15), who realized that it was only envy that made them do it (v. 10). Offended because Jesus had never done anything to curry their favor and resentful of the great power he had to control the multitudes through his teaching and miracles, they feared that if this power continued, the Romans would suspect that a revolt was brewing and would "take away both [their] place and [their] nation" (John 11:47–53). Nor did Jesus' reluctance to be regarded as a king encourage them to think he would exercise his power to help them withstand Rome; in fact, he openly advocated living at peace with their enemy (Matt. 22:21). And when none of this power to save others was exhibited on the cross to save himself, these leaders felt that their rejection of him had been vindicated.

Did the Old Testament Encourage the Rejection of Jesus?

The basic problem that people had with Jesus was thus his lack of concern about Rome's rule over them. The Jews expected the promised Messiah to be a leader powerful enough to deliver them from this rule and restore Israel to a place of prominence in the world. Thus it came as a complete shock to Peter and the disciples after Jesus' acknowledgment that he was indeed the Christ to hear him say that he must "suffer many things and be rejected by the elders, chief priests and teachers of the law, and that he must be killed and after three days rise again" (Mark 8:31). Peter rebuked him for such talk, but in response was himself sharply reprimanded: "Get behind me, Satan! . . . You do not have in mind the things of God, but the things of men" (vv. 32–33).

But can one really hold Zechariah, John the Baptist, Peter, the disciples, and Israel in general responsible to realize that the heir to David's throne, who would redeem Israel, must first suffer and be crucified before he could reign over them in glory? Jesus thought so, for to the two disconsolate disciples walking home to Emmaus he said, "How foolish you are, and how slow of heart to believe all that the prophets have spoken! Did not the Christ have to suffer these things and then enter his glory?" And then, "beginning with Moses and all the Prophets, he explained to them what was said in all the Scriptures concerning himself" (Luke 24:25–27). We wonder what passages Jesus used, for was not the kingdom promised by the prophets one characterized by glory and power? It was indeed, but did they also talk of his sufferings?

The late British scholar F. F. Bruce (1910–90) argued that the Old Testament itself, particularly Isaiah 52:13–53:12, necessarily implied that the future Messiah must suffer.[9] His line of argument was to show that the "servant" who figures so prominently in Isaiah 40–55 could not properly be understood as referring either to some individual existing around the time this passage was written or to a certain group of people. The Jewish interpretation for the servant, echoed as far back as Origen's *Against Celsus* (1:50) in the third century A.D., is that it refers to the Jewish nation.[10] Indeed, in one place God does address Israel as his servant: "You are my servant, Israel, in whom I will display my splendor" (Isa. 49:3). But the idea of a complete identity between the servant and Israel does not hold up. Unlike the servant who obeys God fully ("the Sovereign Lord has opened my ears, and I have not been rebellious" [50:5]), the servant Israel was deaf, blind, and inattentive and thus sorely punished (42:19). Furthermore, Israel needed forgiveness from her sins (43:24–25), but the servant makes this forgiveness possible (53:5, 11).

The understanding of the servant as different from Israel while still closely identified with it was possible because, as Bruce observed, "In ancient societies with a sacral kingship . . . the king was not only his people's representative before God and men but was a representative of God to his people—[and] in Israel [this would be the Lord's] anointed one [the Messiah]" (89). Since none of Israel's past kings fit the picture of the servant (90), he must be Israel's future Messiah. One confirmation is that "while the Servant is sometimes spoken of in the past tense, the principal part of his ministry lies in the future [in Isa. 40–55]" (89). Then too Isaiah had said, "In that day the Root of Jesse [King David's father] will stand as a banner for the peoples; the nations will rally to him" (Isa. 11:10).

Two elements in this clear reference to Israel's future Messiah receive further emphasis in Isaiah 55:3–5, where God links up the servant both with past promises to David and with an outreach to the Gentiles in the future: "Give ear and come to me; hear me, that your soul may live. I will make an everlasting covenant with you, my faithful love promised to David. See, I have made him [the servant] a witness to the peoples. . . . Surely you [the servant] will summon nations you know not, and nations that do not know you will hasten to you, because of the Lord your God."

A third aspect of this servant is that he is to suffer and die vicariously for the sins of others:

> It was the Lord's will to crush him and cause him to suffer,
> and though the Lord makes his life a guilt offering, he [the
> servant] will see his offspring and prolong his days. . . . By his
> knowledge my righteous servant will justify many and he will
> bear their iniquities. Therefore I will give him a portion
> among the great [note the glorification] . . . because he poured
> out his life unto death and was numbered with the transgres-
> sors [note the suffering]. For he bore the sins of many, and
> made intercession for the transgressors. (Isa. 53:10–12)

This passage is explicit in saying that the glorification of
the Messiah comes on account of his sufferings. But down
through the ages Judaism has apparently been repelled at
the thought of a suffering Messiah. In the Septuagint, these
verses set forth a somewhat different picture:

> The Lord is also pleased to purge him from his stroke. If ye
> can give an offering for sin, your soul shall see a long-lived
> seed: the Lord also is pleased to take away from the travail of
> his soul, to shew him light, and to form him with understand-
> ing; to justify the just one who serves many well; and he shall
> bear their sins. Therefore he shall inherit many, and he shall
> divide the spoils of the mighty; because his soul was
> delivered to death: and he was numbered among the trans-
> gressors; and he bore the sins of many and was delivered
> because of their iniquities.[11]

Thus Strack and Billerbeck say concerning this Greek
translation that it is "ambiguous" and that it permits understanding the servant of Isaiah 53 to be the Jewish nation.

Despite the difficulties of making the "servant" one and
the same throughout Isaiah 40–55, this has continued to be
the Jewish understanding of Isaiah 53 during the Christian
era. Although Origen cited such an interpretation in the third
century, Bruce has noted that there are also "traces of a
tradition of a suffering Messiah . . . present in Judaism" (93).
The tractate *Sanhedrin* 98b in the Babylonian Talmud
queries regarding the names of the Messiah and answers,
" 'The Leper of the house of learning is his name,' as it is
said: 'Surely he has borne our sicknesses and carried our
pains, yet we esteemed him a leper, smitten by God and
afflicted' " (94). There is also a passage in a hymn by the poet
Eleazar ben Qalir, written sometime between the seventh

and tenth centuries, that speaks of forgiveness as being made possible only by the Messiah, who "is wounded for our transgressions. He bears on his shoulders our sins to find pardon for our iniquities [and] may we be healed by his stripes !" (94).

We may conclude, therefore, that the servant of Isaiah 40–55 must be the long-awaited Jewish Messiah, since this interpretation yields a coherent meaning to these chapters. We may also conclude from the Hebrew wording of Isaiah 53:10–12 that the Messiah must first suffer and then be glorified. So it was indeed proper for Jesus to scold his disciples on the road to Emmaus for being disillusioned because the Jesus whom they hoped would deliver Israel from Roman rule had instead suffered and died on a cross. They could have known that he must first suffer and only afterward be glorified because it would have been possible for them to get a proper translation of the Hebrew of Isaiah 53:10–12. Thus after Jesus had expounded the Old Testament Scriptures and shown them this truth, their hearts burned with joy (Luke 24:32).

To be sure, Jews, like Peter, have recoiled from the idea of a suffering Messiah. But just because Israel did not want to believe this, their people were not exonerated from following what the Scriptures taught. Not wanting to believe constitutes only moral, not physical, inability and therefore does not release one from responsibility. Hence Jesus was justified in chiding his disciples for not understanding the Scriptures' teaching that the Christ must suffer and then enter into his glory.

Therefore, since the future kingdom in the Old Testament prophets included both the sufferings and the glory of the Messiah, Jesus did not radically reinterpret the Old Testament when he came to give up his life as a ransom for many and at the same time said, "The time has come.... The kingdom of God is near" (Mark 1:15). Without question, many details as to how the Messiah could both suffer and be glorified had not been revealed to the prophets, but these blanks were filled in by further New Testament revelations that are called mysteries.

Review Questions

1. What blessings of the kingdom of God are yet to come in its consummation (not its fulfillment, which took place during Jesus' first advent)?
2. Why could there have been no kingdom of God if Jesus had consummated the kingdom at his first coming?
3. Why could Peter and others be held responsible to know that the Messiah must first suffer, although Peter had no moral ability even to consider such an idea?

NOTES

[1] As explained in chapter 20, the law of Moses did not enable justification because for the most part it was given to Israel without the regenerating power of the Holy Spirit to provide the spiritual empathy needed to respond to the spiritual law. Acts 13:38–39 does not have to mean that the law itself was, as Calvin taught in his commentary on Rom. 10:5, "opposed to Christ." See Appendix.

[2] John Bright, *The Kingdom of God* (New York: Abingdon, 1953), 197.

[3] Cullmann, *Salvation in History*, 183.

[4] Ladd, *Jesus and the Kingdom*, 152.

[5] See ibid., 134–44, for a detailed exegesis supporting this translation.

[6] *Fulfillment without consummation* during Jesus' ministry is the basic thesis of Ladd's *Jesus and the Kingdom*. Cullmann emphasizes the point that in Jesus there is both what has already been fulfilled and that which awaits fulfillment.

[7] Reinhold Niebuhr, *The Nature and Destiny of Man*, 2 vols. (New York: Scribner's, 1945), 1:203. See also chapter 21 above.

[8] Josephus: "So great is [the Pharisees'] influence on the masses, that even when they speak against a king or high-priest, they immediately gain credence" (*Jewish Antiquities* 13.10.5).

[9] F. F. Bruce, *New Testament Development of Old Testament Themes* (Grand Rapids: Eerdmans, 1968). Page numbers in parentheses in the text indicate locations of quotations in Bruce.

[10] Strack and Billerbeck, *Kommentar*, 1:481.

[11] This translation of Isa. 53:10–12 is taken from *The Septuagint Version of the Old Testament and Apocrypha, with an English Translation* (Grand Rapids: Zondervan, 1972).

25

The Present Realm
of God's Kingdom

We have just seen how the Old Testament itself explicitly taught that the Messiah must first suffer and then be glorified. But according to Peter, the Old Testament prophets "searched intently and with the greatest care, trying to find out the time and the circumstances to which the Spirit of Christ in them was pointing when he predicted the sufferings of Christ and the glories that would follow" (1 Peter 1:10–11). In the New Testament, however, three specific new revelations are given that provide considerable help in understanding the way God is directing redemptive history during the period between Christ's sufferings at his first coming and the manifestation of his glories when he returns to earth. Added light is also cast on the way in which redemptive history then comes to a climax and God's purpose that "the earth shall be filled with the knowledge of the glory of God as the waters cover the sea" (Hab. 2:14) is finally fulfilled.[1]

In each of these three passages there is talk of a *mystērion* ("mystery") that is being revealed. The term in these contexts meant "the secret thoughts, plans, and dispensations of God which are hidden from the human reason, as well as from other comprehensions below the divine level, and hence must be revealed to those for whom they are intended."[2] This idea is expressed in Romans 16:25–26: "[The] gospel [is] . . . according to the revelation of the mystery hidden for long ages past, but now revealed and

made known through the prophetic writings by the command of the eternal God, so that all nations might believe
and obey him." From its associations here and elsewhere,
the term "mystery," or "secret," is seen as a revelatory truth
that before a certain time was hidden but then is made
known to people. So, for example, one mystery about the
gospel that is revealed clearly in the New Testament is the
teaching on the resurrection and eternal life: "[Christ] has
destroyed death and brought immortality to light through the
gospel" (2 Tim. 1:10). Such things were hinted at in the Old
Testament but were explicitly spelled out only in the New
Testament. Let us then consider the first "mystery" passage,
Jesus' seven parables in Matthew 13:1–52, and the explanation of the first two.

The Mysteries of the Kingdom

Jesus termed these parables he was about to give "the
secrets [or mysteries] of the kingdom" (Matt. 13:11). He set
forth these new revelatory truths in this way so that they
would not be understood by the multitudes, who in general
were unhappy that he did not fit the pattern expected of the
Jewish Messiah. But Jesus did interpret two of these
parables to his disciples, who in the main had shown
themselves willing to remain committed to him, despite the
obstacles presented by his insistence that he must first suffer
before entering his glories. From the general drift of the first
two parables, in which he made clear the strange realm in
which God's kingdom, or *right to rule,* would now manifest
itself, it is possible to make an educated guess as to the
meaning of the remaining five. Here we are shown what will
be true for the people of God during the time between Jesus'
first coming to suffer and his second coming, when he will
be openly glorified. In general the point is made that even
though God's people are benefiting from the blessings of his
right to rule made possible by Jesus' suffering and death, yet
they too will suffer as they await Jesus' second coming.

The Parable of the Four Soils
(Matt. 13:3–9, 18–23)

Many passages in the Old Testament dealing with the future glory of the kingdom describe its full sway over Israel and the nations. For example, Jeremiah 31:34 tells how people in Israel, from the least to the greatest, would then have full knowledge of the Lord. Isaiah 2:2–3 also affirms that when the kingdom is established at Jerusalem, "Many peoples will come and say, 'Come, let us go up to the mountain of the Lord. . . . He will teach us his ways, so that we may walk in his paths.'" And Daniel 2:44 declares that the coming of the kingdom means such an exercise of God's mighty power that no one can stand before it: "In the time of those kings, the God of heaven will set up a kingdom that will never be destroyed, nor will it be left to another people. It will crush all those kingdoms and bring them to an end, but it will itself endure forever." These kingdoms will then serve and obey the people of the Most High (Dan. 7:27).

Yet in this parable Jesus taught that during the interval before his glorious second coming, the majority of people on earth would not be under his sway. Rather, he likened their varying receptivity to the kingdom's message to four different kinds of soil. Only in the good soil of the fourth category would the kingdom of God rule in people's hearts.

Such a realm carries on the ambiguity that had characterized Jesus' ministry during his first coming. Despite the great manifestations of the power of God, only a small percentage responded positively and entered his kingdom. And ever since, the citizens of this kingdom have, like Jesus, experienced both its healing powers and the onslaughts of Satan and his seed. There is therefore a similarity between this minority of genuine citizens of Jesus' kingdom and the small remnant in Israel before Jesus' first coming, for we recall how these who were regenerated were often persecuted by the ungodly Israelites who greatly outnumbered them (e.g., Num. 14:10).

The Parable of the Weeds and the Wheat
(Matt. 13:24–30, 36–43)

The view of the Old Testament prophets that the future kingdom would effect a complete separation between good and evil was summed up by John the Baptist when he said, "[God] will clear his threshing floor, gathering his wheat into the barn and burning up the chaff with unquenchable fire" (Matt. 3:12). But this parable, like the preceding one, teaches that the kingdom will not universally prevail between Jesus' first coming in suffering and his second coming in glory. In addition to the "sons of the kingdom" (13:38) or "the righteous" (v. 43), representing the "wheat," there will be "sons of the evil one" (v. 38), who cause sin and are themselves doers of evil (v. 41). These are the "weeds," and they will exist in the closest proximity to the wheat until the close of the age, when God himself will make the final separation between the wicked and the righteous. Thus just as the fulfillment of the kingdom of God during Jesus' earthly ministry left social patterns largely intact, so the kingdom of God during the ensuing intermediate period continues to invade "history without disrupting the present structure of society." Indeed, "the Kingdom has come; but society is not uprooted. This is the mystery of the Kingdom."[3]

Like the preceding parable, this one stresses that the kingdom of God will only partially prevail in the intermediate period, but it adds the knowledge that the "sons of the kingdom" will never group themselves together so perfectly that they will succeed in having pure societies of righteous people in distinction to the wicked. Instead, wheat will be so interspersed among weeds that any attempt to effect a separation between the two before the consummation would succeed only in uprooting some wheat as well.

NOTE. It would thus seem that all attempts to establish a pure society, like that of the Puritans, or a pure church, like that of the modern voluntary separatists, are doomed to failure. The history of voluntary separatism indicates that often one separation leads but to another, until finally only a few individuals are left who can agree with one another. (There are, however, instances where a separation that takes place along cultural lines can greatly aid church growth, since a new church is now able to style its worship service and general appeal to people who think more or less alike.) For example, with the establishment of the Orthodox Presbyterian Church in June 1936, J. Gresham Machen proclaimed a purified Presbyterian church. But four months later this church too had split over the issues of premillennialism and the moderate use of alcohol, with the newly formed "Bible Presbyterian Church" finally espousing premillennialism and forbidding the use of both alcohol and tobacco. Yet even then the church had not achieved purity, for there were at least two further splits.

To be sure, Jesus' command to allow the wheat and the tares to grow side by side until God effects the separation does not mean that church discipline is abandoned or that people who refuse to turn from open sin should not be excommunicated. But his command does imply the impossibility of devising a test or procedure that will keep all weeds out of any local church.

Nor does this parable invalidate the separation of Luther and Calvin from Rome, for neither of them initiated this division. It was the pope who expelled them because of their efforts to reform the church from within. John Wesley's conduct is also instructive. As he gained thousands of converts, especially from England's poor, who were nominally members of the Anglican church, Wesley resisted every attempt to gather them together into a separate church. Instead he established "class meetings" of about a dozen converts, led by a mature Christian who helped these new Christians learn the basics of the Christian life. These groups then belonged to larger "societies," which in turn belonged to "circuits," for whom a full-time minister was responsible. In 1797, however, six years after Wesley's death and sixty years after he had organized his first societies, certain of Wesley's circuits held a stormy conclave and decided to found the Methodist church.

Our guiding principle should therefore be to hold the truth in love in whatever group we find ourselves, separating from those around us only when they somehow hinder us in doing the work of the gospel. As long as believers can be edified in the local church and the gospel advanced from it, we should make every effort to keep our church holding to its historic ties.

Another new insight provided by this parable of the weeds is that the wheat will no longer exist primarily in the one nation Israel. Rather, "the field [in which the wheat will now grow] is the world" (Matt. 13:38). This point fits in with Jesus' statement to Israel that "the kingdom of God will be taken away from you and given to a people [the Gentiles] who will produce its fruit" (21:43). "People" in this verse is a rhetorical expression for other ethnic groups and was used to show the Jews that other peoples besides them could be citizens of God's kingdom.

We should not conclude, however, that the gospel is no longer to be preached to Israel, for obviously they are still one of the peoples to which the gospel should go. At the end of Matthew's gospel Jesus made it clear that all ethnic groups are to be evangelized: "And this gospel of the kingdom will be preached in the whole world as a testimony to all nations, and then the end will come" (24:14). Thus "the history of the Kingdom of God has become the history of Christian missions,"⁴ and the great purpose of the kingdom between the past fulfillment and future consummation is to see that each of the peoples of earth, allowed to go their own ways since the dispersion at the Tower of Babel (Gen. 11), now receives the message of redemption. In this way Jesus' blood will indeed have "purchased men for God from every tribe and language and people and nation" (Rev. 5:9). This stress upon *every* people indicates that God's concern is not just with numbers but also with the whole spectrum of earth's diverse cultures.

The Parables of the Mustard Seed and the Yeast (Matt. 13:31–33)

The new thing revealed by these two parables is not that the kingdom of God will eventually be a realm enveloping the whole earth, for this idea appears in Ezekiel 17:23, where the figure of a tree was used to describe the universality of God's future kingdom. What is new here is that the kingdom starts from very small, apparently insignificant beginnings, such as the motley group of fishermen and tax-collector types who worshiped Someone who died on a cross. Yet from this beginning a mighty realm emerges that will someday spread to every ethnic group. Not everyone in these groups will be converted, for we must remember the teaching from the parable of the four soils. But when Christ returns, he will establish his rule upon earth from Jerusalem, and during the millennium a much larger percentage of people will be converted, for Paul argued that "if [Israel's] transgression [in rejecting Jesus at his first coming] means riches for the world [and it certainly has!] . . . how much greater riches will their fullness [at Jesus' second coming] bring [in terms of an ingathering of more Gentile converts]!" (Rom. 11:12).[5]

Then when the new heavens and earth are established at the end of the millennium, the only inhabitants on earth will be the righteous, and at that time the kingdom will indeed be like the tree when full-grown, and the measure of meal when wholly leavened. The Old Testament said nothing about such meager beginnings, and yet the idea fits in perfectly with its teaching that the Messiah must first suffer.

The Parables of the Treasure Hidden in a Field and the Pearl of Great Value (Matt. 13:44–46)

The newly revealed truth here is not that the kingdom of God is a possession whose worth outranks all else, for this teaching could surely be inferred naturally from the prophets' promise regarding the future kingdom. What is new is that even the beginnings of the kingdom, so small and insignificant, are nevertheless of incomparable worth. Here we see that the kingdom's value for an individual in no wise depends upon the extent of its realm. The kingdom, it is to be remembered, is primarily a reign and only derivatively a realm. For one to have the kingdom of God is to have God, bound by an oath to save, employing all his love, power, and wisdom to give us freely all things and to pursue after us to do us good. But the greatest of all his gifts is that of fellowship with him.

The Parable of the Net (Matt. 13:47–50)

More emphatically than the parable of the wheat and the weeds, this parable shows that inside the net of the kingdom are bad things from the world that are right alongside God's good things. The separation of evil from the good and the establishment of a holy community will occur only at the consummation of the kingdom.

These parables, then, outline the kind of realm that the kingdom of God will produce during the time gap that was not fully understood by the Old Testament prophets. To be sure, many predictions of the Old Testament prophets have been fulfilled. The kingdom of God is here, because Jesus himself at the commencement of his public ministry made its existence official. Thus the apostles throughout their epistles speak of its continued working after Jesus had ascended to heaven (Rom. 14:17; 1 Cor. 4:20; Col. 1:13; Heb. 12:28). There was also fulfillment in that Jesus the Messiah did come and performed the miracles predicted by Isaiah 35:5–6 and is now reigning at God's right hand, having accomplished all that is necessary to defeat the powers of Satan and evil and bring in a new heavens and earth (Acts 2:30–35). Likewise, at the Last Supper he openly inaugurated the new covenant (1 Cor. 11:25), which is always operative where the kingdom is operative. Nevertheless during this time gap the realm formed by God's active, saving will accords more with the fact that Jesus had to suffer than with the glorious realm he will found in the future.

What, then, do we who live and preach during this intermediate period do with the prophetic promises of the future, more-glorious millennial kingdom? Can we really, in good conscience, preach the glories predicted for that future kingdom as applying today to the church? We certainly can and must, for the God who is bringing about that future realm is the same God active in the realm in which we are presently living. Therefore we take promises such as Jeremiah 32:41 ("I will rejoice in doing [Israel] good . . . with all my heart and soul") and, making the appropriate changes, preach it as what is true for us today. We leave out the promise of the land to Israel in this verse because that is the work of the kingdom of God in the final period of redemptive history, before God transfers all his people to his new heavens and earth.

Peter's sermon at Pentecost (Acts 2) gives precedent for this procedure. Taking the prophecy of Joel 2:28–32, which will be fulfilled literally and fully only when the new heavens and earth are established, Peter pronounced it "fulfilled" when the realm of the kingdom of God had taken the special form described in Matthew 13. At Pentecost the moon did not turn to blood, the sun did not darken, and neither was the Spirit of God poured out on all flesh. But the Spirit was poured out on people from many different nations, and Peter was thus justified in regarding this outpouring as a token fulfillment of what would occur at the final establishment of the age to come.

Likewise in Acts 15 James cited Amos 9:11–12 as being "fulfilled" in the Gentile mission spearheaded by Paul. In reality Amos was talking about the reestablishment of Israel as a kingdom during the millennium, when the nations of earth would resort to it to learn the ways of God. But James saw that there was an analogy between this yet-future ingathering of the Gentiles and the present Gentile mission. Since the same saving will of God that would produce the future ingathering was bringing in so many Gentiles now, James was warranted in using Amos's prediction as a proof text to justify the Gentile mission and the abolition of circumcision as a condition for Gentiles to receive the promised blessings of the covenant. Certainly David's temple was not then being rebuilt, nor were all Gentiles turning to God. But it was evident that God was working with the Gentiles in a way that was analogous to the future ingathering, and consequently there was a sense in which Amos's prophecy was and is being partially fulfilled in this realm in which the kingdom of God presently manifests itself.

Such examples provide hermeneutical guidelines

whereby the rich teachings of the prophets regarding the future can be applied for the edification of the church today, living at a time when the kingdom of God is working in a special way never envisioned by the prophets. What mandates applying the predictions regarding Israel to the church is that the same right to rule—the essence of the kingdom of God—is benefiting God's people now in our peculiar realm, as it will benefit Israel in another kind of realm during the millennium. Accordingly, we must preach the blessings predicted by the prophets for believers today.

The Mystery That the Gentiles Are Fellow Heirs

One element in the mysteries of Matthew 13 concerned the exercise of the kingdom's powers throughout the world (v. 38). Jesus had said that the kingdom would be taken from the Jews—its proper subjects in the prophets' incomplete view of the future—and given to others: "Many will come from the east and the west, and will take their places at the feast with Abraham, Isaac and Jacob in the kingdom of heaven. But the subjects of the kingdom will be thrown outside, into the darkness, where there will be weeping and gnashing of teeth" (Matt. 8:11–12). This new people to whom the kingdom is given are those from every tribe and nation who bring forth appropriate fruits (21:43). The benefits they will enjoy, the "blessing given to Abraham" (Gal. 3:14), were considered back in chapter 20 and are identical to those of the new covenant inaugurated by Jesus (Luke 22:30; 1 Cor. 11:25).

That the Gentiles, then, should have all the blessings of the kingdom and the new covenant is surely implied by the data in the Gospels. But it is not until we come to Paul's teaching in Ephesians 3:1–13 (cf. Rom. 15:15–21) that this mystery is unveiled and stated explicitly. According to this apostle to the Gentiles, Jewish and Gentile believers are now "one new man" (Eph. 2:15), and through Christ both "have access to the Father by one Spirit" (v. 18). Thus Gentiles are "fellow citizens with God's people and members of God's household" (v. 19). Paul declared that this truth is a mystery "which for ages past was kept hidden in

God ... [in order] that now, through the church, the manifold wisdom of God should be made known to the rulers and authorities in the heavenly realms" (3:9–10).

Paul defines this mystery as the revelation "that through the gospel the Gentiles are heirs together with Israel, members together of one body, and sharers together in the promise in Christ Jesus" (Eph. 3:6). In the Greek the equality the Gentiles now enjoy in the people of God is stressed by the prefix *sun-*, which is repeated in the terms translated as "heirs *together*," "members *together* of one body," and "sharers *together* in the promise." Since Paul regarded this truth as a mystery, it was not, in his thinking, revealed with full clarity to the Old Testament prophets. So we need first to discover what those prophets did say about the blessings the Gentiles are to enjoy in the future kingdom in order to grasp Paul's new insights.

The Status of Gentiles in the Old Testament Prophets' View of the Kingdom

Many passages in the Prophets tell of how Gentiles will participate in and benefit from the future kingdom promised to Israel. God's statements to the servant of Isaiah 40–66 make it clear that his ministry is to embrace the gentile world as well as Israel. "It is too small a thing for you to be my servant to restore the tribes of Jacob and bring back those of Israel I have kept. I will also make you a light for the Gentiles, that you may bring my salvation to the ends of the earth" (Isa. 49:6). "Foreigners who bind themselves to the Lord to serve him, to love the name of the Lord, and to worship him, all who keep the Sabbath without desecrating it and who hold fast to my covenant—these I will bring to my holy mountain and give them joy in my house of prayer. Their burnt offerings and sacrifices will be accepted on my altar; for my house will be called a house of prayer for all nations" (56:6–7).

Far from being inferior to Israel in the restored kingdom, these Gentiles will in fact help spread the message of salvation to the nations, and their converts from these nations will even be made priests in the temple!

"And I, because of their actions and their imaginations [the preceding verse has been talking about the abominations people practice], am about to come and gather all nations and tongues, and they will come and see my glory. I will set a sign among them, and I will send some of those who survive to the nations—to Tarshish, to the Libyans and Lydians (famous as archers), to Tubal and Greece, and to the distant islands that have not heard of my fame or seen my glory. They will proclaim my glory among the nations. And they will bring all your brothers, from all the nations, to my holy mountain in Jerusalem as an offering to the Lord—on horses, in chariots and wagons, and on mules and camels," says the Lord. "They will bring them as the Israelites bring their grain offerings, to the temple of the Lord in ceremonially clean vessels. And I will select some of them [Gentiles] also to be priests and Levites," says the Lord. (Isa. 66:18–21)[6]

In the passages just cited it appears that the Gentiles have equal status with Israel in the future kingdom. But there are other passages from the Prophets in which these converts seem to some extent to be second-class citizens. The following passages are arranged so that the inferiority becomes more pronounced as one proceeds:

Many nations will be joined with the Lord in that day and will become my people. I will live among you [apparently the resulting people made up of Jew and Gentile] and you will know that the Lord Almighty has sent me to you. The Lord will inherit Judah as his portion in the holy land and will again choose Jerusalem [thus Israel would still seem to have priority]. (Zech. 2:11–12)

This is what the Lord Almighty says: ". . . many peoples and powerful nations will come to Jerusalem to seek the Lord Almighty and to entreat him. . . . In those days ten men from all languages and nations will take firm hold of one Jew by the hem of his robe and say, 'Let us go with you, because we have heard that God is with you.'" (Zech. 8:20–23)

In that day Israel will be the third, along with Egypt and Assyria, a blessing on the earth. The Lord Almighty will bless them, saying, "Blessed be Egypt my people, Assyria my handiwork, and Israel my inheritance [thus Israel seems still to occupy the central place]. (Isa. 19:24–25)

Aliens will shepherd your flocks; foreigners will work your fields and vineyards. And you will be called priests of the Lord, you will be named ministers of our God. You will feed on the wealth of nations, and in their riches you will boast. Instead of their shame my people will receive a double portion, and instead of disgrace they will rejoice in their inheritance; and so they will inherit a double portion in their land, and everlasting joy will be theirs. (Isa. 61:5–7)

Foreigners will rebuild your walls, and their kings will serve you. Though in anger I struck you, in favor I will show you compassion. Your gates will always stand open, they will never be shut, day or night, so that men may bring you the wealth of the nations—their kings led in triumphal procession. For the nation or kingdom that will not serve you will perish; it will be utterly ruined. . . . The sons of your oppressors will come bowing before you; all who despise you will bow down at your feet and will call you the City of the Lord, Zion of the Holy One of Israel. (Isa. 60:10–14)

The Lord will have compassion on Jacob; once again he will choose Israel and will settle them in their own land. Aliens will join them and unite with the house of Jacob. Nations will take them and bring them to their own place. And the house of Israel will possess the nations as menservants and maidservants in the Lord's land. They will make captives of their captors and rule over their oppressors. (Isa. 14:1–2)

It should be noted that in the latter part of this list, where subservience to Israel becomes explicit, there is nothing said about the spiritual attitude of the aliens. These verses thus perhaps do not describe the status of Gentile converts but show what will be necessary for Jesus to do in order to rule the nations with an iron scepter (Rev. 19:15; cf. Ps. 2:9). Not all people will be converted during the millennium, for at its end Satan will be able to marshal an army and mount a war against the people of God (Rev. 20:7–9). However, great multitudes will be converted then, and the way they will relate to Israel is described in the earlier passages, some of which appear to give Gentiles complete equality. And possibly where Israel does seem to have the privileged position, it is simply because it will be the nation through whom the message of salvation will go to the world. Such

passages would then fit in well with those teaching that
Gentiles could even be Levites.

The picture, however, is not crystal clear. Thus Paul
declared that the new revelatory truth that believing Gentiles are now so completely on a par with believing Jews that
there is no distinction (Gal. 3:28) "was not made known to
men in other generations *as* it has now been revealed by the
Spirit to God's holy apostles and prophets" (Eph. 3:5). This
"as" is interpreted by Abbot in the ICC commentary on
Ephesians to mean "not with such clarity as now."

The Gentiles as Fellow Heirs of the Promise

This later Pauline revelation thus teaches that through the
gospel Gentiles are now heirs together, members together of
one body, and sharers together in the *promise*—one of the
most important terms in the vocabulary of holy history. In
Scripture it is used so often to mean the promise of God that
the "of God" can be left off without any loss of meaning.
Summing up the totality of all that God engages to do in the
full salvation to which he brings his people, the promise is
also called the *inheritance* (Gal. 3:18; cf. v. 29; Rom. 4:13),
life (Gal. 3:21; Rom. 4:17), and the *Holy Spirit* (Gal. 3:14;
Eph. 1:13). Thus the promise constitutes the whole package
of the blessings the redeemed will enjoy in the new heavens
and earth. It is in Christ that God's truthfulness in making
promises throughout redemptive history is confirmed: "For
no matter how many promises God has made, they are 'Yes'
in Christ" (2 Cor. 1:20; cf. Rom. 15:8), for he accomplished
all that was necessary in order to free the love of God to bless
people.

The blessings promised for the age to come are guaranteed
by Jesus' resurrection, for this act proved that he had
completed the work of redemption, and the spiritual body
with which he rose (cf. 1 Cor. 15:44, 50) demonstrated the
firstfruits of the new creation (v. 23). So to the Jews at
Antioch of Pisidia Paul said, "We tell you the good news:
What God promised our fathers he has fulfilled for us, their
children, by raising up Jesus" (Acts 13:32). And when the

Jews rejected his message, Paul took the very same promise and offered it to the Gentiles there (vv. 46–48).

To be sure, we do not possess the full blessings of the new creation at present, for Romans 8:19–23 points up vividly that we still live in bodies subject to the curse. Verses 24–25 even speak of salvation as that which is still future for the Christian: "For in this hope [the adoption as sons] we were saved. But hope that is seen is no hope at all. Who hopes for what he already has? But if we hope for what we do not yet have, we wait for it patiently." Christ's resurrection, however, has fulfilled and confirmed the promise of the new creation, and as a result all those who are "in Christ" are new creatures (2 Cor. 5:17). They have the guarantee of the inheritance of the future blessings, in that they are sealed with the Holy Spirit, "who is a deposit guaranteeing our inheritance until the redemption of those who are God's possession" (Eph. 1:13–14). This "firstfruits of the Spirit" (Rom. 8:23) that Christ after his ascension poured out on believers (Acts 2:33) thus ensures the Holy Spirit's full blessings in the age to come. And so in the realm presently formed by the working of the kingdom of God, both Jewish and Gentile believers enjoy the guarantee of these unexcelled blessings of the future. So whatever question the prophets had about the status of Gentiles in the kingdom is thus cleared up by this "mystery" revealed by Paul.

Review Questions

1. What new facets of knowledge about the future kingdom were made known by the parables of Matthew 13?

2. Why should one not split off from his or her denomination?

3. How does understanding the kingdom as basically a right to rule rather than a realm help greatly in showing us why we must apply such a glorious promise as Jeremiah 32:41 to ourselves and others today?

4. How do Peter's use of Joel 2:28–32 (Acts 2:14–21) and James's use of Amos 9:11–12 (Acts 15:13–18) justify

applying promises for a later realm of the kingdom to a situation in an earlier realm?

5. What is there in the prophet's predictions about the future status of the Gentiles that justifies Paul's regarding the subject as a mystery?

NOTES

[1] Concerning the details of what will happen at the Second Coming and after it, however, we find ourselves, like the Old Testament prophets, mystified as to how all that is said in Scripture will come to pass.

[2] William F. Arndt and F. Wilbur Gingrich, *A Greek-English Lexicon of the New Testament and Other Early Christian Literature*, 4th ed. (Chicago: University of Chicago Press, 1957), 531–32.

[3] Ladd, *Jesus and the Kingdom*, 259, 229.

[4] K. E. Skydsgaard, "Kingdom of God and Church," *Scottish Journal of Theology* 4, 1 (March 1951): 391.

[5] See the first part of chapter 26 below for an explanatory note regarding the general scheme of future redemptive history that is being followed in this book.

[6] There is some difficulty in knowing to whom the pronouns in this passage refer. Some wonder whether Isaiah really meant that God would make Levites out of the Gentiles. To this question Bright replies, "If reference is only to Jews there would seem to be no point in saying it. Many Jews in other lands were already priests and Levites by birth. The idea [that Gentiles could be Levites], though startling, is quite in line with the prophet's theology" (*Kingdom of God*, 145n).

26

The Conversion of Israel

A third mystery in the New Testament provides information about the end of the present realm of God's kingdom, whose basic features were described in Matthew 13 and Ephesians 3. Romans 11:25–26 is the essential statement of this mystery, where Paul says, "I do not want you to be ignorant of this mystery, brothers, so that you may not be conceited: Israel has experienced a hardening in part until the full number of the Gentiles has come in. And so all Israel will be saved."

NOTE. This phrase "until the full number of the Gentiles has come in" has been interpreted by John Murray to mean that part of Israel will be hardened until the gospel has been fully preached to the Gentile nations of earth. He argues that it cannot represent the end of Gentile evangelization, since 11:12 has spoken of how Israel's future conversion will bring "much greater riches" for the Gentiles than those they had enjoyed as a result of Israel's rejection of Christ at his first coming. So great are these riches that in verse 15 they are designated as "life from the dead." Murray understands this phrase to refer to the greater number of Gentiles who will be saved after the conversion of all Israel.[1]

Many commentators, however, have understood "life from the dead" to mean the climactic event of the future resurrection. For example, C. E. B. Cranfield argues that since in 11:25 Israel's conversion comes *after* "the full number of the Gentiles has come in," the phrases "riches for the world," "riches for the Gentiles," and "reconciliation of the world" (vv. 12 and 15) must designate the full evangelization of the Gentile world and the salvation of all Gentiles destined to be saved.[2] Then since both verses 15 and 25 place Israel's conversion *after* this goal is reached, these interpreters see the "greater riches" (v. 12) and "life from the dead" (v. 15) as consisting not in a further and more successful evangelization of the Gentiles but in the final resurrection, the full upgrading of the spiritual condition of all saved Gentiles as well as Jews.

Murray rejected this view, however, for had Paul meant the "greater riches" and "life from the dead" to refer to the resurrection, he would surely have used the explicit term *anastasis*, as he does elsewhere when speaking of the future resurrection (e.g., Rom. 1:4; 6:5; 1 Cor. 15:12, 13, 21, 42; Phil. 3:10). Here, however, he felt no need to use the unambiguous term, choosing instead the vaguer phrase "life from the dead." Its nearest parallel is "alive from the dead" (lit. trans.) in Romans 6:13, where it refers to people's newness of life as Christians. Clearly, "life from the dead" represents a blessing from God that is of great worth, and therefore in a class with the "greater riches" that result from the conversion of Israel alluded to in verses 12 and 15. But "life from the dead" is not the ultimate blessing of the resurrection. Therefore Murray argued that the wording to be supplied in the last half of 11:12 should be the following italicized words carried over from the first half: ". . . how much greater riches *for the Gentile world* will Israel's fullness [conversion] bring." And he concluded by suggesting that we interpret the phrase "until the full number of the Gentiles has come in" as "an unprecedented quickening for the world in the expansion and success of the gospel."[3]

Accepting this interpretation of the "much greater riches" and "life from the dead" requires us to draw two conclusions. First, according to Romans 11:25–26, Jesus' second coming will cause the conversion of all ethnic Israelites alive at that time, for this is the obvious way to construe Paul's placing their conversion in verse 25 alongside the appearance of the deliverer in verse 26. This understanding is confirmed by Zechariah 12:10, where God says, "I will pour out on the house of David and the inhabitants of Jerusalem a spirit of grace and supplication. They will look on me, the one they have pierced, and they will mourn for him as one mourns for an only child." John 19:37 then regards the Roman soldier's piercing of Jesus' side as the fulfillment of this passage, and Revelation 1:7 uses it in speaking of Jesus' second coming: "Look, he is coming with clouds, and every eye will see him, even those who have pierced him, and all peoples of the earth will mourn because of him." That all Israel will assuredly one day be saved was prophesied by Jeremiah, who said, after speaking of how Israel will in the future be regenerated, "No longer will a man teach his neighbor, or a man his brother, saying, 'Know the Lord,' because they will all know me, from the least of them to the greatest" (Jer. 31:34).

The second conclusion is that Jesus' second coming will initiate a much more fruitful evangelization of the Gentile nations of earth than that occurring between his first and second coming. As Murray emphasized, this "full number" cannot be the final total of Gentile converts but represents those converted during the "times of the Gentiles" mentioned in Luke 21:24: "[Israel] will fall by the sword and will be taken as prisoners to all the nations. Jerusalem will be trampled on by the Gentiles until the times of the Gentiles are fulfilled." This understanding would suggest a literal fulfillment of the many passages in the Old Testament prophets that speak of the Gentiles' learning about God from the Jews, such as Isaiah 2:3 and Amos 9:11–12.

In chapter 25 we noted how James used the Amos passage that refers to a yet-future evangelization of the Gentiles to justify the Gentile mission that Paul had initiated. This mission between Jesus' first and second coming, then, is the type to be fulfilled by the later Gentile mission to be carried out both by converted Israel and, as we have seen (also in chap. 25), by the Gentiles that are

converted during this time. The end of redemptive history
will then come at the conclusion of this greater mission.

The period of time during which this greater mission
will occur is usually called the millennium, Christ's reign
on earth that on the basis of Revelation 20:5–7 is seen as
lasting for a thousand years. Verses 11–15 imply that at the
end of this period, the final resurrection, God's judgment
on all, and the final separation between the righteous and
the wicked will take place. Then there will be a new
heaven and a new earth, with the people of God as the
"new Jerusalem coming down out of heaven from God" to
dwell upon it (Rev. 21:1–2). The dwelling of God will
then be with his people; "he will live with them . . . [and]
wipe every tear from their eyes. There will be no more
death or mourning or crying or pain, for the old order of
things has passed away. . . . I [God] am making everything
new" (vv. 3–5).

Jesus also speaks of this transition to a new order: "I tell
you the truth [*amēn*], at the renewal of all things, when the
Son of Man sits on his glorious throne, you who have
followed me will also sit on twelve thrones, judging the
twelve tribes of Israel" (Matt. 19:28). The present world
order will then be destroyed: "The heavens will disappear
with a roar; the elements will be destroyed by fire, and the
earth and everything in it will be laid bare" (2 Peter 3:10).

It is beyond the scope of this book to consider how other
prophetic events such as the great tribulation (Matt.
24:21–24), the rise of the "man of lawlessness" (2 Thess.
2:3–12), the rapture of the saints (1 Thess. 4:13–18), and
the battle of Armageddon (Rev. 16:16) fit in with Jesus'
second coming and the end of the millennium. But they
will surely have a part to play in bringing redemptive
history to the climax of filling the earth with God's glory.

According to the Old Testament prophets, the glorious
establishment of the kingdom of God would signal the
conversion of the entire nation of Israel. We have considered
Jeremiah's declaration that when God established the new
covenant with Israel, all would know God—from the least of
them to the greatest (Jer. 31:31–34). This same idea is in

Paul's quotation of Isaiah 59:20 that "the deliverer will come from Zion; he will turn godlessness away from Jacob" (Rom. 11:26). In order to be this deliverer, however, Jesus first had to make an atonement for people's sins, so during his first coming he suffered rather than being openly glorified (see chap. 24 above). This suffering climaxed in his crucifixion and death, in which the people and leaders of Israel played a large role, but not without the Gentiles' help in the person of Pontius Pilate, the Roman governor of Judea. Then just before Jesus ascended to heaven forty days after his resurrection, he commanded his apostles and followers to preach the gospel to all the world.

Israel's rebellion against God, which had contributed to Jesus' crucifixion, welled up again in expelling many Christians from Jerusalem as described at the beginning of chapter 24. But this expulsion, far from weakening the Christian movement, greatly strengthened it as large numbers of Gentiles, along with many Jews in Gentile areas, came to enjoy the blessings of the kingdom of God. So the outlines of the realm of the kingdom of God between Jesus' first and second coming began to take shape. One aspect of this realm is the suffering that believers (the wheat) endure as they are in close proximity to people who are the seed of the serpent (the weeds). But during these trials believers are enjoined "to set [their] hope fully on the grace to be given [them] when Jesus is revealed [at his second coming]" (1 Peter 1:13).

One question that must have mystified the Old Testament prophets as they foresaw the sufferings and glory of the Christ (1 Peter 1:11) was that of Israel's response to God in connection with these sufferings. Paul cleared up this mystery by his affirmation that, except for the remnant (Rom. 11:7), Israel would remain in rebellion until Jesus' return (vv. 25–26).

This question had played an exceedingly important role in Paul's own postconversion days. Before he began the Gentile mission, he was confident that Israel would turn to Christ now that he himself had been converted (Acts 22:17–21). Thus when he realized that Israel would not accept even the irrefutable evidence of his own conversion, his agony of spirit was great: "I speak the truth in Christ—I am not lying, my conscience confirms it in the Holy Spirit—I have great sorrow and unceasing anguish in my heart. For I could wish that I myself were cursed and cut off from Christ for the sake of my brothers, those of my own race" (Rom. 9:1–3). But then the mystery stated in Romans 11:25, and the whole theodicy of God's purpose in redemptive history outlined in Romans 9–11, turned him from this anguish of spirit to the greatest doxology in the Bible: "Oh, the depth of the riches of the wisdom and knowledge of God! How unsearchable his judgments, and his paths beyond tracing out![4] 'Who has known the mind of the Lord? Or who has been his counselor?' [Isa. 40:13]. 'Who has ever given to God, that God should repay him?' [Job 41:11]. For from him and through him and to him are all things. To him be the glory forever! Amen" (Rom. 11:33–36).

This mystery that part of Israel should be hardened until the gospel had been fully preached to the Gentile nations of earth is an aspect of the basic pattern running throughout redemptive history: God does not terminate evil immediately after commencing his redemptive process but allows it to have power in various forms down to the close of this age. The first evidences of this pattern were seen at the beginning of chapter 17: why did not God inaugurate the Noachic covenant earlier so that the violence that almost annihilated the seed of the woman would not have had to be ended by a flood? Why did God deal mainly with only one nation from the time of Abraham to the time of Christ? Paul's problem as to why Israel should remain largely in unbelief after its Messiah had come is another aspect of this same pattern. But in Romans 9–11 he singles out three segments of redemptive history where this pattern emerges, and after showing the benefits for subsequent redemptive history that accrue from it, he breaks out into doxology.

Why Only Some of Abraham's Descendants Were the Seed

At the outset Paul had been tempted to think that God's word to Israel in covenants and promises had really failed to come to pass (Rom. 9:4–5). But then he realized that God had specifically said both to Abraham and to Isaac that not all of their seed would enjoy his oath-bound promises. To Abraham he had said, "It is through Isaac that your offspring will be reckoned" (v. 7), and of Isaac's sons, "The older will serve the younger" (v. 12). Thus Jacob rather than his twin, Esau, got the blessings.

But what possible benefits could come from so limiting the enjoyment of God's promises? In Ishmael's rejection in favor of Isaac the lesson for subsequent redemptive history is this: to be the children of God does not depend on any inherent advantage, such as being the descendant of Abraham, but only and wholly on what God does in his sovereign grace. If the children of Abraham's flesh were saved simply because of parentage, they would be prone, as the subsequent history of Israel so amply proves, to boast in this distinctive. But if God created the world for his glory, it follows that his work of saving people and bringing the world to reflect his glory must be carried on under the terms of Ephesians 2:8–9: "For it is by grace you have been saved, through faith—and this not from yourselves, it is the gift of God—not by works, *so that no one can boast.*"

The same point is made by the selection of Jacob instead of Esau. Here Paul makes it unmistakably clear that the selection was not made because of what Jacob and Esau would do but solely "that God's purpose in election might stand: not by works but by him who calls" (Rom. 9:11–12; cf. 11:5–6). In other words, while he elected Jacob unconditionally, that is, without being obligated by what Jacob would be in himself, God was certainly not arbitrary in choosing him instead of Esau, for in so doing, he expressly excluded any grounds for the boasting in which elder sons were prone to indulge and so provided a lesson for all subsequent history.

Paul, however, was aware of the objections that such teachings would raise and so proceeded to answer them in Romans 9:14–24. But first we need to understand the sense in which God is the author of sin.

NOTE. The Westminster Confession of Faith asserts:

"God from all eternity did, by the most wise and holy counsel of his own will, freely and unchangeably ordain whatsoever comes to pass; yet so as thereby neither is God the author of sin ..." (3.1). Such wording may sound like double-talk until it is understood that to be an author of evil means to will evil as evil, that is, as what should ultimately exist. Edwards's statement on this topic is helpful: "That we should say, that God has decreed every action of men, yea, every action that is sinful ... and yet that God does not decree the actions that are sinful, as sin, but decrees them as good, is really consistent.... By decreeing an action *as sinful*, I mean decreeing it for the sake of the sinfulness of the action. God decrees that they shall be sinful, for the sake of the good that he causes to arise from the sinfulness thereof; whereas man decrees them for the sake of the evil that is in them."[5]

The first objection to what Paul had said about God's dealings with Isaac and then Jacob is that he is unjust to elect people without any regard to their own distinctives. But Paul answered that God's righteousness consists only in his unswerving commitment to uphold his own glory in all that he does. If he acted from a sense of obligation to anything but the worth of his own goodness, he would cease to be all-glorious—and therefore no longer be God. In support Paul cited Exodus 33:19, which begins with God's words to Moses: "'I will have mercy on whom I have mercy, and I will have compassion on whom I have compassion.' It [election] does not, therefore, depend on man's desire or effort, but on God's mercy" (Rom. 9:15–16). The *hon an* in the Greek of verse 15 ("I will have mercy *on whom* I have mercy") emphasizes God's sovereignty in dealing with humanity. The same idea is brought out in 9:18: "Therefore God has mercy on whom he wants to have mercy, and he hardens whom he wants to harden."

In exercising his sovereignty, God is not at all arbitrary, for his hardening of Pharaoh's heart was done for a good purpose that was completely consistent with his righteous design that the earth should fully reflect his glory. Paul makes this understanding clear in quoting what God said to

Pharaoh through Moses: "I raised you up for this very purpose, that I might display my power in you and that my name might be proclaimed in all the earth" (Rom. 9:17). His repeated hardening of Pharaoh's heart (Exod. 4:21; 7:3, 22; 8:19; 9:12, 35; 10:1, 20, 27; 11:10; 14:4, 17) gave God the occasion for bringing glory to his name by triumphing over the Egyptians through the ten plagues, inflicted "so that you [Pharaoh] may know there is no one like the Lord our God" (Ex. 8:10). And because God exalted his name even more by destroying Pharaoh's army in the Red Sea, the people of God in the ages to come can sing "the song of Moses . . . and the song of the Lamb: 'Great and marvelous are your deeds, Lord God Almighty. Just and true are your ways, King of the ages. Who will not fear you, O Lord, and bring glory to your name? For you alone are holy. All nations will come and worship before you, for your righteous acts have been revealed'" (Rev. 15:3–4). Since such singing is creation's appropriate response to the glory of God manifested in history, it thus fulfills God's purpose in bringing it into existence. God's creation of the world is then consistent with his love for his own glory, for the history of the world, in having externalized the perfections of God, incites his people to render wholehearted love to him.

But the objector, while perhaps conceding that in order to be righteous, God must simply act for his own glory, still argues that he is not righteous if he persists in holding people whose wills he controls accountable for their deeds. "One of you will say to me: 'Then why does God still blame us? For who resists his will?'" (Rom. 9:19). But Paul counters that people have no more right to call God in question for his dealings with them than clay has in telling a potter into what shape it should be formed (vv. 20–21). Not surprisingly, many find Paul's reply here unacceptable. James Denney in his commentary on Romans in the *Expositor's Greek Testament* says (ad loc.), "To this objection [of v. 19] there is really no answer, and it ought to be frankly admitted that the apostle does not answer it." Likewise C. H. Dodd argues in the *Moffatt New Testament Commentary* (ad loc.): "The objector is right. Paul has driven himself into a position in which he has to deny that God's freedom of action is limited by moral considerations. 'Has the potter no right over the clay?' It is a well-worn illustration. But the trouble is that a man is not a pot; he will ask, 'Why did you make me like this?' and he will not be bludgeoned into silence. It is the weakest point in the whole epistle.".

The trouble with these commentators, however, is that they construe Paul's reply to mean that people have no right to question God but must blindly accede to what he does without seeing any reason for it. But it should be observed that in verses 22–24 Paul does set forth the purpose controlling God's exercise of his sovereignty. To be sure, people have no right to ask God to cease to be God by surrendering any of his sovereignty. But humankind is not asked to submit blindly, for God's exercise of his sovereignty is as purposeful and nonarbitrary as the way potters use clay. Just as it is altogether right for potters to use clay so that they may make evident the full range of their skill, so it can only be right for God to deal with people in such a way that the full range of his glory becomes externalized. A consideration of these crucial verses, with the ellipses in the NIV filled in with the words in brackets, provides clarification: "What [objection can be made] if God, choosing to show his wrath and make his power known, bore with great patience the objects of his wrath—prepared for destruction? [And] what [objection can be made] if he did this to make the riches of his glory known to the objects of his mercy, whom he prepared in advance for glory—even us, whom he also called, not only from the Jews but also from the Gentiles?" When these rhetorical questions are restated declaratively, they assert that it is perfectly fitting for God to work with his creation so that it will externalize *all* aspects of his glory: on the one hand, his wrath and power; on the other, his mercy.

But he has a greater purpose than simply to show the full range of his glory, for he would not be showing himself as he really is if he set forth his wrath and power as coordinate and equal to his love and mercy. God delights far more in his mercy than in his wrath. So in order to show the priority of his mercy, he must place it against a backdrop of wrath. How could God's mercy appear fully as his great mercy unless it was extended to people who were under his wrath and therefore could only ask for mercy? It would be impossible for them to share with God the delight he has in his mercy unless they saw clearly the awfulness of the almighty wrath from which his mercy delivers them. Thus to show the full range of his glory God prepares beforehand not only vessels of mercy but also vessels of wrath, in order that the riches of his glory in connection with the vessels of mercy might thereby become more clearly manifest. Here again Edwards is most helpful.

> It is proper that the shining forth of God's glory should be complete; that is, that all parts of his glory should shine forth, that every beauty should be proportionately effulgent, that the beholder may have a proper notion of God. It is not proper that one glory should be exceedingly manifested, and another not at all; for then the effulgence would not answer the reality. . . . It is highly proper that the effulgent glory of God should answer his real excellency . . . for the same reason that it is proper and excellent for God to glorify himself at all. Thus it is necessary, that God's awful majesty, his authority and dreadful greatness, justice and holiness should be manifested. But this could not be, unless sin and punishment had been decreed; so that the shining forth of God's glory would be very imperfect, both because these parts of divine glory would not shine forth as others do, and also the glory of his goodness, love, and holiness would be faint without them; nay, they could scarcely shine forth at all. If it were not right that God should decree and permit and punish sin, there could be no manifestation of God's holiness in hatred of sin. . . . There would be no manifestation of God's grace or true goodness, if there was no sin to be pardoned, no misery to be saved from.[6]

Thus it is surely right for God to prepare vessels of wrath, for it is only by so doing that he is able to show the exceeding riches of his glory, the capstone of which is his mercy. For God not to prepare vessels of wrath would mean that he could not fully reveal himself as the merciful God. Thus creation could not honor him for what he really is, and God would then have been unrighteous, for in the act of creation he would have done something inconsistent with the full delight he has in his own glory.

But he is indeed righteous, not only in preparing vessels of wrath but also in finding fault with such vessels and visiting wrath upon them. To prepare such vessels but then to fail to visit wrath upon them would be to act with complete disregard for his own glory. God acts consistently with his love for his glory only as he opposes all who disdain finding delight in his glory. If he did not act this way in the world he freely created, he would cease to be God. Hence the objection of verse 19 that God should not blame those whom he hardens is shown to be without substance.

NOTE. It should be pointed out that in Romans 9:19–24 Paul is answering the question not of why people are responsible for their actions but of why the sovereign God is righteous to inflict punishment on evil. It is 1:18–20 that answers the question of why people who are slaves to sin are themselves without excuse, so that their punishment is just. There the basis of people's accountability lies in their having access to the knowledge that God should be worshiped as God. The fact that they do not want to worship him properly and in their rebellion hold down the truth that he should be worshiped does not excuse them at all from their responsibility to do so and to thank him for all his benefits. We should note how our own consciences work on this same principle: they condemn us for failure to do right when the reason is simply that we wanted to do something else. But if the failure is because we were physically hindered from knowing or doing the right, then conscience is quiet. Why conscience should act this way when motives are ultimately given and not chosen is a reflection of the fact that God is sovereign. Yet he is also glorious and righteous, so conscience accuses for failure to do right brought about by ill-advised motives. If God is God, it could not be otherwise.

NOTE. The most extensive exegetical justification for these and other matters in Romans 9:1–23 is set forth in John Piper's *The Justification of God: An Exegetical and Theological Study of Romans 9:1–23* (Grand Rapids: Baker, 1983). Concerning Piper's work, a seminary professor wrote in a review, "Theology aside, [this book] is a work of scholarship in its own right and the best on Romans 9." (G. K. Beale, *Westminster Theological Journal*, 46,1 [Spring 1984], 197).

Why Israel's Trespass Brings Salvation to the Gentiles

In Romans 11:11 Paul asked, "Did [Israel] stumble so as to fall beyond recovery? Not at all! Rather, because of their transgression, salvation has come to the Gentiles to make Israel envious." Here is an excellent illustration of the principle set forth in the preceding section, that God does not ordain evil as an end in itself but only that holy and righteous purposes might thereby be realized. In Pauline thinking, Israel's stumbling is ultimately the work of God, for verse 32 declares, "God has bound all men over to disobedience so that he may have mercy on them all."[7] Thus while this stumbling was decreed by God, the evil of it was not decreed as an evil but in order that the highly prized benefit of bringing salvation to the whole world might be gained. Similarly verse 12 speaks of Israel's transgression and loss as meaning riches for the Gentiles, while verse 15 describes Israel's rejection as being the reconciliation of the world.

In chapter 21 we considered how Israel's failure to keep the law as a law of faith and her resultant punishment constituted a lesson book to stop the mouths of all who assumed that they could please God by their works. Through Israel's example this law of faith made clear to the surrounding nations that they too would be punished for trying to earn God's favor. Then with the Great Commission this lesson book began to be taught to the Gentiles. But it would never have been available had God not hardened the great majority of nonremnant Israel (Rom. 11:7–10). Because of his working, however, and as the Holy Spirit opens hearts, the lesson from this book strikes home and turns proud people into humble ones willing to entrust themselves to God to give them an eternity of happy tomorrows.

Likewise, if circumcision had not become, through Israel's stumbling, a sign of unrighteousness, it would have continued to be the sign for God's covenant people. As we have already considered (see chap. 22), such a continuation would have hindered the gospel from going outside the bounds of Judaism. Then too, had there been no sacrificial system, there would have been no typology to facilitate the preaching of the gospel to the nations. There would have been no contrast with Christ's work, so that we might appreciate it the more, nor would there have been any continuity with it to provide the concrete symbols and object lessons that the New Testament writers used to communicate more effectively what Christ has done.

Thus it becomes evident how Israel's stumbling, trespass, failure, and rejection have indeed meant blessing for the Gentiles: mercy, salvation, riches, and reconciliation. By decreeing evil on one nation, therefore, and that for a limited span of time, God has made it possible for the gospel to go to all nations, and in such a way that they would render far greater praise to him for the blessings they have received.

However, it was not only Israel's rejection of God up to the cross but also after it that functions in a salutary way for the Gentiles. In Romans 11:17–24 Paul speaks of a cultivated olive tree whose roots are the patriarchs Abraham, Isaac, and Jacob, with whom the Abrahamic covenant was made and confirmed. As this tree grew, it developed branches, most of which represent nonremnant Israel. At the time of Christ, after sufficient history had occurred to make the failure of these branches evident, they were broken off as the kingdom of God was taken away from Israel and given to a people who would produce good fruit (Matt. 21:43). Paul likened this people, the Gentile believers, to the branches from a wild olive tree grafted in at the point where the nonremnant branches had been broken off. These grafted branches were now able to flourish from the rich nutrients coming up from the roots. In other words, they enjoyed the blessings of the covenant God had made with the patriarchs.

But it would be a grave mistake for these Gentile believers to suppose that they were grafted in because of some distinctive that made them more desirable than those dead Israelite branches. Thus they must not exalt themselves over those branches, because their status rests solely on the support and nourishment coming up from the roots, that is, from God's mercy extended to them in the Abrahamic and new covenants. Indeed, to boast in their position over the broken-off Jewish branches would be to repeat the very unbelief that caused the downfall of the latter. So from the fact that the nonremnant branches were broken off and remain so because of unbelief, all believers today, Gentile and Jew alike, have the lesson strongly emphasized that they enjoy the blessings of the Abrahamic covenant only as they persevere in trusting God.

However, while this faith then excludes boasting and pride, it includes fear (Rom. 11:20). Faith is genuine only as it both greatly values the kindness of God made visible preeminently in Christ and as it fears by realizing that it will remain in this kindness only as it continues to trust in what God has promised to do. This truth is enforced by the observation that most of Israel's branches are lying dead on the ground and have been undergoing all kinds of trouble down to the present time. But if believers among the Gentiles should fail to work out their salvation by fearing the sternness of God's threats against unbelief, and if they should fail to value the unmatched blessings that will come from persevering faith, they will likewise be removed from his kindness (v. 22).

Hence from Israel's continued exclusion from the olive tree the lesson is unmistakably clear: "You stand [only] by faith" (Rom. 11:20). And the fact that Israel, as a nation, continues to be hardened until this present day should stimulate Gentile believers to cleanse their hearts from all boasting about their presumed prerogatives and, having confidence only in what God has promised, give all glory to him. Since Israel's example thus strengthens faith, God receives even greater glory, for it is only by faith that we honor him (cf. 4:20).

Why the Gentiles' Salvation Brings Salvation to Israel

God's hardening of Israel functions to bring good not only to the Gentiles but finally to Israel itself, for the salvation Israel brings to the Gentiles in turn makes the Jewish people envious (Rom. 11:11). In fact, one of Paul's great purposes in heading up the Gentile mission was somehow to "arouse

[his] own people to envy and save some of them" (v. 14). We
see examples of this reaction in Acts (13:45; 17:5), where the
Jews became jealous as they saw how eagerly the Gentiles
accepted the gospel, and how Paul then offered Gentiles the
enjoyment of the blessings of Abraham simply on the basis of
repentance and faith in Christ. The Jews bitterly resented
Gentiles' receiving the blessings that they considered their
exclusive right. But this arousal of jealousy built up in them a
potential for welcoming God's mercy at a later time with far
greater appreciation.

Nor is such jealousy lessened as, during the period before
Jesus comes again, the gospel is furthered until finally a full
number of Gentiles from every tribe, nation, and tongue is
brought in. This response by itself, of course, does not cause
them to turn to Christ, for they will repent only when the
deliverer comes from Zion to take away their sins (Rom.
11:26–27). But just as Israel's abuse of the law and consequent terrible punishments became a book that helped the
peoples of earth avoid the same mistake, so too the jealousy
and provocation that they feel because of the joy that
Gentiles have in claiming Abraham's blessing will heighten
their fervor when they "look on [him], the one they have
pierced, and . . . mourn for him as one mourns for an only
child, and grieve bitterly for him as one grieves for a
firstborn son" (Zech. 12:10). When blindness is removed
from Israel, they will see that they have missed the great
blessings the Gentiles have been enjoying because, unlike
the Gentiles, they have not received these blessings like
humble clients but have tried to earn them and thus satisfy
their ego more fully. Then their very zeal for these blessings,
and anger against the uncircumcised Gentiles claiming to
have Abraham's blessing, will become sanctified through
regeneration to create a more fervent desire for God's mercy
that will give him the praise his glory deserves. All this will
come to pass when God "[pours] out on the house of David
and the inhabitants of Jerusalem a spirit of grace and
supplication" (Zech 12:10).

Thus we can see how, according to Romans 11:31, Israel
will receive mercy by means of the mercy God has shown to
the Gentiles. Just as the Gentiles received mercy by means

of Israel's disobedience, so Israel will receive mercy because of the grace God has shown the Gentiles. And just as Israel's disobedience has caused the Gentiles to appreciate salvation the more, so also God's mercy to the Gentiles will, by the jealousy it has provoked, cause the Jews to love Christ the more.

Then once the sufficient antecedents of God's strange work are in place in history to incite both Jews and Gentiles to have fervent love for God, the last and final step in redemptive history will be taken. Thus in Romans 11:12 we read that the riches that the Gentiles have realized through God's rejection of Israel will be increased all the more by Israel's full inclusion. At the beginning of this chapter I have argued that this means many more Gentiles will believe on Christ after Israel is saved. And we have seen in chapter 25 what the Old Testament prophets said about the multitudes of Gentiles who would be saved when Israel's kingdom was established. During the millennium the fervor with which Jew and Gentile will come to love God will be so much more intense than before the Second Coming that it will be like life in comparison with death (v. 15).

In looking back over redemptive history, therefore, it should be plain that the earth will render proper worship to God not only to the extent that it is filled with those who worship him but also to the extent of the zeal with which they worship him. Had it not been vital for God to order holy history so that later generations would worship him the more fervently, it is conceivable that there would have been no need for a redemptive history that consists in an extended overlap between this evil age and the glorious age to come. However, we know that God's own intense love for his glory cannot settle for anything less from the world he has created, for Jesus said that he would spit out of his mouth those who had mere lukewarm love for him (Rev. 3:16). Therefore God ordained a redemptive history whose sequence fully displays his glory so that, at the end, the greatest possible number of people would have had the historical antecedents necessary to engender this fervent love for God. Thus Paul sums it all up in Romans 11:32: "God has bound all men over to disobedience so that he may have mercy on them all."[8]

Viewing redemptive history in this light then evokes in Paul the doxology of verses 33–36.

But some might ask, Why does God not use his omnipotence to make everyone sing such a doxology from the start and thus avoid the extended overlap and the problem of evil that redemptive history entails? The answer is that God could find no delight in a creation that, puppetlike, was forced to love him. His love for himself arises freely, that is, because he sees clearly that he is indeed worthy of all his own worship. And unless creation's delight in God is also a free act, arising from the full display of all his glory in the sequence of redemptive history, creation would not be consonant with God's delight in himself, and God could not tolerate it.[9]

The one thing, therefore, that God is doing in all of redemptive history is to show forth his mercy in such a way that the greatest number of people will throughout eternity delight in him with all their heart, strength, and mind. When the earth of the new creation is filled with such people, then God's purpose in showing forth his mercy will have been achieved. The "glorious freedom" (Rom. 8:21) that will then be enjoyed by the children of God and the complete orderliness of all creation, in contrast to the "frustration" that now prevails (v. 20), will represent the fullness of God's glory by showing that he was so sufficient in himself that he could find complete fulfillment and blessedness simply in mercifully imparting the ultimate blessing to creation, with no ulterior purpose beyond that. All the events of redemptive history and their meaning as recorded in the Bible compose a unity in that they conjoin to bring about this goal. Earlier revelation, though incomplete at many points, is not reinterpreted by that which follows it but is structured in such a way that it is open to receive and thus cohere with later revelation.

Thus once one understands the function of each part of redemptive history as it relates to God's particular dealings at that time, and once one understands how each of these dealings makes its contribution to God's purpose for creation, then one is able to grasp the intended meaning of each of the biblical writers who, taken together, yield the revelation God intended to impart to us. Only by seeing the whole of God's purpose in creation and redemptive history can one appreciate God's individual actions in realizing this purpose. It was on the basis of the goal toward which creation and redemptive history moved that Jonathan Edwards was planning to write his systematic theology. "To know ... how a workman proceeds, and to understand the various steps he takes in order to accomplish a piece of work, we need to be informed what he *intends* to accomplish; otherwise we may stand by, seeing him do one thing after another, and be quite puzzled, because we see nothing of his scheme."[10] It is to help others understand God's scheme, his loving purpose in salvation history, that this book has been written.

Review Questions

1. Explain how God's election of Jacob in preference to Esau was not arbitrary, though it was unconditional.

2. How does Romans 9:14–19 answer the objection that God was unjust to elect Jacob unconditionally?

3. Though God was sovereign in hardening Pharaoh's heart, why was he not arbitrary to do so?

4. Why would God have been sinful if he had not hardened Pharaoh's heart?

5. Why will God judge all of the human race, even though no one has ever resisted his sovereign will?

6. Why would God have been sinful not to have unconditionally predestined the reprobate to be reprobate?

7. Why would God be sinful if he did not punish the reprobate, whom he predestined to be such, for their sins?

8. What has to be true about people before they can be held responsible for their sins and punished for them?

9. Why would God not be God unless motives are finally given and not chosen?

10. Why would God not be God unless our consciences condemned us for doing wrong?

11. Though God does ordain evil, why is he nevertheless not the author of it?

12. List the antecedents that must be in place in redemptive history and tell how each is necessary to effecting God's goal in creating the world.

13. I have said that God elects as many as possible. What keeps him from electing all?

14. Why did God not use his omnipotence to make everyone disposed to praise him with full fervency so there would have been no Fall and no protracted terrible evil in redemptive history?

NOTES

[1] John Murray, *The Epistle to the Romans*, 2 vols. (Grand Rapids: Eerdmans, 1962–65), 2:94–95.

[2] Cranfield, *Romans*, 2:562–63.

[3] Murray, *Romans*, 2:84.

[4] Paul remembered how, by himself, he could not understand why Israel would reject Christ—Israel, the very nation to whom belonged "the adoption as sons; . . . the divine glory, the covenants, the receiving of the law, the temple worship and the promises, . . . the patriarchs, and from them is traced the human ancestry of Christ" (Rom. 9:4–5). It was incomprehensible to him that Israel could remain in unbelief even after his own conversion. But it did not remain so after the revelation of the mystery. To the contrary, the whole of Rom. 9–11 is a setting forth of the reason for it all.

Calvin said that one should not try to answer the question of why Israel's posterity rather than its ancestors would receive Christ: "He who here seeks a deeper cause than God's secret and inscrutable plan will torment himself to no purpose" (*Institutes*, 21:978 [3.24.12]). But since Paul does answer this question, the statement in his doxology about the inscrutability of God's ways is to be understood not of what is true after the revelation of the mystery of Rom. 11:25 but of what was true, especially for Paul, before this mystery was revealed.

[5] Edwards, *Works*, 2:527.

[6] Ibid., 528.

[7] The same point is also made in Rom. 8:20–21: "For the creation was subjected to frustration, not by its own choice, but by

the will of the one who subjected it, in hope that the creation itself will be liberated from its bondage to decay and brought into the glorious freedom of the children of God." To be sure, most commentators arbitrarily exclude Adam and Eve, the only moral agents in the original creation, from this verse. But the German commentator Otto Michel says, "This sentence is understandable only when *ktisis* ['creation'] means the complete sum of all that is made (without limitation) and all is placed over against 'God's sons' [8:23–25] as the ones who are obviously singled out" (*Der Brief an die Römer*, 4th ed. [Göttingen: Vandenhoeck & Ruprecht, 1966], 201).

8 As the context indicates, the "all" does not mean that everyone will be saved, but that God finally reaches out to every ethnic entity and saves as many as will make for the most fervent worship of his glory. Nothing in the flow of thought leading to Rom. 11:32 intimates that this verse teaches that those who died in impenitence—as for example nonremnant Israel, who remained hardened (v. 7)—will finally be saved.

9 To be sure, only through the enablement of the Holy Spirit will people give God the praise his glory deserves. But the Holy Spirit's work is never to do more than cause us to own up to the truth of the knowledge to which we have access. Since the Holy Spirit works simply to make people reasonable, their subsequent acts are done out of the freedom of knowing how well-advised they are.

10 Edwards, *Works*, 1:535. Edwards never fulfilled his dream of writing a systematic theology in this way. He had received a smallpox vaccination before the process was at all perfected and came down with such a severe case that the doctor told him that he would die in a matter of hours. At first Edwards was greatly distressed because he would thus be unable to realize his ambition of many years. But soon all his theology came home to him; content, then, for God to do with him as God saw fit, Edwards died resting in the Lord's mercy.

Appendix
The Nature of the Mosaic Law

Calvin regarded the following three passages as foundational for understanding the nature of the law. The following exegetical arguments based on them are given to support the thesis of chapter 21 that, contrary to Calvin, the law and the gospel are a continuum rather than a contrast.

Galatians 3:15–24

A superficial reading of Galatians 3:17–18 seems to say that Paul regarded the Mosaic law given at Sinai as something opposite to the promises God had previously given to Abraham:

> [17] The law, introduced 430 years later [c. 1500 B.C.], does not set aside the covenant [with Abraham] previously established by God and thus do away with the promise. [18] For if the inheritance depends on the law, then it no longer depends on a promise; but God in his grace gave it to Abraham through a promise.[1]

What suggests this antithesis is that in verse 17 Paul was clearly talking about the actual law as it was given to Moses at Sinai. So when he refers again to the "law" in verse 18, the conclusion seems inescapable that he is talking about the same law and is affirming that that law was totally opposite to the promise requiring faith from Abraham and not works. There are two reasons, however, for understanding "law" in verse 18 as different from the revelatory law of verse 17.

Paul's Meaning of "Law" in Galatians 3:17

We must keep in mind that in writing Galatians, Paul was in a life-and-death struggle with the Judaizers, who were trying to turn the churches in Galatia (an area in what is now central Turkey) away from the teachings they had heard when Paul first preached the gospel in that region. Therefore he had to base his arguments on common-ground data that the Judaizers would also accept as

459

true. But if Paul were in fact saying that the intended meaning of the law given at Sinai was opposite to the promises made to Abraham, the Judaizers would have scoffed at the idea and used this obvious misunderstanding effectively to discredit Paul with the Galatian Christians.

The way these Judaizers and the Jews in general saw Abraham and the law can be reconstructed from the rabbinic teachings of the early centuries of the Christian era, as well as from certain passages in the Old Testament Apocrypha and pseudepigrapha, which also comport with Jewish thinking in the first century. These writings are unambiguous in affirming that Abraham was fully obedient to the Mosaic law.[2] According to 2 Baruch 57:2, "The unwritten law was in force among [Abraham, Isaac, and Jacob], and the works of the commandments were accomplished at that time."[3] And according to rabbinic *Kiddushin* 4:14 in the Mishnah, "We find that Abraham our father had performed the whole Law before it was given, for it is written [Gen. 26:5], '... that Abraham obeyed my [God's] voice and kept my charge, my commandments, my statutes, and my laws.'" From such citations Strack-Billerbeck concluded that, in the old rabbinic understanding, "all promises were made to Abraham exclusively on the basis of his having lived righteously according to the law."[4]

For good reason, then, we believe that the Judaizers also understood Abraham as the perfect exemplar of one who lived according to their interpretation of the law and on this account received promised blessings. But in 3:18 Paul completely contradicts this view by contrasting the law with the promises. He could do so because he believed he had already established the conclusion that God's blessings came to Abraham's children simply by believing his promises, and not because they had earned it by works or distinctives in which the recipient could boast (3:6–9). In verse 8 Paul had cited Genesis 12:3, that "all peoples on earth," with their widely differing customs, would be blessed through Abraham, knowing the Judaizers would also accept this verse as authoritative. Then on the basis of this common ground, he argued that Abraham's blessing had to come to each ethnic people group simply on the basis of their faith in God's promise and not because of some particular distinctives they possessed, like circumcision and a kosher diet—distinctives the Judaizers were trying to force on the Galatian churches. If the blessing were to come on such a cultural basis, then the equal access to blessing implied by Genesis 12:3 would be a fiction, for those peoples whose culture pattern was closer to Jewish distinctives would have an advantage over peoples whose cultures were far different.

So when Paul said in Galatians 3:15 and 17 that the later Mosaic law could not in any way modify or annul the Abrahamic covenant, he believed he had already irrefutably proven that God's blessings came to all peoples in a way that would be equally easy (and hard!) for every group; that is, each equally had to entrust their future to the loving God and his promises and to regard their nonsinful distinctives as irrelevant. Thus when he declared in verse 17 that the law could not annul the teaching of the Abrahamic covenant that forgiveness and its consequent blessings came simply by faith, he was by no means affirming that the law taught what was contrary to faith and the promises. For the sake of argument he was simply saying that even if the Judaizers were right in understanding the law as teaching that Abraham's blessings came by the good works and distinctives in which people can boast, such an understanding still could not annul the previous affirmation of the Abrahamic covenant as proven from Genesis 12:3: righteousness and every consequent blessing come to all peoples, including Jews, simply as they bank their confidence on the promises of God.[5]

Thus in construing verse 17 in this way, Paul to make his point was assigning not his but the Judaizer's meaning to the law given to Moses at Sinai. They regarded the Mosaic covenant as a law of works (Rom. 3:27; 9:32), a job description listing the various things people should do as patrons helping the client God to fulfill his needs and realize his goals. It is no wonder, then, that in verse 18 Paul drew such a contrast between the blessing coming to Abraham by the promise and that which supposedly came through the "law" as misinterpreted by the Judaizers and the Jews as a whole. And when Galatians 3:17–18 is understood in this way, it becomes impossible to use this passage, as did Calvin, to argue that Paul regarded the Mosaic covenant as something opposite to the gracious promises of the Abrahamic covenant and the gospel.

The Argument from Galatians 3:21–24

[21a]Is the law, therefore, opposed to the promises of God? Absolutely not! [21b]For if a law had been given that could impart life, then righteousness would certainly have come by the law. [22]But the Scripture declares that the whole world is a prisoner of sin, so that what was promised, being given through faith in Jesus Christ, might be given to those who believe. [23]Before this faith came, we were held prisoners by the law, locked up until faith should be revealed.

[24] So the law was put in charge to lead us to Christ that we might be justified by faith.

A second support for our interpretation of Galatians 3:17–18 is Paul's vehement denial in verse 21a that the content and thought structure of the law was any different from that of the promises made to Abraham. After this denial he declared that the law's only difference from the promise was, generally speaking, its lack of power to turn unregenerate people's hearts to God (v. 21b). Thus in giving the law to the Israelites, God did not, as he did with Abraham, also give a regeneration of heart so that Israel would want to become God's humble client, obeying the law as a law of faith rather than of works. In that the law is a law of faith whose commands call for an "obedience that comes from faith" (Rom. 1:5; cf. 16:26), which then produces works of faith (1 Thess. 1:3; 2 Thess. 1:11), its conditional promises are no different from the conditional promises that God made to Abraham and his seed.

But since God had not regenerated Israel as a whole, the sin that rules in every heart had perverted the people's understanding of the law (v. 22). Thus Israel had stood it on its head, interpreting it as a "law of works" instead of a "law of faith";[6] it had distorted the "holy, just, . . . good," and "spiritual" law (Rom. 7:12, 14), thus becoming "utterly sinful" (v. 13). The Jews had therefore been imprisoned by their perverted understanding of the law, locked up by sin until the coming of Christ (Gal. 3:23–24).[7]

Hence Calvin's claim that Galatians 3:17–18 proves that a contrast existed between the essential law and the gospel is invalid. But we must also examine the two other Pauline passages—Romans 10:5–8 and Galatians 3:10–12—that Calvin claimed showed "most clearly" an antithesis between the law and the gospel (20:746 [3.11.17]).

Romans 10:5–8

We shall concentrate on these four verses, but not without recognizing that this passage belongs to the larger literary unit of Romans 9:30—10:10.

[5] Moses describes in this way the righteousness that is by the law: "The man who does these things will live by them [Lev. 18:5]." [6] But [Greek *de*] the righteousness that is by faith says: "Do not say in your heart [Deut. 8:17], 'Who will ascend into heaven?' [Deut. 30:12]" (that is, to bring Christ down) [7] "or 'Who will descend into the deep?' [Deut. 30:13]" (that is, to bring Christ up from the dead). [8] But what

does it say? "The word is near you; it is in your mouth and in your heart" [Deut. 30:14], that is, the word of faith we are proclaiming.

In the English the conjunction "but" introducing verse 6 suggests that Paul is placing Deuteronomy 30:12–14 in opposition to Leviticus 18:5. But lexicographers agree that the *de* in the Greek does not have to be interpreted as implying a strong contrast, such as the conjunction *alla* regularly does. Indeed, *de* often indicates simply that a transition is being made from one point of view to another.

A much stronger argument for seeing a contrast is provided by Philippians 3:8–9, which uses phrases similar to those in Romans 10:5–6 to set up an unmistakable antithesis between the "righteousness of law" and that of faith. There Paul says, "For [Jesus'] sake I have lost all things. I consider them rubbish, that I may gain Christ and be found in him, not having a righteousness of my own that comes from the law, but that which is through faith in Christ— the righteousness that comes from God and is by faith." Three considerations, however, argue against seeing the same contrast in Romans 10:5–8 as is found in Philippians 3:8–9.

Paul's Use of Two Pentateuchal Verses in Romans 10:5–8

If we suppose that Paul meant to set up a contrast by quoting Leviticus and then Deuteronomy in these verses, then we are faced with one of two difficulties. If we try to say (along with Zahn, Leenhardt, and Hodge) that Paul honored the intended meaning of Leviticus 18:5 to establish a "law righteousness," but then read his own theology into Deuteronomy 30:12–14 to establish a contrasting "faith righteousness," then we have to concede that Paul felt quite free to give his own interpretation to Moses and other parts of the Old Testament at any time he pleased. In his Romans commentary F. F. Bruce does agree that here Paul interpreted the Deuteronomy passage in his own way but confesses that it is not as easy for us moderns as it was for Paul to pit Deuteronomy in verses 6–8 against Leviticus in verse 5.

One reason for this difficulty is that a part of Paul's purpose in Romans is to show his submission to the authority of the Old Testament—probably because of the Jewish element of the church at Rome. Thus in the salutation he emphasized that the gospel he was about to expound was promised by the Old Testament prophets and that Jesus Christ, the center of the gospel, was the descendant of David (Rom. 1:3). Then in 3:1–2 and 9:1–5 Paul listed the advantages the Jews have had in being the physical descendants of Abraham (e.g., possessors of "the very words of God," "the covenants," "the promises"). He stressed, as though answering an objector, that his teaching, far from undermining the law, in fact upheld it (3:31), and in Romans 7:1 said, "I am speaking to men who know the law." So he would have undermined this desire to uphold the authority of the Old Testament if he read his own meaning into Deuteronomy 30:12–14.

Another reason for this difficulty is that much of Romans was written in a debating style, where an objector's question is raised and then answered (e.g., "What shall we say then? Shall we go on sinning so that grace may increase? By no means!" [Rom.6:1–2]). There is considerable agreement that Paul used this argumentative style, not because he was trying to correct an error in the Roman church,[8] but because he wanted that church to feel his burning zeal to defend and propagate the gospel. Paul had now finished his third and last missionary journey on the northern shores of the eastern Mediterranean, and "there [was] no more place for . . . [any new] work [there]" (15:19, 23). Therefore he wanted the church at Rome to become his base for missionary operations in the western Mediterranean, particularly in Spain (v. 24), as the church of Antioch in Syria had been the base for his missionary journeys in the East. In his previous missionary efforts Paul had spoken to Jewish enclaves first (Acts 13:5, 14; 14:1; 17:1, 10, 17), a strategy that had led to many heated discussions as he "vigorously refuted the Jews in public debate, proving from the [Old Testament] Scriptures that Jesus was the Christ" (Acts 18:28). So in writing Romans it was both natural and desirable to write in his usual debating style, which would help the church to feel his zeal for the gospel and so be willing to back him up as he went onward to Spain.

Hence in seeking to win Jews over to faith in Christ by arguing on the common ground of the Old Testament, Paul could never have replaced the intended meaning of Deuteronomy 30:12–14 with a meaning that came from his own Christian presuppositions, for he would thereby have undone all his efforts to convince both the Romans, whom he needed as his friends, and the Jews and others whom he sought to win to Christ of his loyalty to the Scriptures. Thus this second consideration makes it impossible to suppose that Paul would ever have treated the Old Testament in such a way.

At this point one might then suppose that Paul regarded the Pentateuch itself as speaking of both a works-righteousness (Lev. 18:5) and a faith-righteousness (Deut. 30:12–14), the former which he then suppressed in favor of the latter. But such a hypothesis raises a third difficulty, for in quoting the Old Testament elsewhere, there is no instance where he ever did this. "It was not the custom of Paul to seek out contradictions in the scripture and to quote the Old Testament as meaning that one of its statements is no longer valid."[9] Rather, in Romans 10:5–8 he was waging war against the difficult works-righteousness that the Pharisees demanded of people in order to be saved. So after quoting Leviticus 18:5 in verse 5 as setting forth the righteousness based on law and just before paraphrasing Deuteronomy 30:12–14 in verses 6–8, Paul inserted the command, "Do not say in your heart . . ." (Deut. 8:17, lit. trans.) to give imperatival force to his citation. In so doing, he was rebuking the Pharisees for regarding the law's righteousness to consist of works done for God and, to use the words of Peter at the Jerusalem Council, "putting on the necks of the disciples a yoke that neither we nor our fathers have been able to bear" (Acts 15:10). One interpreter puts the case as follows:

> To be sure, Moses required that a person must do the righteousness required by the law in order to live [Lev. 18:5]. But this requirement is not fulfilled by superhuman achievements ("to climb into heaven," "to climb down into the abyss," which was Paul's way of expressing the impossible tasks which the Jews, through their zeal for the righteousness of works, wanted to produce and fulfill by their own efforts). [The righteousness required by the law] is fulfilled rather through the Word which is in the heart and in the mouth—which according to [Rom] 10:10 is faith and confessing the Lord: "for with the heart one believes (and this leads) to righteousness, and with the mouth one confesses (and this leads) to salvation." The life that Moses promises according to [Lev. 18:5 and Rom.] 10:5 is therefore to be enjoyed by those who believe and confess. The obedience of faith thus becomes the proper fulfilling of the law, which requires righteousness and promises life to those who do righteousness.[10]

The Argument from Romans 9:30–33

A further evidence for concluding that the law, like the gospel, commands an obedience of faith comes from Romans 9:30–33. The following is a literal translation that supplies in brackets words necessarily implied.

> [30]What then shall we say? [We say] that the Gentiles, who did not pursue righteousness, have obtained it, a righteousness that is by faith; [31a]but Israel, [although it] pursued a law of righteousness, [31b]has not attained [that law]. [32a]Why not? [Israel did not attain that law] [32b]because they pursued [the law of righteousness] not by faith,

but as if it were [attained] by works. [32c]They stumbled over the "stumbling stone." [33]As it is written, "See, I lay in Zion a stone that causes men to stumble and a rock that makes them fall, and the one who trusts in him will never be put to shame" [Isa. 28:16].

We observe that the function of verses 32a and 32b is to give the reason for Israel's failure to comply with the law (v. 31b) and that this reason is stated in the Greek only in adverbial modifiers consisting of the prepositional phrases—"not by faith, but as by works." This reason emphasizes that Israel's failure was not in seeking to comply with the law but rather in the manner in which Israel sought to do so—"not by faith, but as if it were by works." Since the objective after which Israel was pursuing would itself prescribe how it should be attained, then a necessary implication from what Paul is saying in 9:32ab is that the Mosaic law itself forbade works to earn blessings and enjoined nothing but the obedience of faith to obtain mercy. He therefore was clearly affirming that the Mosaic law was a law of faith. But Calvin and much of the Protestantism he influenced so greatly have insisted that the Mosaic law was a law of works telling people what they must do "thoroughly to earn God's benevolence."[11] Such an idea, however, would have to turn verse 32a upside down and make it say that the reason Israel failed to attain the law was because the Jews did exactly what it required—an obvious contradiction.

That Paul regarded the Mosaic law itself as forbidding works is enforced by his use of "as" *(hōs)* in "[Israel] pursued [a law of righteousness] not by faith but *as* if it were by works." In commenting on the "as," the grammarian George Winer observed that "[the expression] 'by faith' [in 32b] denotes the objective standard [required by the law]; [and] 'as of works' [denotes] the purely imaginary [standard]."[12] So Israel's efforts to comply with the law as a law of works came purely from her imagination, which arose from her sinful inclination to exalt the ego, even at the expense of completely denying the evidence that the Mosaic law was a law of faith. The law therefore was in fact like the health regimen that sick patients follow because they trust the physician who prescribed it and are depending on that expert to restore them to good health. But Israel, purely out of their sinful imagination, regarded the law to be a law of works, like a job description, in which they, functioning as patrons for God, would perform the services he, as a needy client, wanted them to do for him. Thus Israel "through the commandment [became] utterly sinful" (Rom. 7:13). For client human beings to seek to switch places with God, becoming his patron lords while he appears as a needy client, is a cosmic role reversal that constitutes ultimate blasphemy and sinfulness.

So we may conclude that Romans 9:31–32ab, as well as Romans 10:6–8, is best interpreted if we take the *de* between Romans 10:5 and 6–8 as signifying not a contrast but a continuum between what Paul meant by the righteousness of the law and the righteousness of faith. Since the obedience that stems therefrom is precisely what the law taught and since the works of trying to earn or obligate God's favor are precisely what the law forbade, then the righteousness of the law, which Paul cites Moses as describing in Leviticus 18:5, is the very righteousness of faith described in Deuteronomy 30:12–14.

The Argument from Romans 10:3–4

These two verses further support the conclusion that Paul intended no contrast between the "righteousness that is by the law" and the "righteousness that is by faith." In Romans 10:2 he had said concerning Israel, "I can testify about them that they are zealous for God, but their zeal is not based on knowledge," and this comment echoes what he had said in 9:31. Israel had zealously sought to comply with the law but had gone about it in the wrong manner and so had failed to conform its life to the law. The reason her zeal for God was not based on knowledge is found in verse 3: "Since they did not know the righteousness that comes from God and sought to establish their own, they did not submit to God's righteousness." From what Paul had just said in Romans 9:31–32ab, the righteousness of God, to which Israel would not submit, must be the righteousness of faith set forth in the Mosaic law itself.

It should also be noted that Israel's failure to know the kind of righteousness God requires was not because it was hidden from them. To the contrary, it was clearly evident in the Mosaic law itself, right in the middle of the Ten Commandments, where Exodus 20:6 quotes God as promising his mercy (not a recompense) to those keeping his commandments. Since the blessing resulting from obedience is mercy, none of God's commands can ever be likened to the recompense one receives for works done for him. Works do not obtain mercy; to the contrary, they obligate a client employer to respond to the patron employee with a recompense equivalent to the value of the service rendered. A tit-for-tat recompense is not mercy.

So Israel's ignorance of God's righteousness of faith was a volitional ignorance, in which its desire for ego fulfillment shut out any thought of being needy, dependent clients, utterly cast upon the God who works for those who wait for him. This understanding of Israel's ignorance is stressed in the Pentateuch itself, where Moses recalled that Israel's promise to keep the law was short-lived. To be sure, the people had asked Moses to "tell us whatever the Lord our God tells you. We will listen and obey" (Deut. 5:27). God's response, however, was, "Oh, that their hearts would be inclined to fear me and keep all my commands always" (v. 29). But this was not the case, as was evident when, forty years later, Moses said, "To this day the Lord has not given you a mind that understands or eyes that see or ears that hear" (29:4). And Paul saw this same lack of understanding persisting down to his own time and onward until the second coming of Christ (Rom. 11:7, 25).

This same hardness of heart that caused Israel to reject the law as a law of faith also caused the nation to reject Christ. After saying that Israel had failed to pursue the law as a law of faith (Rom. 9:32ab), Paul immediately, with no conjunction, declared that Israel had stumbled over a stumbling stone (v. 32c), which as verse 33 and 10:11 make clear, is Christ.

So if the hardness of heart that kept Israel from realizing that the law was a law of faith also caused her to reject Christ, then it follows that the condition Jesus sought for people to meet in order to have eternal life was the same as that for the blessings promised in the law: obedience to the law as a law of faith. This connection helps us understand why Romans 10:4, "[For] Christ is the *telos* ["goal"][13] of the law so that there may be righteousness for everyone who believes," is introduced in the Greek by the conjunction *gar* ("for"), which indicates that Paul intended verse 4 to argue for verse 3. In verse 3 he spoke of how Israel, in its zeal to establish its own righteousness, had rejected the righteousness of God set forth in the law of faith. And we have just seen that this rejection of God's righteousness extended to their repudiation of Christ as well. So in order to support his assertion that Israel has rejected God's righteousness in these two ways, Paul tied Christ and the law of faith together as a continuum in saying that Christ was the goal, or full embodiment, of the law.

To be sure, many interpreters construe Romans 10:4 to mean that Christ was the termination, or "end," of the law, arguing that verse 5 with its quotation of Leviticus 18:5 is introduced with a "for," which means that a supporting argument follows for what precedes. This interpretation would make sense if Paul intended to say that the righteousness of faith (vv. 6–8) has superseded that of the law, for then Christ's coming would have made an end to the

Old Testament "righteousness that is by the law" (v. 5). But we have already shown that both in verse 5 and verses 6–8 Paul was affirming that the law in fact set forth the righteousness of faith. Then verses 5–8 together support the idea of Christ as the continuum and climax (i.e., the goal) of the law as a law of faith.

But before rejecting Romans 10:5–8 as one of Calvin's "most clear" statements affirming the contrast between "faith righteousness" and "law righteousness," we must consider again the similar phraseology in Philippians 3:9. Here Paul spoke of a "righteousness of my own that comes from the law" as something sinful and completely opposite the "righteousness that comes from God and is by faith." It is significant that this righteousness to be rejected, which comes from the law, is Paul's own—and this wording echoes his declaration in Romans 10:3 that the Jews, in order to establish their "own righteousness," had rejected that of God. This line of thought argues that there are two very distinct types of righteousness stemming from the law, one's own (to be repudiated), and that which is identical with the righteousness that comes from faith (which is to be credited). But then we must understand Paul as using the word "law" *(nomos)* in two diametrically opposed ways: to represent either (1) the revelatory Mosaic law, which is holy, righteous, and good, or (2) the monstrosity the Jews had made out of it as their proud egos stood the law of faith on its head and regarded it instead as a law of works.

Support for Paul's twofold usage of "law" comes from two noted New Testament scholars. According to C. F. D. Moule,

> The many shades of meaning attaching to *nomos* have to be deduced from the ways in which the word is used; and it is clear that *nomos* is used by Paul in (among others) the two quite distinct connexions which may be called respectively "revelatory" and "legalistic" . . . This contrast between the two contexts in which *nomos* is used [he had just cited Rom. 7:12 as a "revelatory" usage, and 3:28—"the works of the law"—as a "legalistic" use] is perfectly familiar to all students of Paul.[14]

C. E. B. Cranfield has made the same point:

> It will be well to bear in mind the fact (which, so far as I know, has not received attention) that the Greek language used by Paul had no word group to denote "legalism," "legalist," and "legalistic". . . . In view of this, we should, I think, be ready to reckon with the possibility that sometimes, when [Paul] seems to be disparaging the law, what he really has in mind may be not the law itself but the misunderstanding and misuse [of it] for which we have no convenient term.[15]

As we have noted, Paul never quoted the Old Testament to bring forward an idea that he would then discard. Nor did he ever do so with Moses, whom elsewhere in his writings he regards as an authority for what he himself was teaching, never as someone whose teachings could be set aside (e.g., Rom. 10:19; 1 Cor. 9:9; cf. Acts 26:22; 28:23). Calvin, however, had no qualms about regarding much of Moses' teaching as something to be superseded: "The law has a twofold meaning; it sometimes includes the whole of what has been taught by Moses, and sometimes that part only which was peculiar to his ministry, which [part] consisted of precepts, rewards, and punishments." Indeed, Moses had

> this common office—to teach the people the true role of religion. Since it was so, it behoved him to preach repentance and faith; but faith is not taught, except by propounding promises of divine mercy, and those gratuitous: and thus it behoved him to be a preacher of the gospel; which office [Moses] faithfully performed. . . . But as evangelic promises are only found scattered in the writings of Moses, and these also somewhat obscure, and as the precepts and rewards, allotted to the observers of the law, frequently occur, it rightly appertained to Moses as his *own* and *peculiar* office [italics added], to teach what is the real righteousness of works, and then to show what remuneration awaits the observance of it, and what punishment awaits those who come short of it. . . . And whenever the word law is thus strictly taken, Moses is by implication opposed to Christ [!]: and then we must consider what the law contains, as separate from the gospel. Hence what is said here [Rom. 10:5] of the *righteousness* of the law, must be applied, not to the whole office of Moses, but to that part which was in a manner peculiarly committed to him.[16]

But since Paul and the Jews, Calvin to the contrary, never let one statement of Moses supersede another, we must understand his use of *nomos* in Romans 10:5 in this light. Thus when Paul said, "Moses describes in this way the righteousness that is by the law," we should reject out of hand any thought that this was somehow a righteousness of God that is to be set aside. Even though Philippians 3:9 speaks of the righteousness of the law as rebellion against that of God, this is one's own righteousness. And Romans 10:3 is in complete agreement that such a righteousness is sinful. But as we have seen, there is no reason to give the reference in Romans 10:5 to "the righteousness of the law" the same meaning it has in Philippians, for in verse 5 *nomos* is to be construed in its revelatory rather than its legalistic sense.

Still a problem remains. It has been objected that Galatians 3:12 uses the wording of Leviticus 18:5 to say unequivocally that "the law is not based on faith; on the contrary, 'The man who does these things will live by them.'" Calvin regarded this verse and the train of thought leading onward from verse 10 as the second passage that "most clearly" taught that the revelatory law is antithetical to faith and the gospel. So we must now turn to the exegesis of Galatians 3:10–12.

Galatians 3:10–12

10aAll who rely on [works of the law, lit. trans.] are under a curse, 10bfor it is written, "Cursed is everyone who does not continue to do everything written in the Book of the Law" [Deut. 27:26]. 11aClearly no one is justified before God by the law, 11bbecause, "The righteous will live by faith" [Hab. 2:4]. 12aThe "law" is not based on faith; 12bon the contrary, "The man who does these things will live by them" [Lev. 18:5].

In verse 12 Paul was clearly setting up a contrast between the "law" and faith. But in following C. F. D. Moule's advice to let the immediate context indicate whether by this word Paul meant "revelatory law" or the "legalism" resulting from the Jewish misinterpretation of the law, we have placed law in quotation marks for the time being. First, we will examine the train of thought beginning at verse 10 for clues to the meaning of "law" in verse 12. Then we will look to Galatians 2:15–18 for further help in understanding the term "works of the law," which also appears in verse 10 and sets the direction for the line of thought ending at verse 12.

"Works of the Law" in Galatians 3:10

After Paul had founded the Galatian churches, certain Jews regarding themselves as Christians had arrived. These Judaizers were attempting to discredit Paul as an authoritative teacher and to persuade his Gentile converts to agree to circumcision as the sign of the covenant (Gal. 5:2), with possibly other Jewish distinctives as well (4:10). In writing this epistle, therefore, Paul saw himself as engaged in a life-and-death struggle. He regarded the "gospel" these Judaizers taught as false and under God's condemnation (1:8–9), and he warned the Galatians that if they submitted to circumcision, they would have fallen away from grace and lost all of Christ's benefits (5:2–4). So to refute the Judaizers' attempts successfully, Paul had to base his arguments on data that they would also accept as true.

How, then, would a Judaizer have reacted to Galatians 3:10? In

attempting to answer this, we start with verse 10b, whose wording
of Deuteronomy 27:26 resembles the Septuagint: "For it is written,
'Cursed is everyone who does not continue to do everything
written in the Book of the Law' [Deut. 27:26]." From this sentence
Calvin inferred Paul to mean that "if [the law] be not obeyed—
indeed, if one in any respect fail in his duty—the law unleashes
the thunderbolt of its curse. For this reason [he] says: '. . . "Cursed
be every one who does not fulfill all things"' [Gal. 3:10; Deut.
27:26 paraphrase]. [Paul] describes as 'under the works of the law'
those who do not ground their righteousness in remission of sins,
through which we are released from the rigor of the law" (20:363
[2.7.15]).

But there are two reasons why such an interpretation would
have scored no points against the Judaizers. First, they did not
regard the commands of the law in Moses' writings as separate
from the merciful promises of the forgiveness of sins, as did Calvin.
For example, in Exodus 34:6–7 God proclaimed himself to Moses
as "the Lord, the Lord, the compassionate and gracious God, slow
to anger, abounding in steadfast love and faithfulness, . . . forgiving
wickedness, rebellion and sin." No Judaizer would have agreed
that a momentary failure to keep a single part of the law would
consign one to a curse, as long as he or she was trying to live by it.
In fact, the Judaism of Paul's day regarded everyone as having
failed to live up to the law. In a midrash on Psalm 143:2, "Enter
not into judgment with thy servant, for no one living is righteous
before thee," the following statements appear: "Who can say, 'I
have purified my heart' (Prov. 20:9)?" No man, by himself can
regard himself as righteous at the day of judgment. Why? . . .
'There is no man who has not sinned (1 Kings 8:46)'[!]. . . .
Therefore Psalm 143:2 says, 'For before you [God] there is no one
living who is righteous.' "17

Rabbi Eleazar (c. A.D. 150) too affirmed that "God forgives the
repentant."18 And one of the great authorities on ancient Judaism
has lamented the propensity of Protestants to forget that forgiveness, on the basis of repentance, is central to Jewish thought.19 So
we can easily imagine the reply of a Judaizer to the customary
Protestant interpretation of Galatians 3:10: "Indeed, we have all
sinned in failing to live up to the commands of the law, but Moses
himself wrote in Exodus 34:6–7 that God forgives the repentant."
So they would never have agreed with Calvin's view that seeking
to obey the law could only bring one under a curse.

A second problem the Judaizers would have had was Paul's use
of Deuteronomy 27:26 to support the conclusion (Gal. 3:10a) that

"all who rely on the works of the law are under a curse." In the ordinary parlance of Judaism, "works of the law" represented doing what the law commanded. A very similar expression is found in 2 Baruch 57:2, which was written early in the second century A.D.: "At that time the unwritten law was in force among [the patriarchs Abraham, Isaac, and Jacob], and *the works of the commandments* were accomplished at that time."[20] From this and other examples the commentators Strack and Billerbeck, among others, affirm that

> Were an individual, according to his duty, to have been led by the Torah, so would his deeds be regarded as *opera praeceptorum*, that is works to which the Torah [the Pentateuch] had given direction, and which arise from obedience to the Torah. The apostle [Paul] has attached the same meaning [?] with his [Greek] words *erga nomou* ["works of law"]: they are works which are the result of the observance or performance of the law.[21]

But if Paul meant this meaning when he mentioned the "works of the law," then his quotation of Deuteronomy 27:26 does not argue at all that those who rely on them are under a curse. How could all who do what the law commands be under a curse because Deuteronomy 27:26 said, "Cursed be those who do *not* do what the law commands"? Only if Paul used the term "works of law" as representing something violating the law would Galatians 3:10 make sense.

Most interpreters, however, are convinced that Paul attached the Jewish meaning to "works of the law." Hence they must insert wording somewhere between verses 10a and 10b to indicate that "no one keeps the law perfectly." Randall, for example, in the *Expositor's Greek Testament*, says, "Paul urges that [resting on the law] entails a curse of a broken [!] law." For Schmoller, "[The citation of Deut. 27:26 in Galatians 3:10] proves . . . that 'as many as are of the law are under a curse,' provided [!] a non-continuance [in obeying the law] can be established." Schlier declares that "to show that a curse is over all those who live by the law, the decisive thought *must be added:* there is no person who can fulfill the law" [italics added].[22]

We have just seen, however, that the Judaizers would have scoffed at the idea that one had to keep the law perfectly to avoid being under what Calvin called "the thunderbolt of its curse." Therefore it is impossible to suppose that Paul expected his antagonists at Galatia even to have thought of supplying such an idea between Galatians 3:10a and 10b. Consequently I argue that Paul departed from the Jewish understanding of "works of the law" and used it instead to mean an attitude of mind and its resulting conduct that was entirely opposed to the teaching of the law. Then the argument in verse 10 makes good sense. The logic would simply be that those guilty of violating the law by engaging in its "works" were under a curse, for (to follow the Hebrew rendering of Deut. 27:26 rather than the LXX) they had done something to undermine the law rather than uphold it.

"Works of the Law" in Galatians 2:15–18

No doubt the Judaizers at Galatia would have objected to Paul's giving a meaning to the "works of law" that was opposite to the customary one. But if he could show good reason for using this term to designate activity that undermined the law, he could both silence them and keep the Galatian churches loyal to him. Galatians 2:15–18 helps clarify the negative sense Paul gave to the term "works of the law." This term is repeated three times in the Greek of 2:16, in a context that provides justification for giving it Paul's negative meaning. The passage reads as follows:

> [15]We who are Jews by birth and not "Gentile sinners" [16a]know that a man is not justified by [works of the law, lit. trans.], but by faith in Jesus Christ. [16b]So we, too, have put our faith in Christ Jesus [16c]that we may be justified by faith in Christ and not by [works of the law], [16d]because by [works of the law] no one will be justified. . . . [18a]If I rebuild what I destroyed, [18b]I prove that I am a lawbreaker.

First, observe that this statement comes right after the paragraph recounting Paul's clash with Peter at Antioch on the matter of Jewish dietary regulations (Gal. 2:11–14). Note also that the threefold reference to the "works of the law" occurs in a sentence beginning with a reference to how Jews, adhering to their distinctives, considered themselves as superior to Gentile "sinners." Modern expositors agree that Paul was not using "sinner" in verse 15 in the usual sense of one who had, in fact, disobeyed God's will, but rather with a peculiar Jewish sense in which the word is a virtual synonym for a Gentile.[23] As Jews proudly reflected on their great zeal in keeping the law, and particularly its more ceremonial aspects such as dietary regulations and circumcision, it was easy for them to regard Gentiles as "sinners" simply because they were indifferent to such sacred ceremonial or cultural commands of the law.

So one significant fact for determining what Paul meant by the "works of the law" in this passage is that in the immediately preceding context his attention has been focused not at all on the moral injunctions in the Mosaic law but rather on its ceremonial aspects. The Jews' zealous observance of these aspects of the law fueled their pride in regarding themselves as superior to the rest of humankind. Thus when the "works of the law" are seen in this context of Paul's thinking, it becomes clear that for him, this term represented the Jews' belief that doing such works distinguished them from other peoples and thereby gained them acceptance with God. Another significant clue for grasping Paul's understanding of the term is the emphatic contrast he drew three times in 2:16 between it and faith in Christ. He regarded the pride arising from what people do to distinguish themselves from others as totally incompatible with deriving one's confidence solely from what Another has done to make salvation possible.

But Calvin in his commentary on Galatians argued that the meaning of this term in 2:16 must not be derived from the preceding context concerning the dietary regulations of the Mosaic law—which was how the Romanists in his day interpreted this verse. According to them, Christ's coming had made these Jewish ceremonies outdated, and so Paul's statement in 2:16 means that people are saved, not by persisting in these ceremonies, but by following Christ. So loyalty to Christ excluded only the ceremonial aspects of the Mosaic law but left its moral precepts untouched. Thus it was easy for the Romanists to regard faith in Christ as going hand in hand with obedience to these moral precepts as part of the work they must do to earn salvation.

Calvin, of course, wanted to keep faith in Christ completely free from any of the commandments or conditions in the Mosaic law for receiving the promises. He conceded that Paul had been thinking only about the ceremonial law up to verse 16. But beginning with that verse, Calvin emphasized that "the moral law is also comprehended in [the 'works of the law'], for everything that Paul adds [from 2:16 on] relates to the moral rather than the ceremonial law" (commentary on 2:15). As Calvin saw it, only if one understood the "works of the law" as referring to all that the Mosaic law really commanded could one honor the antithesis Paul drew between the law and faith in Christ. According to Calvin, not Paul's line of thought up to Galatians 2:16 but the way he used *nomos* ("law") after 2:16 was decisive for determining the meaning of the "works of the law" in that verse. This failure to let the immediately preceding context determine the meaning of the term was certainly faulty exegetical procedure.

Another argument against Calvin's saying that the moral law is spoken about after 2:16 is that in verse 18 Paul's attention is still focused upon the law's ceremonial aspects. There he talks about how terrible it would be for him to do as Peter had done at the church in Antioch: "If I rebuild what I destroyed, I prove that I am a lawbreaker." Peter's action at Antioch (Gal. 2:11–14) was surely a "building up" of one of the distinctives upon which Jews prided themselves. But Paul reminded Peter that they had both "destroyed" any thought that such distinctives gave them an advantage with God. From that time on, they had both preached that reconciliation with God came only by entrusting oneself to Christ, who had paid the penalty for one's sins. But now Peter, by breaking off table fellowship with the Gentile believers when emissaries from the Jerusalem church arrived, had again built up one of these distinctives. Such an action encouraged the Gentile believers at Antioch to think that the observation of the Jewish distinctives would now be a vital part of being a Christian, rather than dependence upon God's mercy alone in order to be his children.

Thus Paul would have nothing to do with building such a frame of mind up again, especially when he remembered how in his previous zealous adherence to the Jewish distinctives he had succeeded only in becoming the chief of sinners. He therefore regarded Peter's action of avoiding table fellowship with Gentile believers at Antioch and insisting on kosher food was a major violation of the Mosaic law. We have already seen (see n. 6 above) how Exodus 20:6 declared that it was blessings of mercy alone that came to people for keeping God's commandments. This emphasis on mercy kept all of the law as a law of faith. But the Jews, in priding themselves on their distinctives, were guilty of standing the law on its head, perverting it into a law of works in which they could boast. Since in so doing they were not upholding the law but injuring its basic integrity, they were guilty of the great transgression, and as a result the curse of Deuteronomy 27:26 was over their heads.

In repudiating the "works of the law" in verse 16, Paul was thus not repudiating the Mosaic law as a law of faith, but only that legalistic frame of mind in which the Jews regarded their adherence to certain distinctives as making them superior to others and thereby earning God's favor. Such a meaning for "works of the law" would fit in well with Galatians 3:10, which then would be saying that all who, like the Jews, prided themselves on their distinctives were under the curse of Deuteronomy 27:26, because they had not honored the law's intention to impart God's mercy to

people who obeyed its commands simply because they trusted
him.

The Line of Thought in Galatians 3:10–12

When it is understood that the "works of the law" in Galatians
3:10 refers to the Jews' pride in their distinctives, it becomes clear
that Paul in the main clause of that verse was speaking of the law
as the legalistic way the Jews had distorted it, demonstrating an
attitude of heart that excluded faith. Verse 11 in quoting Habakkuk
2:4, "The righteous will live by faith," is explicitly contrasting the
humility of one supplicating mercy with the pride of those who
boast in their distinctives as obligating God's blessing. So Paul
uses this verse as an argument to support the curse the law
imposes on those who undermine it by perverting it from a law of
faith: "All those who pride themselves on Jewish distinctives are
under the curse of Deuteronomy 27:26, because it is evident from
Habakkuk 2:4 that people enjoy fellowship with God by faith in
what he does, rather than by means of the legalistic pride that
stems from what they do in distinction to other people" (para-
phrase of 3:10–11). Then Paul goes on to say in verse 12 that this
legalism is not of faith but is dependent on what one does. And
since he talked about the legalistic perversion of the law in 3:10
and then contrasted that legalism with faith in verse 11, there is
every reason to suppose that by "law" in verse 12 he likewise
means the legalistic frame of mind that is incompatible with faith.
Thus this verse in no way supports Calvin's contrast between the
conditional promises of the law and the gracious promises of the
gospel.

But it may be objected that "law" in Galatians 3:12 must mean
the objective law itself, since Paul cites the wording of Leviticus
18:5, the passage he also used to speak of "the righteousness of the
law" in Romans 10:5. In the Galatians passage, however, he does
not cite Moses as an authority for pitting the law against faith. This
failure to cite Moses indicates that here Paul was referring to the
decidedly different meaning the Jewish legalists gave to Leviticus
18:5 as they constantly quoted it in their teaching. For example, in
the Psalms of Solomon, regarded as representing the orthodox
position of the Pharisees, Psalm 14:1–2 echoes Leviticus 18:5 in
this fashion: "The Lord is faithful to those who truly love him, to
those who endure his discipline, to those who live in the
righteousness of his commandments in the Law, which he has
commanded for our life."[24] It must be emphasized that "law" in

Galatians 3:12 has a legalistic meaning, not because of some distinctive way Leviticus 18:5 was worded, but because the Pharisees expounded it in a very different way from Paul.

Therefore Calvin's claim that Galatians 3:12 showed "most clearly" that much of the revelatory law in Scripture is antithetical to faith has problems that simply cannot be surmounted. Thus in his commentary on Galatians, in order to make sense out of 3:10, he had to inject into it the idea that no one can keep the law perfectly. But at the suggestion that God ever expected perfect obedience the Judaizers at Galatia would have scoffed. Furthermore in defining the "works of the law" in Galatians 2:16, Calvin refused to let the preceding train of thought, concerned exclusively with the Jews' zeal for an outward aspect of their ceremonial law, determine the meaning of this term in a verse where it appears three times.[25]

In this Appendix, then, we have examined the three places where Calvin felt that Paul drew a sharp contrast between the law, on the one hand, and faith and the promise, on the other— Galatians 3:17–18, Romans 10:5–8, and Galatians 3:12—and have concluded that no such contrast was intended. The law therefore is indeed a "law of faith" as Exodus 20:6 and Romans 9:32 unmistakably affirm.

NOTES

[1] Regarding v. 18 Calvin said, "Here is the reason why [Paul] so often opposes the promise to the law, as things mutually contradictory: 'If the inheritance is by the law, it is no longer by promise' [Gal. 3:18]; and [other] passages in the same chapter [e.g., Gal. 3:10–12] . . . express this [same] idea [of the opposition of the Mosaic law to the promise]" (*Institutes*, 20:747 [2.11.17]).

[2] The same point was made in another connection in chapter 20 above.

[3] A. F. H. Klijn, "2 (Syriac Apocalypse of) Baruch," in James H. Charlesworth, ed., *Old Testament Pseudepigrapha*, 2 vols. (New York: Macmillan, 1983, 1985), 1:641.

[4] Strack and Billerbeck, *Kommentar*, 3:204.

[5] In our world today an oath comes the closest to being like a covenant in the days of Abraham. "Oath" is better than "testament" or "will" because people can amend their wills many times during their lifetimes, and in some cases their heirs can get them amended after death. (In Heb. 6:13–20, esp. v. 16, the promise God made to Abraham is confirmed by an "oath.") When one

understands "covenant" to be virtually an oath, then there is no difficulty in citing examples of how once an oath is taken, it cannot be annulled or amended. For example, one spouse cannot ask the other to revise a part of their marriage vows, nor can the President of the United States make any changes in the oath of office taken at inauguration.

⁶The best proof text to show that the law and all of God's commands are laws of faith is Ex. 20:6: "[God shows] mercy to a thousand generations of those who love [him] and keep [his] commandments" (cf. Deut. 7:9). Mercy is not a blessing that a patron benefactor receives as an equivalent recompense for services performed for a needy client, but rather what a benefactor *gives* to people who humble themselves and take the stance of those *deserving nothing*. Acts 17:25, "[God] is not served by human hands as if he needed anything," also shows that God could never give any commands, even hypothetically, with the thought that they are part of a job description informing finite, sinful people what they must do to render needful service to him, the Creator, so as to earn a blessing as an equivalent recompense. Calvin failed to see this point when he said, "So also ought we to recognize that God's benevolence has been set forth for us in the law, if we could merit [*demereo*, 'thoroughly merit'] [benevolence] by works" (*Institutes*, 20:804–5 [3.17.2]).

⁷Why this period lasted until Christ was explained in chapter 21.

⁸In Rom. 15:14 he said concerning his readers, "I myself am convinced, my brothers, that you yourselves are full of goodness, complete in knowledge and competent to instruct one another."

⁹Felix Flüeckiger, "Christus, des Gesetzes *telos*," *Theologische Zeitschrift* 11, 2 (March/April 1955): 155.

¹⁰Ibid.

¹¹See note 6 above.

¹²George B. Winer, *A Grammar of the Idiom of the New Testament*, trans. J. Henry Thayer, 7th ed. (Andover, Mass.: Warren F. Draper, 1897), 617.

¹³The Greek word *telos* is often translated "end" or "termination." In many instances in the New Testament, however, it has the meaning "goal." Understanding it to have this meaning in verse 4 gives coherency to Paul's line of thought in Rom. 10:3–8.

¹⁴C. F. D. Moule, "Obligation in the Ethic of Paul," in *Christian History and Interpretation: Studies Presented to John Knox*, ed. W. R. Farmer et al. (Cambridge: Cambridge University Press, 1967), 392–93.

[15]C. E. B. Cranfield, "St. Paul and the Law," *Scottish Journal of Theology* 17, 1 (March 1964): 55. In the next section of the Appendix I present the argument that Paul used the Greek of the rabbinic phrase for the "works of the law" to represent the legalistic misuse and misunderstanding of it. But since this phrase was rather cumbersome, he sometimes simply used the word "law" (as in Phil. 3:9) to represent not the revelation given by Moses but the legalistic misunderstanding of the law that the majority of the Jews had espoused since the time of Moses.

[16]See Calvin's remarks on Rom. 10:5 in his *Commentaries on the Epistle of Paul the Apostle to the Romans,* ed. and trans. John Owen (Grand Rapids: Eerdmans, 1948), 386–87.

[17]Strack and Billerbeck, *Kommentar,* 3:157, on Rom. 3:9.

[18]Ibid., 1:637.

[19]George Foote Moore, *Judaism,* 3 vols. (Cambridge: Harvard University Press, 1927), 1:507, 521.

[20]Klijn, "2 Baruch," 1:641.

[21]Strack and Billerbeck, *Kommentar,* 3:160–61.

[22]Frederic Rendell, "The Epistle of Paul to the Galatians" in *The Expositor's Greek New Testament,* ed. W. Robertson Nicoll (Grand Rapids: Eerdmans, n.d.), 3:168. Otto Schmoller, *The Epistle of Paul to the Galatians*vol. 7 of *Commentary on the Holy Scriptures,* the Lange series, ed. Philip Schaff, 1870, [New Testament]), trans. C. C. Starbuch and M. B. Biddle (Grand Rapids: Zondervan, n.d.), 68. Heinrich Schlier, *Der Brief an die Galater* in Kritisch-exegetischer Kommentar über Das Neue Testament, Begründet von Heinrich August Wilhelm Meyer, 12th ed. (Göttingen: Vandenhoeck and Ruprecht, 1962), 7:132–33.

[23]Clear evidence for such usage is how Matthew uses the word "Gentile" in 5:47 (RSV), whereas the parallel passage in Luke 6:32– 33 uses the word "sinner" instead.

[24]R. B. Wright, "Psalms of Solomon," in *Old Testament Pseudepigrapha,* 2:663.

[25]We must not, however, be too hard on Calvin. He did not have the benefit of the efforts of modern biblical theologians, several of whom have concluded that in passages where Paul contrasts the law and faith, as in Gal. 3:12, he was contrasting the Jews' legalistic perversion of the law with the faith that the law wanted to call forth.

Bibliography

Arberry, Arthur J. *The Koran Interpreted.* New York: Macmillan, 1955.

Arndt, William F., and F. Wilbur Gingrich. *A Greek-English Lexicon of the New Testament and Other Early Christian Literature.* 4th ed. Chicago: University of Chicago Press, 1957.

Barth, Karl. *Church Dogmatics.* Translated by Geoffrey W. Bromiley et al. Edinburgh: T. & T. Clark, 1936–75.

Beckwith, Roger. *The Old Testament Canon of the New Testament Church.* Grand Rapids: Eerdmans, 1985.

Bertram, Georg. "Ergon." In *Theological Dictionary of the New Testament,* 10 vols., edited by Gerhard Kittel and Gerhard Friedrich, translated by Geoffrey W. Bromiley, 2:635–55. Grand Rapids: Eerdmans, 1964–76.

The Bhagavad Gita. Translated by Shri Purohit Swami. London: Faber & Faber, 1978.

Bright, John. *The Kingdom of God.* New York: Abingdon, 1953.

Bruce, F. F. *The Canon of Scripture.* Downers Grove, Ill.: InterVarsity Press, 1988.

————. *New Testament Development of Old Testament Themes.* Grand Rapids: Eerdmans, 1968.

————. "Some Thoughts on the Beginning of the New Testament Canon." *Bulletin of the John Rylands Library* 65, 2 (Spring 1983): 37–60.

A Buddhist Bible. Edited by Dwight Goddard. New York: E. F. Dutton, 1952.

Bultmann, Rudolf. "Eleos." In *Theological Dictionary of the New Testament,* 10 vols., edited by Gerhard Kittel and Gerhard Friedrich, translated by Geoffrey W. Bromiley, 2:477–87. Grand Rapids: Eerdmans, 1964–76.

————. "The New Testament and Mythology." In *Kerygma and Myth,* edited by Hans Werner Bartsch, translated by Reginald H. Fuller, 1–44. London: S.P.C.K., 1957.

––––––. "Prophecy and Fulfillment." In *Essays on Old Testament Hermeneutics,* edited by Claus Westermann, 50–75. Richmond: John Knox, 1963.

Calvin, John. *Commentaries on the Epistle of Paul the Apostle to the Romans.* Edited and translated by John Owen. Grand Rapids: Eerdmans, 1948.

––––––. *Institutes of the Christian Religion.* Edited by John T. McNeill, translated by Ford Lewis Battles. The Library of Christian Classics, vols. 20 and 21. Philadelphia: Westminster, 1960.

Charlesworth, James H., ed. *The Old Testament Pseudepigrapha.* 2 vols. New York: Doubleday, 1983, 1985.

Clark, W. Malcolm. "A Legal Background to the Yahwist's Use of 'Good and Evil' in Genesis 2–3." *Journal of Biblical Literature* 88 (1969): 266–78.

Conze, Edward. *Buddhism: Its Essence and Development.* New York: Harper & Row, 1959.

Cranfield, C. E. B. *A Critical and Exegetical Commentary on the Epistle to the Romans.* 2 vols. International Critical Commentary. Edinburgh: T. & T. Clark, 1975.

––––––. "St. Paul and the Law." *Scottish Journal of Theology* 17, 1 (March 1964): 43–68.

Cullmann, Oscar. *Salvation in History.* Translated by Sidney G. Sowers. New York: Harper & Row, 1967.

––––––. "The Tradition." In *The Early Church,* edited by A. J. B. Higgins, translated by A. J. B. Higgins and S. Godman, 55–99. Philadelphia: Westminster, 1956.

Dalbiac, Lilian, ed. *Dictionary of German Quotations.* New York: Frederick Ungar, n.d.

Dunn, James D. G. "2 Corinthians III.17—'The Lord Is the Spirit.'" *Journal of Theological Studies,* n.s., 21, 2 (1970): 309–20.

The Ecclesiastical History of Eusebius Pamphilius. Translated by Christian F. Cruse. Grand Rapids: Baker, 1955.

Edwards, David L. *Evangelical Essentials: A Liberal-Evangelical Dialogue.* Downers Grove, Ill.: InterVarsity Press, 1988.

Edwards, Jonathan. *Observations Concerning the Scripture Economy of the Trinity and Covenant of Redemption.* New York: Scribner's, 1880.

––––––. "Treatise on Grace." In *Puritan Sage: Collected Writings of Jonathan Edwards,* edited by Vergilius Ferm, 534–73. New York: Library Publishers, 1953.

————. *An Unpublished Essay of Edwards on the Trinity.* Edited by George P. Fisher. New York: Scribner's, 1903.

————. *The Works of Jonathan Edwards.* Revised and corrected by Edward Hickman. 2 vols. Carlisle, Pa.: Banner of Truth Trust, 1974.

————. *The Works of President Edwards.* 4 vols. New York: Leavitt & Allen, 1858.

Eichrodt, Walther. *Theology of the Old Testament.* Translated by J. A. Baker. 2 vols. Philadelphia: Westminster, 1961.

Ellis, E. Earle. *Paul's Use of the Old Testament.* Grand Rapids: Eerdmans, 1957.

Fernando, Ajith. *The Christian's Attitude Toward World Religions.* Wheaton, Ill.: Tyndale House, 1987.

Flüeckiger, Felix. "Christus, des Gesetzes *telos.*" *Theologische Zeitschrift* 11, 2 (March/April 1955): 153–57.

Fuller, Daniel P. *Easter Faith and History.* Grand Rapids: Eerdmans, 1965.

————. *Gospel and Law: Contrast or Continuum?* Grand Rapids: Eerdmans, 1980.

Gesenius' Hebrew Grammar. Edited by E. Kautzsch and A. E. Cowley. 2d ed. Oxford: Clarendon Press, 1910.

Glueck, Nelson. *Hesed in the Bible.* Cincinnati: Hebrew Union College Press, 1967.

Hasel, Gerhard F. *Old Testament Theology: Basic Issues in the Current Debate.* Grand Rapids: Eerdmans, 1972.

Hirsch, E. D., Jr. *Validity in Interpretation.* New Haven: Yale University Press, 1967.

Hodge, Charles. *Commentary on the Epistle to the Romans.* Rev. ed. of 1886. Reprint. Grand Rapids: Eerdmans, 1953.

Johnson, Marshall D. "Genealogy of Jesus." In *The International Standard Bible Encyclopedia,* 4 vols., edited by Geoffrey W. Bromiley et al., 2:428–31. Grand Rapids: Eerdmans, 1982.

Johnstone, Patrick. *Operation World: A Day-to-Day Guide to Praying for the World.* 4th ed. Pasadena: William Carey Library, 1986.

Justin Martyr. *Dialogue with Trypho.* Edited and translated by Alexander Roberts and James Donaldson. The Ante-Nicene Fathers, vol. 1. Grand Rapids: Eerdmans, n.d.

Klijn, A. F. H. "2 (Syriac Apocalypse of) Baruch." Ed. James H. Charlesworth, *The Old Testament Pseudepigrapha.* Vol. 1.

Kümmel, Werner Georg. *The New Testament: The History of the Investigation of Its Problems.* Translated by S. MacLean Gilmour and Howard Clark Kee. New York: Abingdon, 1972.

Ladd, George E. *Crucial Questions About the Kingdom of God.* Grand Rapids: Eerdmans, 1952.

————. *Jesus and the Kingdom.* New York: Harper & Row, 1964.

Lewis, C. S. *Beyond Personality.* New York: Macmillan, 1948.

Liddell, Henry George, and Robert Scott. *A Greek-English Lexicon.* Revised by H. S. Jones and R. McKenzie. 9th ed. Oxford: Clarendon Press, 1940.

Luther, Martin. "The Freedom of a Christian." In *Martin Luther: Selections from His Writings,* edited by John Dillenberger, 42–85. New York: Doubleday, 1961.

Machen, J. Gresham. *The Virgin Birth of Christ.* New York: Harper & Brothers, 1930.

Metzger, Bruce M. *A Textual Commentary on the Greek New Testament: A Companion Volume to the United Bible Societies' Greek New Testament (third edition).* London: United Bible Societies, 1973.

Michel, Otto. *Der Brief an die Römer.* 4th ed. Göttingen: Vandenhoeck & Ruprecht, 1966.

Moore, George Foote. *Judaism.* 3 vols. Cambridge: Harvard University Press, 1927.

Morris, Leon. *The Apostolic Preaching of the Cross.* Grand Rapids: Eerdmans, 1955; reprinted 1974.

Moule, C. F. D. "Obligation in the Ethic of Paul." In *Christian History and Interpretation: Studies Presented to John Knox,* edited by W. R. Farmer et al., 389–406. Cambridge: Cambridge University Press, 1967.

Niebuhr, Reinhold. *The Nature and Destiny of Man.* 2 vols. New York: Scribner's, 1945.

The Old Testament Pseudepigrapha. Edited by James H. Charlesworth. 2 vols. New York: Doubleday, 1983–85.

Orr, James. *The Problem of the Old Testament.* London: James Nisbet, 1907.

Pascal's Pensées. Translated by H. F. Stewart. New York: Pantheon Books, 1950.

Pinnock, Clark. "Fire, Then Nothing." *Christianity Today* (March 20, 1987), 40–41.

Piper, John. "How Redeemed People Do Battle with Sin." *Decision* (January 1990), 12–13.

————. *The Justification of God: An Exegetical and Theological Study of Romans 9:1–23.* Grand Rapids: Baker, 1983.

Provence, Thomas E. " 'Who Is Sufficient for These Things?' An Exegesis of 2 Corinthians ii 15–iii 18." *Novum Testamentum* 24, 1 (1982): 54–81.

Rendall, Frederic. "The Epistle of Paul to the Galatians." Ed. W. Robertson Nicoll, *The Expositor's Greek New Testament.* Vol. 3. Grand Rapids: Eerdmans, n.d.

Rengstorf, K. H. "Apostolos." In *Theological Dictionary of the New Testament,* 10 vols., edited by Gerhard Kittel and Gerhard Friedrich, translated by Geoffrey W. Bromiley, 1:398–447. Grand Rapids: Eerdmans, 1964–76.

Robertson, A. T. *An Introduction to the Textual Criticism of the New Testament.* Nashville: Broadman Press, 1925.

Rowley, H. H. *Unity of the Bible.* Cleveland, Ohio: World Publishing, Meridian Books, 1957.

Schaff, Philip. *The Creeds of Christendom, with a History and Critical Notes.* 4th ed. 3 vols. New York: Harper, 1877.

Schlier, Heinrich. *Der Brief an die Galater.* Kritisch-exegetischer Kommentar über Das Neue Testament. Begründet von Heinrich August Wilhelm Meyer. Vol. 7. 12th ed. Göttingen: Vandenhoeck and Ruprecht, 1962.

Schmoller, Otto. *The Epistle of Paul to the Galatians.* Ed. Philip Schaff. *Commentary on the Holy Scriptures,* the Lange series. Vol. 7 (New Testament). Trans. C. C. Starbuch and M. B. Biddle. Grand Rapids: Zondervan, n.d.

The Septuagint Version of the Old Testament and Apocrypha, with an English Translation. Grand Rapids: Zondervan, 1972.

Skydsgaard, K. E. "Kingdom of God and Church." *Scottish Journal of Theology* 4, 1 (March 1951): 383–97.

Snaith, Norman H. *The Distinctive Ideas of the Old Testament.* London: Epworth Press, 1950.

Stoebe, H. J. "Hesed." In *Theologisches Handwörterbuch zum Alten Testament,* 2 vols., edited by Ernst Jenni and Claus Westermann, 1:599–621. Munich: Chr. Kaiser, 1971–76.

Strack, Hermann L., and Paul Billerbeck. *Kommentar zum Neuen Testament aus Talmud und Midrasch.* 3d ed. 6 vols. Munich: C. H. Beck'sche, 1963.

Tasker, R. V. G. *The Old Testament in the New Testament.* Philadelphia: Westminster, 1947.

Terkel, Studs. *Working.* New York: Avon Books, 1972.

Tournier, Paul. *The Meaning of Persons.* Translated by Edwin Hudson. New York: Harper & Brothers, 1957.

Toynbee, A. J. "How and Why I Work." *Saturday Review* (April 5, 1969), 22.

von Rad, Gerhard. *Genesis.* Translated by J. H. Marks. Rev. ed. Philadelphia: Westminster, 1972.

———. *Old Testament Theology.* Translated by D. M. G. Stalker. 2 vols. New York, Harper & Row, 1962–65.

Vos, Geerhardus. *Biblical Theology.* Grand Rapids: Eerdmans, 1961. Reprint.

Weatherhead, Leslie. *The Christian Agnostic.* New York: Abingdon, 1965.

Wesley, John, "On Free Grace: Rom. 8:32." *The Works of the Rev. John Wesley, A.M.,* 7 vols., 3d ed., 1:482–90. New York: Eaton & Mains, 1896.

———. "The Use of Money." *Works of John Wesley.* Vol. 2. Ed. Albert Outler. Nashville: Abingdon, 1984–85.

Winer, George B. *A Grammar of the Idiom of the New Testament.* Translated by J. Henry Thayer. 7th ed. Andover, Mass.: Warren F. Draper, 1897.

Winter, Ralph D. "The Diminishing Task." *Mission Frontiers.* 13, 1 (1991).

Wright, R. B. "Psalms of Solomon." Ed. James H. Charlesworth. Vol. 2. *Old Testment Pseudepigrapha.*

General Index

Aaron, 376, 380
Abel, 37, 41, 224, 225–30, 231,
    233, 239, 305, 390
    regeneration of, 230, 391
Abimelech, 259, 308, 329
Abraham, 23, 46, 102, 215, 361,
    362, 376, 383, 392, 430, 450,
    452, 473
    covenant of. *See* Abrahamic
        covenant.
    faith in God's promises and.
        See Abraham's faith.
    forgiveness of. *See* Abraham's
        forgiveness.
    Islamic view of, 87, 89
    Israel's historical destiny and,
        31, 32, 33
    justification of, 310–16, 322
    Mosaic law and, 351, 358, 459,
        460–61, 462, 464
    persevering faith of,
        See Persevering faith
    regeneration of, 229, 301,
        304–5
    seed of. *See* Abraham's seed.
Abrahamic covenant, 251, 253,
    325–26, 328–29, 332, 341,
    387, 388, 390, 392, 398,
    450–51, 461
    circumcision significance in,
        325, 330, 331, 365–70
Abraham's faith, 151, 254, 258,
    269–98, 336–37
    futuristic orientation of, 270,
        271–76, 298, 301, 303
    past orientation of, 276–78
    unbelief fought with, 279–97,
        298
Abraham's forgiveness, 251–65,
    317–18
    Israelite interpretation of, 253,
        256–57

Paul's interpretation of,
    255–56, 257–65
Abraham's seed, 325–43, 345,
    346, 462
    blessings for, 325–29
    God's people as, 335–37
    identity of, 330–35
    physical descent and, 330–32,
        334, 337–43, 442–49
    regeneration of, 341, 343
Absalom, 395–96
Acts, 22-24, 66
    apocryphal books of, 61–62
Adam, 132, 140, 176, 181, 182,
    183, 187, 227, 228, 232, 233,
    235, 387
    God's mercy toward, 184–85,
        205–6
    nakedness significance to,
        177–79, 180
    regeneration and, 229, 230
Adonijah, 396
Adultery, 373
A fortiorti argument, 277, 278
Against Apion (Josephus), 35
Against Celsus (Origen), 416
Against Heresies (Irenaeus), 63
Allah, 87, 88, 89
Amitabha, 80, 81, 82, 83, 85
Amitayus, 80
Amnon, 395
Angels, 88, 182, 234–35
Animism, 74
Annihilation, 196–201, 202
Antitypes, 379, 382, 383
Anxiety, 284
Apocrypha, 61–62, 66, 256, 460.
    See also specific works.
Apostolic authority, 47–54
Arahatship, 77–78
Arjuna, 70–71, 72–73
Ark of the covenant, 383
Armageddon, 440

Scripture Index

The Unity of the Bible was typeset by the
Photocomposition Department of Zondervan Publishing House,
Grand Rapids, Michigan, on a Mergenthaler Linotron 202/N.
Compositor is Sue Koppenol.
Manuscript editing by Craig Noll and Leonard G. Goss
Production editing by Robert D. Wood
Imprint Editor for Academie Books is Leonard G. Goss

The text was set in 11 point Caledonia, a face designed by
W. A. Dwiggins in 1938, inspired by a face cut around 1790 by
Scottish designer William Martin for Bulmer's press.
It was first issued by the Mergenthaler Linotype Company.
Among modern types, Caledonia has the reputation of being
one of the most readable for text, and is a popular book face.
This book was printed on Lyons Falls 50-pound Pathfinder paper by
R. R. Donnelley & Sons, Harrisonburg, Virginia.